WBI DEVELOPMENT STUDIES

The Challenge of Urban Government

Policies and Practices

Edited by
Mila Freire and Richard Stren

The World Bank Institute
Washington, D.C.

The Centre for Urban and Community Studies
University of Toronto

The World Bank Institute was established by the World Bank in 1955 to train officials concerned with development planning, policymaking, investment analysis, and project implementation in member developing countries. At present the substance of WBI's work emphasizes macroeconomic and sectoral policy analysis. Through a variety of courses, seminars, workshops, and other learning activities, most of which are given overseas in cooperation with local institutions, WBI seeks to sharpen analytical skills used in policy analysis and to broaden understanding of the experience of individual countries with economic and social development. Although WBI's publications are designed to support its training activities, many are of interest to a much broader audience.

ISBN 0-8213-4738-1
Library of Congress Cataloging-in-Publication Data

The challenge of urban government : policies and practices / edited by Maria Emilia Freire, Richard Stren.
      p.cm. -- (WBI development studies)
      Includes bibliographical references.
      ISBN 0-8213-4738-1
      1. Municipal government. 2. Metropolitan areas. 3. City planning. 4. Urban poor. I. Freire, Maria Emilia, 1948- II. Stren, Richard E. III. Series.

JS78 .C8 2000
352.16--dc21

00-034950

On demand printing - LSI

Contents

    Editor's Introduction *193*
        Richard Stren

    Public-Private Partnerships for Urban Services *199*
        Richard Batley

    The Role of the Private Sector in Municipal Solid Waste
        Service Delivery in Developing Countries: Keys to Success *215*
        Carl R. Bartone

    Public-Private Participation in the Provision of Infrastructure to
        Tirrupur, India *225*
        Usha P. Raghupathi and Om Prakash Mathur

6. Land and Real-Estate Markets *235*
    Editor's Introduction *235*
        Richard Stren

    Land Markets and Urban Management: The Role of
        Planning Tools *239*
        Alexandra Ortiz and Alain Bertaud

    Tools for a Land and Housing Market Diagnosis *253*
        Ayse Pamuk

    Property Taxation *269*
        Enid Slack

    The Portland Experience *281*
        Charles Hales

7. Urban Poverty *287*
    Editor's Introduction *287*
        Richard Stren

    The City Poverty Assessment: An Introduction *291*
        Jesko Hentschel and Radha Seshagiri

    Poverty Reduction in Urban Areas: Employment and
        Income Generation through Partnerships *315*
        Camilo Granada

Foreword

In the coming decades, as much as 80 percent of population growth and most economic growth in the developing world will occur in cities. In this context of rapid urbanization accompanied by pervasive globalization, the challenges that local governments and city managers face have increased in both scope and complexity because of the lack of resources, the continuing migration toward large cities, the deteriorating infrastructure, and the need to tap a solid economic and financial base while maintaining the incentives necessary to attract investment and generate employment. In most of the world's largest cities, those responsible have introduced innovative ideas to improve the quality of urban governance. Some cities have begun preparing city development strategies that include integrated and participatory action plans to promote and sustain economic growth and improve living conditions for city residents. These developments bring with them the need for capacity building in a variety of disciplines, especially among those tasked with managing cities.

The World Bank Institute (WBI) has responded to the challenges of urban development and city management by launching a number of important initiatives. Chief among these is the program on Urban Challenges of the 21st Century, under which the Institute developed a number of courses on urban and city management that have been conducted worldwide. These courses were designed in the context of a new urban strategy in the World Bank. The strategy recognizes that cities are crucial in efforts to address poverty and other development issues, but acknowledges that this potential will not be realized unless cities are livable, competitive, well-governed and managed, and bankable—all themes that are explored in this book.

The book is the result of the first such course, which was held in Toronto, Canada, in May 1999. The course was jointly organized by WBI, the Canadian Urban Institute, the City of Toronto, and the University of Toronto, and was sponsored by the Canadian International Development Agency and the government of Spain. Among the participants were mayors, city managers and administrators, local-level policymakers, urban planners, and directors of urban training institutes, as well as experts from the World Bank, the Inter-American Development Bank, and several well-known academic and research institutions. The book's chapters correspond to the course's ten modules on such topics as globalization and city management, city strategy and local governance, urban financial management, private sector participation in infrastructure provision, urban environmental management, and urban poverty reduction.

This book stresses the kind of analytical thinking that promotes greater understanding of the complexity of urban issues; of innovative policies, programs, and management tools; and of successful practices in addressing issues of urban governance. We hope that it will be a valuable information resource for all involved in efforts to improve the management and governance of cities.

John Flora, Director   Vinod Thomas, Vice President
Urban Development Department   World Bank Institute
The World Bank

Acknowledgments

This manuscript is a product of the first Urban and City Management course, offered in Toronto in May 1999. That initiative marked the beginning of a successful series of national and regional courses that have now been offered in four continents and six different countries. They have their basis in the conviction that managing cities requires not only a special way of looking at a reality but also a passion for urban issues in all their complexity, dynamism, and interconnections with many complementary disciplines.

In putting together the manuscript—a set of the best papers prepared for Toronto accompanied by selected pieces to illustrate important issues—we have benefited from the help and intense work of a large team of colleagues in several countries and the support of several organizations and individuals. At the risk of omitting some, we mention several of those who have contributed to this project. First, we acknowledge our gratitude to the three cosponsoring institutions—the World Bank Institute; the Canadian International Development Agency, which supported the initiative from the very early planning stage; and the government of Spain. Second, we recognize the coordinators of the course modules: Michael Cohen, Angela Griffin, Victor Vergara, Bob Ebel, Antonio Estache, Alexandra Ortiz, Carl Bartone, John Flora, and Tim Campbell. They accepted the challenge of identifying the major message—analytical and practical—to be given to city managers through the different modules, which correspond to different chapters in the book. Third, we thank our colleagues who collaborated in the pedagogical aspects of the course and in the preparation of the manuscript, notably Erin Hagar and Alexandra Ortiz, who were committed from the first day, and Judith Bell whose extraordinary commitment to clear writing and organization has made this book of readings possible. Fourth, we thank our eminent reviewers from three continents who took on the effort of reading the extensive manuscript and who gave us fundamental suggestions on both the content and format. Finally, we thank our colleagues in the Bank—notably Danny Leipziger, Daniel Kaufmann, Tony Pellegrini, Jennifer Clark, and James Quigley; and in the University of Toronto, Laila Smith, who worked so imaginatively to widen the scope of the book.

Mila Freire   Richard Stren
World Bank Institute   University of Toronto

Contributors

Rebecca Abers is a researcher at the Nucleo de Pesquisa em Politicas Pública's of the Department of Political Science of the University of Brasília.

Anton Baare is a social anthropologist with Nordic Consulting Group in Taastrup, Denmark.

Najib Balala, formerly Mayor of the city of Mombasa, Kenya, lives in Mombasa.

Carl R. Bartone is Principal Environmental Engineer in the Urban Development Division of the Infrastructure Group at the World Bank.

Richard Batley is Director of the International Development Department of the School of Public Policy at the University of Birmingham, England.

Alain Bertaud is an urban planner who has recently retired from the World Bank where he was a Principal Urban Planner.

Richard M. Bird is Adjunct Professor, Rotman School of Management, University of Toronto.

Jordi Borja, formerly a member of the municipal government of Barcelona, is with Urban Technology Consulting in Barcelona.

Larry S. Bourne is Professor of Geography and Planning at the University of Toronto.

Manuel Castells is Professor of City and Regional Planning and of Sociology at the University of California, Berkeley.

Robert Cervero is Professor of City and Regional Planning at the University of California, Berkeley.

Michael Cohen is Visiting Fellow at the International Center for Advanced Studies at New York University.

Robert D. Ebel is Principal Economist, World Bank Institute Program in Intergovernmental Relations and Local Finance.

Israel Fainboim Yaker is a research associate in Fedesarrollo, Fundación para la Educación Superior y el Desarrollo, in Bogotá, Colombia.

John Flora is Director, Transport Sector in the World Bank.

Mila Freire is Course Director of the Urban and City Management Program in the World Bank and Sector Lead Economist/Specialist in the Latin America and Caribbean Region.

Camilo Granada is senior advisor to the Secretary-General of the Organization of American States; he was formerly in the Partnerships for Poverty Reduction program of the World Bank Institute.

Michael Greenberg is Professor of Urban Studies and Community Health at Rutgers University, New Jersey.

Angela Griffin is a Senior Urban Advisor in the World Bank, responsible for assisting in the implementation of the city management and governance aspects of the Bank's Urban Strategy.

Sumila Gulyani is an Infrastructure and Urban Specialist at the World Bank.

Charles Hales is a City Commissioner in Portland, Oregon, and manages the Portland Department of Transport and the Office of Planning and Development Review.

Nigel Harris is Professor Emeritus of the Economics of the City at the Development Planning Unit of University College London.

Jesko Hentschel is a senior economist and social planner in the Poverty Group of the World Bank.

Rajendra Kumar is Commissioner of Coimbatore City Municipal Corporation, India.

Om Prakash Mathur is Professor of Housing and Urban Economics in the National Institute of Public Finance and Policy, New Delhi.

Pratibha Mehta is Senior Technical Adviser (Local Governance) and Global Coordinator, Life Programme, in the United Nations Development Programme, New York.

Colleen O'Manique is an international development specialist with Conseil Equilibrio Consulting in Quebec.

Molly O'Meara is a researcher with the Worldwatch Institute in Washington, DC.

Alexandra Ortiz is an urban economist and task leader for several programs in Latin America in the World Bank

Ayse Pamuk is an assistant professor at the University of Virginia, where she teaches qualitative research methods and housing policy to urban planning students.

Rajesh Patnaik is a research fellow in anthropology at Andhra University in Visakhapatnam, India.

Usha P. Raghupathi is an associate professor in the National Institute of Urban Affairs, New Delhi.

Radha Seshagiri is a research analyst in the Poverty Group of the World Bank.

Enid Slack is a Toronto economic consultant, specializing in municipal, education, and intergovernmental finance.

Pilar Solans is Senior Municipal Finance Specialist for the World Bank. She was previously Financial Director and Coordinator of Municipal Companies and Agencies for the City of Barcelona.

Richard Stren is Professor of Political Science at the University of Toronto.

François Vaillancourt is Professor of Economics and Research Fellow in the Centre de recherche et développement en économique (CRDE) at l'Université de Montréal.

Franz Vanderschueren is a technical advisor with the Urban Management Programme, UNCHS (Habitat) in Nairobi.

Ellen Wasserman is a researcher and consultant specializing in health policy; she is based in Washington, DC.

Glossary of Abbreviations

AIC	Average incremental cost
BOT	Build, operate and transfer
BSUDP	Bolivia Sustainable Urban Development Project
CBD	Central business district
CBO	Community-based organization
CDS	City Development Strategies
CEPAL/ECLAC	United Nations Economic Commission for Latin America and the Caribbean
CIDA	Canadian International Development Agency
CMA	Census Metropolitan Area
CPA	City poverty assessment
DANE	Colombian Statistical Institute
DHS	Demographic and health surveys
ECAM	Equipo de comunicación alternativa con mujeres
EPZ	Export processing zone
FAR	Floor/area ratio
GDP	Gross domestic product
GDPP	Gross domestic provincial product (Canada)
GIS	Geographic information system
GTA	Greater Toronto Area
ICLEI	International Council for Local Environmental Initiatives (Toronto)
IIED-AL	International Institute for Environment and Development–America Latina
IMF	International Monetary Fund
INEGI	Instituto Nacional de Estadistica Geografía e Informatica (Mexico)
INEI	Peruvian Statistical Institute
INI	National Ecology Institute (Mexico)
IS	Information systems
KShs.	Kenyan Shillings (55 KShs. approximately equivalent to US$1)

LAA	Land administration authority
LPA	Local Planning Authority
LRMC	Long-run marginal cost
LSMS	Living Standard Measurement Study surveys
MDF	Municipal Development Fund
MDP	Municipal Development Program
MTEF	Medium-term expenditure framework
NAFTA	North American Free Trade Association
NGO	Non-governmental organization
NIC	Newly industrialized country
NTADCL	New Tirrupur Area Development Corporation
NVA	National Valuation Agency (Guatamala)
PAHO	Pan American Health Organization
PDT	Partido Democratico Trabahista (Democratic Labor Party [Brazil])
PT	Partido dos Trabalhadores (Workers' Party [Brazil])
Rs.	Indian Rupees (1 rupee approximately equivalent to US$ 0.024)
SDC	Swiss Development Cooperation
SITM	Integrated System of Mass Transportation, Bogotá
SRMC	Short-run marginal cost
TADP	Tirrupur Area Development Plan
TEA	Tirrupur Exporters Association
UAMPA	Union of Neighborhood Associations of Porto Alegre
UDA	Urban development authority
ULB	Urban local body (India)
UMP	Urban Management Program
UNCED	United Nations Conference on Environment and Development
UNCHS	United Nations Center for Human Settlement (Habitat)
UNDP	United Nations Development Programme
UNEP	United Nations Environment Programme
USAID	United States Agency for International Development
UTUI	University of Toronto Urban International
VAT	Value-added tax
VKT	Vehicle kilometers of travel
WHO	World Health Organization
WRI	World Resources Institute

The Challenges of Urban Government

Introduction
Mila Freire

Cities and towns are marvelous and vital instruments of exchange, vital for the development of economic systems and social organizations. As Paul M. Hohenberg (1988) suggests, the extent of urbanization largely defines the place of exchange in economic life, and with it the extent of specialization and the role of markets, money, and credit. Cities provide the network and the nodes for transport and for communication, both for goods and services, and for knowledge. Literacy is at home in the town, as the town is the base for counting and measuring, accounts, schools, books, records, and documents. More than most human achievements, cities have historically represented a challenge to the precariousness of life. The fact that even poor societies, at the edge between subsistence and dearth, have organized the retrieval of meager surpluses to support urban life testifies to the great efficiency of the urban institution in bringing amenity and civilization to human lives. The peasant may not always pay those taxes willingly, but the city dweller throughout history has represented wonders to the peasant working in the field.

The survival of cities against the odds testifies to their economic productivity, however elusive and disguised that role may be. It is apparent that urbanization and economic growth are well correlated, although the causal relationship is hard to prove (Bairoch 1988; Mokyr 1995).[1] As countries develop, more national income is produced in urban areas, accounting for 55 percent of gross national product (GNP) in low-income countries, 73 percent in middle-income countries and 85 percent in those of high income (World Bank 1999).

---

1. Very few historical economists have examined the contribution of urbanization to the great transformation in Europe (the Industrial Revolution). Joel Mokyr is among the few who stress the role of the urban in technological change.

Cities are also the very place where political activity occurs; where constituents elect their representatives and leaders, where urban dwellers make their elected leaders accountable for the taxes collected and for the implementation of promises made during election campaigns. Cities and municipalities are the basis of the political structure of any democratic country, even if they may sometimes seem like the end of a long chain in a heavy decentralized or deconcentrated political and fiscal structure.

Cities do, however, face tremendous challenges. In a world of increased competitiveness and complexity, cities simultaneously have to be attractive to business as a way of generating income and employment opportunities, to provide a good livelihood for their inhabitants, to generate enough resources to finance infrastructure and social needs, and to take care of their poor. Cities have provided an avenue for upward mobility, and for that reason have remained a magnet for rural migrants. But at the very bottom, in the space usually occupied by the most recent arrivals and other excluded social groups, living conditions have remained below what is considered the threshold of acceptability. Cities, often overwhelmed by the continuous influx, have frequently been unable to keep up with the provision of basic services. Thus, in 1994 at least 220 million urban dwellers (13 percent of the developing world's urban population) lacked access to clean drinking water; almost twice as many had no access to even the simplest latrines. Between a third and two-thirds of the solid waste generated went uncollected, piling up on streets and in drains, contributing to flooding and the spread of disease. In addition, cities' domestic and industrial effluents are often released into waterways with little or no treatment (World Bank 2000).

The last two decades of the twentieth century have brought fundamental changes in our way of life, our perception of our home, our workplace and indeed our future (Lo and Yeung 1998). Structural change on a global scale, together with waves of technological innovation, have made our world more interdependent; and globalization processes of diverse kinds have penetrated every corner of the world. These powerful changes have seen the ascendancy of large cities and have opened the opportunity for creative management; but they have also exposed the weaknesses of urban management and urban structures in dealing with complex problems such as poverty.

By their very nature, urban dilemmas are almost always multisectoral (Stren 1996) and city management has to be studied from a variety of angles and disciplines. Today, solutions to problems at the local level, as well as urban success in the global environment, require a nonideological and multisectoral approach as well as popular participation in decisionmaking. Recently, Alexandra Ortiz (1998) asked a set of Latin

American mayors what they would need to know the day after their election to office. The mayors answered that they would like to understand several things including: how global influences will affect their city and the way their city relates to the external world, how to prepare and implement a strategic plan, how to generate and administer the resources required for daily tasks and development projects, how to partner with the private sector while keeping the public interest in sight, how to favor or orient the spatial location of the city's activities, how to reduce poverty, curb environmental problems, and use the transport infrastructure to improve the wellbeing of their constituents. This wide-ranging and integrated view permeates the way policymakers and development agencies look today at urban management issues.

The World Bank: A Changing View of Urban Development

Development agencies have experienced first hand the challenge of expanding perspective in studying urban problems. The World Bank's urban projects during the 1970s and 1980s, for example, focused on particular components of urban development—frequently infrastructure. The Bank's new urban strategy document (World Bank 1999) recognizes that, while these projects brought benefits, they fell short of a sufficient recognition that achieving sustainable urban development requires a more integrated approach across the physical environment, infrastructure networks, finance, and institutional and social activities.

Urban assistance in the 1970s focused on poverty alleviation through investment in basic infrastructure and housing for low-income residents. The aim was to test the feasibility of providing low-cost improvements that could be replicated for large numbers of the underserved population. The slum-upgrading projects or project components generally met this objective, with sometimes dramatic results. The first generation of upgrading projects was less successful, however, in achieving even indirect cost recovery through property taxation. Although the projects incorporated extensive community participation before this became the norm in other sectors, local counterpart institutions (both municipalities and nongovernmental organizations [NGOs]) were insufficiently developed to sustain and expand the projects. Many other multisectoral urban projects that had a less clear focus than urban upgrading, acquired ill-prepared and poorly integrated components that suffered from weakness in borrower ownership and implementation capacity. The need for a better enabling policy environment for all urban activities, based on supportive intergovernmental relations, became very clear.

During the 1980s, urban development projects therefore became reoriented towards strengthening the policy, financial, and institutional frameworks. Housing assistance, for example, shifted from shelter investment to the reform of housing-finance policies, and the restructuring or dismantling of housing banks and public housing agencies. The Bank began devoting a much larger share of its lending to municipal development projects that aimed to effect broad capacity-building and financial reforms within municipal government, coupled with credit lines to support investments and help municipalities establish credit records. Single-sector projects in urban areas, notably urban transport, water, and sanitation, also became popular in some country programs.

The solid base of urban policy analysis that was developed during the late 1980s and early 1990s—building in part on Bank-supported research—remains a sound guide for the Bank's assistance activities.[2] This policy work substantiated, for example, the impacts of the regulatory regime for land and housing on the costs and demand-responsiveness of these markets, particularly for the poor; the necessary conditions for sustainable municipal credit and markets for housing finance; the critical role of intergovernmental frameworks in defining incentives for municipalities to be effective; and the growing importance of urban environment and urban poverty issues in sustainable urban development. These messages were reflected increasingly in the projects funded in the mid-1990s, that have taken on an ambitious agenda of municipal policy, institutional change, and market reform.

This shift in the Bank's approach to urban development is articulated in its new urban strategy, which maintains that if cities and towns are to promote the welfare of their residents and of the nation's citizens, they must be sustainable in four respects: they must be "livable," that is, they must ensure a decent quality of life and equitable opportunity for all residents; they must also be productive and "competitive"; they must be well governed; they must be well managed; and financially sustainable, or "bankable." Each dimension implies preconditions of appropriate national-level policies, including a sound macro-fiscal environment and a strong financial sector, as well as specific local-level policy and institutional requirements.

---

2. World Bank policy papers issued in this period include *Urban Policy and Economic Development: An Agenda for the 1990s*, 1991; *Housing: Enabling Markets to Work*, 1993; *Better Urban Services: Finding the Right Incentives*, 1995; and an unpublished sector review, "An Agenda for Infrastructure Reform and Development," INU, 1993, which served as an input to the Bank's 1994 *World Development Report*.

Building Blocks of the Strategy

The proposed multi-dimensional urban policy agenda provides broadly common goals for all cities and local governments.

NATIONAL URBAN STRATEGIES. There is recognition that one needs to work with national and local counterparts to understand and articulate better how the urban transition can contribute to national goals of economic growth and poverty reduction. National urban strategies are needed to promote the appropriate national policies and especially to promote the institutional conditions for sustainable cities and towns, notably in terms of: (a) inter-governmental fiscal relations; (b) safety nets; (c) regulations affecting urban environmental improvement; (d) national regulatory conditions affecting the business climate and incentives for public-private collaboration in urban infrastructure; and (e) development of domestic financial markets as a basis for municipal credit.

SUPPORT TO CITY DEVELOPMENT STRATEGIES. Technical advice would be provided for the preparation of city development strategies that originate with, and are wholly owned by, local counterparts. These exercises would outline the stakeholders' vision for the city, analyze the city's prospects for economic development, and identify priorities for assistance (including investment from the Bank) to implement the strategy. Strategies would focus on the issues of greatest local concern for livability, and the implied requirements in terms of enhancing city productivity, management, and financing. Components of city development strategies are described in Chapter 2 of this volume.

SCALING-UP SERVICES FOR THE POOR, INCLUDING UPGRADING OF LOW-INCOME URBAN NEIGHBORHOODS. Basic infrastructure for the poor continues to be the first priority of multilateral assistance expressed by respondents in the World Bank's recent urban client survey.[3] The Bank would support initiatives that have demonstrated good outcomes and wide support from beneficiaries and originating institutions (often community-based organizations and NGOs). Scaling-up would hinge on agreement among key stakeholders (local and central

---

3. As an input to the development of the Bank's recent strategy on urban and local government issues, consultants conducted an external client survey to obtain feedback on past Bank-financed urban operations and future demands in 14 countries. This has provided the Bank with excellent information on the views of our major clients.

government, utilities, private developers, donors) and would be integrated into the question of access to a modicum of income-generation opportunities, which in itself relates to the need for education—less than 20 percent of heads of households in these areas have finished high school, and technical capacitation opportunities are very limited.

ENHANCED ASSISTANCE FOR CAPACITY-BUILDING. Project assistance and direct training in municipal development ("retail" approaches) would be complemented by new emphases. The first would be on channeling support to intermediary networks ("wholesaling") for exchange of knowledge and expertise among municipalities and other agencies involved in urban management and service delivery; including dissemination of good practices, training, and technical assistance which would be promoted through support to national and regional associations of local governments, training institutes, and research centers, and facilitation of "city twinning" arrangements. The second emphasis would be on nonlending advisory services; and these would permit more flexible and timely provision of technical assistance, outside the context of Bank lending, on a variety of urban management issues.

Sharing Knowledge: The First Urban and City Management Core Course

The time was right, then—given the broader understanding of urban development and the commitment to increase capacity-building efforts—to develop a learning program that reflected these trends. The logical theme on which to base this course was urban management, since those responsible for managing cities confront the complexity and the interrelationships of urban issues on a daily basis. However, while managers and mayors face these issues, they may not have had sufficient exposure to the wide-ranging and complicated topics that affect their cities; and they may not have had the opportunity to review successful policies and practices implemented by their international colleagues. The Urban and City Management Core Course[4] was designed to respond to this challenge. For two weeks, urban and city managers, mayors, policymakers, and trainers met in Toronto to explore and discuss ten "windows" of urban management.

---

4. The course took place in Toronto in May 1999. It was organized by the Bank in collaboration with the City of Toronto, the University of Toronto, the Canadian Urban Institute, and the course's co-sponsors—CIDA and the Government of Spain.

The objective of the course was to expose the participants to those topics, and to new concepts and practices. It gave the "big city picture," and provided materials and networking that would allow individual topics to be addressed in depth at a later time.

Given the complexities of urban management, narrowing the content of the course was a challenge. In order to clarify priorities, the course team relied heavily on consultations with mayors, as well as with professional colleagues from inside and outside the Bank. An additional preliminary step included a survey mission conducted at the Fourth Inter-American Mayors Conference in Miami, in which mayors and urban officials were asked what topics would most suit their needs. On the basis of their answers, and guided by a number of peer reviews, the training program was designed on a set of windows of urban development—the pillars of our training program.

The primary purpose of this volume is to assemble a set of readings that can assist city and municipal managers, students of urban management, and the general public to get acquainted with the main issues that urban managers face in their everyday life. Most of the contributions were prepared for the first Core Course in Toronto mentioned above. Other readings have been added to complement those and to provide information on key issues.

Globalization and Metropolitan Development

In economic literature, globalization refers to a situation of nations' increasing closeness in economic terms through trade, capital flows, and a new international division of labor. For Alan Gilbert (1990), globalization is the third most important reorganization of the international division of labor, the first having been the use of colonies as suppliers of raw materials, and the second the industrialization of developing countries through the medium of local or foreign entrepreneurs. Accompanied by rapid technological innovation and falling raw materials prices, globalization has brought about the tertiarization of old metropolises, such as London, and the increase in manufacturing in "younger" economies attractive to foreign direct investment. According to Gregory Ingram (1998), urban development patterns in both industrial and developing countries with market-oriented economies show strong regularities consistent with basic urban location theory: i.e., large metropolitan areas are converging into similarly decentralized structures with multiple subcenters, decentralized manufacturing, and more centralized service employment.

Has globalization affected the creation of megacities or metropolises? According to Yue-man Yeung (1995), one of the most interesting developments since World War II has been the rapid urbanization in developing countries and the concentration of urban populations in large cities. Between 1950 and 1990, the number of "million cities" in the world more than tripled, from 78 to 276, and is now projected to reach 511 by 2010. In 1990, 33 percent of the world's population lived in "million cities," and 10 percent in cities of more than 8 million inhabitants. Our expectation is for 26 megacities (cities of 10 million or more inhabitants) in the world by the year 2015, when the three largest urban agglomerations will be Tokyo, Bombay, and Lagos (U.N. 1998).

In the future, trade liberalization and financial integration will reinforce the importance of urban agglomeration economies, and localized networks for production will be essential underpinnings of global competitiveness (Gertler 1997). Manufacturing will increasingly emphasize intermediate service inputs connected with technology use, such as computer software, programming, and engineering services. An example is Sydney, whose transformation into a global city translated into a 25 percent increase in job creation and a radical shift toward financial and business services between 1971 and 1991 (Yeates 1997).

The consequences of globalization on city management, especially in conditions of weak public institutions and poor governance, have sometimes been dramatic. In several cases, the worsening of urban poverty and urban income inequality has been aggravated by the skewed allocation of resources in urban public investment and by technology which favors highly skilled labor as well as by the relative weakness of public institutions and public policy in responding to problems, and the gradual fragmentation of the metropolis and its institutions.

From an operational viewpoint, the capacity to address the critical management needs of metropolitan areas, in particular megacities, is often limited, given the usual absence of a metropolitan agency that is empowered to lead often a dozen or more component municipalities. In some instances the World Bank has supported the creation of umbrella agencies. For example, the Metropolitan Development Authorities in Manila and Calcutta have played important roles in the institutional constellation of the city, but without the powers required to address interjurisdictional issues effectively. More recently, the focus has been on metropolitan-wide management of specific sectoral or subsectoral activities such as water, public transport, or solid waste, where there is a rationale for cross-border collaboration, and externalities are tangible. City strategy exercises have also been key instruments in the identification of shared stakeholder interests and concerns in metropolitan cities where a coalition exists with vision and broad credibility, even in the absence of a formal executive agency.

City Strategy and Governance

Good city governance and management is a prerequisite for competitiveness and livability in any city. Governance is defined here in terms of accountability and transparency in the use of public funds, coupled with the knowledge and capacity required to execute local government responsibilities in response to the constituency's demands. Several issues are at stake in this area: first, what the requirements are for good governance; second, how to tackle the challenge of drawing a vision for one's city; and third, how to get the stakeholders' participation in the government process.

On the first issue, a prerequisite for good governance is a clear national framework of intergovernmental relations, one which determines incentives and the accountability of each level of government. It is widely recognized today that intergovernmental frameworks are a key part of the policy dialogue, especially as decentralization forces are remapping relations among cities, provinces, and the center. The participation of communities and entrepreneurs also mobilizes ideas, skills, and resources for better management, as does working with municipal associations, professional groupings of city managers, and newer national or subregional associations. The examples of the Municipal Development Program (MDP)[5] in Sub-Saharan Africa, and SACDEL, with several chapters in Latin American countries (supported by the World Bank Institute), attest to the importance of local associations in catering to, and channeling knowledge to, their partner individuals or institutions.

What about competitiveness? The aim of local strategic planning is to help the city identify market signals and its capacity to respond. The ingredients of this approach include: (a) analysis of what is actually happening in the local economy and surrounding markets; (b) participation by all the city stakeholders—private firms, labor, officials, financiers, community groups, infrastructure providers, universities, and research institutes—in

---

5. The MDP was established in 1991 and has become increasingly independent in its planning, execution, and financing. It provides technical assistance, consulting, training, and policy analysis by Africans to African local governments at their request.

defining how they want the city to evolve, what bottlenecks and requirements need to be addressed, and what they are prepared to contribute to the process; and (c) formation of active partnerships as commitments to implementing the strategy.

Understanding the city's economy is a vital component of city management. Pressed by emerging globalization and decentralization trends, city managers need to know about the economic strengths and weaknesses of their city, the dangers of declining sectors, and the opportunities of high-growth sectors. They need to be aware of the consequences of international integration (e.g., Mercosur), and they need to collect and use information. Cities are changing fast, and managers need to recognize some prototypes, including the "de-industrializing" city and the "serving" city. The latter refers to cities that have lost manufacturing but gained tourism, information, health, higher education, and new exportable goods.

Cities' productivity derives from economies of urban scale and agglomeration, as well as from natural assets, such as proximity to mineral resources, universities, trade corridors, and historical or cultural roots. Cities can enhance their productivity, or competitiveness, by developing policies and institutional frameworks that reinforce these sources of advantage and prevent diseconomies of agglomeration. Cities therefore need efficient factor markets and infrastructure, as well as a supportive and predictable climate for business. Facing a competitive global and national economy, local governments increasingly seek to become more proactive to enhance their growth. Strategies of local economic development that consist of trying to lure industries with tax breaks and other incentives often result in weakening the city's finances without producing net private investment; at best, they prompt a transfer of firms from another region. Studies of industrial location decisions show that firms are more influenced by elements affecting major labor and transport costs, and by the overall structure of taxation, than by special tax incentives that local authorities are able to offer (Bradbury, Kodrzycki, and Tannenwald 1997).

How to get the stakeholders together and draw on their energy and enthusiasm? In its support of City Development Strategies (CDS)—as part of its own urban strategy discussed earlier—the Bank has recognized the paramount importance of the people's participation in urban policy and change and, in many instances, has acted in the role of facilitator. CDS forms one of the main building blocks of the World Bank's urban strategy and the core of the recently formed City's Alliance. The approach calls for building broad coalitions of local stakeholders and development partners, both local and international, to work together to develop a strategy for a particular city/urban area that reflects a broadly shared understanding of the city's socioeconomic structure, constraints, and prospects (the analytical assessment), and a shared vision of goals, priorities, and requirements (the strategic plan of action). The CDS is both a process and a product that together identify ways to create the conditions for sustainability of the city on four dimensions: livability, competitiveness, good management and governance, and bankability. The process of CDS is defined by the cities themselves; each is therefore unique. The strategies reflect the priorities as perceived by the stakeholders, such as pressing concerns with unemployment (e.g., in Cali), poverty and crime, environmental deterioration, and so on. CDS are in preparation in more than 40 cities around the world; the most advanced are probably those developed by Coimbatore in India, Kampala in Uganda, Cali in Colombia, seven cities in the Philippines, Sofia in Bulgaria, and Johannesburg in South Africa.

City/Municipal Financial Management

To exploit the benefits of agglomeration, cities must provide an attractive place to do business and to live. To this end, cities need to invest in infrastructure and to provide the basic services necessary for economic growth. Pressure for investment is particularly concentrated during a country's urban transition—the years of rapid urban population growth. It is estimated that urban residents will increase by 2.4 billion over the next 30 years. This will require further investment in housing, water and sanitation, transport, power, and telecommunications. Asia alone will need to invest $280 billion a year over the next 30 years (Brockman and Williams 1998).

The private sector can finance a significant part of the infrastructure, notably housing, water, and telecommunications. However, publicly financed infrastructure will still be needed. In the case of streets, cost recovery is difficult; in the case of social infrastructure, it is undesirable. In many developing countries, central governments have traditionally mobilized the resources needed for public financing through domestic taxation, external debt, or donor assistance; with the tendency towards decentralization, local governments have gained a much greater role in financing investments.

Local governments can finance new responsibilities in several ways, notably through development fees, connection charges, and local tax revenues (property taxes and business taxes are the most important sources of local revenues for World Bank clients). In all cases, however, the revenue possibilities of the local governments are much lower than their expenditure needs, leading to a significant finance gap. In 1989, 62 percent of local expenditure in 18 developed countries was financed out of local revenue; in 18 developing countries, the proportion was less than half. Covering this gap requires transfers from higher levels of governments. In addition, local governments can resort to debt financing, especially when it is used to finance long-term investments such as roads, schools, pipelines, etc.[6]

While cities have a good idea of how much financing they need, revenue sources are often dependent on other levels of government. Issues of financial management relate not only to the wisdom of the budgetary process and allocation (which in principle should be carried out according to well-defined rules and processes of participation) but also to relations with upper tiers of government, notably the central government. Understanding financial management therefore requires a good perception of the links between levels of government, the assignment of responsibilities among those levels, and the relationship between those responsibilities and the revenue authorities for collecting taxes. Only in an environment of trust and open communication can the alternatives open to local government be broached. It is today well accepted that sound financing and good overall city management involve establishing linkages between services provided (directly or indirectly) by the city, and payment for them by users and beneficiaries, either directly through charges and tariffs, or indirectly through taxes.

A major focus of the World Bank's urban development program is the provision of technical assistance and policy advice to local and national governments on the fundamentals of sound subnational finance. These interrelated elements include rational intergovernmental *assignment of functions* as well as: (a) *expenditure management* (capital and recurrent budgeting and investment selection practices), including decisions to transfer activities and investments out of local government departments to separate corporations such as utilities or project companies, and/or enhancing the participation of the community in the preparation and execution of the municipal budget (see the readings on Porto Alegre's participatory approach); (b) *revenue mobilization and cost recovery* (sound pricing for public services, the use of suitable fees and charges to promote economic efficiency, property and other local taxation, and demand-side or willingness-to-pay approaches)—also depending on decisions about what activities should be financed privately, e.g., on a nonrecourse basis;

---

6. The use of debt instruments by local governments needs to be assessed with care, as imprudent borrowing may lead to fiscal indiscipline and macroeconomic imbalances (Freire, Huertas, and Darche 1998).

(c) *intergovernmental transfers* that are predictable and consistent with "hard budget" incentives; (d) *financial administration*, including generally accepted accounting, auditing, disclosure, asset and liquidity management, procurement, and payment procedures; and (e) *access to credit*, based on a legal and regulatory framework that allows municipal bankruptcy, collateralization, and prudent mechanisms of credit enhancement, such as revenue escrows and intercepts of fiscal transfers. Financing strategies could include choices between bank credit and bonds (general obligation or revenue bonds) for various purposes (Freire, Huertas, and Darche 1998).

To instill these practices, Bank operations have supported specialized municipal finance institutions (often called municipal development funds [MDFs]), in countries where a municipal credit market is virtually nonexistent. In Brazil, the Bank financed a sustained program of municipal development in five states covering more than 700 municipalities. While some MDFs have had ambiguous mandates and have politicized their lending, many have introduced sound municipal lending practices, have helped their clients to adopt the good financial management needed for creditworthiness, and have thereby contributed to establishing effective local government demand for a formal credit market.

For many cities, the ultimate goal is to become sufficiently creditworthy to access banks and capital markets. Ahmedabad, for example, turned its financial performance around in a few years to become the first city in India to be rated by a domestic agency, and successfully issued an investment bond. But for all cities, financial soundness is a worthwhile objective in itself, as it is reflected in respect for hard budgets and in efforts to mobilize fully and to use judiciously even weak resource bases.

Private-Sector Involvement in Public Service Provision

As cities look for more fiscally prudent ways to provide services, an increasingly common strategy is to contract some services to the private sector. The model of urban management relying on the public sector has often failed to yield satisfactory outcomes, prompting calls for the state to withdraw from the role of provider and to assume the role of regulator, relying on the private sector for the production and delivery of services. However, the historical record suggests that private provision might not be enough. In the late nineteenth and early twentieth centuries in England and the United States, gas, water, canals, trolleys, highways, and electricity were mostly provided privately. By 1890, 57 percent of the waterworks in the United States were owned by private companies. Services were often provided under long-term franchise contracts between municipalities and private firms, primarily for financing reasons because cities lacked capital and national subsidies were limited (Tynan and Cowen 1998).

Over time, however, dissatisfaction with private providers increased. Complaints centered on lack of coverage, high prices, poor quality, and political corruption. In the case of water, increasing volumes of wastewater began to pollute local sources, and private companies proved reluctant to invest in more distant sources. Disagreements also arose with municipalities over supply of water for fire-protection services, as fire-fighting technology changed and required water at greater pressures. Contracts proved hard to regulate, and courts of law found it difficult to cope with the complex regulatory problems that arose in disputes over these issues (Shugart 1998).

It is well accepted today that the private provision of public services has an important role to play in urban management and that it can lead to higher levels of efficiency and consumer satisfaction. It should, however, be avoided in the case of pure public goods, natural monopolies, and market failures. In all cases there is a need for effective regulation of private providers by public agencies. The experience of private provision in France is instructive in this regard; the decentralized public-private system of municipal concessions which has developed over a hundred years has proved to be very successful, but the French experience also shows that such a system is not always easy to implement and calls for a strong monitoring mechanism (Shugart 1998).[7]

Chapter 5 contains an interesting account of the benefits and possible problems associated with the privatization of some services or the use of the private sector to provide those services. The conclusions are clear: the private sector works better, provided that there is competition, political will, technical capacity, and accountability. A collaborative donor program established through an initiative of the Swiss Development Cooperation (SDC), the Urban Management Program (UMP), and the World Bank is focusing on how to improve public-private partnerships, developing guides for the preparation of contracts and bidding documents, and understanding the role of informal private-sector groups.

---

7. Associations of local governments have now created a consulting agency to help them with contract negotiation and regulatory design. Also, several laws have been passed that require concessionaires to make their accounts accessible to the public. This has substantially improved the situation and led to a restoration of confidence in water concessions (*Les Echos*, 25 March 1999).

The World Bank frequently re-evaluates its advice to clients who are considering particular arrangements with the private sector to improve efficiency or cash flow in particular sectors. One area of steady demand is the development of a strong and independent regulatory capacity, that can guarantee contracts and supervise agreed financial conditions. Many contracts have failed, or have had to be renegotiated, because of poor preparation by the public entity (sometimes the city) which failed to recognize the need for mutual respect, or to observe conditions necessary for success.

Land and Real-Estate Markets

Land management is a fundamental function of municipal governments, and one that has major impacts on city growth and efficiency. The ability of firms and households to make efficient location decisions within cities has big implications for urban economic growth. Local governments regulate the operation of land markets in several ways. The most usual form is through zoning, which typically assigns possible uses—residential, retail, commercial, industrial, mixed—to land in different parts of the city. It may also dictate intensity of use through maximum or minimum limits on lot sizes, floor space, or ratios of floor space to lot area.

The quality of land and real-estate policies has important (and sometimes damaging) effects on business and household welfare. In fact, most urban land markets are constrained by unnecessary regulation, strict zoning and rent controls, and lack of suitable land titling and registration systems. In Peru the adjudication process for state land takes more than three years; in Malaysia about half of any land parcel remains usable for construction after the approvals process is complete. In addition, legislation restricting land redevelopment, sale, or rental increases, produces delays and creates land rationing as well as rampant opportunities for corruption.

Delays in land registration and unclear property rights deter private investment in land and housing, and prevent collateralization for mortgage finance. Inappropriate codes for building construction and settlement density, often borrowed from more developed countries, make illegal the housing and infrastructure that the poor could afford. In addition, governments commonly fail to protect minimal rights of way in the face of rapid urban growth, thus forcing up costs for later installation of infrastructure networks, and requiring more resettlement.

Governments also influence the location of economic activity through controls over public land and the location of transport improvements. Up to half of urban land is in the public domain—for roads, highways, sidewalks, parks, and public buildings and facilities. How that public portion of urban land is utilized determines the spatial configuration of a city—where industry locates, how congested the city is, how dense neighborhoods are—and how the city will develop. Cities expand through progressive additions of transport corridors and ring roads, allowing economic activity to spread out in more or less progressive additions of concentric circles. Failure to expand facilities delays needed deconcentration and suburbanization of people and industry, resulting in exceedingly dense core cities with poor living conditions, and noncompetitive land and wage costs.

From an urban perspective, land, shelter, and infrastructure are closely linked. Access to legal and affordable land and shelter by poor dwellers in cities around the world has been very difficult for several decades and is worsening, leading to increasing percentages of the population living in so-called slums, under illegal occupation: an estimated 44 percent of the population in Caracas live in informal settlements, 35 percent in Guatemala City, 60 percent in Mexico City, and 40 percent in Lima (Gilbert 1996). Among city leaders who attended the Competitive Cities Congress in May 1999, about 50 percent see housing and land-tenure issues among the main challenges facing cities today, and 68 percent see this as the main urban challenge for the next decade (*Urban Age* 1999, p. 28). Such opinions confirm the urgency of reconciling competing demands for land, whether it be for shelter, factories, transport systems, waste disposal, agriculture, recreation, or green areas.

The impact of this problem on poverty amplifies the concerns of policymakers. Although informal settlements represent the only chance of some sort of shelter for many people, environmental problems in slums are serious: notably, poor access to potable water, bad (if any) drainage and sewerage systems, deficient solid-waste collection, very limited transportation options, and overcrowding, among others. The proliferation of urban slums is due, in part, to obsolete regulatory, legal, and institutional frameworks.

Urban Poverty

Poverty is probably the single most complex and daunting challenge facing any city manager. We know how cities have attracted migrants from depressed rural areas, and how the vagaries of economic cycles have led to shifts of income and the spreading of informal settlements; and we know how these settlements degenerate into slums as a result of years of rapid urbanization combined with poorly functioning housing and land markets, and the inability of the public sector to keep up with the investments needed for basic sanitation and health services. Residents are caught in a vicious, and often helpless, circle, lacking education, healthcare, and income-generating opportunities.

Evidence suggests that poverty and inequality lead to higher rates of crime and violence, with both offenders and victims predominantly from disadvantaged social groups. Urban dwellers in poor districts of metropolitan areas are particularly vulnerable (Bourguignon 1998). According to the World Health Organization (WHO), the annual global cost of injuries from violence is almost $500 billion in medical care and lost productivity (Zaidi 1998). Across regions, estimates of the social costs of crime and violence range from about 2 percent of GDP in Asia to a very high 7.5 percent of GDP in Latin America (Bourguignon 1998).[8]

While poverty should be addressed as a national issue, as should most redistributive programs (at least in the fiscal realm), local policies and institutions can influence the quality of life and health of the urban poor. In particular, community-driven public work schemes—often nationally funded but locally designed—have emerged as an effective means of reaching the poor by expanding their income-earning potential. When designed as a public guarantee of work with below-market wages, such schemes can screen out the non-needy and equalize opportunities across households; they can also create infrastructure of value to communities, especially when the communities themselves identify and determine the public works.

At the institutional level the main operational instrument to deal with poverty has been the integrated development project for low-income neighborhoods, typically called slum upgrading, which the World Bank started supporting in the mid-1970s. It is a way of providing specific urban or periurban settlements with basic improvements in water, sanitation, transport (footpaths and access roads), lighting, drainage, solid waste collection, community social service facilities, and increased security of tenure.

After some change in the configuration of these projects over time (as discussed earlier), there is today a renewed demand for Bank assistance for urban upgrading, as well as housing and land market/policy reform projects, to help governments improve access to urban land markets. Important programs are already underway in Brazil and Venezuela. Furthermore, in Guatemala City, the Bank worked with local partners to disburse a significant loan for housing, land titling, street construction and paving, storm drainage,

---

8. A recent estimate for South Africa placed the costs of crime and violence as at least 6 percent of the country's GDP (*Business Times*, 14 February 1999).

public lighting, and solid waste. The innovative aspect of these more recent projects is that they were initiated by the community rather than by the government, and many involve the private, for-profit, sector.

Understanding urban poverty requires proper definitions and measures, mainly to facilitate diagnosis of the issue and the monitoring of policy actions designed to alleviate the problem. Chapter 7 provides a clear path through the use of poverty assessments, measures of absolute and relative poverty, and city poverty profiles. These are important tools that enable city managers and policymakers to understand the degree and severity of the poverty of their poor residents and monitor the success of established or new policy actions. Creative solutions arrived at with the participation of the community are mentioned at length as successful experiences that are worthy of replication elsewhere in the urban world.

The Urban Environment

In addition to reducing poverty, good city management includes creating a healthful urban environment, minimizing crime and the risk of violence, establishing a civil protection system, and making urban amenities more accessible (Evans 1998; Kessides 1998). The environmental problems of urban areas (the "brown" agenda) include air pollution from vehicles, household energy use, and industrial and power plants; land and water pollution from solid wastes and untreated sewage; and traffic congestion, accidents, and noise. These problems have more direct and immediate negative impacts on human—especially poor people's—health and safety, and on business productivity, than do the issues addressed by the "green" environmental agenda. [9]

In addition to removing public health threats in slum neighborhoods, improving livability of the broader urban area requires protection of land, air, and water across a city and across jurisdictions. Top priority should normally be given to the near-term environmental threats to human health, notably from automobile and street-level emissions of lead and fine particulates, from inadequate water supply and sanitation, and from overcrowded urban residential quarters with inadequate ventilation. Air pollution, a negative externality contributed by economic growth, seriously impinges on the life chances and health of children, as well as of adults. Especially affected are those already suffering from malnutrition and

---

9. Several studies show that urban environmental quality is more closely associated with morbidity than is income per se (Harriss 1989).

infectious disease, conditions that lower their threshold for resisting chemical pollutants. For most children in large cities in developing countries, breathing the air is as harmful as smoking two packs of cigarettes a day. For example, in Delhi the incidence of bronchial asthma in the 5–16 age group is 10 to 12 percent, and air pollution is one of the major causes (Chhabra, Gupta, and Chhabra 1998). A 1990 study of lead pollution in Bangkok estimated that 30,000 to 70,000 children risked losing four or more IQ points because of high lead levels, and many more risked smaller reductions in intelligence (WRI 1996, p. 24.). China, another dramatic example of potential health risks, has nine of the top ten cities with the worst air quality in the world, measured by total suspended particulates.

Safety risks from traffic accidents and losses from potential industrial or climatic disasters require measures of prevention or mitigation. Cultural assets of cities, such as historic neighborhoods, are rapidly deteriorating as a result of pollution or population pressure, and encroachment is destroying parks and open spaces.

There is an increasing recognition that stand-alone interventions are most effective when guided by a consistent environmental policy framework. Such an approach requires methodologies and tools (e.g., comparative risk assessment) to improve understanding of the linkages between economic development, land use, environmental impacts, and social effects and mechanisms for consensus building and "mainstreaming" environmental priorities into policies and actions within sectors and subsectors (water/sanitation, transport, industry, solid waste, etc.).

Traditionally, the main lines of environmental assistance have rarely targeted urban environmental issues in a comprehensive way. Today, there is recognition that the environmental agenda must be seen as a central problem of urban management. This implies the need to work with the most appropriate level of government—increasingly, capacity building and technical assistance should be focused on the lower levels of government—and to find mechanisms to harness private initiatives and capital for lasting environmental improvements. In addition, emergency assistance to urban disasters needs to be mainstreamed and made proactive through disaster prevention and mitigation.

Urban Transport and Metropolitan Development

Urban transport and its management play key roles in the economic and social development of a city and its citizens. Transport systems are vital for any city, particularly in parts of the world where transport accounts for 40 percent of public-sector expenditures (Leinbach 1995). Transport is an issue for the local manager as population changes and economic development bring important pressures—increasing demand for transport, congestion, air pollution, and the lack of resources or technical skills to address these questions (Kitano 1998). Transport is a key issue from the point of view of poverty alleviation: the urban poor are often excluded from adequate public transportation, so mainstreaming transport into urban clusters is a high priority. The readings in Chapter 9 deal notably with the function of transport policies in increasing access and affordability, adjusting to changes in global patterns, increasing responsiveness to consumers, and to rapid motorization, which has led to traffic congestion[10] and significant air pollution.

Transport policies need to be sustainable, financially, socially, and environmentally. Financial sustainability is crucial to the life of a transport system and to the ability of the local government to support it. It implies on the one hand running the system at the lowest possible cost, generally calling for private-sector participation, along with adequate regulation, and bidding and concession mechanisms; and, on the other hand, passing costs to the users, or beneficiaries. In addition, to allow the poor to use the system at prices affordable to them, transparent subsidies should be used, financed by the authorities.

Social sustainability means including the poor and often underserved, particularly women, into the urban management picture, by increasing access and affordability. Transport systems need to improve physical access to jobs and to provide all people with mobility. In Latin America the lowest-income people live outside the central city where the jobs are; this requires the reduction of barriers to the informal sector, rather than keeping the informal sector out.[11] Affordability requires systems of direct subsidy to poor riders. In addition, land and transport planning need to be brought together to prevent developers' neglect of poor people's needs. Equally, community participation is essential, so that the public can decide the type and level of services it desires.

---

10. Estimates for Bangkok indicate a daily loss of about $4 million as a result of traffic congestion; in the United States, $43 million is lost every year.

11. The physical re-ordering of highly dense urban slums is given priority in an upgrading project that the Bank is financing in Venezuela. Access is currently so limited that the average slum dweller must walk for eight minutes to reach an accessible street. It then takes 20 minutes to reach formal-sector transportation—either subway or surface. Improvements in internal access are estimated to reduce travel times by over 20 percent—a potential saving of $3–4 million annually in time costs.

Environmental sustainability, above all, must include initiatives for road safety, as well as lowering levels of air pollution through cost-effective reduction of particulates and use of alternative fuels and cleaner gasoline. Pollution from transportation in Latin American cities accounts for 70 percent of all air pollution. Urban transport projects supported by the Bank in Brazil assist local governments with the design and implementation of integrated urban transport, land use, and air quality strategies; promote modal integration; improve investment planning; and undertake railway rehabilitation and concession programs.

International experience shows three key factors for any transport system: (a) a well-designed basic infrastructure network—lack of roads and connections leads to congestion and excessive demand in some parts of the system; (b) proper management of the traffic system—low-cost improvements such as computerized signal systems, turn restrictions, and pedestrian crosswalks can significantly improve the flow of traffic; (c) public transportation and buses—the public and private-sector roles—with priority for buses, dedicated bus lanes, and integrated facilities. And, as traffic grows, other alternatives play a role: train, metro, integrated modes of transportation, and integrated transportation planning. While in Bangkok the lack of transportation management is the primary problem, it seems that in Paris, Tokyo, and São Paulo, cities where the system works well, three critical elements are present: a well-developed rail network, effective traffic management, and facilities for pedestrians.

Future challenges are on the horizon and will need serious consideration. To prevent congestion prices eventually need to come into play—higher fuel prices, fees in congested areas (as in Singapore), and better articulation of private and public services. Again, Latin America seems to have produced good examples (Buenos Aires, São Paulo, Santiago) that could be used elsewhere, and we hope that this will continue to be true for quite a while.

Looking Ahead

The glimpses of improvement in cities and parts of cities offer hope and direction for the future. Land use and transportation in Curitiba, the participatory budget process in Porto Alegre, sustainable income programs in Argentina, private-sector management of solid waste in the Philippines—all are significant achievements. The challenge now is to bring such achievements to every city, a challenge worthy of the twenty-first century and by no means out of reach.

The sectoral examples reaffirm the importance for cities of developing appropriate institutions that get the most from the private sector and civil society. The much-appraised experience of Porto Alegre (Chapter 3) is an example of such an arrangement.[12] A key institutional innovation in that city's process is the municipal budget forum where project priorities are discussed by community representatives elected by different neighborhoods or districts; and the opportunity to articulate community demands creates an incentive for neighborhoods to organize themselves as well.

All the evidence we have presented makes clear that, despite the significant gains of the recent past, the unfinished urban agenda needs attention, and that efforts to improve urban livability can have significant effects in terms of increased wellbeing for millions of households. The challenge is to find the most cost-effective and inclusive ways of achieving the objective. Capacity-building and improved managerial skills of urban and city managers are key factors in facing this challenge.

Most of the issues examined in the following chapters are discussed from a technical point of view, abstract from the political aspects of the urban economy. Politics and the city are, however, intimately related. Both politics and cities have to do with social interdependence and both have undergone a revolution in the twentieth century. Cities became true urban centers at the end of the century with the introduction of social amenities—water and sanitation, public transportation, schools—offering their inhabitants a lifestyle inconceivable in any other environment. It was in these cities that the democratic revolution had its greatest impact and it was the institutionalization of democracy that led to deep changes in society resulting in what is called "urban lifestyle" (Singer 1994). The growth of cities makes democracy probable and the existence of democracy "urbanizes" the cities. In several countries, fiscal and political crises have led to a substantial decline of resources in their cities, and to the inability to maintain urban service provision at the same level. Lower levels of urban services (including personal safety and well-being) have led to the outflow of the most affluent residents, leaving the opposite pole of unemployment and poverty in the very core of the city itself. Some authors would argue that privatization, or the reduction of the role of the state, has been at the root of this crisis; others would claim that the urban crisis is the result of the weakening of nation states. Independently of which forces are at play in diverse circumstances, evidence abounds to attest to the importance of community participation, accountability, and adequate governance mechanisms in restoring the quality of urban services and in revitalizing the life of our cities.

---

12. Participatory budgeting has also been practiced in several other Brazilian cities, as well as in cities in Mexico and Venezuela. See Coelho 1996; Campbell 1998.

References

Bairoch, Paul. 1988. *Cities and Economic Development.* Chicago: University of Chicago Press.

Bourguignon, F. 1998. "Crime As Social Cost of Poverty and Inequality: A Review Focusing on Developing Countries." World Development Report Background paper. Washington, DC: World Bank.

Bradbury, Katherine L., Yolanda K. Kodrzycki, and Robert Tannenwald. 1997. "The Effects of State and Local Public Policies on Economic Development: An Overview." *New England Economic Review* March/April: 3–12.

Brockman, Royston C., and Allen Williams. 1998. *Urban Infrastructure Finance.* Manila: Asian Development Bank.

Campbell, Tim. 1998. *The Quiet Revolution: The Rise of Political Participation and Local Government with Decentralization in Latin America and the Caribbean.* World Bank, Washington, DC. Processed.

Chhabra, S.K., C.K. Gupta, and P. Chhabra. 1998. "Prevalence of Bronchial Asthma in School Children of Delhi." *Journal of Asthma* 35(3): 291–96.

Coelho, Magda Prates. 1996. "Urban Governance in Brazil." In Patricia L. McCarney, ed., *Cities and Governance: New Directions in Latin America, Asia and Africa,* pp. 39–55. Toronto: Centre for Urban and Community Studies, University of Toronto.

Evans, Peter. 1998. "Looking for Agents of Urban Livability." In *A Globalized Political Economy.* Draft manuscript.

Freire, Maria E., Marcela Huertas, and Ben Darche. 1998. *Subnational Access to Capital Markets: The Latin American Experience.* Washington, DC: World Bank.

Gertler, Meric S. 1997. "Globality and Locality: The Future of 'Geography' and the Nation-State." In Peter Rimmer, ed. *Pacific Rim Development: Integration and Globalisation in the Asia-Pacific Economy,* pp. 12–33. St. Leonards, Australia: Allen and Unwin.

Gilbert, Alan G. 1990. "Urbanization at the Periphery: Reflections on the Changing Dynamics of Housing and Employment in Latin American Cities." In D. Drakakis-Smith, ed., *Economic Growth and Urbanization in Developing Areas,* pp. 73–124. London: Routledge.

Gilbert, Alan G. 1996. *The Mega City in Latin America.* Tokyo: United Nations University Press.

Harriss, John. 1989. "Urban Poverty and Urban Poverty Alleviation." *Cities* 6(3): 186–94.

Hohenberg, Paul M. 1998. "Urban Systems and Economic Development: The European Long Term and Its Implications." Background Paper for the *World Development Report 1999/2000*. Washington, DC: World Bank.

Ingram, Gregory K. 1998. "Patterns of Metropolitan Development: What Have We Learned?" *Urban Studies* 35(7): 1019–36.

Kessides, Christine. 1998. "A Strategic View of Urban and Local Government Issues: Implications for the Bank." Working Level Draft. Washington, DC: World Bank.

Kitano, Naohiro. 1998. "Analysis of Spatial Organization and Transportation Demand in an Expanding Urban Area Using Centrographic Methods." Sendai 1972–1992. Paper for WDR Tokyo Workshop.

Leinbach, T. 1995. "Transport and Third World Development: Review, Issues, and Prescriptions." *Transportation Research A* 29(5): 337–44.

Lo, Fu-chen, and Yue-man Yeung. 1998. *Globalization and the World of Large Cities*. Tokyo and New York: United Nations University Press.

Mokyr, Joel. 1995. "Urbanization, Technological Progress, and Economic History." In H. Giersch Paul, ed., *Urban Agglomeration and Economic Growth*. Berlin: Springer.

Ortiz, Alexandra. 1998. "Survey of Selected Latin American Mayors on Priorities on Urban and City Management Training Needs." World Bank, Washington, DC. Processed.

Shugart, Chris. 1998. "Decentralization and the Challenges of Regulation for Local-Level Public Services in Central and Eastern Europe." Extended version of a commentary delivered to European Bank of Reconstruction and Development seminar on Commercial Infrastructure Challenges in Transition Economies, London, 12 April.

Singer, Paul. 1994. "Politics and the City." *Urban Age* 2(2): 3.

Stren, Richard. 1996. "The Studies of Cities: Popular Perceptions, Academic Disciplines, and Emerging Agendas." In Michael Cohen, Blair Ruble, Joseph Tulchin, Allison Garland, eds., *Preparing for the Urban Future: Global Pressures, Local Forces,* pp. 392–419. Washington, DC: Woodrow Wilson Center Press.

Tynan, Nicola, and Tyler Cowen. 1998. "The Private Provision of Water in 18th and 19th Century London." Department of Economics, George Mason University. Draft.

United Nations. 1998. *World Urbanization Prospects: The 1996 Revision*. New York: U.N.

Urban Age. 1999. "Urban Age Survey Probes City Leaders' Views on Issues, Challenges." *Urban Age* 7(1): 28.

Yeates, Noel R. 1997. "Creating a Global City: Recent Changes to Sydney's Economic Structure." In Peter Rimmer, ed., *Pacific Rim Development: Integration and Globalisation in the Asia-Pacific Economy*, pp. 178–96. St. Leonards, Australia: Allen and Unwin.

Yeung, Yue-man. 1995. "Globalization and World Cities." In Richard Stren with Judith Bell, eds., *Urban Research in the Developing World: Vol. 4, Perspectives on the City*, pp. 189–226. Toronto: Centre for Urban and Community Studies, University of Toronto Press.

World Bank. 1999. *Elements for a New Strategy on Urban Development and Municipal Issues*. Washington, DC: World Bank.

World Bank. 2000. *World Development Report 2000*. Washington, DC: World Bank.

WRI (World Resources Institute). 1996. *The Urban Environment 1996–1997*. In collaboration with UNEP, UNDP, and IBRD. New York: Oxford University Press.

Zaidi, Akbar S. 1998. *Urban Safety and Crime Prevention*. UNCHS Regional Symposium on Urban Poverty, Fukuoka, Japan, October 27–29.

1

Metropolitan Issues

Editor's Introduction

Richard Stren

As many commentators remind us, we are living in an age of "globalization," in which increasingly rapid and intense flows of capital, labor, and technology circulate relentlessly around the world—creating new productive, social, and institutional structures. The sociologist Manuel Castells describes the process as one of great historical significance:

> Toward the end of the second millennium...events of historical significance have transformed the social landscape of human life. A technological revolution, centered around information technologies, is reshaping, at an accelerated pace, the material basis of society. Economies throughout the world have become globally interdependent... in a system of variable geometry... [Moreover] capitalism itself has undergone a process of profound restructuring, characterized by greater flexibility in management; decentralization and networking of firms both internally and in their relationships to other firms; considerable empowering of capital *vis-à-vis* labor... [This process includes] intervention of the state to deregulate markets selectively, and to undo the welfare state, with different intensity and orientations depending upon the nature of political forces and institutions in each society; stepped-up global economic competition, in a context of increasing geographic and cultural differentiation of settings for capital accumulation and management (Castells 1996, pp. 1–2).

While some writers point out, with justification, that economic internationalization is far from a new phenomenon (Hirst and Thompson 1996), the rapidity and geographic spread of these forces at the end of the twentieth century is unprecedented. One well-known author refers to globalization as an "overarching international system shaping the domestic politics and foreign relations of virtually every country." The same writer goes on to argue that the defining characteristic of this system is speed— "[the] speed of commerce, travel, communication and innovation" (Friedman 1999, pp. 7, 9).

Cities have been caught up in these changes in many significant ways, although it is important to understand that not all of the major transformations taking place in cities can be directly attributed to globalization. Looking at urbanization trends over the past 25 years, Michael Cohen comments on the intimate relationship between urban and national development, with cities constituting "powerful engines of growth, in many cases more powerful than national economies." But, in spite of improvements in urban incomes and productivity, in many cities there is growing poverty, inequality, reduced social cohesion, and a decline in the effectiveness of public institutions and public policy. Urban sprawl arising from disproportionate investment in highway and road transport (as in North America) or from the absolute lack of urban facilities in the peripheries (in many Latin American countries) is a serious challenge to productivity and the urban quality of life.

On the more positive side, we are witnessing a rebirth of local participatory processes in many areas (such as Latin America), especially when decentralization policies are effectively applied, and urban environmental challenges are becoming increasingly understood. Looking at the largest cities and their governance structures, Cohen argues that they require new institutional frameworks that can manage both internal transformations and the impact of global forces, while at the same time improving urban productivity, reducing urban poverty and inequality, and sustaining the natural balance of the urban environment. Finding the appropriate metropolitan solutions to the problems of social differentiation and spatial fragmentation, he suggests, is a major response to the global challenge.

Pursuing the metropolitan governance theme in detail, Jordi Borja reflects on some of his experiences in Europe and Latin America. Borja understands metropolitan administration not only as a given structure, but also "a project... an outcome of action, an outcome of a strategy." Managing large city regions in which many who live outside the city use central-city services and cultural institutions, and in which—at least in developing countries—the majority of the population lives at a subsistence level, while a small minority lives in affluence and comfort, requires a strategic plan and political innovation. Part of this planning must be aimed at creating city centers that cater to the large spatial extensions of the metropolis, but another must be to achieve some coherence in both transport and social policies. Some of the flavor of these planning challenges is conveyed in box examples from Barcelona scattered through Borja's paper. For example, Barcelona has completed a number of remarkable cultural projects since 1995—including a new opera house, a "City of Theater" project, and a plan to revitalize the museums in the Gothic quarter of the city. In partnership with the private sector, the city has promoted the establishment of three large new centers of commercial activity outside the central business district. And it has set up a new Metropolitan Transport Authority to coordinate administrative and planning issues for the multiplicity of public transport agencies within the metropolitan area. Of course, each city is different and must develop its own institutional approach, but metropolitan solutions "should guarantee coordination, decentralization, and equal rights of all citizens that live in the same territory."

These reflections on metropolitan governance are followed by a detailed case study of Toronto, Canada. This analysis, written by Larry S. Bourne, deals with the experience of Toronto in developing planning mechanisms to respond to the dynamic changes that have been taking place in that large Canadian city since the end of World War II. The current population of the "City of Toronto" (an amalgamation of one upper-tier and six lower-tier municipalities) is approximately 2.3 million, in a larger urban region (called the "Greater Toronto Region," or GTA) of 4.6 million. The history of planning in Toronto shows extreme fluctuations—at times planning decisions were popular and acceptable, at other times they were virtually ignored. But a key player was always the Ontario provincial government, within whose constitutional jurisdiction the municipality of Toronto (whatever its form and functions) has been located since Canada became a sovereign nation in 1867. The current situation, in which there is a City of Toronto for the old built-up area of the GTA, and four independent regional governments covering the rest of the GTA, represents a "retreat from regional planning and development regulation" on the part of the provincial government. The senior level of government, which draws much of its political support from regions outside the built-up area of Toronto, has essentially resisted the creation of a metropolitan government covering the whole urban region, leaving in its place a weak structure (the Greater Toronto Services Board) with limited powers of cordination. Such coordination is important, says Bourne, since as Toronto has expanded outward, it in effect has become differentiated spatially, socially, and economically into three different cities: the central city, the older suburbs, and the outer-ring suburbs. Given these emerging differences, and the political and jurisdictional conflicts that can easily arise, the city faces a serious challenge in redistributing costs and benefits of urban growth over the entire region, and in coordinating services and other investments. Like so many large conurbations in North America and elsewhere, Toronto needs a more comprehensive metropolitan-level planning framework of some kind; but as in almost all other cases, a combination of historical, political, and institutional factors inhibits the emergence of proper metropolitan governance for this important city region.

References

Castells, Manuel. 1996. *The Rise of the Network Society*. Oxford: Basil Blackwell.

Friedman, Thomas L. 1999. *The Lexus and the Olive Tree: Understanding Globalization*. New York: Farrar, Strauss, Giroux.

Hirst, Paul, and Grahame Thompson. 1996. *Globalization in Question: The International Economy and the Possibilities of Governance*. Cambridge: Polity Press.

The Impact of the Global Economy on Cities

Michael Cohen

Two fundamental issues should guide our efforts to understand the impact of the global economy on cities: the importance of globalization for city management, and the changing meaning of local responsibility. To avoid an only theoretical, or even rhetorical, discussion, we should place our discussions in real time, in mid-1999, a moment of intense discussion about the evils and opportunities of globalization. How do global economic and technological processes affect cities? What do we know? What needs more research? What is the meaning of local responsibility under these new circumstances? If global factors appear to be beyond local control, how can local governments respond?

I shall begin by asking whether the major features of the urbanization experience over the past 25 years have been significantly affected by the processes of globalization. I shall capture this question in nine general observations, placing them within the growing debate about the potential of metropolitan solutions to urban problems. I shall conclude by proposing an activist perspective on the meaning of local responsibility in a global age.

Looking Back at the World's Urbanization Experience

My first observation is that we know that urbanization over the past 25 years has been a major factor in the overall improvement of incomes and quality of life in developing countries. Increases in economic productivity, improvements in literacy, health status, and life expectancy have, in most countries, resulted from urban-generated economic surpluses. Cities are powerful engines of growth, in many cases more powerful than national economies. While the world's leaders have been worried about short-term global economic crises, we should not forget the longer-term lessons of comparative history: in 1960, Korea and India had equal per capita incomes; 40 years later, there is no question that Korea is one of the world's largest economies, with tremendous investments in human capital, technology, and infrastructure, and much of this growth has come from urban-based industry and trade. India, in contrast, has experienced slow growth, mired in rural poverty, and has been unable to develop urban policies to encourage efficient private investment.

Over the same period, Ghana, richer than Korea in 1957, failed to convert its agricultural surpluses into investment in people and, more importantly, people in cities. Accra and Kumasi deteriorated badly, leaving the country with no commercial infrastructure to export its crops once production restarted in the 1980s. Industrial investment stalled and existing residential infrastructure deteriorated badly. At one point, conditions were so bad that the residents of Accra were leaving the city to find food and shelter in the countryside. City performance matters. Indeed, when urban investment is managed badly, unsustainable financial liabilities can provoke debt crises and deep recessions, as suggested by the Latin American experience of the 1980s, and the Asian crisis of 1997–98. Yet, despite these problems, the gross domestic product (GDP) of Rio de Janeiro and São Paulo together is bigger than the GDP of the Andean countries.

We can conclude that the productive contribution of urbanization to national welfare may change as a result of global economic processes, but its overall role in providing more than half of GDP, and much more in some countries, will continue and increase in importance. The economic future of countries will depend to an increasing degree on the productivity of urban-based economic activities.

My second observation is that, despite increases in urban incomes and urban productivity, there is growing urban poverty in most countries. The absolute numbers of people living below US$1 or $2 a day is in the billions. Demographic growth—initially rural-urban migration, and subsequently natural increase—has been faster than the increase in the capacity of public institutions to provide needed infrastructure. Demographic increases and new entrants into the labor market have combined to create massive unemployment and under-employment in cities in developing countries. Urban poverty and unemployment are affected by globalization. A recent study by Samuel Morley (1998) concludes that urban poverty appears to be disproportionately related to macro-economic performance: when macro-economic growth rates drop, urban poverty increases at a faster rate, and appears to be slower to decline when growth resumes. This suggests that, when global and regional economic crises introduce more instability within individual national and local economies, these forces will have longer-lasting effects than might be expected. The effects of the "tequila crisis" of 1995, for example, are still felt in Argentina.

Third, absolute poverty is accompanied by growing inequality within cities, much of which can be attributed to the skewed allocation of resources, in urban public investment, for example, and in the access of the poor to urban infrastructure services. These differences in living conditions, coupled with varying levels of education and professional training, combine to create cumulative patterns of inequality in employment, incomes, and social mobility. These patterns appear to be exacerbated by the globalization of the world economy, where high financial returns come to individuals able to benefit from technological and industrial progress, while individuals without skills are trapped in low-wage jobs. As the global economy comes to value these higher-wage skills, existing patterns of inequality are worsened.

The costs of urban life determine levels of welfare as well as social mobility. For the growing numbers of urban poor, no longer does the city promise a better life for one's children. Programs to assure basic education for all, rather than to provide equally high-quality programs for the poor, in some sense contribute to the problem: in order to compete, young people must have skills that can add quality to the production of goods and services. Yet providing "quality" education is perceived as prohibitively expensive in many cities. Only where strong family and community incentives exist, as in some Asian cultures, can these opportunities become vehicles for true upward social mobility.

Inequality, therefore, may be exacerbated by social programs which, while seeking to provide minimum or basic levels of education, actually limit opportunities for the more able students.

Fourth, economic distress in all parts of the world, whether Jakarta, Cairo, or Los Angeles, is accompanied by, and worsened by, declining social cohesion: crime, street violence, household violence and abuse, drugs, youth unrest, and a breakdown in traditional family and community structures and values. Crime data such as the figure of 25 murders per day in São Paulo suggest an apocalyptic view of the future. Urban insecurity is no longer news, yet 25 years ago it was not a major issue in many developing-country cities. There is no particular reason why the global economy *per se* is responsible for these patterns of behavior, although historically, the incidence of economic, social, and political unrest has increased dramatically during periods of instability—for example, in the period from 1929 to 1932, when the world experienced many regime changes. It is true, nevertheless, that increased economic deprivation provides the motivation for violence, crime, and other social manifestations of economic stress, as seen recently in Ecuador and Indonesia, and over the past several years in Russia.

Social polarization, between rich and poor, between long-time residents and recent arrivals, and between racial and ethnic groups, exists not only in developing countries, between Malays and Chinese, for example, but also in New York between African-Americans and Koreans. Growing differences and competition, reflected in residential location, social mobility, and quality of life, all tend to increase segregation, manifest in the quality of schools, concentrations of poor children, crime, unemployment, and in fundamentally different land-use patterns.

A recent study of 100 U.S. cities (Galster 1998) provides some of the first rigorous econometric analysis of this process. It shows that shocks to labor markets in specific cities are reflected in individual and aggregated social behaviors such as the rates of crime, school dropout, and female-headed households. These, in turn, magnify the initial shock, affecting the metropolitan opportunity structure, because these elements are mutually interactive; labor, housing, and mortgage markets respond to changes in them. Differences, therefore, become deeper over time.

A fifth feature of urbanization has been the relative weakness of public institutions and public policy in responding to problems, and the growing recognition that non-public actors in civil society have major roles to play; for example, in the management of infrastructure, or in community development. The ideological shift of the 1980s towards the private sector and redefined roles of the state in many countries is, among other things, simply a reflection of weak public institutions. This has been captured by one writer as "strong societies and weak states." As demand grew and public resources and capacities became proportionately smaller to apply to these challenges, the state evolved from being a dependable to an undependable service provider and, more recently, to a weak and frequently corrupt regulator of privately provided services. The trend towards privatization occurred before globalization; the importance of non-public actors in urban management therefore cannot be attributed to globalization, but the sharing of this experience at a global level between countries has probably accelerated privatization.

The weaknesses in privatization of services without adequate public institutions to ensure equitable access to such services enhances differentiation within the metropolitan area. Commonly held public perceptions of the great differences in income between neighborhoods, barrios, and quartiers in cities such as Abidjan, Nairobi, Karachi, or Caracas, can now be easily supported by rigorous data on the distribution of infrastructure investment, social services, poor households, youth violence, and other indicators.

Pockets of wealth and poverty reflect the consolidation of economic and social power, and its translation into political power as well. These patterns are thus also spatial. For example, shortages in basic infrastructure, such as water supply, electricity, sanitation, transport, and housing, impose heavy private costs on urban households at the periphery. A 1992 World Bank study in Ciudad Juarez, a busy and growing city along the Mexican-U.S. border, found that households living on the "poor side of town" spent 29 percent of their income on transport to work. Residential location is a powerful predictor of socio-economic status and future earning potential. Robert Hackenberg, studying Davao, the Philippines, in the late 1970s suggested a "concentric theory of urban income distribution," with the richer households living in the center, often with the difference between rich and poor being the opportunity for a secondary wage earner in the household to take advantage of central locations.

My sixth point is that weak centralized public institutions have also given way to greater decentralization of responsibility for policy and services, both to local units at the city and intra-urban level, and to the private sector. This process seems to be leading in many countries, such as Mexico, Brazil, and the Philippines, to greater local democracy and, in some cases, to increased efficiency in urban service delivery. It is probably too early in most developing countries for a solid judgement on the equity of private-sector service delivery. In Argentina, with an extensive privatization program, major improvements have clearly been made in urban transport, telecommunications, water supply, and sanitation, yet the citizens of Buenos Aires experienced an electricity blackout for 10 days during the summer heat of 1998, leading to many new views about the value and efficacy of private sector management. While there have been few comparative studies of the incidence of these changes, it is fair to say that this process also appears independent of globalization.

The meaning of decentralization within metropolitan areas is at least twofold: it refers, first, to the decentralization of governmental institutions from downtown locations into neighborhoods; or second, to a parallel process of decentralization of economic activity to the periphery of cities. The first is clearly happening as "City Hall" becomes farther and farther away, both spatially and culturally, from individual neighborhoods. In its place are outposts of the city government and, in many cases, new forms of neighborhood and regional administration and participation. Neighborhood councils and specialized districts for schools, water supply, and other services have created new forms of urban governance that bring public decision-making closer to the population.

These institutional processes also reflect new urban spatial configurations and interests. William Morrish (1999) has analyzed, in Minneapolis, the varying interests of "suburban rings," neighborhoods whose economic, social, infrastructural, and environmental interests are based on their age— when they were built and where they are in the life cycle of their public and private investments. The first- and second-ring suburbs have faced similar problems, but at different times. As a result, their relationships to the downtown core, which is itself in varying cycles of boom and bust, are very different. At the same time, however, many metropolitan studies in the United States have demonstrated that the economic status of suburban and central-city areas is interdependent. These new spatial forms are thus far more complicated and multi-nodal than the central business district/ suburban models of the 1950s.

Although the process of fragmentation of metropolitan areas is driven by economic and social processes, its first indicator has historically been institutional; the process begins when communities and their local government units no longer perceive that their "natural" links are with the metropolitan core. Jurisdictional affinities become closer to non-central institutional units, to provinces or neighboring units of different sizes. These institutional leanings reflect economic and social realities. This process was described in Brazil 10 years ago as "demetropolization." Examples included communities located on the periphery of Rio de Janeiro, and along the transportation corridor towards São Paulo; they no longer looked to downtown Rio, but were more concerned with how their infrastructural lifeblood would be managed, and how growing traffic and trade in the direction of São Paulo would influence local production, municipal services, and incomes. The Rio metropolitan area was literally breaking down, on the periphery. Similar examples occurred in São Paulo, as the economic hinterland of São Paulo State became more important than the downtown Avenida Paulista.

This process is well underway in Buenos Aires, now with a population of 11.5 million persons, of which only 3 million live in the *Capital Federal*. The remaining 75 percent live in *municipios* dependent on the Province of Buenos Aires, under the control of a Governor from a political party different from that of the Mayor of downtown Buenos Aires. If the downtown holds the valued *patrimonio* of the past, the province is clearly the locus of the future: its aspirations, technology, and investment. This is similar to patterns in Chicago, Los Angeles, or Manila.

This institutional fragmentation is compounded by the growing importance of markets for goods and services beyond the city, and now, in a globalized world, even in other countries. For some enterprises, the most important location in the city is the port or the airport. These locational shifts reflect economic realities, and are evident in the extraordinary growth of factories, depots, offices, and hotel facilities near transport nodes. The historical connections of cities to water transport have now been amplified by high-speed trains, superhighways, and airports.

Seventh, decentralization, particularly in Latin America, has also strengthened local participatory processes in many countries, and has permitted higher levels of accountability and transparency in some localities. There are few studies, however, of the impact of decentralization of public responsibilities on income levels, infrastructure service quality, social cohesion, crime, or environmental quality. Robust conclusions about the relationship between institutional form and performance remain elusive. The management of urbanization is increasingly decentralized, but the trend is not materially affected by globalization.

Eighth, it is also clear that urban environmental problems are becoming increasingly understood. Yet, with less regulation of the private sector, green space and other natural resources are severely threatened by over-consumption and poor management. This unsustainable pattern is reflected in the increasing marginal cost of water in almost every city in the world. Beijing is now bringing water from sources 800 miles from the city. It is apparent that the growing importance of the market, and the spreading private management of infrastructure, is negative for the natural environment. Private enterprises rarely have the public interest at heart in their calculations of profit and loss, when it comes to factoring in longer-term environmental costs. This is not, in most cases, a result of globalization, although foreign capital may be less sensitive to sustainable uses of locally available natural resources.

An important part of this story also involves the management of the physical landscape of cities. Not only are there major issues of the absolute levels of consumption of natural resources within metropolitan areas—witness the growing dramas about water supply in cities such as Beijing or Los Angeles—but also who will have access to natural resources, including public space. Patterns of private residential investment and patterns of public management of green spaces can contribute to increasing vulnerability to so-called natural disasters.

A ninth characteristic of the urbanization experience is the parallel process of urban concentration in megacities, and the accelerated growth of secondary cities and towns. While it is difficult to prove that globalization increases urban population concentration, the forces that have attracted populations are magnified by globalization, the creation of employment, and opportunities for trade. The focus on the biggest cities, which dominated attention in the early 1990s, has given way to appreciation of the fast-growing secondary cities. This is appropriate for many reasons, including the fact that there are many more of these so-called secondary cities. Countries such as China, Brazil, India, Indonesia, Mexico, Turkey, and the Philippines all have multiple cities of over a million people. This process would have occurred regardless of globalization.

The issue of city size also needs to be related to institutional capacity. We used to hear about Mexico City and Calcutta, but industrial accidents in Guadalajara and Bhopal demonstrated that even more serious problems might exist in secondary cities where public institutions have less capacity to manage fast-growing problems. Increased economic and environmental complexity increases vulnerability to various kinds of risk, such as health or industrial accidents. But, again, this vulnerability cannot be attributed to the global economy.

When one takes all these general characteristics of urbanization into account, it is apparent that the global economy increases local vulnerability to macro-economic changes—in part because of the pace of change and the lags in response—and this may be reflected in rapid changes in economic opportunities dependent on trade, industrial production, and technology. These patterns need more study to develop a truly robust theory or explanation of the relationships. It is nevertheless useful to identify some of the indicators of impact and change that have already been experienced over the past few years.

Indicators of Impact and Change

We know that the increasing interdependence of markets for all kinds of goods and services within the global economy, within countries, regions, and localities, has resulted in new patterns of production, consumption, demand, and supply. For example, over the last ten years, 50 percent of the jobs in Buenos Aires have changed from one sector to another. These changing patterns are reflected in new prices: for capital, labor, technology, skills, land, infrastructure, and many other institutional services, such as trading and commercial services. These prices in turn mean that the local demand for labor, for example, will depend no longer on local markets, but on a range of international markets. All these patterns—production, consumption, demand, supply—and their indicators, such as prices, should be monitored at the local level to ascertain the nature of the changes that are going on.

These short-term changes may occur in export markets and in the tourism industry. Export markets are frequently of critical importance in local economic life, as Argentina is discovering since Brazilian markets for Argentine-produced cars have quickly contracted with the financial crisis. This has direct consequences for producers of steel, automobile parts, and other ancillary industries in, for example, Cordobà, a city of 1.5 million persons. It also has an immediate impact on tourism within Mercosur: if fewer Brazilian tourists visit Mercosur cities, demand for facilities is likely to be reduced. One interesting impact will be the reduction in municipal tax revenue from sources tied to tourism, such as hotel receipts, airport taxes, and other such charges. It will also have an impact on the demand for labor in the tourism industry.

If these changes can be relatively rapid, as the impact of the Brazilian crisis shows, other impacts have longer incubation periods and longer duration. For example, the establishment of industrial parks in response to markets in neighboring countries takes time, but, once created, they have longer-term spatial impacts. These kinds of changes occur both within cities and within the urban structures of countries and regions, giving rise to what Saskia Sassen (1994) has termed "new geographies of margins and new peripheries."

Another type of impact lies in physical changes in land use. For example, many of the foreign investments in specific cities bring with them their own proportions and dimensions, that frequently bear no relation to the existing city plans, grids, layouts, and codes of land use or construction. In Buenos Aires, the Argentine architectural historian, Margarita Gutman, has pointed out that many of the buildings which do not seem to "fit" within the land-use plans or architectural style of a particular neighborhood are financed from external sources. This subject deserves some comparative research as another manifestation of globalization.

Metropolitan Solutions to Urban Change

My view of metropolitan institutions is essentially as a framework to manage externalities, secondary, and tertiary impacts, both positive and negative in nature. Historically, metropolitan government has often been useful in managing new impacts—for example, of transportation planning. However, as suggested by the case of Toronto, these institutional forms may be useful for a certain time and then may appear less effective when the impacts change in scale or significance. One such case involves managing environmental impacts such as air or water pollution, that spread first beyond municipal boundaries, then beyond metropolitan jurisdictions to have regional effects.

In this regard, metropolitan frameworks need to be judged according to longer-term criteria for urban management. Three criteria, or urban policy objectives, might be used: Do metropolitan frameworks help to assure and improve the productivity of urban areas? Do metropolitan frameworks help in efforts to reduce poverty and urban inequality? Do metropolitan frameworks help to manage the urban environment more effectively?

Each of these criteria, of course, involves definitions and needs specification in terms of measurement. But institutional forms should, in my mind, be designed and adopted in relation to policy objectives, not the other way around. Institutional forms should not be assumed as a "given," nor to exist forever. Rather, they need to be seen in dynamic terms, as responses to ever-changing needs and challenges.

Metropolitan Areas: A World of Differences

In applying these criteria, it is important to emphasize that the metropolitan areas of the world are, above all, marked by their differences: differences in access by individuals, households, and communities to services, resources, opportunities, and, most of all, quality of life. Most cities in the developing world, and many in the industrialized world, are experiencing deepening and cumulative patterns of inequality. Recent metropolitan studies in the United States suggest some interesting categories for analysis of metropolitan processes. In a 1997 study called *Chicago Metropolitics*, Myron Orfield, a state legislator and keen analyst of metropolitan patterns, identified the following types of change in metropolitan Chicago: fragmentation, differentiation, growing inequalities, poverty concentrations, decentralization, polarization, and what he refers to as a "spatial mismatch," whereby problems are located in spatial areas or jurisdictions lacking the resources to address them. These categories are also useful when applied to developing countries.

While the studies of Chicago show the predominance of poverty on the city's South Side, they also reveal growing numbers of poor households in other parts of the city, on the solidly African-American West Side, and more recently, in the older white suburban neighborhoods. While not in the spectacular form of the slums of Calcutta or Madras, these areas are nevertheless concentrations of poverty in Chicago. They are reinforced by poor schools and inadequate transport services. They are compounded by social disorganization, declining property values, and business disinvestment. Recent evidence from Los Angeles shows that most banks have moved out of poorer districts of the city, leaving behind only automatic teller machines. An estimated 300,000 monthly welfare checks in Los Angeles are sent to commercial addresses where poor households pick them up; their residential addresses are neither secure nor permanent.

Can the Differences be Sustained?

Given the forces that fragment, divide, and polarize metropolitan areas, what conclusions can be drawn for the sustainability of metropolitan societies over time?

First, it seems clear that some aspects of the diversity of urban areas that contribute to their economic and cultural vitality, can also undermine social cohesion, economic productivity, and, eventually, future social mobility and opportunity.

Second, there is a growing tension between the promise of metropolitan growth in economic terms, both at the urban and national levels, and growing economic and social differences between individuals, households, and communities.

Third, short-term economic differences are becoming structural in the sense that they are reflected in patterns of residential investment and neighborhood quality of life. Spatial and physical differences in turn deepen social and economic differences and inequalities, giving rise to polarization.

Fourth, these structural differences are reflected in radically different perceptions of politics and social justice across neighborhoods and, not surprisingly, give rise to what are politely called antisocial behaviors. One example was the stoning of cars driving on the *autopista* in Buenos Aires, by residents of the adjacent *villas miserias*. Another, more constructive, reaction was the turning inward by residents of *favelas* in Rio to strengthen neighborhood organization and quality of life.

Fifth, it is not surprising that these inward-looking behaviors are occurring at all income levels, as witnessed by the rise of gated communities in both rich and poor countries. These "fortress communities," well described by Edward Blakely and Mary Gail Snyder (1997), are powerful testimonies to the intended exclusion of people.

Sixth, while these patterns are proliferating, their impacts on economic productivity and social cohesion are receiving uneven attention. Much attention is given to declining crime rates in New York, and the consequent surge in tourism and, hence, in employment. So-called "zero-tolerance" approaches are being transferred from New York to other cities, even recently to Amsterdam, which hardly has the problems of a large Latin American city. But in reality, the basic acceptance of growing inequality is perceived as a necessary evil in the face of globalized economic competition. Local governments perceive many of the patterns described above as beyond their control. Relatively little attention has been devoted to urban social policy. Whether the rhetoric of the "Third Way" can be translated into urban social policy that can affect inequality, remains to be seen.

Conclusions: Accepting Local Responsibility

The challenge of urban management is fundamentally one of political leadership. If leaders can communicate in words and action that the diverse members of the urban community have shared interests, there are possibilities for shared futures. If not, the tendencies for fragmentation and polarization, particularly within metropolitan areas, will grow and become reflected in physical and spatial structures. These will in turn reinforce differences beyond the power of public policy to change them.

This process exists in cities in both developing and industrialized countries. The case of residential segregation in the United States is an excellent example. Residential segregation became reinforced by using local property taxes to finance public education; this in turn excluded certain types of housing and, hence, lower-income people, mostly African-Americans, from whole areas of the city. The drama of housing policy in the past decade has not been whether or not to subsidize the poor, but rather where they should be located. In this sense, location within the metropolitan area became a code word for "race" and the key variable of social policy.

Finally, if it is the differences found in the metropolis that make it attractive and productive, it is important that these differences be explicitly managed to avoid their becoming the chronic sources of metropolitan collapse. Here, the attraction of a collapsing Calcutta during the 1940s and 1950s, or a hopelessly congested Bangkok in the 1990s, suggest that vigilance is necessary.

But what values should guide policy and vigilance? The first step is to assert local social responsibility. The forces affecting metropolitan growth are not beyond the effective control of political leaders. The tools of residential integration, service delivery, and land use are not determined in the far-away financial centers of New York or Tokyo; they are local. Building codes, methods of school finance, training, and management of green spaces are not to be found on the Internet; they are the responsibility of local governments and local leaders. While the challenges are difficult, they are not so daunting as to be impossible. They require building public support in constructing a future in which differences once again become strengths, and not weaknesses.

References

Blakely, Edward J., and Mary Gail Snyder. 1997. *Fortress America: Gated Communities in the United States*. Washington, DC: Brookings Institution.

Galster, George. 1998. *An Econometric Model of the Urban Opportunity Structure: Cumulative Causation among City Markets, Social Problems and Underserved Areas*. Washington, DC: Fannie Mae Foundation.

Morley, Samuel A. 1998. *The Impact of the Macroeconomic Environment on Urban Poverty*. U.N. Economic Commission for Latin America.

Morrish, William. 1997. "Placing Metropolitan Problems in Real Time and Space: The Case of Minneapolis." Paper presented to the World Bank Institute's Urban and City Management Core Course, Toronto, 2–14 May.

Orfield, Myron. 1997. *Chicago Metropolitics: A Regional Agenda for Community Stability*. Washington, DC: Brookings Institution.

Sassen, Saskia. 1994. *Cities in a World Economy*. London: Pine Forge Press.

The Metropolitan Project: The Management of a Variable Geometry

Jordi Borja

I have some experience of the metropolitan subject, but about 12 years ago, when I became the director of the Barcelona metropolitan area during the pre-Olympic games period, I had never before faced anything so complex. I learned that the best policy, when confronting complex problems, is to remember that solutions need to be simple—looking for complex solutions to complex situations rarely solves the problem.

Metropolitan space is a perfect illustration of complexity. Metropolitan space is a space of variable geometry; we don't know where it starts and where it ends, and, even less, how it will be in 10 or 20 years. In this space of variable geometry, one is inclined to say that urbanization is happening without the city, where the urban entity as a dense and central force is being diluted. There are even people who get excited by the disintegration of the city's boundaries, despite the fact that we know all too well that this increases functional costs, that it fragments social life and makes governing the city very difficult. In fact, the destruction of the city in the process of urbanization promotes a ghettoization of the territory.

Perhaps we need to change the "chip" that we have in our heads, that makes us think that a given territory is just a collection of data given to us by certain political and administrative structures. The laws of territorial organization, regional or local, such as a municipality, province, or department, present the same characteristics: population, territory, and organization or institutions. This is no longer a sufficient definition. In this space of variable geometry, the territory is not only data, it is also a project; it is an outcome of action, an outcome of a strategy. When a decision is made for a group of projects in a city or an area, it is necessary to define the scope of social demand that the projects are to cover, and also the scope of financing possibilities to maintain the infrastructure.

We worry about where the money will come from in order to make these projects possible. I think this problem is secondary to that of where to find the money to maintain what has already been done. Finding money to invest is certainly a problem, but it is probably an easier one to resolve than the problem of maintenance. One of Latin America's biggest problems, even bigger than the lack of investment in urbanization, is the maintenance of the urbanization that has already taken place. One example is the amount of water that is lost in the cities while millions of people

---

Box 1.1.   Cultural Facilities Built in Barcelona since 1995

The recent cultural transformation of Barcelona is truly remarkable. With its new facilities added to those that already existed, the City's intention is to make culture more accessible to its citizens and to assure Barcelona a place among the top European cities in music, museums, and theater.

The Liceu Opera House has a special symbolic importance. Five years after the fire that destroyed the old building, the new Liceu opened the 1999 musical season in September, following inauguration of its auditorium in March of that year. The complex houses symphony halls as well as the Museum of Music and the Conservatory. The "City of Theater" project is based on the integration within a small area of theaters, dance theaters, concert venues, theater and dance schools, and research centers for the performing arts.

The City is completing its plan for new central district libraries; these will complement the existing neighborhood reading rooms. The last five years have witnessed the start of a program to revitalize the museums in the Gothic quarter. This program includes enlargement of the Picasso Museum and construction of a new municipal museum, the Barbier-Mueller Museum of Pre-Colombian Art, inaugurated in 1996. Urban renewal projects include the conversion of old buildings to new uses; for the most part these buildings are old factories with historic value that are rehabilitated as civic facilities such as schools, libraries, or museums.

—Pilar Solans

---

struggle for access to clean drinking water. Therefore, when we say, "We are going to create infrastructure for the city," we must also ask how many people will use it?

A group of cultural infrastructure projects were planned during the 1980s in Barcelona, and are currently being developed. For a city that aspires to capital status, with its concomitant centralization of facilities and functions, we must have museums, great exhibitions, opera houses, theater festivals, competitive orchestras, and so on. We calculated the population that we needed to make this cultural purpose possible. We counted two million in the city, three million in the urban sprawl, four million in the metropolitan area, six million in the region of Catalonia, and came to the conclusion that we needed nine million more. The strategic plan of Barcelona eventually defined and agreed upon a coordination of projects with six other Spanish regions, and two in France. The plan included important cities in the south of France, like Montpellier, a city with one of the oldest universities in the world, and Toulouse, but stopped short of Marseilles. The Mayor of Marseilles came to Barcelona and asked, "Why not include us? We prefer to build our connection with you rather than with Paris, because Paris represents more pressure for us, but with Barcelona we can have a relationship of equals."

Box 1.2.   New Central Areas in Barcelona

In the 1990s, the City of Barcelona promoted the establishment of new centers of commercial activity outside Barcelona's central business district. These introduced a new concept of compatibility of uses by combining commercial, financial, and service facilities in locations far from the traditional center. One of these new central areas is the L'Illa center, a retail and office complex including 35,000 square meters of retail space, 45,000 square meters of office space, and hotel and leisure facilities. The L'Illa center was developed by the Winterthur Insurance Group. A second new central area is Plaça de les Glories, a 250,000 square meter retail, office, and leisure complex, developed by a group consisting of Continente, Consorcio de la Zona Franca, and Caisse des Dépôts. A third center is being developed by Hines: the Diagonal Mar project involves the construction of 342,000 square meters of housing, retail, and office space.

—Pilar Solans

The City of Places

Metropolitan regions, and the strategic territory of a great city, present not just one center, but a system of centralities. We should therefore not be afraid of the complexity of the relatively uncontrollable dynamic of metropolitan spaces; instead, we should define a strategic territory within which we will try to structure what we have closer to us, through the capacities of the municipality, department or province. For this, we need the cooperation of other political structures, and sometimes of other countries. This approach does not resolve the daily routine issues generated in multiple municipalities that are also of variable geometry; rather, it raises the important problems of how these separate entities interconnect.

In Buenos Aires, situations of spillover occur frequently; that is, people who live outside a large city use the services of the large city. This is not abuse, it is a necessity; the need for the hospitals, the schools, the cultural events, transportation, and so on. People have the right to use these services and public spaces, yet this raises a political problem—who can make a democratic decision about the use of public spaces in the city center? Not long ago, an interviewer with an Italian radio station remarked, "Look at the horror of Rome on weekends, when the downtown gets overcrowded with young people coming in from the suburbs." And I said, "Lucky that they have downtown, considering how awful the suburbs of Rome are—at least they have this."

This city of "places" is in crisis. Existing centers have become overcrowded or have been degraded, while the suburbs have not achieved the quality of a city with complementary central areas. Not only is there an urbanization process without the development of a city beyond the

---

Box 1.3.   Metropolitan Transport Authority of Barcelona

Public transport in Barcelona and its metropolitan area is provided by the central, regional, and local governments, and by private operators. The different governments have competed to improve existing transport lines, but the system is not integrated. Some areas have very good service, while in others it is inadequate. In 1997 the Metropolitan Transport Authority of Barcelona was formed to institute cooperation between the administrations involved in public passenger transport within Barcelona's metropolitan area. The Authority's tasks include the preparation of integrated infrastructure plans for public transport, the review of price rates, and the development of medium-term contract programs among the various administrations that subsidize public transport.

—Pilar Solans

---

central city, but also in the central city itself there is a process of disintegration. I have discussed this with colleagues from Latin America, warning them (because they—as in many cities—have dense cities with the famous square grids) that if they allow them to degrade now, that if they allow the urban grid to be broken because of a speculative policy of developing isolated blocks, they will lose the best that their city has, and they will be creating new problems of segregation, fragmentation, and a malfunctioning of the urban system.

A new subject is emerging in urban planning, and that is the challenge of how to create a city over an existing city. This does not refer to creating a city where there is none, but rather to creating a city where one already exists, thereby giving the suburbs elements of centrality. The next question is, whose responsibility is it to figure out how to address this challenge? Which political institution will move through the chaos of countries, regions or departments, and (in the case of the metropolitan city) of different municipal entities? For an example of political and administrative inflation, just look at metropolitan cities. Nothing is more difficult to handle than political and administrative organization, because it obscures political relations and therefore the decision-making process. There is no perfect metropolitan solution.

There is a political and administrative fragmentation that contributes to a regressive redistribution of public spending. One need not be a radical to realize that urban planning plays an important role in social redistribution. Social redistribution is not only carried out through peoples' wages, the classic welfare state that gives security of employment, education, and health care; it is also accomplished through land use and the quality of

Box 1.4.   The Urban Renewal of Barcelona

At the beginning of the 1980s, urban renewal operations were oriented towards recovering the urban landscape. Operations were localized and were not designed to affect the overall structure of the city. During the early years of the first democratically elected municipal government, intervention in public space was limited to specific operations intended to regenerate the surrounding neighborhoods; examples include the work done on the Plaça Reial, the Parc de l'Espanya Industrial, the Plaça del Sóller, and the Via Júlia. At the same time, the first plans for inner-city reform were put into action in the Raval, Carmel, and Torre Baró areas. These plans soon turned into effective tools for the renewal of entire neighborhoods and for citizen participation in this renewal. Residents welcomed the plans because of the speed with which action followed proposals for solutions to specific problems, whether they involved physical neglect of the area, lack of facilities, or the need to reshape the urban layout.

When Barcelona was chosen as the site of the 1992 Olympic Games, a new stage of urban renewal was begun. This lasted from 1987 to 1992 and was characterized by the recovery of large areas and their conversion into the Montjuïc "Olympic Ring," the Poblenou and the Vall d'Hebron Olympic Villages, and the Diagonal sports complex; and by the construction of strategic road infrastructure to connect different areas of the city (ring roads, tunnels, and junctions). This stage was also one of strong economic growth and coincided with foreign investment attracted by Spain's entry into the European Community in 1986. In addition to these operations carried out at the urban level, the city continued its smaller-scale operations in the neighborhoods.

The Barcelona that emerged after the Olympic Games was a renewed city that was closing one cycle of urban renewal and opening another that would reach out to include the entire surrounding metropolitan area. This new stage was marked by respect for the environment and sustainable growth; by the desire for the international, economic, and cultural projection of the city; and by concern for the need for suitable, accessible housing and improved urban mobility.

—Pilar Solans

those uses. We have experienced this clearly in Barcelona. If we give urban quality to land or territory, we reduce socio-economic disparities. If we open a public space of quality, everything improves in that territory, but with one condition: income structure of the population must be of a certain minimum level.

When a majority of the population lives at subsistence level, it is very difficult to promote development dynamics through urban planning alone. The appropriate urban policy is to facilitate a redistribution of income. It is unacceptable when the combination of planning procedures in large regions (the metropolitan area of variable geometry), combined with political and administrative fragmentation, cause a regressive redistribution. Putting this another way, it is not acceptable when the citizens of rich areas receive up to 10 times more in public spending than the citizens in poor areas, as is currently happening. There is ample evidence of this in public spending per capita in fragmented cities. In the case of Santiago de Chile, it was especially difficult when, during the military dictatorship, the country was divided into 34 local districts, with a great gap in public spending between them. With democracy, the public spending has been reduced, although disparities still exist. Nevertheless, these differences create tendencies to excessive competition inside the same political boundary. As a result of decentralization, everyone is competing for urban plans, and proceed to create plans that define areas for offices while excluding social housing, because the latter is not profitable.

Implementing the Metropolitan City

I propose two approaches to implementing the metropolitan city idea: facilitating the creation of a city in the periphery, and avoiding the parallel processes of congestion and degradation of the central areas. First of all, a structure is necessary. This might be called the structure of the real, or metropolitan, city, or the city of daily mobility, with at least two functions: to coordinate public investment and to negotiate joint services. These two things require a minimal vision of the future, and this is why strategic plans are so critical. Coordinating public investments and negotiating public services like transportation, environment, water, police, and public housing programs, is very important.

Second, this structured approach has a political and administrative dimension that requires a representative political structure that has legitimacy to coordinate these investments and to negotiate these services, whether the negotiation is public or private. A metropolitan government can be of multiple shapes; it can be congruent with the province or department, or it can be an emanation of the municipalities, but, whatever the shape of the metropolitan government, representation has to legitimize it. People who follow the same laws, and people who need the same services, need to have the same rights. Therefore we have to be open in every city to political innovation because history, culture, and territorial relations are different; the uniformity that nineteenth-century states imposed over regional and local territorial realities is absurd in the modern day.

Political innovation should guarantee coordination, decentralization, and equal rights of all citizens who live in the same territory. The youngsters of the periphery who use the city center must have the same rights as the youngsters who live there. No one is the sole proprietor of their district or suburb; residents of any area are not the exclusive owners of that area, and participation does not mean indecision. Confrontation is the starting point of a dialogue that should lead towards a decisionmaking process.

Box 1.5.   The Strategic Plans for Barcelona and the Metropolitan Area

In the preparation of the first strategic plan for Barcelona, approved in 1989, one problem became evident: that of the development of the city's central areas in relation to its periphery or neighboring townships. The participation of the metropolitan area municipalities in the planning process has therefore contributed to developing strategic objectives and actions on metropolitan issues; these include the articulation of the surrounding metropolitan area, the improvement of the territory's internal accessibility, and policies oriented to rebalancing the metropolitan area.

—Pilar Solans

I will conclude with an example that is very common in large cities. I am thinking of big projects—like the renovation of ports, the conversion of military or railroad sites into public or commercial spaces, housing programs, or projects of access to the city. The tendency is to think of a great project as having a leader, an institution, a public body, or a private body, and that it has a function—a shopping mall is a shopping mall, a highway is a highway, a program of public housing is a program of public housing. I suggest that we should change the "chip" in our thinking about this: we should not think that each project or action is going to resolve a single problem, but that each action or project should resolve several problems, on several scales and with several functions.

When we contemplate the necessity of a ring road, for example, it is not only to resolve a traffic problem, but to resolve an issue of new metropolitan centers, to create public spaces, to bring quality to the periphery. Such diversity of functions implies a proper design and also implies agreement between different parties. We should never let a single party do a big project, or let one single project perform only one function, or make it perform at only one scale.

The reality of 17 million inhabitants, more than half living in São Paulo, and the rest on the periphery, requires alternative centers. São Paulo is an overcrowded city that has created centers on a speculative basis, with hardly any articulation between them, and that can barely function. So, what should be done is to create alternative centers in order to change this picture; because the metropolitan city of São Paulo and the future triangle that is going to be one of the biggest settings of the south—with Belo Horizonte and Rio—cannot function with these overcrowded metropolitan centers.

First of all we need a proposal for a metropolitan city. Second, a proposal to articulate the new centers. The nucleus should give continuity, even visibility, to the new centers, in a way that makes people feel that they are citizens of the same reality. It is very important that a design give continuity to the urban reality. And third, we should create an engine that increases the number of existing centers.

In this way we have three different scales; and I think this principle applies to everything. Big urban projects should not have only a single function or be of only one dimension. It is just as important to plan communication and mobility at the metropolitan level as it is to generate mobility within every suburb, in relation to the total metropolitan area. In a large city, mobility is a democratic right as important as the right to vote. Mobility allows us to exercise urban freedom.

All of this requires a great effort of coordination, of consultation, and of cooperation between different parties. I think that the cooperation between a public and a private party is very simple—everyone knows their role. The cooperation becomes more difficult between two public parties. Perhaps the political culture that we need to develop in order to facilitate greater cooperation lies in the realm of a contractual culture, rather than the hierarchical and compartmentalized culture that is so prevalent in the way we manage cities today.

Designing a Metropolitan Region: The Lessons and Lost Opportunities of the Toronto Experience

Larry S. Bourne

Setting the Context

Cities, especially large metropolitan areas, sit at the intersection of transitions in the economy, demography and social order, as well as in culture, technology, and politics. They are, in effect, the local venues where most innovations occur and where the impacts of external forces are most prominently expressed. They are the arenas in which economic linkages and social networks are constructed and deconstructed, and where political conflicts that invariably occur within and between these forces of change are worked out. Historically, of course, cities have always played this role (Lemon 1996; Hall 1998). What is different now is the massive scale and complexity of metropolitan regions, the rapidity of change, the level of uncertainty attributable to the globalization of markets and cultures,[1] and the large number of actors, agents, and institutions involved in the urban development process. How does society "manage" such complex entities? What kinds of organizations, institutions, strategies, and policy instruments are most appropriate? What geographical delimitation of a metropolitan region is most suitable for management and planning?

As a contribution to the debate on these questions, both in Canada and abroad (OECD 1998), this study provides an overview of the experience of the Toronto metropolitan area in managing urban development, designing urban forms, and adapting institutions to social and economic change. It emphasizes the context in which planning is practiced, including the dynamics of urban development itself, and broad shifts in the frameworks through which that development has been managed. The objective is to highlight both the successes and opportunities lost in Toronto's post-war experiment and to extract from that experience general lessons that might have relevance elsewhere.

---

1. For Ontario, and specifically Toronto, the term "globalization" is more accurately described as "continentalization"; that is, increasing continental integration with the United States in both markets and culture. The most obvious example of globalization, in the sense of being tied to the rest of the world, is foreign immigration.

For present purposes, the term Toronto refers to the entire metropolitan region, not any local municipality (Figure 1.1). There are two variations in defining this region: the census metropolitan area (CMA) and the greater Toronto area (GTA). The former is a typical functional region, combining a city (or urbanized core) and those adjacent suburbs that are closely integrated with the urbanized core, as measured by commuting to work and other forms of interaction. In effect, the CMA is considered to function as single labor and housing markets, albeit with distinctive sub-markets. The GTA is a close approximation in both size and population to the combined Toronto and adjacent Oshawa CMAs, but its outer boundaries are those of the four suburban regional government units—Halton, Peel, York, and Durham regions—that surround the new City of Toronto (the former Metro Toronto). At the 1996 Census, the population of the GTA was over 4.6 million, spread over an area of 7,100 square kilometers, with roughly equal population numbers in the City and the four suburban regions (Table 1.1). It is this region, not its individual parts, that is our subject of interest, and, in light of the recent and massive overhaul of local governments and regulatory agencies, the question is: who is now managing, designing, and planning the Toronto region?

Toronto's recent experience in urban management should be of wide interest. Toronto is Canada's largest metropolitan region, and it dominates the country's economy and social life, as well as its media and cultural institutions. Montreal, which Toronto passed in terms of population in the mid–1970s, is now (with 3.3 million people) a distant second in the national urban hierarchy, and serves primarily as a regional service centre for Quebec and for French-language cultural institutions. Within the North American context, the GTA ranks seventh in the urban size hierarchy, roughly on a par with the metropolitan areas of Philadelphia, Boston and Detroit.[2] Like these three, Toronto is also dependent on New York for many highly specialized services, but unlike them, it also provides a wide range of functions nationwide within Canada. Furthermore, Toronto is one of only three large metropolitan areas in all of eastern North America (north of Florida) that have been growing rapidly—the other two are the Washington-Baltimore and Atlanta metropolitan areas.

---

2. The six larger metropolitan areas are New York, Los Angeles, Chicago, Washington-Baltimore, San Francisco-Oakland-San Jose, and Philadelphia. These are defined in the U.S. Census as Consolidated Metropolitan Statistical Areas.

Figure 1.1.　　The Toronto Region, 1997

Source: The Cartography Office, Department of Geography, University of Toronto.

A Simple Policy Framework

Neither public policies in general nor specific instruments of planning emerge in a vacuum. They are, in large part, place-specific and historically contingent. While some universal concepts and principles in regulating urban development can be extracted from the Toronto experience, most of the underlying principles, and the criteria on which we evaluate success and failure, are produced in other countries of the developed world. They are then diffused almost everywhere through means of information dissemination dominated by professionals in those same countries.

There are at least two preconditions for effective management and public policy formulation. One is the knowledge base—that is, our understanding of the nature and trajectory of the system that we intend to manage, in this case understanding the urban development process writ large. It is as important to recognize what we do not know about cities as it

Table 1.1.   Population Growth and Suburbanization, Greater Toronto Area, 1961–96

	Population by region, (000s)					
Year	Metro[a]	Peel	York	Durham	Halton	GTA
1961	1,620	110	110	150	110	2,110
1971	2,090	260	170	210	190	2,920
1981	2,140	490	260	280	250	3,420
1991	2,280	730	500	410	310	4,240
1996	2,385	852	593	459	340	4,629
	Region as percent of GTA population					
Year	Metro[a]	Peel	York	Durham	Halton	Four suburban regions
1961	76.9	5.3	5.3	7.2	5.3	23.1
1971	71.6	8.9	5.8	7.2	6.5	28.4
1981	62.6	14.3	7.5	8.2	7.3	37.3
1991	53.8	17.3	11.8	9.7	7.3	46.1
1996	51.5	18.4	12.8	9.9	7.4	48.5

a. Metro Toronto became the new City of Toronto after amalgamation, January 1998
Source: Census of Canada, various years.

is to identify what we do know. The second is an awareness of what forces or elements of the urban process we can actually influence or manipulate—these become the policy variables or instruments—in contrast to those forces over which we have little influence or control—these become the external or exogenous variables. In terms of urban policy, the former might include land-use control by-laws and zoning; the latter includes macro-economic policies and conditions, demographic change, technological innovations, and societal preferences, deriving from both national and international forces. The key for public policy is to use the policy variables in such a way as to achieve stated public goals, while minimizing the negative side-effects of those policies, and at the same time recognizing, adapting to, and then accommodating, changes in the exogenous variables. As the process of globalization continues, the relative importance of exogenous forces also increases, thereby increasing the degree of uncertainty in policy formulation.

It is also important to note that the management and regulation of urban development is considerably broader than the specific instruments of planning and urban policy formulation. Nevertheless, planning and other forms of development regulation, what we may call "local regulatory frameworks," remain important precisely because they are the responsibility of local and provincial governments. In Canada, the key element in this context has been the strong role and interventionist style of the provincial governments, that essentially have complete control over local governments within their jurisdictions.[3]

Regulating Urban Development in Toronto: A Brief History

Toronto has a long history of attempting to shape urban development and to manage the quality of the living conditions that it provides. The city is widely regarded as a success story; as an urban area that has been able to maintain a relatively high level of employment opportunities, a more-or-less balanced distribution of public goods and services, a viable and livable downtown core, and an attractive quality of life in general. It has, at least to date, managed to avoid many of the sharp social divisions, racial tensions, capital disinvestment, and fiscal problems that have plagued many other cities in eastern North America. It is, in particular, known for its innovative experiment in metropolitan government, its extensive public transit system, and its attempts at designing an integrated and equitable urban form for the entire metropolitan region. Are these images still warranted? What role did planning, management and state intervention play in enhancing the quality of life? And, are these conditions likely to persist?

Toronto, like many frontier towns, in fact started as a "planned" settlement in the 1790s, on a site selected because of its protected harbor, accessibility to a new hinterland, and its distance from the U.S. border. As it grew it faced many of the same social problems—of poor health, sanitation and housing conditions, and haphazard fringe developments—as other frontier communities. Growth was uneven, characterized by frequent booms and periods of slow growth. The city's population reached 10,000 in 1835; 30,000 in 1850; and 200,000 at the end of the century. By 1915, after another spurt of growth, the city and its environs had a population of almost 500,000.

The early twentieth century witnessed sporadic efforts at addressing the social consequences of growth, and at preparing formal "plans" for Toronto (Lemon 1985; Sewell 1993). Although few of these designs were

---

3. Under the Canadian constitution, municipalities are the "creatures" of the provincial governments, and can be created, dissolved or amended as the provinces see fit. The federal government has no direct role in urban development or management.

realized, they did, in combination with other initiatives, leave a legacy of knowledge, legislative experience, and a network of community organizations that underlie most post-war planning policies. For example, extensive improvements were made in public health, through upgrading of water and sewer facilities, and by improving housing conditions in older neighborhoods.

The severe depression of the 1930s, however, set the stage for dramatic policy shifts at the national level, and set in motion a reinvigoration of planning practice, and of state intervention generally. The 1930s, for example, witnessed the establishment of the outline of a social welfare system—the social safety net—and commitments to employment generation and a national housing policy. As part of post-war reconstruction, and in anticipation of rapid urban growth, the city and the provincial government established new institutions of planning and the legislative frameworks and professional associations necessary to support those institutions. The new City Planning Board was created in 1942, and quickly produced a new plan for the city in 1943 that laid out a 30-year trajectory of growth. In 1946 the province also passed a new and relatively progressive Planning Act that, among other details, allowed—indeed strongly encouraged—municipalities to develop blueprints or "official plans" for their respective communities. As population growth in the region accelerated during the late 1940s and 1950s, in response to the pent-up demand from the depression and war years, combined with a rising birth rate and increased immigration, the regulatory frameworks for planning and service delivery were placed under considerable strain. These pressures were particularly evident with respect to the increasing difficulties and costs of servicing suburban fringe developments, the need to upgrade older infrastructure, increasing traffic congestion, a shortage of housing, and the challenge of slum clearance.

A few public-sector decisions stand out in this period as having significant and lasting implications for how the urban region developed subsequently. One was the creation, in 1953, of the Municipality of Metropolitan Toronto (or Metro). This act of the provincial government, perhaps the most important since the initial Municipal Act of 1849, combined the City of Toronto and 12 local municipalities (reduced to six in 1966) into a two-tier government structure for the entire urbanized region. It divided functions between Metro and local (or area) municipalities, and, of particular importance, it permitted Metro to levy taxes and exert planning power over the thinly populated rural municipalities beyond its immediate borders.

Although the Metro experiment, the first on the continent, has not been without its critics, and has not evolved in the ways that many observers, past and present, anticipated (*Plan Canada* 1984; GTA Task Force 1996; Lemon 1996; Frisken et al. 1997), there is little question of its immense impacts and its contributions to the challenges of managing a rapidly growing region. Building on the city's tax base, Metro was able to facilitate the provision of high-quality infrastructure, social services and transit throughout the region (as it was then defined). It also increased the standards of suburban development, eased the usual problems of raising capital financing for new development, redistributed resources to municipalities with weaker tax bases (e.g., for schools), and allowed for the dispersion of public housing construction among both city and suburb to a greater extent then would otherwise have been possible.[4] The newer suburbs benefited from the city's commercial tax base and its infrastructure; the city in turn benefited from the suburbs' sharing of the costs of accommodating the less fortunate, and from a transit system oriented to the downtown core. In addition, Metro was able to restrain the growth of new suburbs outside its boundaries, and this in turn contributed to a relatively more "compact" urban form.

Another critical decision was the establishment of the Metropolitan Toronto and Region Conservation Authority (MTRCA), hastened by a disastrous hurricane in 1954. This regional agency, designed to provide flood protection throughout the watershed, has also contributed to the preservation of the region's extensive ravine systems as open space and parkland. These ravines, and the conservation areas that serve as headwater reservoirs, have become the backbone of the metropolitan park system and the green "lungs" of greater Toronto.

The third decision, made in 1946, was to build a 4-kilometer underground subway line, the first in post-war North America, along congested Yonge Street. Opened in 1954, that subway was the first segment in what is now a system of 70 kilometers of subway, combined with efficient and fully integrated bus and streetcar connections. The entire TTC (Toronto Transit Commission) system now carries over 390 million passengers a year—the second largest public transit system on the continent—despite being the most reliant on farebox revenue. Improved transit, especially the subway, has contributed to higher development densities overall. It has also been instrumental in maintaining the employment concentration of the central core, in retaining and encouraging new investment in the older housing stock, and in attracting young professionals to settle in older inner-city

---

4. The government of Ontario also established the Ontario Housing Corporation, as a developer of social housing, in 1964.

neighborhoods. Land and housing values have risen in the central core, further increasing the attractiveness of the inner city. In other words, a cumulative cycle of investment and re-investment in the built environment has taken root in much of the inner city, in part due to policy decisions to improve infrastructure and living conditions.

As rapid metropolitan growth continued through the late 1960s and into the 1970s, pressures increased for further revisions to regulatory frameworks, and to the organization of government, in the region. The population of the region (GTA) grew from 2.1 million in 1961 to 2.9 million in 1971 and 3.4 million in 1981, driven again by the "baby-boom" and immigration. As a result, the suburbs boomed, but more in the typical low-density style of American suburbs (e.g., large lots, shopping centers, etc.). At the same time, the pace of redevelopment in the downtown core and at selected nodes in the central city accelerated. A series of commissions, task forces and study groups were established, and an entire shelf of staff reports set out new agendas and often competing proposals for reform. This was the period when regional planning reached its peak in Ontario; what some have since called the "golden age of planning" (*Plan Canada* 1984).

The 1970s ushered in a new set of conditions, new planning philosophies, and a host of other—often conflicting—initiatives at both local and regional scales. This was the decade of "citizen participation" and advocacy planning. The City, in its 1974 Central Area Plan, moved to introduce caps on office construction in the central area in an effort to encourage further decentralization and to protect inner neighborhoods (even though the market was already doing so). The provincial government halted three expressways headed for downtown through built-up areas, essentially terminating the city's proposed expressway network. At the same time, the province funded modest extensions to the subway system, established a new regional commuter rail system (GO Transit), and encouraged third-sector (non-profit) housing construction through provincial and federal subsidies. Ratepayer organizations, at least in elite and middle-class areas, assumed considerable political power, as evident in their ability to prevent further redevelopment in older established neighborhoods and in opening the regulatory process to public scrutiny. Citizen participation increased in almost all aspects of planning. A reform-minded city council also ended efforts at slum clearance, encouraging instead new in-fill housing (both market and social) downtown, and shifting the emphasis to preservation and conservation of the existing stock. By that time, a long-standing decline of population in the central city had ceased, and the resident population started to grow.

The emergence of a new planning regime within the City, whatever its merits and demerits, also seemed to contribute to a shift away from regionally based thinking and political action. Metro lost its planning authority in areas immediately outside its political jurisdiction, at precisely the time when population and jobs were spilling rapidly over its borders. With the constraints removed, the outer suburbs boomed, but with little coordination with either development or service provision within Metro.

Meanwhile, frequent efforts at reorganizing the metropolitan federation, and specifically at extending its territorial jurisdiction (not simply its planning powers) to include new suburbs outside Metro, produced few results, and no boundary extensions. Instead, during the 1970s the provincial government created four new two-tiered regional governments in the suburban region surrounding Metro, and in effect opened those regions to full-scale development. In so doing, the province also lost the opportunity to create a new "Metro2," to replicate the success of the initial experiment in metropolitan government, and to bring the structure of governance into line with the economic and social realities of this expanding urban region. The result was to re-introduce fragmentation in government, in public service delivery and tax rates, and variability in the regulation of urban development. The mold was then set for a more dispersed, lower-density, competitive, and automobile-dependent suburban landscape.

In the two decades since, numerous plans and proposals have come and gone; with plans for the City (City of Toronto 1991) and Metro (Metroplan 1980, 1991) and proposals for the entire region (OGTA 1991, 1992; GTA Task Force 1996). Few have been fully or even partially implemented. In fact, the 1980s may be considered a decade of lost opportunities. Few improvements were made in the public transit system, the structure of government remained ossified, and social housing production slowed. Nevertheless, the economy of the region boomed during the middle and late 1980s, and increased levels of immigration maintained population growth. Housing and land prices rose again, and development pressures increased. As a result, planning again became more central to local politics and policy-making, but often as a commercial "partnership" with the private sector. The thrust of these proposals was to accommodate and manage growth, as reflected in proposals to concentrate more commercial development in nodes, both in the suburbs and the city (OGTA 1992), building on trends established in the 1960s. At the same time, efforts were made to encourage residential intensification, mixed uses, and "reurbanization" within the older urban fabric. The stated objective was to create a more compact and livable metropolis, that was also efficient, although these terms were not clearly defined.

The deep recession of the early 1990s, followed by the election of an austerity-minded conservative provincial government in 1995,[5] initiated another phase of reform in governance and another shift in the philosophy of how to manage urban development in the Toronto region. The recession highlighted the weaknesses in the regional economy, the high costs involved in servicing new and more distant suburbs, and the inefficiencies resulting from lack of region-wide coordination in service provision and land use designation. Evidence mounted on the increasing polarization of incomes in the older city and suburbs, the negative impacts of rapid development on the natural environment, the loss of affordable housing, increased homelessness, and the fiscal strains facing municipal budgets and the transit system.

The response, at least since the 1995 provincial election, has been a complete rewriting of municipal structures, a re-ordering of sources of funding and responsibilities, and dramatic revisions to older regulatory frameworks. Property tax reform was (finally) implemented, hospitals and school boards were amalgamated across the province, rent controls were removed, social housing production ceased, and some funding responsibilities were downloaded to municipalities. Unfortunately, this downloading included functions that almost everyone agrees should be managed, and certainly funded, at the regional, provincial or national level—notably social housing, welfare, and public transit. Unexpectedly, Metro Toronto and its six area municipalities were also amalgamated by the province into a new single-tier city of Toronto, despite considerable local opposition. The provincial planning act was also revised and streamlined.

The combined result of these initiatives suggests that we are moving to a new "culture of regulation" and a new down-sized planning system. That system could be characterized as more modest, more decentralized, and more flexible and permissive in application; it also became more privatized. This new culture, driven by deregulation, is akin to a "corporate" model of planning; supported by a neo-conservative philosophy of "leave-it-to-the-market." In effect, the province has passed on much of its authority and responsibility for monitoring and approving development proposals, for reviewing the plans and planning decisions of local governments, and for negotiating solutions to local conflicts, to local governments, the courts, and the private sector.

---

5. This government was re-elected in 1999.

The latest stage in this exercise of reorganization involves deciding what to do in the changing climate of the 1990s, and in the absence of a metropolitan government for the entire region. The GTA Task Force was established in 1994 to recommend solutions to continued economic and property tax difficulties, and to suggest alternative forms of governance for the region. The Task Force's report (GTA Task Force 1996) recommended region-wide coordination of economic development initiatives, and the establishment of strong regional service authorities with responsibility for a selected range of services. In compensation for losing certain functions, local governments were to be given more powers and responsibilities. The Task Force, however, stopped short of recommending a new level of government.

A subsequent report by the special advisor on the possible establishment of a Greater Toronto Services Board (GTSB 1997) also recommended a regional authority, with moderate, but still significant, powers. The provincial government, however, resisted both initiatives. In January 1999, a GTSB did come into existence as a regional service agency, but it is a thin agency with only one function to administer—GO Transit (now called Greater Toronto, or GT, Transit), no taxing powers, and limited authority. The debate continues on how the GTSB should evolve, and what specific functions and powers it should have. The province's retreat from regional planning and development regulation has become almost complete. On the other hand, perhaps surprisingly, the provincial government has recently agreed to some degree of "revenue pooling" across the entire region.

The situation has become even more confused through the proliferation of competing "visions" for what constitutes an ideal urban form. Various proposals have been put forward, at least since the 1970s, for more "compact" cities, including attempts to limit sprawl, encourage in-fill (intensification), adaptive reuse, and more downtown housing—e.g., "reurbanization" (Breheny 1995; Bourne 1996; Tomalty 1997). The recession galvanized efforts to create a more "competitive" city, as mirrored in the strong economic mandate given to the GTA Task Force (1996) and to the City's recent official plan review (City of Toronto 1999). Parallel visions have been put forward for what constitutes environmentally "sustainable" cities, visions that respect natural ecosystems, maintain greenlands, and restore blighted industrial districts such as the waterfront (MacLaren 1992; Waterfront Regeneration Trust 1992).

At a minimum, these studies have demonstrated several needs: to link suburban services and development controls with city services and revitalization strategies; to pool regional tax revenues to help the disadvantaged, and formally to incorporate both social and environmental criteria into the traditional land-use planning system and into the agendas of developers and politicians. Still others have offered visions of cities that are at once "safe," equitable, humane and accommodating of social diversity. All of these are laudable objectives and design proposals; what is missing, however, is a sense of how these visions are to be achieved, and how their different and often conflicting objectives are to be rationalized.

The Dynamics of Urban Development

One element of the knowledge base required to design alternative urban futures, and specifically to establish more effective systems of governance, management and service provision, is an appreciation of the scale and rapidity of change in the contemporary metropolis. For example, in only four decades the greater Toronto region grew almost four-fold in population, from just over one million to nearly 4.7 million in 1996. The number of jobs increased from 400,000 to over 2.1 million, with the latter distributed among 80,000 work locations. The social structure has also changed almost beyond recognition. The number of households has increased at a rate 50 percent higher than the population (Foot and Stoffman 1996). In the central core over 40 percent of households now comprise only one person. In addition, over 47 percent of the population is now foreign-born; over 200 different linguistic and ethnic groups are represented in the schools. No one, 40 years ago, could have anticipated this kind of diversity or scale of social transformation. The challenge of responding to this scale of growth is immense. At the same time, the physical extent of the urbanized area increased by 7 to 8 times, as incomes increased and individuals and firms consumed an increasing amount of space per capita.

It is also worthwhile reiterating how much change actually takes place within a given urban environment, even when changes are not evident in the physical landscape or building stock. Consider, for example, the population dynamics of the Toronto region. During the decade 1986–96 roughly 390,000 people moved into the metropolitan area from elsewhere in the country; over 590,000 left; and over 35 percent of continuing residents actually changed their address within the metropolitan area. Over the same 10 years net foreign immigration totaled almost 575,000. At the same time, natural population increase (births less deaths) added 255,000 persons. In other words, of 4.7 million residents in the Toronto region in 1996, over 1.2 million were new residents. With such large population turnovers the potential for rapid social change is obviously very high.

The lesson for urban managers here is two-fold: first is the need to plan for uncertainty, supported by a requirement for effective information systems to monitor trends in urban development and social change. A small shift in urban living conditions or in the underlying determinants of spatial change can lead to very large population shifts. Second, policymakers must be cognizant of the fact that policies directed to particular individuals and population groups may not in fact benefit those individuals. Policies take considerable time to design, and even longer to implement; but the target populations do not stay put. There is clearly a time lag involved. Far too often, policies are introduced for problems that have largely passed, or at least changed their shape. One reason that many of Toronto's grand planning proposals of the past have not been implemented, or if implemented have often not had the expected results, is that they frequently dealt with yesterday's problems. One plausible explanation for the myriad changes introduced by the latest provincial government is simply inertia: that previous administrations, both provincial and local, had not been able to modify and adapt the system of regulation and governance in the region for decades.

Three Cities, Three Worlds?

The outcome of this historical record of development and regulation (or lack thereof) is the creation of three different urban landscapes—three different worlds—that together comprise the contemporary built form and social landscape of the Toronto region. First is the inner city, especially the pre-1930 landscape, characterized by relatively high densities, mixed uses, retail strips, and high levels of transit dependence. This area corresponds roughly to the old City of Toronto and parts of its adjacent pre-war suburbs, and has a current population of about 900,000. That population is also the most polarized in the region, accommodating many of the region's elite and professional classes, together with a large proportion of its poorest citizens.

The second world consists of the ring of immediate post-war suburbs, built largely in the 1950s and 1960s, and characterized by lower densities, single-family bungalows, and a mix of transit and expressway access, sprinkled with high-rise housing (including social housing), shopping centers and older—often decaying—industrial parks. The ring corresponds to the older suburbs within the former Metro Toronto, but now includes parts of some of the older suburbs outside Metro's boundaries. That area currently has a population of about 1.6 million, and by the 1990s it had become at least as socially diverse as the old central city, and the home of an increasing proportion of the disadvantaged. The mounting problems of these older suburbs, notably poverty and the absence of services appropriate to an increasingly diverse and needy population, are not new; they were noted 20 years ago, for example, by the Social Planning Council of Metro Toronto (1979), and have recently been re-emphasized in a report from the United Way charitable agency on communities "at risk" (1997).

The third world is the ring of post-1970 suburbs located largely outside the old Metro boundaries. This massive envelope of suburbanization is characterized by much lower densities, especially for commercial and industrial uses, large homogeneous blocks of related activities, massive "designer" subdivisions, upscale shopping complexes, and new industrial and office nucleations, all oriented around, and dependent on, an extensive highway and expressway system. That ring (called the 905 zone because of its telephone area code) now encompasses more than two-thirds of the urbanized area of the GTA, and accommodates almost 90 percent of its new population growth; its current population is about 2.4 million. This is, in effect, a post-modern landscape, an eclectic mix of uses, functions and building styles, both neo-traditional and modernist, many in the big-box style. Although increasingly diverse in social and ethnic terms, largely through immigration, the third Toronto is becoming richer relative to the older suburbs, and its four regional governments increasingly see themselves as autonomous jurisdictions, not exactly as edge cities (Garreau 1991), but close, and increasingly removed from the old city and inner suburbs of Toronto and their social problems.

There are, then, three different Torontos; three urban forms and living environments that mirror the conditions, policies, and attitudes prevailing at the time of their construction. Unfortunately, there are few common denominators between the three rings. For those who view the older inner city and its adjacent suburbs as a "success" story—because of their compact forms, higher densities, pedestrian access, transit-orientation, and the initial experiment in metropolitan government that shared resources and redistributed the costs and benefits of urban growth more-or-less equally—the outer ring of suburbia is a social and planning disaster, another set of opportunities lost. Transit is poor, streets are for cars, not pedestrians, distances are vast, social services are strained by rapid growth, and there is little coordination at the macro-scale between the location of residential development and jobs, transit or public services among the four suburban regions, or between those regions and the former Metro. Instead of region-wide cooperation there is intensified competition; instead of a seamless transit system for the region, with the exception of GO Transit, there is fragmentation (with 12 suburban transit systems outside the former Metro).

To those living in the outer ring, on the other hand, the new suburbs are a success story. To many of those residents, the older city is seen as congested, polluted, unsafe, and often ugly. The new suburbs, in contrast, provide a relatively high quality of housing and well-designed neighborhood and community facilities; they have a rapidly expanding employment base and offer ease of access to jobs, shopping and recreation, at least for those with automobiles. Except for a few high-rise condos and offices, and the odd GO commuter train, however, these regions look more like the suburbs almost anywhere in North America, and less like the inner two rings. This partitioning of urban space is both an outcome of past structures of governance, and a constraint on the emergence of any new structures.

Some Lessons from the Toronto Experience

What can we learn from the Toronto experience in terms of governance and the management and regulation of change in metropolitan environments? It is, of course, far too early to evaluate the consequences of the numerous legislative and policy changes of the last few years. The system is still in flux. We can, however, offer a few general comments on the evolution of urban governance and management in the Toronto region, and then offer a summary of more specific lessons learned.

Among those lessons is the recognition that the particular configuration of government, institutions and regulatory agencies is less important than the process through which decisions are made. Moreover, it is often the case that the formal mechanisms of regulation and management are less important than the informal and implicit. It is also clear that plans, and planning proposals, are important even if not implemented. They often serve as informal guides for development and the continuing exercise of plan formulation and public consultation contributes to our understanding of how a metropolitan region grows and changes. Based on the Toronto experience, two particular prerequisites for effective metropolitan management, in addition to an improved information base, stand out:

- Urban areas require pro-active, involved governments at higher levels;
- There must be some mechanism in place for redistributing the costs and benefits of urban growth over the region that actually generates that growth.

Toronto, despite its current problems, has indeed done reasonably well, at least relative to comparable metropolitan areas in other parts of North America. Success, however, depends at least as much on context and circumstance, and on what is not done, as on what is done. Unlike its immediate American neighbors, Toronto has not had a recent influx of low-income, poorly skilled rural migrants. Immigrants, in contrast, the driving force in Toronto's population growth, have tended to be relatively highly skilled. Neither does Toronto, unlike nearby U.S. metropolitan areas such as Pittsburgh, Cleveland or Detroit, have a legacy of outmoded heavy industry. Nor has Canada seen income inequalities increase during the 1970s and 1980s as in the United States. Extensive systems of transfer payments to individuals and governments, and higher overall tax rates in Canada, have restrained income differentials attributable to the operation of the labor market. Nor were Canadian cities subjected to the equivalent of the interstate highway and urban renewal programs in the United States, that removed thousands of older low-rent dwellings in the inner cities, while increasing accessibility for those who drive in from the suburbs.

In addition, Toronto has benefited from its position as provincial capital, from a dedicated civil service, and—in the past—from the actions of a more pro-active provincial level of government than is common in most U.S. states. It is also true, in the Toronto case, that municipal government intervention in general, and planning in particular, have played a fundamental—and frequently controversial—role in managing urban growth and maintaining a high quality of life. And, equally important, the systems through which Toronto has attempted to manage development have been relatively transparent and open to public scrutiny and debate.

A number of lessons derive, directly or indirectly, from the above review:

- The elements of the urban milieu that are the slowest to adapt to changing conditions are the structure of governance and the supporting network of institutions.
- There is no single model of planning, regulation or service delivery that necessarily works everywhere. Similar structures of governance, regulatory institutions, and policy instruments can produce quite different results on the ground.
- The single most important component in designing a regulatory system is an improved understanding of the processes of change—both market and public-sector decision processes—that are shaping the region. Far too often, policies are devised and implemented as if the problems, and the populations and activities involved, were static in time and space.
- In the typically fragmented metropolis of today, the basic strategic requirement is for "region-wide" coordination of metropolitan development and management. This coordination, involving all

relevant levels of government—local, regional, provincial—may or may not involve the establishment of formal regional governments. Whatever their form, however, the regulatory institutions must have exclusive powers, veto rights, and access to a secure funding base. They must also be open and accountable to the electorate.

- The key element in region-wide coordination, and in maintaining uniform service facilities across the metropolitan area, is the sharing of the costs and benefits of urban growth and change. This is usually expressed as the ability of regional authorities (or senior levels of government) to redistribute revenues from richer to poorer local jurisdictions (e.g., through fiscal transfers or direct service provision).
- As a precursor to more effective coordination in metropolitan regions, there is a clear need to develop a stronger "sense-of-urban-region," a regional consciousness and feeling of cooperative citizenship, that transcends local self-interests and attachments to place.
- In a politically fragmented metropolitan environment, local governments, left on their own, are unlikely to enter into cooperative agreements that impose redistributive taxes on their own residents, especially for social and welfare needs arising elsewhere in the region.
- Even with a structure in place for improved regional coordination, effective implementation of any strategy requires the active participation of senior governments. Neither local nor regional governments have the powers or resources to manage metropolitan regions on their own.
- Uncertainty with respect to rates of change in the economies, technologies, and social structures of the modern metropolis, also suggests the need for "flexibility" in both management strategies and the instruments of regulation, but set within a context of known "rules" of development.
- Within any format proposed for regional coordination, there must be improved cooperation between those institutions, agencies and other stakeholders involved in the development process. Obvious examples include the need to establish closer links between land-use planning and transportation, housing and finance, social services, and housing provision.
- A basic requirement is to encourage diversity in terms of housing types, employment locations, and development options, and thus in the choices presented to both producers and consumers.
- Urban management is itself a learning process, and thus the system must be able to evolve as conditions and policy issues change.

- Even if we accept the importance of competitiveness as a reasonable objective of public policy at the scale of individual metropolitan areas, local economic development strategies must incorporate the maintenance and upgrading of social overhead capital (e.g., universities, research institutes, social institutions, cultural facilities, etc.) as a priority.

None of these lessons learned, of course, is entirely new or original.

Conclusions

Toronto continues to provide a relatively high quality of life for most of its citizens (Frisken et al. 1997). It has been, on balance, a competently administered urban region, despite its current fragmentation, that delivers a relatively high level of services and employment opportunities. Moreover, it has often served as a textbook example of effective management (Sharpe 1995). To many observers, Toronto illustrates how the presence of a metropolitan government, a uniform service delivery system, metro-wide revenue-sharing, good quality public transit, strategic housing policies, and proactive planning at both local and regional scale, can contribute positively to creating a healthy urban environment. Its overall success, at least in part, can be attributed to deliberate efforts to regulate urban development and to direct that development toward specific goals; but in part it is also attributable to circumstance, timing and good luck. What proportion of the successes, and of the failures, is attributable to management, broadly defined, and regulation, is impossible to estimate. Regulation is also expensive, but so too is the absence of regulation.

Continued success is not guaranteed. Serious challenges remain.

References

Bourne, L.S. 1996. "Reurbanization, Uneven Urban Development and the Debate on New Urban Forms." *Urban Geography* 17: 690–713.

Bourne, L.S. 1999. "Governance, Efficiency and Equity in Large Urban Agglomerations." In A.G. Aguilar and I. Escarmilla, eds., *Problems of Megacities: Social Inequalities, Environmental Risk and Urban Governance*, pp. 159–73. Mexico City: UNAM Press.

Breheny, M., ed. 1995. *Sustainable Development and Urban Form*. London: Pion.

City of Toronto. 1991. *The Official Plan Proposals Report (Cityplan '91).* Toronto: Planning Department.

City of Toronto. 1999. *Economic Development in the Learning City: Toronto's Competitiveness in the Global Knowledge Economy.* Consultant's report. Toronto: City of Toronto.

Foot, D., and D. Stoffman. 1996. *Boom, Bust and Echo: How to Profit from the Coming Demographic Shift.* Toronto: Macfarlane Walter Ross.

Frisken, F., L.S. Bourne, G. Gad, and R. Murdie. 1997. *Governance and Social Well-Being in the Toronto Area: Past Achievements and Future Challenges.* Research Paper 193. Toronto: Centre for Urban and Community Studies, University of Toronto.

Garreau, J. 1991. *Edge City: Life on the New Frontier.* New York: Doubleday.

Gertler, M. 1990. *Toronto: The State of the Regional Economy.* Toronto: Ontario Ministry of Supply and Services.

Greater Toronto Area (GTA) Task Force. 1996. *Greater Toronto: Report of the Task Force.* Toronto: Queen's Printer.

Greater Toronto Services Board (GTSB). 1997. *Getting Together. Report of the Special Advisor* (M. Farrow). Toronto: Office of the Special Advisor, GTSB Project.

Hall, P. 1998. *Cities in Civilization: Culture, Innovation and Urban Order.* London: Weidenfeld and Nicolson.

Kjellberg Bell, J., and S. Webber, eds. 1996. *Urban Regions in a Global Context: Directions for the Greater Toronto Area.* Major Report 34. Toronto: Centre for Urban and Community Studies, University of Toronto.

Lemon, J. 1985. *Toronto Since 1918: An Illustrated History.* Toronto: James Lorimer.

Lemon, J. 1996. *Liberal Dreams and Nature's Limits: Great Cities of North America since 1600.* Toronto: Oxford University Press.

MacLaren, V. 1992. *Sustainable Urban Development in Canada: From Concept to Practice.* 3 vols. Toronto: ICURR Press.

Metropolitan Toronto Planning Department. 1976. *Metroplan: Concepts and Objectives.* Toronto: Municipality of Metropolitan Toronto.

Metropolitan Toronto Planning Department. 1991. *Towards a Liveable Metropolis: A Discussion Paper (Plan Review Report 13).* Toronto: Metro Planning Department.

Municipality of Metropolitan Toronto. 1980. *Official Plan for the Urban Structure of Metro Toronto (MetroPlan)*. Toronto: Metropolitan Toronto Planning Department.

Office for the Greater Toronto Area (OGTA). 1991. *GTA 2021: The Challenge of Our Future*. Toronto: Office for the GTA.

Office for the Greater Toronto Area (OGTA). 1992. *Shaping Growth in the GTA: A Commentary Report*. (Report prepared by Berridge Lewinberg Greenberg Ltd. for the Greater Toronto Coordinating Committee). Toronto: Office for the GTA.

Ontario, Commission on Planning and Development Reform in Ontario. 1993. *New Planning in Ontario: Final Report* (John Sewell, Chair). Toronto: Queen's Printer.

OECD. 1998. *Better Governance for More Competitive and Liveable Cities*. Report of the OECD Toronto Workshop. OECD, Group on Urban Affairs, Toronto Corporate Policy and Planning Office.

Plan Canada. 1984."Ontario Planned? Special Issue on the Golden Age of Planning in Ontario, 1966–75." *Plan Canada* 24(3/4).

Sewell, John. 1993. *The Shape of the City: Toronto Struggles with Modern Planning*. Toronto: University of Toronto Press.

Sharpe, L.J., ed. 1995. *The Government of World Cities*. London: Wiley.

Social Planning Council of Metropolitan Toronto. 1979. *Metro's Suburbs in Transition: Evolution and Overview*. Toronto: Social Planning Council.

Tomalty, R. 1997. *Compact Cities: Growth Management and Intensification in Vancouver, Toronto, and Montreal*. Toronto: ICURR Press.

United Way of Greater Toronto. 1997. *Metro Toronto: A Community at Risk*. Toronto: United Way.

Waterfront Regeneration Trust. 1992. *Regeneration: Toronto's Waterfront and the Sustainable City* (Hon. David Crombie, Commissioner). Toronto: Queen's Printer.

2

City Strategy and Governance

Editor's Introduction

Richard Stren

In an increasingly global (or at least international) context, the growth and/
or decline of urban economies is seen as—at least partially—the result of
urban policies that make particular cities more or less *competitive*. Competitiveness is notoriously difficult to measure. But experience suggests
that cities and city regions that are *more* competitive should, for example,
attract more international (or even local) investment; and should demonstrate rising levels of such indicators as retail sales, manufacturing value
added, professional employment, business services receipts, high-quality
business and residential construction, and the like. By contrast, cities that
are *less* competitive tend to display higher levels of unemployment and
dependency, a deteriorating business and manufacturing environment, and
overall, a more sluggish economy.[1]

In the late 1990s, it was the conventional wisdom among urban managers and planners around the world to plan for urban economic development on the premise that to produce such a plan—or planning process—
would make their cities more competitive in relation to other cities of similar size and potential, both nationally and internationally. Study after study
of such major European cities as Paris, Lyon, Lille, and Barcelona show

---

1. For some useful measures of urban competititiveness, see Kresl and Singh 1999.

that major infrastructural projects and involvement in such international competitions as the Olympics, or lobbying for international headquarters of important organizations, were the hallmark of planning in the 1980s and 1990s. Even in the case of London—considered by such an authority as Saskia Sassen (1991) as one of the world's major "global cities," there was, from 1991 to 1998, an "unprecedented series of major studies" of the urban region, sponsored by different government bodies, suggesting different strategies to enhance the city's competitive position (Gordon 1999).

In his foreword to a book entitled *Competitive Cities: Succeeding in the Global Economy,* Charles Royer, a former mayor of Seattle, argues that cities must learn from each other, since "[s]uccessful cities of the future, both large and small, and regardless of where they are on the world map, must use all their resources if they hope to compete and prosper in a new world economy" (Royer 1995, p. x).

Planning for a stronger urban economy, then, has been a central preoccupation of urban leaders for some time. In this exercise, at least three elements seem to be crucial—at least on the basis of the evidence presented in the papers in this section. First, there must be systematic knowledge (based on research where possible) of the strengths and weaknesses of the economy of any city or city region. Second, there must be strong and committed political leadership, especially in the difficult process of developing a "vision" of a desirable future which the city and its residents must strive to attain. Third, there needs to be an effective consultation process of the major stakeholders in the city—business, community groups, educators, political parties, and major institutions—who must in the end "sign on" for planned investments, and important social and other changes to take place. Each city will have its own answer to the challenge of strategic planning but, as the papers in this section indicate, there are many common elements. One of the most important elements is the elaboration of a "governance" strategy, whereby decisions and plans formulated by the city leadership are accountable and transparent to the citizenry, and where administrative decisions and the implementation of public services are equitable and efficient.

In his paper, "Preparing an Economic and Strategic Vision for a City," Nigel Harris emphasizes the changing economic dynamics of cities in the context of globalization and decentralization. Noting important trends such as the restructuring of the workforce (into more informal and less industrial occupations), as well as a shift in the territorial distribution of workers, he stresses the importance of urban leaders understanding the operation and needs of the new economic sectors. Among these new sectors are finance and business support services, trade, hotel and restaurant businesses, information processing and management, tourism, and transport. Important for local purposes are health services, education, culture, and sport, although these can also become important as a means of attracting investors. While many cities "score" well on the development of some of the new economic sectors, few succeed in building a good quality of life and in "creating a city which is clean, safe, and beautiful, without major environmental hazards or desperate transport congestion." But, for this to be possible, the city must organize regular meetings with leading groups, and attempt to reach a political consensus on the best direction for development. This requires educated professionals, and a strong research capacity, without which different options and choices cannot reasonably be considered.

To help us imagine what a successful strategic planning exercise would look like, we have the example of New Zealand presented by Angela Griffin. In her article, which is framed by the four major objectives of the World Bank's new Urban and Local Government Strategy (according to which cities should be first sustainable, but also livable, competitive, bankable, well managed, and well governed), Griffin reviews New Zealand's urban management reforms since the late 1980s. The essence of these reforms was the separation of governance and management in 86 regional and district authorities, and the application of rules for accountability, transparency and contestability. The accountability objective is partly achieved through requiring the mayor and other elected representatives to consult with their local community on a 10-year Strategic and Financial Management Plan, and to deliver this plan in an organized fashion, subject to consultation. Since these reforms were put into practice, there has been an increase in spending on regulatory functions, on social infrastructure, and on social programs. In general, local authorities in New Zealand are operating on a much sounder financial footing than was the case before the reforms. At the same time, local democracy has become more active, with a steady increase in the number of female councilors across the country. At the end of her article, Griffin addresses some of the practical requirements needed to achieve success in the production of an effective vision and urban strategy.

As an example of what a strategic planning process looks like in a city in the developing world, we have the case of Coimbatore, in southern India. Coimbatore, a city of some 1.1 million, was facing two major problems in the late 1990s. While economically the city was prospering due to an expansion in its textile and engineering industries, that very expansion was creating serious problems of urban sprawl and lack of coordination of land-use decisions. But merely servicing and administering a rapidly growing urban population was also hampered by an internal organizational structure that was at once understaffed and inexperienced in important areas. In the light of the 74th Constitutional Amendment of 1992 (which gave more power and explicit responsibilities to municipal governments throughout India), the city set out to establish a "strategic vision," with major goals formulated through a broad process of consultation involving citizens, elected representatives, business and community stakeholders, and government agencies. This process has already led to improvements in the tax reporting and tax collection system, which in turn has improved significantly the revenue obtained from the collection of property tax. Since this effort is still a work in progress, the overall results of this planning strategy will require some time to assess.

While the Coimbatore case may give the impression that the initiation of a strategic planning process is relatively straightforward and unproblematic, the reading selections also include a more challenging example. In this case, which involves the city of Mombasa, Kenya (a city of 1.5 million people on the East African coast), the newly elected Mayor attempted to use the political process to improve the regulatory procedures, the administration of services, and the collection of local revenues. This is a very personal document. As Najib Balala writes, many of his initiatives were popular with the citizens of the town, and successful in the short term, but he soon found that there was political resistance to some of his policies from among sitting councilors and business interests in the town. At the same time, the structure of central government oversight and control over the Council—whereby major decisions had to be ratified by the Minister of Local Government in Nairobi—produced serious delays in obtaining legal clearance for local decisions. As a result of his inability to move the local government system towards his objectives, he made the decision to resign from office after only one year in the position. His resignation in early 1999 was a highly publicized event in Kenyan political life. Aside from its importance in the East African context, this case illustrates all too well the very real obstacles to policy and institutional change that can exist in many cities, in spite of the emergence of a dedicated local leader and the clear and pressing need to undertake strategic reforms.

The final article in this chapter addresses an all too common challenge in contemporary cities: the problem of crime and violence. We have included Franz Vanderschueren's article in this section because, in many important respects, a city that wishes to be competitive in relation to other cities must not be seen to have a "crime problem," let alone a "violence problem." In his article, Vanderschueren first traces the growth of various kinds of crime and violence in relation to urbanization in different parts of the world. Urbanization leads to crime and violence as a result of such factors as the poverty of low-income neighborhoods, a poor urban environment, the limitations of protection services (both public and private), the absence of social controls in the city, and the coming of age of young people who for various reasons are prone to violence. Given the fact that the typical governmental response to crime—imprisonment—is expensive and not very effective, the author examines a number of community responses to criminality. While some of these responses are worse than the problem itself, successful initiatives involve a combination of local partnerships between the municipal authorities, communities, police, and judicial systems close to the people. In the end, extreme inequalities and the absence of gainful employment for youth play an explosive role in the growth of crime, and must be counteracted through imaginative local social policies. Vanderschueren himself favors the notion of "local justice," by which local groups and communities develop their own unique means to deal with what they consider to be unresolved conflicts. These forms of justice, that include neighborhood tribunals in the Philippines, Justices of the Peace in England and Spain, and Resistance Councils in Uganda, are accessible, cheap, and fast. In the end, as the author concludes, the prevention of violence must be everyone's business.

References

Gordon, Ian. 1999. "Internationalization and Urban Competition." *Urban Studies* 36(5/6): 1011.

Kresl, Peter Karl, and Balwant Singh. 1999. "Competitiveness in the Urban Economy: Twenty-four Large U.S. Metropolitan Areas." *Urban Studies* 36(5/6): 1017–27.

Royer, Charles. 1995. "Foreword." In Hazel Duffy, ed., *Competitive Cities: Succeeding in the Global Economy*, pp. ix–x. London: E. and F.N. Spon.

Sassen, Saskia. 1991. *The Global City: New York, London, Tokyo*. Princeton: Princeton University Press.

Preparing an Economic and Strategic Vision for a City

Nigel Harris

Understanding the city economy has become a vital component of city management. This has arisen from two interrelated processes: "globalization"—the integration of formally separate national economies into a single economic system that has changed patterns of local specialization, fueled by trade and capital flows; and decentralization—the tendency of national government to vest responsibilities and powers in subnational levels of government.

City managers thus need to know much more about the economic strengths and weaknesses of their city, the dangers of declining sectors and the opportunities of high-growth sectors, all in order to assist the structural changes and minimize social damage. As the changing structure of the economy is a by-product of integration into an international system, managers similarly have to be aware of the implications for their city of the international changes—the implications of, for example, a free-trade area for the Americas, of Mercosur or bilateral trade agreements (as between Chile and Mexico, Colombia and Mexico), or of innovations in other cities that affect the patterns of production or exports, and might provide opportunities for the city to emulate or service.

The city is both the most productive and the most dynamic component of the territorial economy. Change—in output, in workforce and in territorial distribution of activity—is, therefore, in addition to economic growth, very rapid. To benefit from these processes requires a flexible economy, one capable of reacting swiftly to opportunities and dangers, and one therefore where, for example, public authorities, businessmen and other agencies in the city must work closely together. The measures of economic flexibility are difficult to identify[2] (although rigid public regulations often constitute one impediment to flexibility), but the result can be seen in the cities—for example, in the capacity of Hong Kong over the past half-century to industrialize and deindustrialize without significant unemployment or urban dereliction.

---

2. A Turkish economist described the growing responsiveness of the Turkish (national) economy under the impact of macroeconomic reforms in the following way: "It took six years for the government to react to the first oil price increases, over six months to the major financial crisis of 1983, six weeks to the exchange crisis of 1987, six days to the 1990 Gulf War and now six hours to major external changes."

If high growth impels constant rapid restructuring, albeit on an incremental basis, recession is the most painful test of a city's capacities to survive—the test of its leadership and management. The older industrial cities of Europe and North America in the 1970s and 1980s painfully illustrate the costs of failure in very high rates of unemployment and inner-city dereliction, problems that, in the worst cases, have still not been overcome. When national trends are powerful, it is difficult to counter them, but cities vary immensely in their response to economic downturn, and one factor in that variation is local leadership.

The opening up of national economies appears to have been accompanied by growing "informalization"—that is, a growing share of a city's economy may have slipped below the threshold of the statistical system. Often, the sectors that have disappeared are among the newest and most dynamic, so they have an exaggerated effect on our picture of where the city is going. Take, for example, the textile industry of Mumbhai (Bombay), historically located in the heart of the city. Employment has declined from nearly 250,000 two-and-a-half decades ago, to around 50,000. But the statistically unrecorded "power loom" industry, on the periphery of the metropolitan area, has grown in parallel, adding perhaps 150,000 jobs. The type of output has changed, as has the workforce and its incomes, and the location; but, most important, it has slipped out of the accounts. Some suggest that anything between 30 and 60 percent of the economies of Kiev and Lima are similarly unrecorded. Any strategy for a city must therefore bear in mind the unseen base of this informal economy iceberg. Over time, good city managers—such as officials, businessmen, trade union officials, NGOs—can build up a good sense of what is unrecorded, even if they cannot easily quantify it; but, in the short term, scenarios of the city's future have to be qualified by what we do not know.

What Do We Need to Know about Trends and City Economies?

The Deindustrializing City

After the long historical association of the urban and the industrial, manufacturing is tending to relocate away from cities. This can occur either completely (as seemed to happen to Accra and Santiago de Chile), or as part of the development of much larger industrial regions (as in the central valley of Mexico, where industry is moving northwards from the Metropolitan Zone, and where manufacturing is growing rapidly in cities on the periphery, such as Toluca, Queretao and Puebla. Something similar is occurring in the Central Indian Triangle between Mumbhai, Pune, and Nasik. A prototype might be the Pearl River delta in southern China, where major urban servicing cities—Guanzhou and Shenzhen–Hong Kong—lie at each end, with a scatter of industrial cities, towns, and villages between. Of course, this pattern implies that smaller cities may continue to industrialize, while manufacturing is of declining significance for most big cities. (In relatively rare cases, however, some of the latter have seen rapid industrial growth; for example, Dhaka has added in the order of one million new manufacturing jobs in the past two decades, and Ho Chih Minh City has seen a comparable growth in export-oriented light industry.)

The Servicing City

The service sectors are poorly conceptualized and, therefore, ill recorded; this leads to them being often underestimated. However, almost all large cities in Europe and North America are servicing centers. The shift has been quite dramatic—London, for example, lost 800,000 jobs in manufacturing in the two decades to 1980 but, in the same period, reached 800,000 positions in finance and business services. Again, the change is a change of workforce, of incomes and consumption (and, thus, the retail and wholesale trades), of location and movement patterns. What sorts of services are concerned? Some examples follow:

FINANCE AND PRODUCER SERVICES. The growth of the financial sector of big-city economies has been remarkable as capital markets have opened, governments have liberalized the conditions for foreign investment, developed stock exchanges, and privatized functions. The central business district has had to be reconstructed to accommodate these developments. Furthermore, there has been major growth in business or producer services. In some cases, in Lyons, for example, this service manufacturing is in a large region outside the city. Hong Kong is a declining center for manufacturing, but a key element in its service sector is managing the logistics for world manufacturing—as the case of Li and Fung illustrates (see Box 2.1).

TRADE. Trading and the handling of tradable goods—from giant wholesale markets to the pavement seller and the cyclist carrying wares—is probably the biggest single employer in developing countries and big cities, although surprisingly little is known about the system. National distribution centers are closely related to cities as junction points in the transport system, with warehousing and storage, related processing centers (flour

---

Box 2.1.   Hong Kong's Services

The firm of Li and Fung (of Hong Kong) is a spider's web of manufacturing in 23 countries, with operations in various parts of South-East Asia and also in Latin America, Eastern Europe, the Caribbean, and Mauritius. Mr. Fung explains how the system works. A foreign company will come to him with a modest product—a ballpoint pen, for example, or a simple dress—and ask him to find out where it can be made more cheaply than anywhere else the inquiring company yet knows about. Mr. Fung's people set out to find not only a source of ever-cheaper labor but also somewhere safe from trade restrictions on Chinese production. Take that simple dress. The yarn may be spun in Korea, the fabric woven in Taiwan, the zips bought in Japan and the garment part-finished in China before it passes through a final stitching factory in Indonesia. "What we are doing is finding the best place for every operation," Mr. Fung says. "At the same time, we are lining up factors of production so that we can cut lead times from three months to five weeks."

Li and Fung has a network of 7,500 regular suppliers, employing an average of 200 workers apiece. In other words, about one-and-a-half million workers to some extent depend on this firm (*The Economist* 1998, p. 20).

---

and rice milling, oil pressing, for example), and banking and credit systems. The retail end is vital for the quality of life of the city, and for tourism— indeed, some cities have developed retail networks in order to develop tourism, as have Panama, Singapore, and Bahrain.

Hotels and restaurants. Again, these are decisive for the quality of life in the city and for tourism, a high-growth sector in developing countries in the future. Like trade, they are labor intensive and therefore important in employment and generating city incomes.

Information industries. The "unbundling" of information services, made possible by satellite communications (and paralleling the unbundling of manufacturing so that parts of the manufacturing process of a good can be located in different countries) is producing a wide range of urban export industries responding to demands in developed countries:

- Loading and processing of information—airline ticketing and accounting (Barbados, Mumbhai), legal and criminal records (Ciudad Juarez, Manila), medical records (Barbados), library catalogues, real-estate transactions (Shenzhen); it is possible in the future that many other statistical series of developed countries will be loaded and processed in cities in developing countries, such as population and industrial censuses, and national accounts;

- Software programming for companies in Europe and North America: there are now many centers for this in Asia and Latin America; 12 have been identified in India, though many of these are not engaged in exports; the two best known are Bangalore and Mumbhai;
- Printing and publishing, now important in, for example, Bogotá and Hong Kong.

TOURISM. Tourism is becoming important in many cities, both for end-visits and as transit points in the transport system. It pulls together many of the preceding sectors—trade, hotels, and restaurants—and some discussed below. Again, it can be very labor-intensive, with significant implications for agriculture and manufacturing. Tourism, however, requires a well-ordered city, secure, clean, and healthy; that is to say, the quality of life in the city is fundamental to its capacity to earn income from tourism.

THE "NON-TRADABLE THAT BECOMES TRADABLE". That is, a set of services, often closely related traditionally to free public services for domestic consumption, that can also become commercial export industries:

- *Health services* (including hospitals and clinics, convalescent and retirement homes, pharmacists, and paramedical services; sometimes, backed by teaching and research hospitals, university medical faculties, etc.). Demand is likely to increase steadily here, as populations in the developed countries, closely followed by the newly industrialized countries (NICs), age and their active labor forces decline. Already, in the special circumstances of the United States-Mexico border, Mexican medical services for Americans (especially the increasing number of the aged who winter in the south) have been developed on a significant scale. There are other more specialized centers—for example, Bogotá and Barcelona (for eye surgery), Singapore, etc. as well as centers in the developed countries for upper-income consumers (such as La Jolla, London, Zurich, Vienna).
- *Higher education* (and, in some places, secondary education). The number of students now attending, and staff servicing, city universities and colleges makes them a significant component of a city's consumer markets with important multiplier effects in retail consumption and transport. For example, Cairo has possibly 500,000 students in public and private tertiary educational institutions (many of them from other Arab countries or elsewhere—that is, generating export revenues). In the same way, most Latin American cities are

major student centers—with Mexico City probably exceeding Cairo in numbers. North Cyprus has developed a deliberate export strategy based upon creating five English-speaking universities to attract students from Turkey, the Middle East and South Asia.

- *Culture and sport:* A number of cities have begun deliberately to develop cultural and sporting facilities as elements of an export strategy to attract both ordinary tourists and those visiting for special purposes (for example, executives coming to work temporarily in the financial or other sectors, participants in business conventions, and so on.). In the early 1990s, employment in the provision of cultural activities in London was estimated at 215,000, a not insignificant sector of the economy. Expansion in urban cultural activities has also been enhanced by "festivalization," that is, the holding of special occasions to attract consumers—major international drama, film or music festivals, fiestas or traditional ceremonies, commemoration events. Something similar happens with international sporting contests. Barcelona's exploitation of the opportunity of the 1992 Olympic Games is well known in this respect.

TRANSPORT. A globalized economy implies that an increasing proportion of domestic output is moved, as it is traded internationally; and that an increasing proportion of the world's population (both consumers and providers of services) is also internationally mobile. Since cities are often the major junction points in the transport system—between sea, air, rail, and road—both a globalized economy and the city's prosperity depends upon the urban infrastructure and its daily management. Major investments have been channeled into new airports (and, particularly in future, the high-growth sector of air transport and air freight) and the containerization of ports, without the necessary improvements being made to the road and rail feeder systems—and often traffic management is so poor that half the advantage of these investments is lost. High costs in the transport system can eliminate any comparative advantage a country might have in particular exports. Furthermore, port modernization often implies relocation of the wharves away from old inner-city dock areas, opening up central areas of derelict land for redevelopment (the same is sometimes true of inner-city railway lands) to, as it were, retool the city for new economic functions (some of the redevelopment schemes are now well known, such as those in Barcelona, Cape Town, Yokohama, London, Sydney, and New York).

Many of these servicing sectors are mutually reinforcing; for example, New York's financial activities are strengthened by the city's vigorous cultural life that the financiers can enjoy after work. Lyons has employed its universities to create a university quarter, a "Left Bank" of small theaters, galleries, and restaurants that focus on tourism. Other cities have tried to use their universities as a basis for science parks, located near airports and highway junctions.

However, an economic precondition for building a well-functioning servicing city is an adequate quality of life, creating a city that is clean, safe, and beautiful, without major environmental hazards or desperate transport congestion. Few cities score well here and some score really badly—Bangkok's transport system is now notoriously a deterrent to visitors. Tourists visiting Mexico City to see the volcanoes, or Santiago de Chile to see the Andes, will be disappointed, as the traffic haze now hides a key comparative advantage much of the year. Medical tourism will hardly work if patients are afflicted by polluted water; cultural tourism can be destroyed by poor security. Thus, the old agenda of municipal service provision now becomes a condition for the success of the new city economy.

At a disaggregated level, each city is unique, and it is at this level that the innovations occur that ultimately transform the city. This implies a unique relationship to the world economy, a unique history and physical form, and a unique inheritance of human capital, the key to economic growth. City managers are in great danger of error if they read off what they should do from a standard model of a city economy (as witness the numerous empty industrial estates around the world), rather than seeking to understand the unique bundle of attributes in which their city has a real competitive advantage. However, city managers often do not know their city—they have not put together the picture of its strengths and weaknesses.

What Do We Need to Know about the City Economy?

A city's economic structure is continually changing, as shown in three measures: (a) changes in the composition of the value of output, by sector and sub-sector; (b) changes in the distribution of the labor force by sector and sub-sector; and (c) changes in the physical distribution of activity within the city, the metropolitan area and, possibly, neighboring districts.

The greater the degree of disaggregation, the greater the changes, but also the greater the problems of handling the data (and, sometimes, in finding it). But only at a disaggregated level does one identify just what is expanding—not "electrical and electronic equipment," but " transistor radios" (as in Hong Kong in the 1970s)—and what the employment and territorial implications of this are.

Part of this exercise is also to identify the changing composition of the city's exports (that is, what leaves the city as opposed to what is consumed in the city), and thus its emerging competitive advantages, as well as the expected demands upon its transport system. This is part of a separate analysis: of the city as a junction point in flows of people, goods, finance, and information; and of the means to minimize transaction costs between modes. In addition, we need to put together the much more familiar picture of the support services—the educational system and its adequacy in supporting the right combinations of skills, the capacity of the health system to sustain the population, housing and public services.

All this needs to be placed in a dynamic context. This includes the likely impact on the city of external economic changes in, first, the international economy, for example, Europe 1992, the implications of the Asian and Brazilian economic crises, the changing value of the dollar or the yen, the implications of declining oil prices, of new innovations, of trade agreements, and so on—the kind of exercise common enough in national ministries of finance, but more rare for subnational layers of government; and, second, in the domestic economy (changes in government policy, effects of major new infrastructure spending, and so on).

We can then begin to understand the likely future evolution of the city's economy, its demand for labor (and hence possible immigration) and skills, for additional infrastructure, for adjusting the regulatory structure, for the redevelopment of old sites or the opening up of new ones. The exercise in essence is not an expert one, although there may be some expert inputs. Often, the available data do not allow the identification of innovations until they are well advanced, even though such changes have been known to the business community concerned, or to others in partial or anecdotal form. Making sure this partial knowledge informs the process of defining a city strategy requires an institutional form for pooling all resources. The City Forum (where government officers and councilors meet representatives of business associations, trade unions, political parties, universities, NGOs, community organizations, and other groups) is one mechanism for putting information together and, in the process, reaching a political consensus on what the direction of development should be. Consensus planning—agreement on a desired set of scenarios that incorporate allowance for flexibility—is replacing the old 20-year master plan, with its emphasis on statutory long-term targets and norms (a plan that can no longer be achieved, although elements of infrastructure planning still require longer-term planning horizons).

All this requires up-to-date and appropriate data on a regular basis. Without such data there can be little transparency in government, little responsible citizen participation, and little flexibility in responses. Information is crucial to transparency, accountability and to the promotion of the city. Ideally, as in the national government, each city should have its annual statistical yearbook with, in some cases, quarterly bulletins to allow continuing strategic thinking by the city managers, the promotion of the city (to business, for instance), and citizen participation (consultation processes cannot be successful if the city managers are ill-informed).

Some cities have gone further, by setting up city research centers (for example, Bogota's Siglo XXI) to service the City Forum or the local authority, or local business (indeed, the Chamber of Commerce plays this research role in some cities) with reports on different sectors, appraisals of the impact of external changes on the city, and briefing documents for city officials and others. Some of this work has also been internalized in local government through departments of economic development, economic advisory units attached to the mayor's office, or embodied in separate public agencies, such as economic development corporations or partnership alliances. There is a wide range of options, with different merits and demerits attached to each, but the overall aim is the same: to make the economic management of the city and the political consensus underlying policy increasingly better informed, more precisely targeted, and more effective.

Finally, planning is not about producing a plan; it is about the continuous adjustment of the behavior of the local authority and other stakeholders to a changing economic and social environment.

References

The Economist. 1998. Supplement. 20 June.

Harris, Nigel, ed. 1992. *Cities in the 1990s: The Challenge for Developing Countries.* London: UCL Press.

Harris, Nigel. 1994. "The Emerging Global City: Transport." *Cities* 11(5): 332–6.

Harris, Nigel. 1997. "Cities in a Global Economy: Structural Change and Policy Responses." *Urban Studies* 34(10): 1693–1703.

Harris, Nigel and Ida Fabricius, eds. 1996. *Cities and Structural Adjustment.* London: UCL Press.

Peterson, George, Thomas Kingsley, and Jeffrey P. Telgarsky. 1991. *Urban Economics and National Development.* Washington, DC: USAID.

UNCHS. 1996. *An Urbanizing World: Global Report on Human Settlements 1996.* New York: Oxford University Press.

The Promotion of Sustainable Cities

Angela Griffin

The aim of the World Bank's new Urban and Local Government Strategy is to promote sustainable cities and towns that fulfill the promise of development for their inhabitants—in particular by improving the lives of the poor and promoting equity—while contributing to the progress of the country as a whole.

Sustainable cities are first and foremost *livable, competitive, bankable, well managed,* and *well governed.* A well-managed and well-governed city is one where there is representation and inclusion of all groups; with accountability, integrity, and transparency of government actions in pursuit of shared goals; and with strong local government capacity to fulfill public responsibilities based on knowledge, skills, resources, and procedures that draw on partnerships.

There is now increasing pressure on governments at the subnational level to perform new roles in their communities as a result of the worldwide trends of globalization, decentralization, urbanization, and the reform of government, all involving changes in the roles of the public and private sectors.

Efficient and effective subnational governance requires an intergovernmental institutional framework that clearly specifies the responsibilities of each level of government; provides the appropriate authority to coincide with the delegated responsibilities; and specifies and enforces a code of conduct. It is usual for central government to legislate this framework, and for the activities of subnational governments to be restricted to its requirements; and where the framework is based on democratic principles the legislation will provide for the election of community representatives to make decisions within it. Some countries, like New Zealand, are more advanced than others in developing those enabling frameworks.

Local Government in New Zealand

New Zealand has attracted considerable interest since the 1980s for its pursuit of national and subnational public-sector reform that has clarified the role of government and introduced measures to improve its performance.

In 1989, following the successful reform of its state sector, the national government introduced legislation that restructured local government by creating 86 regional and district authorities in which the roles of governance and management are separated, with the intention of improving performance through *accountability, transparency,* and *contestability.* The legislation specified the functions of local government for the first time. It also required: the appointment of a City Manager with responsibility to employ and manage the staff; the introduction of accrual accounting to track the full cost of services and the levels of investment to maintain the value of the community's assets; the involvement of the community through mandatory consultation; publicly available annual spending plans; and independently audited annual public reporting on performance. The stipulations on the appointment of a city manager are an important feature of the twin objectives of separating the roles of governance and management, and achieving full accountability of elected representatives to their community (governance), and of managers to the elected representatives (management).

The emphasis of the reform was, first, to achieve autonomy in terms of a local authority's ability to manage community affairs, including the right to raise funds through property taxes and other charges, with minimum intergovernmental transfers; second, to emphasize the role of the local authority as a purchaser of goods and services from public and private sources that offer choices and deliver benefits to the community, while at the same time efficiently managing resources; and third, to corporatize publicly owned trading activities (such as energy) into arms-length companies that operate in a commercially neutral way with no non-transparent public subsidy.

The Principles of Accountability, Transparency, and Contestability

The legislation ensures the underlying principles of the reform:

- *Transparency*—public access to information and decisionmaking forums so that the public knows what is happening in its name;
- *Accountability*—so that the public can identify who is responsible for making decisions; and
- *Contestability*—so that the public can be assured of optimum performance through the introduction of competition and private-sector business practices.

Transparency is achieved in a number of ways: through the Official Information Act 1982, and the Privacy Act 1993, which promote public access to information and open decisionmaking; requirements to consult with and report to the public annually on planned activities; enforcement of regulations by officers who are not also responsible for determining those regulations; and, finally, purchasing of goods and services through contractual relationships with internal staff or the private sector. All of these have the effect of mitigating the risk of corruption by making information statutorily available and by ensuring the making of transparent public policy and decisions.

Accountability is achieved when the person with authority to make or influence a decision about use of resources (inputs) is held also to be responsible for the effective delivery of the goods or services purchased (outputs and outcomes). New Zealand has created a local government hierarchy of accountability. The first tier is the Mayor and Councilors, accountable to the public; the second tier is the City Manager, accountable to the Mayor and Councilors; and the third tier is the staff, accountable to the City Manager for clearly defined results.

The Mayor and other elected representatives are required to consult with their community on a 10-year Strategic and Financial Management Plan, and deliver that through annual plans and budgets, also subject to consultation. Accountability is further enhanced through the annual report on progress against promised outcomes and performance standards; this is reviewed by independent government-appointed auditors. There is a requirement for regular testing of public satisfaction with local authority performance; this is undertaken in a variety of ways, including surveys.

Contestability was introduced to assure the adoption of practices that enhance the efficiency and effectiveness of local government. Local governments are required to offer choices between different kinds of facilities and services through the adoption of competitive bidding processes and the development of contracting relationships between the purchaser (the local authority) and the deliverer, who can be the local authority or the private sector.

The Roles Now Performed by Local Governments in New Zealand

As a result of reform the roles performed by local governments have become:

- Strategy and policymaking, and the monitoring of the organization's activities, including investments to maintain the value of the community's assets.
- Purchasing services and products through the annual budget and plan, to achieve benefits for the community and to monitor the quality of those services.
- Delivery of services or functions, using public employees or private contractors.
- Enforcement of regulations set by central government or by the local government as policymaker.

Under the separation of the roles of governance and management referred to earlier, the first two functions are the *governance* functions, and the remaining two are *management* functions, although in practice these roles are not so clear cut. Flexibility is required to make the relationship effective.

The benefits of separating these roles are fourfold. First, the elected representatives have access through the City Manager to objective policy advice and options which transparently identify the choices available, the costs and benefits of those choices, and the trade-off that may be required. Second, the elected representatives are free to concentrate on policy and performance, and can hold the City Manager accountable for the efficient achievement of objectives. Third, consistency in professional management can be achieved; this protects the standards of service provision from the volatility caused by politics and elections. Finally, the risk of corruption and manipulation of the rules is reduced, particularly by the separation of the making of policy from its implementation; by separation of regulation enforcement from regulation setting; and by separation of contract letting from contract delivery.

The Benefits of Reform

Recent research has shown that, in the decade since reform, significant shifts have occurred in local government spending patterns and activities. A slight but significant increase has taken place in spending on democracy, suggesting greater investment in reporting, monitoring, and consultation. We see a significant real increase in spending on regulatory functions, and a substantial decline in spending on physical infrastructure, consistent with improvements in efficiency and privatization. There has also been a substantial increase in spending on social infrastructure (McDermott and Forgie 1999); although spending on physical infrastructure is still the largest functional category overall, a visible shift of focus has occurred in urban areas to social functions, such as economic and employment development, housing, health, and safety.

Since reform net operating expenditure of local governments has declined, as has debt, property tax increases have been limited to the rate of inflation, and capital expenditure levels have been retained and assets maintained at reduced costs under a contestable regime (see Figure 2.1). Long-term operating deficits on current accounts have been eliminated.

Despite the reduction in the number of councils, representative democracy has been enhanced, with more active involvement of individuals in local affairs, and a steady increase in the number of female councilors. Local governments have moved to fulfill a governance role as advocates for their

Figure 2.1.   Beneficial Outcomes: Local Authority Performance Index, 1989-95

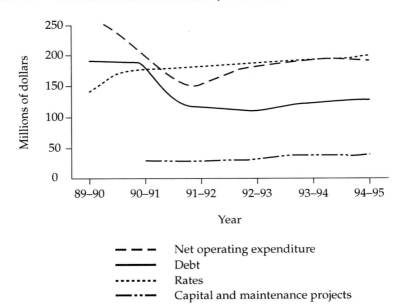

- - -   Net operating expenditure
——————   Debt
·········   Rates
—··—   Capital and maintenance projects

Note: Characterized by: operating deficit eliminated, debt reduced, rates increased with reduced levels of inflation, and capital expenditure levels retained and asset maintenance provided for, at reduced costs, under a contestable regime. Capital and maintenance projects are included in net operating expenditure before 1990–91.
Source: Author.

communities and purchasers of services rather than as service deliverers; the latter function is performed more and more by the private sector through privatization or facilities management. Beneficial outcomes also include increased satisfaction with local authority performance (see Figure 2.2).

While the New Zealand system of local government is only one example of possible government reform, it facilitates an understanding of the principles that underlie good governance and management that can lead to successful and sustainable city development.

The Role of Local Government in City Strategy

Local government is only one of a group of stakeholders that influence a city or governed area. Others include community groups, NGOs, the private sector, central government, and academia. Given its unique position as representative of the community, a local government can become the focal point for, and take the leadership role in, encouraging all

Figure 2.2.   Beneficial Outcomes: Satisfaction with Council Performance, Wellington, New Zealand, 1992–97

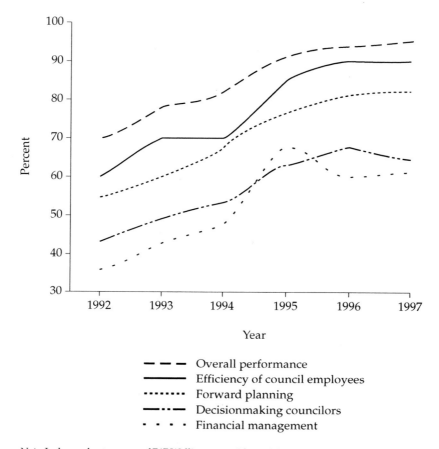

Note: Independent survey of 767 Wellington residents. Measure equals residents who rated services as very good, good, or satisfactory.
Source: Author.

stakeholders to take responsibility for their own unique roles in the development and success of a community.

Elected representatives, in an environment where they are free from day-to-day management duties as a result of separating the roles of governance and management, can shift their energies to strategy, policy, and planning and monitoring the achievement of strategic goals.

A strategic vision developed through the leadership of elected local representatives can provide the framework for the activities of all other

---

Box 2.2.   Questions Worth Posing on the Roles of Local Government/Levels of Autonomy/Code of Conduct; and the Roles of Elected Representatives and Managers

Which is preferable: local financial autonomy in terms of the ability to raise revenue, or a well-defined framework for intergovernmental transfers, with financial dependence on national taxes? Are there issues of equitable redistribution of resources that would override financial autonomy benefits?

What kinds of advantages could be gained from the separation of regulatory enforcement functions from other functions?

What kinds of problems and advantages could arise in a local government if a 10-year strategic plan, financial management plan, annual plan and report, and annual independent audit were required?

If governance and management were separated, how would the local government need to be organized?

What measures would have to be taken in a local government to allow citizens the right of access to all significant information?

If, in competitive bidding for delivery of services, the best bid is one from the private sector, what impact would this have on local authority personnel?

---

stakeholders, and that framework can be a basis for attracting investment and jobs. Key elements of a strategic planning process are:

- *Lead and facilitate* the strategic visioning process;
- *Engage* all stakeholders;
- *Provide* data to facilitate informed discussion;
- *Produce* the city's development strategy, which contains the community's preferred strategic vision and goals;
- *Seek commitment* of stakeholders to develop their own plans for delivering on the vision goals;
- *Develop and cost* the local government strategic plan to fulfill the local authority part of the strategic vision;
- *Agree on* the strategic goals to be achieved each year;
- *Provide resources* through the local government annual budget;
- *Set and monitor* indicators to measure performance;
- *Report back* to the community the achievement of the goals, and continue to lead the community vision.

Important Features of Strategic Visioning and Planning Processes

If a community visioning exercise is to reflect the views of the community, it must engage the public in the process, and promote citizen responsibility and ownership. Each identified group of stakeholders in the community should ideally be encouraged to participate in a process that achieves an agreed vision for the future. To do this they will need to be provided with data relating to trends in the physical, environmental, social, and economic environment of the city, and likely future scenarios. The local authority or an academic institution will frequently take responsibility for providing this information by gathering statistics from all sources, and commissioning specific research or arranging events to enhance understanding as a basis for informed debate and decisionmaking.

It is essential to capture all ideas from all sectors of the community, and to encourage the community to exercise judgement on options and risks and conflicts, so that they can make tradeoffs. As the priority options become more refined and concrete, these need to be costed for choices to be made in the full understanding of implied future funding needs.

Local authorities have devised many ways to engage the public in strategic planning; these include visioning party days, workshops, school events, and neighborhood events. Detailed preparation and advance planning and distribution of material is essential (City of Brea 1997).

Risks and How to Overcome Them

Strategic visioning processes can take one or two years if they are to result in a product that has an ownership wider than the local authority. It takes planning, organization, and resources to succeed in avoiding a process in which only the habitually active in the community are involved. It is essential to avoid capture by pressure groups by providing creative means for all the community to participate, avoiding reliance on traditional meetings.

One of the risks associated with a participative process is that politicians can feel their decisionmaking roles are being undermined; this can be overcome by explaining the distinction between a strategic vision for the city (a city development strategy) and a strategic plan for the local authority based on that vision; and by encouraging the mayor and elected representatives to see the leadership role they can perform in both activities.

Production of an unrealistic vision and strategy should be discouraged through asking questions throughout the process such as: What would an ideal solution enable people to do? Are there some things we have in common? What else could we do? What would happen if we chose that path? Is this fair and just, does this create inequity? Who will pay for this and is it affordable?

Having achieved agreement on the strategic vision for the community—the City Development Strategy—the local government must then produce its own long-term (10-year) strategic plan and proposed actions for

---

Box 2.3.   Questions Worth Posing on City Visioning and Strategy Development

Who are the stakeholders who need to be involved? What techniques could be used to retain their ownership of the process? What might make it difficult to achieve that ownership and consistent involvement? How could those difficulties be overcome?

---

implementing the vision, and encourage the engagement of the other stakeholders as partners.

Features of a Quality Strategic Vision and Plan

The strategic vision and plan should: be responsive to how customers/community see things, i.e., the city vision; be strategic in intent—long term, futuristic, visionary, compelling, understandable, and memorable; reflect strategic choices that have been made—nothing is of equal importance; be simple, not obscure or complex; lay out a critical path and costed sequence of actions; have clear links to the organization's own processes for delivery; have accountability and commitment, with workplans that are open to monitoring.

The Value of a Strategic Vision and Plan

Cities worldwide, including best-practice examples in Barcelona, Brisbane, Quebec, and the cities of Sunnyvale and Brea in the United States, have used strategic planning to influence and guide change and growth in their communities. Benefits include the engagement and representation of all sectors of the community in determining the future; a framework for public investment and activity that is validated against publicly owned long-term objectives; a holistic view of the city, so that interdependencies and synergies are optimized through partnerships; strengthened arguments in support of reform or support from central government; a shared direction and focus that can be used to attract investment; redirection of resources to priority areas that deliver on the strategy; the engagement of local government with its community, and the pursuit of shared goals.

References and Further Reading

Benest, Frank. 1997. "Re-Connecting with Citizens." Washington, DC: ICMA (International City Management Association) University.

City of Brea. 1997. "Shaping the Downtown-Workshop and Idea Fair." City of Brea, California.

McDermott, P., and V. Forgie. 1999. "Trends in Local Government: Efficiency, Functions and Democracy." *Political Science* 50(2): 245–65.

Political Science. 1999. Special issue on local government in New Zealand. *Political Science* 50(2).

State Services Commission. 1996. "New Zealand's State Sector Reform: A Decade of Change." Wellington, New Zealand: State Services Commission.

Wellington City Council. 1997. *Annual Report 1997.* City of Wellington, New Zealand.

See also the City Strategic Plans of Barcelona, St. Petersburg, and Brisbane.

The Coimbatore City Corporate Plan: A Case Study of Strategic Management

Rajendra Kumar

Devised in 1997 as a management tool for overcoming some fundamental problems of local governance, the Coimbatore City Corporate Plan is the first major attempt by an Indian municipality to lay out a strategic plan. The 74th Amendment to the Constitution of India in 1992 granted local government significant powers in managing municipal affairs, but serious issues remained for Coimbatore that impede its control of the city's urban form. These issues involve dealing with competing land-use claims in a rapidly expanding city, and the confusion of bureaucratic roles and responsibilities within the Municipality's management structure.

Coimbatore, popularly known as the Manchester of South India, is situated in the western part of the state of Tamil Nadu; it has a population of 1.1 million, and a land area of 105.5 square kilometers. With its strong textile and engineering base, the city is considered the industrial center of Tamil Nadu, its growth and prosperity linked to an abundant supply of water and power, and to superior educational facilities. The city's employment opportunities are a major attraction for rural migrants from within and outside the district.

The governance problems of Coimbatore have deep roots. From 1688, when the first municipal government in the state was established by formation of the Madras Corporation, Urban Local Bodies (ULBs) have continued to be under the control of state governments, particularly in the area of finance; ULBs were dependent on state governments for grants as their main source of revenue. In 1992 the 74th Constitutional Amendment created a new framework for the widespread changes that have taken place in local government, by strengthening both local institutions and the process of democratic decentralization. The Amendment placed ULBs on a firmer footing by crafting a more equal relationship of functions and powers with the state government, such as ensuring regular elections and arrangements for revenue sharing. New local government powers include the determination of taxes, duties, and fees to help generate revenue. By giving ULBs constitutional status, the 74th Amendment acknowledged local governments as important players in city management, in such areas as planning for economic and social development, and poverty alleviation. The new powers have been timely, given the challenges to urban management that Coimbatore has had to face—the two major ones being the external challenge of urban sprawl, and the internal one of administrative inefficiency and the multiplicity of outside government agencies involved in delivery of basic services.

The Planning Challenges of Urban Sprawl

Over the years, overlapping land-use management powers between different government levels have fueled the problems of the city's rapid expansion. The current Master Land Use Plan for Coimbatore was drawn up in 1991 by the state's Local Planning Authority (LPA) for Coimbatore, for the period until 2001; it cannot meet the current demands of growth, as its provisions have been outstripped by the changing needs of the city.

The weak record of management in maintaining existing city infrastructure has been compounded by the rapid population growth of Coimbatore, a growth that has significantly increased competition in land use. The city now suffers from the illegal conversion of agricultural land within its limits, as well as on its fringes, and, while there has been some senior government legislation over land use and development, the absence of effective policies and regulations has allowed private interests to exploit available land and resources. Consequently, even low-income settlements have been built outside the control of government policies and regulations.

The city's position as an industrial hub attracts large numbers of migrants, leading to the proliferation of illegal slums and squatter settlements that, in the absence of service delivery, are prone to a variety of health-related hazards. In addition, high land prices, inappropriate and unclear land ownership, poor access to credit, and inadequate provision of serviced land, have all contributed to the growth of slums. As the Municipality was not in a position to prevent rapid growth, nor to service such sprawling areas, the Corporation moved to explore the imposition of planning restrictions and the levying of impact fees.

Strides were made in moving towards decentralization within the Municipal Corporation, by giving more powers to local councils and to middle- and lower-level municipal staff. However, while the Corporation has accomplished a range of management reforms, and has taken numerous steps to address the city's service weaknesses, it has been hampered by problems of urban governance and management. These focus primarily on the fragmented functions of the Corporation, and the unclear roles and responsibilities of municipal staff.

The Management Challenges of Bureaucracy

With the functions and operations of the Corporation being reorganized into a local-area form of management, employees are required to manage all aspects of service delivery within such an area. City personnel are ill-equipped, in either organization or expertise, to contend with planning issues or key areas of city management. One major example is that the engineering staff at the area office must handle the additional work of town planning and solid waste management. The resulting increase in workload weakens the department's capacity to delegate work effectively; in addition, it loses the ability to handle even the parent area of operation. This confusion of responsibilities creates administrative backlogs and compromises the staff's capacity to handle the complex challenges of service provision for a sprawling city.

These bureaucratic quagmires are compounded by an unclear delineation of the municipality's town planning powers, under which it cannot even give approvals for new buildings—these have to be referred to the LPA of Tamil Nadu's Directorate of Town and Country Planning. While approvals and sanctions lie with the LPA, the real-estate market has, in many ways, bypassed this process, and the resulting proliferation of unauthorized developments in the suburbs has put immense pressure on the city's infrastructure, the planning and provision of which has itself been hampered by the LPA's control over changes to the Master Land Use Plan. The situation at present is that the LPA has started the process of producing an updated Plan, to be in force for the decade following 2001.

Steps towards Improved Governance: The Coimbatore City Corporate Plan

In accordance with the 74th Constitutional Amendment, the Municipal Corporation is the ultimate "Manager" of the city. The Tamil Nadu Urban Local Bodies Bill of 1997 proposed an entirely new legislative framework governing all ULBs in the state, including Towns, Municipalities and City Corporations. The 74th Amendment established a state finance commission for the devolution of revenue to municipalities, so that they could address issues in urban planning, the regulation of land use, planning for economic and social development, greater provision of municipal services, and targeted approaches to urban poverty alleviation.

Within this new dynamic created by both the 74th Amendment and the state's enabling legislation, the process of developing the Coimbatore City

Corporate Plan began in October 1998 with extensive consultations with citizens, elected representatives, stakeholders, and various government departments involved in providing services within the city. The strategic vision and goals formulated during these consultations focused on six areas of concern—economic development, land-use and growth management, basic services and urban infrastructure, urban environment, social infrastructure, and urban governance—and established performance indicators for each target area; these were set for a six-year period. Overall, the Plan was designed to articulate a vision of how Coimbatore will grow to sustain its citizens' values.

Strategic Plan Outlook

Coimbatore had already formulated separate plans that addressed different components of the city's facilities: the Water Supply Augmentation Plan, the Sewerage Master Plan, the Storm Water Drainage Master Plan, and the Comprehensive Traffic and Transportation Plan. Each of these had been prepared during different periods, and their integration was proposed as part of the strategic planning exercise. A simple set of values emerged from discussions and debates with the stakeholders: Urban Environmental Management, focusing on protecting and improving the quality of the city environment; Community Participation, stressing facilitation and support for a strong sense of community within neighborhoods, and collaboration with residents, community organizations, and institutions to find ways to achieve the Plan's goals; and Economic and Social Development focusing on enhancement of the region's economic prosperity, providing basic services to all sections of society, and alleviating poverty. These core values are the fundamental principles that guide the Corporate Plan, and are the ultimate measure of the Plan's success or failure.

Plan Implementation

An investment strategy has been formulated to achieve the Plan's goals; this involves tradeoffs among many possible investment choices for making resource allocation decisions. The Corporation works with the other line agencies, NGOs, and citizen groups to provide a large number of services. Primary and secondary responsibilities for each of the Plan's elements have been identified and the Corporation has started working with these agencies for implementing those strategies for which it does not have primary responsibility. Table 2.1 describes the services provided by, and the responsibilities of, various agencies.

Table 2.1. Responsibility for Service Provision by Agencies, Coimbatore

Service component	Primary responsibility	Secondary responsibility
1. Economic development	State Government	Coimbatore Corporation
2. Land use and growth management	Local Planning Authority (LPA)	Corporation
3. Water supply and sewerage		
• Source development and transmission	Tamil Nadu Water Supply and Drainage Board	Corporation
• Storage and distribution	Corporation	—
• Sewerage and sanitation	Corporation	—
4. Solid waste management	Corporation	—
5. Storm water drainage		
• Urban drainage	Corporation	—
• Maintenance of water bodies	Public Works Department	Corporation
6. Roads and transportation		
• City roads	Corporation	—
• Major roads/ highways	Highways	Corporation
7. Traffic management	Traffic Police	Corporation
8. Street lighting	Corporation	—
9. Urban environmental management	Tamil Nadu Pollution Control Board	Corporation
10. Social development	Corporation	Government
11. Urban governance and management	Corporation	Commissioner of Municipal Administration

Source: Author.

Plan Monitoring and Evaluation

To facilitate continuous monitoring and evaluation, a set of sustainability indicators was adopted to monitor the change to the economic, social, and environmental conditions in the city brought about by the Plan. Targets were set for each of these areas. Indicators and targets adopted for some components of the Plan are shown in Table 2.2. Monitoring and evaluation will lead both to plan amendments and to an improved ability to project future requirements.

Table 2.2.   Coimbatore Strategic Plan: Indicators and Targets

Component	Performance indicators	Situation, 1998	Targets for 2004
Water supply	• Daily per capita supply	110 lpcd [a]	150 lpcd
	• Supply frequency	2 hours per day, most areas	2.5 hours per day
	• Population served/ total population	81.84%	100.00%
	• Proportion of distribution length/ road length	81.46%	All approved layouts and 90% of road network
	• Transmission and distribution losses/ total supply	38.21%	20.00%
Sewerage and sanitation	• Population covered/ total population	27.92%	70.00%
	• Sewerage network/ total road length	17.41%	47.61%
Storm water drainage	• Proportion of drain length/ road length	88.30%	94.93%
Solid waste management	• Proportion of waste collected	85.00%	100.00%
	• Proportion of vehicle capacity/ waste generated	82.00%	100.00%
Roads	• Percent roads surfaced	92.10%	100.00%
	• Road density	6.47km/sq.km.	7.97km/sq.km
Street lighting	• Average spacing	31.69m	22.70m
	• Percent sodium vapor lamps	24.67%	100.00%

a. lpcd: liters per capita per day
Source: Author.

Strategies for Urban Management

One of the greatest challenges for Coimbatore is to balance urban development and environmental protection. The Corporation sees an efficient urban form as instrumental in aiding economic growth and protection of sensitive resources, and several growth management strategies have been designed to address these objectives.

The first strategy deals with protecting priority resources by restricting development in specific areas and, where necessary, designating and servicing alternative locations; it encourages preservation through tax incentives and improving citywide environmental management.

The second strategy is to strengthen the land market by providing infrastructure to reduce developers' risk, encourage high-density development (where desirable) and establish flexible development standards, while simplifying administrative procedures. For instance, the Corporation can facilitate the redevelopment of certain areas and promote land assembly by offering floor-area bonuses in conjunction with planning restrictions on how open space is used. It is also looking at the possibility of "exactions" or levying "impact fees" to recover part of the cost for improving off-site infrastructure.

A third important strategy involves tax collection, changing the calculation basis for assessment, and supporting that with the creation of an electronic database. With the resulting access to a wider tax base, the Corporation can make financing available to fund development projects.

The introduction of a reporting system has increased the collection efficiency of property and professional taxes. All departments within the Corporation have been extensively computerized. Creation of a website, publication of a Citizens' Charter, and creation of Citizen Service Centers in all local ward council offices have tremendously improved performance in all areas, and have brought about transparency and accountability in the Corporation's services. A computerized system for common receipt has been introduced for all Corporation dues, together with facilities to accept payments through credit cards, another first among municipalities in India. Improved monitoring of tax collection has paid immediate dividends, as the collection of property tax has increased by more than Rs.60,000,000 (rupees) in 1997-98 over the previous year.

Finally, a key strategy is to make better use of the land and real estate owned by the Municipal Corporation, developing this commercially to mobilize financing for the Capital Improvement Program, a multi-year scheduling of public infrastructure improvements and investments.

The issue of urban governance is deeply interwoven with national and state government constitutional and legislative provisions, and only when the pattern of that weave was changed by senior government legislation has the City of Coimbatore been able to establish some control over managing its own future.

Challenges of Local Governance: The Experience of One African Mayor

Najib Balala

I was elected Mayor of Mombasa[3] in early 1998, and resigned the office one year later, on a matter of principle. Never having previously been a politician, the level of challenge and risk that I would face as Mayor was not clear to me when I first took the position; some risks were clearly visible, others lay hidden from sight. As time went by, it dawned on me that the unexpected is the one thing you can always expect in a political leadership position.

True democracy starts and ends with local government, whichever way one looks at it. Mombasa, with a current population of over 1.2 million, is Kenya's oldest urban center, and a one-time capital city. This brief reflection looks at a small facet of Mombasa's recent history, its development and the operations of its local authority, the Mombasa Municipal Council. From my experience I hope we can learn some lessons about what might be necessary for good urban governance.

Some Background

As we arrive at the millennium, it makes one sad to have to look back to the first two decades of Kenya's independence (that came in 1963) with some degree of nostalgia. But we have been repeatedly warned that, if we do not learn from history, we are liable to repeat past mistakes, as part of the progress of human civilization is surely to learn from previous experience.

The portrait of the Municipality of the 1960s and 1970s that the elders had painted to me was in sharp contrast to what I found when I became Mayor. Telling me about those earlier days, they spoke of the Town Hall being a model of intense but orderly activity, with the staff conducting daily affairs with such professionalism that each department jealously

---

3. Mr. Najib Balala was originally nominated in 1998 for the position of councilor from the Government party, KANU; he was elected Mayor by the other councilors. During the year he held the post, he was a well-known and generally popular figure in Mombasa (and Kenyan) politics. He reflects here on his experiences as a public official, in an address delivered at the Urban Governance Round Table during the Biennial Commission for Human Settlements, United Nations Gigiri Complex in Nairobi, 6 May 1999. *Eds.*

guarded its reputation. They spoke of the Town treasurer taking extreme care that the annually audited accounts could withstand not only the scrutiny of the Municipal Council and the central government, but also of Mombasa's residents.

The contrast to today is appalling. When I entered the Mombasa Municipality on 26 February 1998, a picture of doom and gloom confronted me. The following is only a small part of the catalogue of problems I encountered.

Outside Political Control

There was political interference at all levels of decisionmaking. The central government exerts control over the local authority through the appointments of heads of departments and other controls introduced through the Local Government Act (Cap 265) of the Laws of Kenya. This Act has been in operation since the country became independent. While central control has its value, it can also act as an impediment to proper development. For example, whatever proposals the Councilors make—whether for raising revenue or improving services—the Minister's consent has to be obtained before implementation, and this may take a very long time. While the Council has power over a great number of local matters—such as garbage collection, town planning and building standards, primary education and primary health, markets, local roads and road maintenance—it cannot act expeditiously to carry out its functions.

Lack of Effective Authority

The head of the local authority (the Mayor) lacks effective powers, while at the same time there is (in my opinion) too much concentration of power at the center over local authorities; for instance, the Minister for Local Government in Kenya has draconian powers over local authorities. Even though local authorities pay the salaries and pensions of senior council staff, they have no authority to either hire or fire the same officers, a feature of our system that effectively removes their responsibility to the local councilors and, therefore, the local people. As a result, the Mayor has no authority to scrutinize the effectiveness of human resources. I had no alternative to dealing with the reality that heads of departments were unaware of their responsibilities, let alone of who worked for them, or what their role should be in managing human resources. The absence of effective forms of authority, combined with a lack of integrity amongst civic leaders and staff, led to frequent malpractices, such as graft, nepotism, and land grabbing.

Poor Infrastructure and Services

The condition of the municipal infrastructure was terrible. Council buildings had not been given a coat of paint since they were first built in the 1960s. The municipal offices themselves were in a shameful state of disrepair, reflecting the rot that had permeated the Municipality. In addition, the road system was crumbling; cracks had become potholes, and potholes had become craters. Services were equally poor. Garbage collection and disposal services were almost non-existent, and educational services were preposterous for the second most important city in the country. Further, health services were deplorable, community or childcare programs were lacking, and there was little accountability as a result of a poor work ethic. The workers came in and went out just as they pleased; cases were common of workers merely clocking in and then following their own pursuits for the rest of the day.

Inadequate Revenue

Lack of funds and proper planning were major impediments to the operation of good urban governance. The Council was steeped in debt, having been stripped of all its assets by politically insensitive individuals working for it. As a result, budget deficits had become the order of the day. And, as the Council got deeper in debt and could not manage its infrastructure and services, people found ways to evade taxes and Council regulations.

What Went Wrong?

These problems were but the tip of the proverbial iceberg. What was true of Mombasa Municipal Council was true of many other local government authorities all over Kenya. What has gone wrong to bring about this disorientation of service which once was the envy of other third world countries? What has blown us off course? Answering these questions should help us to understand how to correct such malpractices in order to move forward to better urban governance.

Some Preliminary Conclusions

One major factor in the current urban governance debacle in Mombasa has, in my opinion, been the general and systematic emasculation of local government authorities by the central government. Local governments started the Independence era with full legislative powers to appoint virtually all their staff, senior as well as junior. Today, these bodies have no powers to appoint any of their senior officers (a term that, in this case, includes experienced professionals all the way from the Town Clerk to accountants.) In fairness, it should be said that this transfer of authority from the local governments to the central government was provoked in part by the misuse of powers by the local government authorities themselves. One must therefore give the central government the benefit of the doubt as to the original justification for curtailing the abuse of powers. One should go further by saying that this transfer of powers of appointment of senior officers was not done directly by the Ministry, but rather by the Public Service Commission (under Local Government Regulations). But soon, the Public Service Commission itself became more or less a rubber stamp, meekly acceding to the dictates of the Ministry of Local Government.

Once the appointment and transfer of senior officers had become an exclusive prerogative of the Minister of Local Government, one thing followed another. Efficiency was thrown overboard, commitment and dedication became expunged from the local government vocabulary, and massive corruption became the order of the day. "Everybody for himself" became the *de facto* motto. Those seeking appointment to senior local government positions knew where to go to secure them!

While potential, as well as actual, senior officers of local authorities learnt how to secure and keep their jobs, the inevitable switch of loyalty from the local authority to the Ministry was a regular occurrence. In theory, that need not be an unmitigated disaster. In practice, it is. It has a direct effect on the commitment and dedication of the officers. Advancing the welfare of the political godfathers in the central government makes up for what is lacking in efficiency. And this, as we know, can be done in a variety of increasingly complex and sophisticated ways.

What I Tried To Do

When I came into office, I was thrown in at the deep end—and it does not get deeper than the position of Mayor. While the "Lord Mayor" in the British tradition is an honorific position, it is, nevertheless, a position of enormous influence. I soon learnt that there was more to it than the mere exhibition of the chain of office. I decided that I would not accept failure as inevitable. Despite all the odds, I was determined to try to beat them. Here are some of the things I did to try to bring about change.

A New Spirit

One of the first things I did was to call all the Council's staff to a meeting with the Mayor and the councilors. We have no record of any such thing having taken place during the pre-Independence era, and it certainly had not happened since Independence. The novelty of this approach immediately helped to boost morale. Everybody—big and small—felt wanted. It helped to ventilate ideas and air out the vast pockets of despair. By airing views, and giving and taking criticism, we entered a new age of incipient accountability. We cannot pretend that even a few meetings were enough to overcome so many layers of malpractice and absence of transparency. But it is amazing how one good meeting can lay the first seeds of hope, where only despair prevailed before. I was encouraged by the results. Staff began to feel that if they delivered they would be rewarded, and that the only certain route to progress was through hard work and productivity, not political patronage.

A Citizens' Forum

Another early experiment was to bring—again for the first time ever—the entire citizenry of the municipality to a joint meeting with the councilors and the staff. Over a thousand people of all social classes attended. The ground was packed to capacity. It was hugely successful. The citizens had a field day. Nobody was spared. I restrained the councilors and staff from replying. We wanted a cathartic session—an open discussion in which the citizens would pour out their anger and frustrations. The session left citizens feeling as if their problems were being heard, and we in turn were further educated about the deficiencies of our services! When council met following this forum, I made sure that councilors who were in charge of services were committed to pursue their improvement.

Citizen Participation

Mere catharsis may be therapeutic, but it could soon breed cynicism if not followed by positive actions. The first citizens' forum provided the strategic framework for ensuring greater public participation in designing the city's annual plans, and allocating the budgets necessary to implement such plans. Regular citizen *barazas* (public meetings) within each of Mombasa's wards, could then be used as a vehicle to ensure that the people's voice was put forward to local government through constructive channels.

One area in which I involved citizens directly was in programs of beautification. But, knowing as we all did that to entrust private funds to Council officialdom would be the kiss of death for any project, I got the private sector itself to assume overall responsibility for this. And the project took off like wildfire. Roundabouts that had escaped "grabbing" were suddenly rising like the proverbial phoenix from the ashes, to stand up in beautiful tribute to a new spirit. And this was all paid for by the private sector!

Accessibility

As I was keen to listen to, and learn from, the city's residents, I regularly participated in social and community activities, and was an active participant in religious and other functions. I tried to live up to my idea of a "People's Mayor." I was governed by the cardinal principle of providing service to the residents of Mombasa, without concerning myself with their political inclinations, social, religious and other characteristics. I preached and practiced social and religious tolerance, and I encouraged cultural interaction. For instance, I brought together different religious groups with the aim of trying to create a dialogue on how to integrate their respective views into a secular constitution. This dialogue not only facilitated respect between Muslims and Christians when celebrating each other's sacred holidays, but led to an interest on the part of many in both groups to participate in each other's public ceremonies. With this example of social integration in mind, I initiated and organized the first-ever street carnival, which was a resounding success.

Improving Infrastructure and Services

It is an open secret that, when the service charge (a fixed charge deducted from the monthly paycheck of each working person) was introduced, services dramatically declined. The service charge was enacted to provide funds for keeping cities and towns clean but, as soon as it was introduced and the funds were collected, services virtually disappeared! One of the first things we did was to work on an improved system of garbage collection. People began to cheer as they saw tangible improvement being made to their environment. Further, we set up an education task force that involved the Parent Teachers Association, the Head Teachers Association, and the Council, with the aim of improving education standards.

Turning to health, we made certain that the Council's health institutions (mostly primary-care clinics) were supplied with medical necessities to enable them to provide subsidized services to the residents. Public-health functions were strengthened in order to focus on prevention, rather than on curative services. We also had other social services projects, including setting up of a Country Bus Terminal, more effective controls over, and monitoring of, taxi operations, and instilling discipline and sanity in minivan operators within the town.

The potholes and dangerous craters that were a common feature of our roads needed urgent attention. Council had no funds, of course, so I brought together Mombasa's road contractors and convinced them to undertake urgent road repairs at no cost to the Council. I also managed to find a grant from the World Bank for the rehabilitation of suburban roads, which are predominantly in low-income communities.

As for the Council offices and chambers, I insisted on their refurbishment, and this worked miracles. This was done to set the standards for the city's residents, as I am an ardent believer in leading by example. The initiative had a snowball effect and, in a short time, many other residents followed suit, painting and renovating their houses and offices. All of this work generated a "feel-good" attitude and pride in being a Mombasa resident.

Raising Revenue

Mombasa's local revenue comes mostly from land rates and, to a lesser extent, from fees and charges. Improvement in revenue collection was one of the hallmarks of my tenure of office. This was achieved through various methods, such as: providing incentives to ratepayers; strict monitoring of revenue collectors and instilling of discipline and transparency; strict control of expenditure and effective management of funds; and implementing strategic staff changes in collection points. All these measures resulted in improved revenues—which rose from 300 million KShs. (Kenyan shillings) in the 1996–97 fiscal year to 411 million KShs. in the 1997–98 fiscal year.

I also tried to develop alternative sources of revenue. Every local authority in Kenya has the right to benefit from resources within its area of operations. Mombasa is endowed with a major deep-water port, but this unfortunately does not benefit the residents in any direct fashion. To make more of a connection between the Port and the town's services, it was my intention to introduce a US$1 levy on every ton handled at the port. The funds were to be used strictly for infrastructure maintenance and development, and would have been controlled and maintained by the stakeholders—port users such as importers and exporters, shipping companies, and clearing and handling companies. While the Council had approved this measure during my Mayoralty, it was revoked after I resigned.

One other achievement that resulted in a marked improvement in the Council's finances, was tackling the issue of "Ghost Workers." When I joined the Council there were reportedly 4,700 employees on the Council's books. It was well known that many of these people, who were paid by the month, had either died or no longer worked for the Council. By insisting that monthly checks be picked up by the individual workers themselves, I was able to reduce the number of total workers to only 3,500—a reduction of over one-fifth, with a corresponding reduction in the Council's monthly operating expenditures.

Other Malpractices

But there were many more malpractices with which we needed to come to grips. We set out to introduce integrity and a professional approach in all Council matters and business. We intended to root out nepotism, graft, land grabbing, and other social ills, that were contributing to the erosion of public confidence in the authority. This was a Herculean task as we were arrayed against powerful individuals who were benefiting from the existing situation. We tried to curtail the problem by protecting public property, and by not approving the development of dubiously acquired land, such as public park property and road reserves. However, this was not enough, and, judging by the current goings on, Mombasa will soon be one of the only towns in East Africa without any road reserves or public land left.

The Way Forward

Although I am no longer a local councilor in Mombasa, my brief experience suggests very strongly that there is enormous support for a local government whose provision of services is driven by the needs of its residents and consumers, instead of being offered at the convenience or whim of providers, as is mostly the case. To accomplish this, however, local authorities have to remain flexible enough to analyze the specific requirements of their residents, and to develop solutions on an on-going basis. As a starting point, we should introduce directly elected full-time mayors and councils with more local powers—which they would undoubtedly use for promoting their localities. Other priorities of a strategic plan for bringing about improved local governance to Mombasa are:

- Complete overhaul of the current legal structure governing the operations of local authorities, with a view to empowering them to operate without political or other interference.
- Improved efficiency and recruitment of competent staff. The current economic climate has brought increasing pressure on local authorities to cut operational costs. But better and more efficient staff would result in improved revenue collection.
- Introduction of a Local Authority Audit Commission, which should be allowed in the course of its work as the local-authority "watchdog" to publish the names of individual local authorities for the purposes of comparative studies on transparency in local government.
- Local authorities should be obliged to set, or have set for them, targets for their performance, and to publish details of compliance with these targets on a regular basis.
- Introduction of a Charter that should give the residents (consumers of public services) within local authority areas more rights against the monopoly suppliers of those services. The Charter should incorporate checks and balances, for a charter without checks is an empty gesture.

We must only give to the local authorities those functions that will, beyond reasonable doubt, deliver significantly better results because they are performed at a local, and not a national, level.

Successful running of local authorities requires natural ability, hard-earned experience, and a sense of balance. I believe there is only one way to earn respect, and that is through the delivery of quality services. For this to happen requires experience, understanding, innovation and a determination to reject anything but the best. When I became Mayor, I set out on a mission to bring about positive change in local governance, and to introduce accountability, transparency and professionalism to our system. By so doing, I hoped to improve the lives of the residents of Mombasa in particular, and Kenyans in general. Though I am currently out of office, it is my intention to continue this mission with the help of the Kenyan people, the current setbacks I now face notwithstanding.

From Violence to Justice and Security in Cities

Franz Vanderschueren

At least once every five years, 60 percent of those living in cities with 100,000 or more inhabitants are victims of some form of crime. This is true not only in areas that are highly urbanized, such as Europe and North America, but also in Africa, where the urban population is still the minority. In Asia, the figure was 45 percent in 1994. However, levels of violence vary considerably from place to place, and are determined not only by the pattern of urbanization but also by the political and economic climate, by local traditions, and by culture.

In many countries, urbanization has largely been a process of migration from the poverty of the countryside to the cities—hence the growth of urban marginality. Poverty may not automatically lead to violence, but may favor it in certain circumstances. Violence is not a spontaneous phenomenon but, above all, the product of a society characterized by inequality and social exclusion. It is a distortion of social relationships generated within social structures—family, school, peer group, neighborhood, police, justice—which can no longer fulfill their role. The offender has often been stimulated by a social environment dominated by consumerism, competition, and by the mass media, which propagate and legitimize violence.

In a society that promotes consumption to the detriment of sharing, and unbridled competition at the expense of solidarity, young people with no hope of employment or success look for ways to gain a sense of achievement and recognition, if not from society then at least from their peer group. This often leads to, or involves, violence. The analysis presented here is schematic, for it does not go into local or regional detail. Its aim is to describe briefly the forms and causes of urban violence, the responses of the principal actors and, in the light of current experiences, to suggest practices that should facilitate the creation of an urban structure that rests on a foundation of humanity and solidarity.[4]

---

4. The article first appeared in *Environment and Urbanization* 8(1) 1996: 93–112. This revised and shortened version is printed with permission of the author and the publisher of *Environment and Urbanization*.

Growth and Forms of Urban Violence

The current process of urbanization goes hand in hand with a rise in urban violence that outstrips the demographic growth of cities. It is estimated that urban violence has risen by 3 to 5 percent a year over the past two decades, although certain cities show significant variations at different times. Each region, country, and city presents different patterns of change. In Western Europe, there was a rapid growth in petty crime until the beginning of the 1990s, whilst serious crime seems to be under control as a result of modernized policing and criminal justice measures, as well the development of sophisticated international cooperation.

In Third World countries and in Eastern Europe, both petty and violent crime have increased, and the figures from the past few years have been more and more alarming. Even in Asia, where crime decreased between 1975 and 1990 at a national level, cities of more than 100,000 inhabitants have seen a considerable increase in crimes against property, and in drug trafficking (Hagiwara 1995). The development of drug-related organized crime may indeed be a major contributor to the level of violent crime in certain cities, but there is growing evidence of a general rise in crime that, in some Latin American cities, is reaching explosive proportions (see Box 2.4). Globally, youth crime is increasing even in countries where crime growth has been stabilized (Dryden Witte 1996).

Causes of the Growth in Urban Violence

Many reasons have been put forward to explain the phenomenon of rising urban criminality (and, in particular, crimes against property in all its forms), although no one can yet claim to have established an overall theory of urban violence. However, certain key factors have been identified, including the poverty of low-income neighborhoods, the provocative and poorly protected urban environment, limitations of current protection measures, the absence of social controls, the number of frustrated youth, and the crisis in criminal justice systems.

The Utter Poverty of Badly Served Neighborhoods

Certain specialists stress the significance of very poor and overcrowded housing and living conditions, and the lack of security in illegal settlements, in creating fertile soil for the development of violence and in generating a

---

Box 2.4.   Violent Crime in Latin America and its Major Cities

In Mexico City, an average of 543 crimes were reported every day in the first three months of 1995. For a 10-week period, these included 5,843 non-violent car thefts, 3,962 muggings, 3,435 violent car thefts, 3,306 assaults, 416 killings and 250 rapes. Police advisors reckon that the real figure may be 50 percent higher because many people no longer bother to report crimes to the police. In Colombia, police reported an average of one murder every 15 minutes in the first quarter of 1995, 62 percent more than in the same period of 1994. Violence is the principal cause of death in the country, and Bogotá has become one of the most violent cities in the world, with over 5,000 killings a year (*Latin American Weekly Report* 1995).

In Brazil, the two largest cities, São Paulo and Rio de Janeiro, are the main scenes of urban violence. In Rio de Janeiro the number of homicides tripled between 1982 (23 per 100,000 inhabitants) and 1989 (59 per 100,000). Young people's involvement in homicides tripled between 1982 and 1985, with a similar trend observed for crimes against property. The authorities recorded more than 1 million criminal offenses in 1994: 51 percent involved theft, 17 percent were homicides, and 10 percent were drug-related crimes. Violence in Brazil has become the second highest cause of death after heart disease, and accounts for larger numbers than cancer and other illnesses. In Peru in the first three months of 1995, reported homicides were 25 percent up on the same period for 1994 (Sader 1995; Zaluar 1995).

---

sub-culture of violence. This view was stressed in the conclusions of the 1989 Montreal Conference of Mayors on Urban Safety (ICPC 1998): "[T]he basic causes of violence increase: urban growth, with the marginalization of the underprivileged and the isolation of groups at risk, qualitative and quantitative insufficiency of social housing programs and community amenities, unemployment of young people."

Living in illegally occupied areas, deprived of basic services, having to use dangerous and inadequate transport, victims of urban speculation, forced to function in the informal sector, without proper leisure facilities, and surrounded by advertising that invites them to acquire everything, poor urban families in the South are a milieu permeated with social frustrations in which the culture of violence can flourish.

A Provocative and Poorly Protected Urban Environment

Other explanations, whilst not contradicting those outlined above, stress more the contemporary urban environment where attractive and tempting goods are continuously on display, and thus create targets for potential criminals. In cities, particularly in developing countries, the ostentatious display of luxury and prosperity, as in shops or cars, in certain areas provokes those who have not accepted their unfavorable social situation, and engenders an attitude that legitimizes the "redistribution of wealth" through criminal activity.

Three main factors contribute to a growth in lawlessness: a poorly protected (and therefore easy) target; inadequate surveillance or an absence of social control; and individuals who are prone to violence (Wikstrom 1991). Targets are poorly protected because most private individuals or households do not have the means to keep their homes under constant surveillance. Another factor is rapid growth in the amount of space used by the public, from department stores to metro stations and car parks, that are difficult for the police to keep under surveillance.

The Limitations of Current Protection Measures

Private security services can protect organizations or businesses but, outside these areas, private surveillance is of limited value. Its cost places it beyond the means of most homeowners. In Europe, 5 percent of the population uses private security services. In certain Third World countries, they are used more widely by social groups who can afford them—a fact which accentuates the gap between rich and poor, and diverts criminal activity towards unprotected areas.

In addition, police time is taken up with other functions: the fight against serious crime and drug trafficking, traffic management, immigration control (especially in the wealthiest countries), political tasks such as the surveillance of opposition groups, or the protection of municipal property such as markets and sports facilities. Moreover, the spread of free-market ideas, and of structural adjustment programs, has facilitated the corruption of poorly paid police officers.

Furthermore, insurance against theft, for those who can afford it, does not resolve the problem of prevention since it does not halt the theft itself (the breaking of the law) or its consequences. It indemnifies also only about one-third of victims and does nothing to assuage feelings of insecurity and fear. Its only positive impact is that it puts pressures on clients to acquire security systems.

Finally, certain types of theft, such as car theft, have gone from the stage where the main objective was to "borrow" the vehicle, to the level of illegal international traffic which presupposes criminal cooperation on a worldwide scale that is very difficult for the police to control.

The Absence of Social Controls

One effect of the loosening of local community ties is that community protection, which in the nineteenth century was an important form of social control, has lost its power. The community undertook surveillance and, when an offence occurred, worked out some form of reconciliation. Except in cases where a culture has maintained stable ties within neighborhoods, the anonymity of cities has practically eliminated all community intervention.

Unlike rural or poor urban societies that have sometimes maintained support structures for coping with poverty and for playing a role paralleling that of the unions in the development of the working class, modern cities favor anonymity and fragmentation. Rising crime in neighborhoods has exacerbated this tendency.

Frustrated Youth, Prone to Violence

NEGATIVE SOCIALIZATION. Urban violence recruits its principal players from among young men aged between 15 and 25. They are also its principal victims. In the vast majority of cases, it is at this age that most law breakers begin their criminal apprenticeship and, the more serious the offences committed by youths under the age of 25, the more likely it is that they will offend again. The younger the age at which a person enters the world of law breaking, the more difficult it is to rehabilitate them (ICPC 1995).

The negative experiences of youth lead to non-adaptation at school, to a lack of personal discipline, and to low self-esteem. This creates a need to develop psycho-social compensatory mechanisms that lead young people to join groups that become schools of criminality. Anti-social behavior or criminal activity thus become the means of affirming an alternative form of self-esteem recognized by the group or gang itself. At this stage, confrontation with the police or with the law can actually reinforce this tendency. Meanwhile, this alternative social integration blocks entry into the labor market, or limits it to low-paid, low-prestige jobs.

The failure of poorly qualified young men to enter, and remain in, the labor market has a negative impact not only on their desire to conform to social norms but also on their participation in a stable lifestyle. If there is nothing to encourage them to respect the law—for instance through starting a family and/or achieving a place in the community—or to adhere to the norms of the community, there is, for young men, little to be gained from giving up crime or losing their taste for anarchy. This is particularly true if they are physically capable of sustaining this way of life, if their peers continue to draw them, or if the rewards of crime make up for what they may have lost because of their unsuitability for work, for taking care of a family or for achieving stability.

STREET CHILDREN. The phenomenon of street children is one of the most serious, large-scale problems, and one that is typical of large Third World cities. It has many underlying causes: ill-treatment in the family; poverty—especially if the family is headed by a lone mother who cannot maintain her children and has sent them into the streets to earn their keep; and the move in certain Muslim countries from forced begging (*talibé* in West Africa) to living in the streets. It is a familiar process: children work in the streets for a while, then they join others and do not return home. Life with their group revolves around street-corner meeting places. They often take drugs, exploit younger children, earn their living from odd jobs (collecting rubbish, minding car parks), doing errands, or from petty crime or begging. As for the girls, they are sometimes forced (as in Nairobi) to go into prostitution from the age of eight, with all the risks that this implies.

THE CRISIS OF CRIMINAL JUSTICE. International studies confirm the systematic loss of reputation of nations' criminal justice systems. Only 15 percent of the charges brought are dealt with, and only 5 percent of cases are cleared up. If one takes into account unreported crimes, criminal justice systems resolve only 2 to 3 percent of all crimes, and only 25 percent of decisions will be implemented. In other words, the role played by the criminal justice system is more symbolic than real (Marcus 1995). In most of the wealthiest countries, the system may deal effectively with violent crime (at least where corruption or terror do not hamper it) but it is almost totally ineffective with regard to everyday, petty, urban crime. Overwhelmed by the number of cases, it is slow, expensive, overburdened with procedures, hampered by a language that bears no relation to the concerns and needs of inhabitants, and is ill-suited to a rapidly changing urban environment. Most people have little respect for it; the urban poor may have no confidence in it or respect for it at all (Correa and Jimenez 1995; Moncayo 1995).

The effectiveness of police intervention depends on the relationship between the police and the criminal justice system—in other words, it depends on the effectiveness of criminal justice. The modernization of the criminal justice system in North America and many European nations has mostly benefited the fight against serious crime but continues to have little effect upon petty crime. Besides, governments do not have the means to undertake the thorough modernization of the criminal justice system that would be necessary to cope with all the needs created by the rise in petty crime.

Traditional Responses of Governments

The most common response by the state is imprisonment, and in the United States and Russia this has reached a level of more than five persons in prison per 1,000 inhabitants. The average for the rest of the world is less than 1.7 per 1,000 inhabitants, with a mere 0.36 per 1,000 in Japan (International Prison Observatory 1995). This policy is not very effective, for it does not reduce the number of offences committed. It also diverts funds that could be invested in preventive social action, and tends to stigmatize certain groups. One of the direct consequences of preventive imprisonment is the worsening of prison conditions and the overpopulation of penitentiary institutions. This was denounced by the International Prison Observatory (1995).

The "modernization" of criminal justice, with its limited impact on urban crime, is another traditional policy that is increasingly being abandoned in favor of local justice.

The Spontaneous Reactions of Citizens

City dwellers have reacted to violent and petty crime in a variety of ways. In places where the policing is judged to be inadequate, the responses of citizens range from private or community security to "rough justice," and include giving groups powers to assist or replace the police with the task of social "cleansing."

The use of private security firms is an option available only to a wealthy minority. But neighborhood watch, whether undertaken by residents or by persons paid by the community, is growing in some cities and even in many illegal or informal settlements. This system has even been institutionalized in Tanzania, where family groups were organized to ensure their own protection. This type of community surveillance is becoming increasingly common in the middle-class areas and informal urban settlements in countries such as Nigeria, where urban crime is widespread. City forms also adapt to high crime levels. Latin American cities, characterized by sharp geographical and social segregation, ghettos such as the closed villages of Manila, or groups of cloistered houses in African cities, are all direct consequences of rising crime. They also reinforce inequalities and prevent the integrated development of cities.

Spontaneous forms of social cleansing that violate human rights have also appeared in Latin America. They are the death squads that murder children and beggars, first in Brazil and now also in Colombia, and also kill those alleged to be criminals and corrupt officials in Honduras.

What might be termed rough justice, where individuals and groups take the law into their own hands, is less selective but no less inhuman than social cleansing. This is also something that governments ignore or cannot control. Its victims are alleged criminals—more often than not, petty criminals, caught in the act and lynched by the mob. It is a particularly frequent practice in Nigeria and Kenya, where there were more than 100 cases in Nairobi in 1994. Given the increasingly obvious crisis of justice and the ineffectiveness of the police, the practice has also begun to emerge in other countries.

There are in addition "negotiated" agreements with offenders, who accept payment or other benefits in exchange for ensuring the security of the neighborhood and undertaking to limit their activities to other neighborhoods. These methods, which are difficult to detect or evaluate, are semipublic in Guayaquil (Ecuador) and the Dominican Republic, but often discreetly practiced elsewhere. In informal settlements, they have the advantage of preserving the fragile fabric of community relations necessary for survival, whilst giving criminals a sort of legitimacy. It is difficult for the inhabitants of cities to introduce positive measures beyond the level of community surveillance. Without the support of the state, local authorities or the police, most citizens are likely to be paralyzed by a feeling of insecurity, and this can lead to the disintegration of community ties, to the abandonment of neighborhoods that are economically dynamic but judged too dangerous, or to apathy. It can also lead to the appearance of death squads and lynch mobs.

What Is To Be Done? Some Positive Alternatives

Governments, municipalities and NGOs have taken numerous initiatives to change the current situation. Generally these are based on three principles:

- The only effective partnership is one that involves the municipal authorities, organized communities and police and judicial systems close to the people;
- The very varied nature of violence requires up-to-date information and analyses, as well as different treatments, based on a rigorous methodology; and
- Anyone hoping to have an impact on the causes of violence has to

adopt programs aimed at those groups of marginal youth most at risk from engaging in violence.

Coordinated City-Oriented Policies for Dealing with Urban Crime

Several countries have become aware of the fact that violence cannot be dealt with by repression only. They have created security contracts or city contracts in which the state subsidizes a set of initiatives undertaken by the communities at risk.

But it is on a city level that coordinated initiatives in the fight against violence have emerged. Usually, cities set up "crime prevention councils" on which all the key players in a community or area are represented. These councils, found throughout the European Union and in some Latin American cities, discuss the problems of crime and form working parties that define and coordinate programs. They may be run by a local authority or by an independent person, and their success depends on the weight of that authority and the clarity of their official mandate. In essence, they create a partnership that brings together all the players and that, in particular, works with the police and judicial system, or they constitute coalitions around specific themes. For instance, partnerships or coalitions have been established in African cities such as Johannesburg (South Africa), Dar es Salaam (Tanzania) and a few municipalities of the Abidjan agglomeration (Côte d'Ivoire), and in European cities such as Liverpool (England), Charleroi (Belgium), Roubaix (France), Frankfurt (Germany), and Haarlem (Netherlands).

Initiatives in crime prevention and control at the municipal level have emerged in most countries in Europe and North America, and in several Latin American and Arab countries. These initiatives are inspired by conferences, such as the Conference of Mayors on Urban Safety, held in Montreal in 1989, that have focused on the role of cities, and they form the basis of a regional network that allows the exchange of expertise and methods.

Public authorities at all levels must support preventive measures developed at the local level. If crime is to be prevented in cities, solutions are needed that do not rely solely on penal or police justice. Long-term solutions must be set in motion, whilst at the same time immediate needs must be addressed. Prevention has to bring together those responsible for housing, social services, leisure, schools, the police and the law, in order to confront the circumstances that generate or facilitate crime. Those elected at all levels must use their political authority and take on the responsibility of fighting urban crime and encourage solidarity within the community. Without this commitment, our confidence in society, the quality of life in urban centers, as well as human rights, will be threatened. Crime prevention is everyone's responsibility (Conference of Mayors on Urban Safety 1989).

The experience to date makes it possible to identify three major directions of city action:

- The risk of crime is linked to the objective presence of circumstances that facilitate the perpetration of crime; to this situation the response is usually the situational prevention which is described by Ronald Clarke (1995).

- The more or less direct, but obvious, impact on crime levels of the distribution of wealth in the broadest sense, that includes not only the distribution of income but also of jobs, access to health care, education, and the availability and quality of housing.

- The nature of values, the way they are shared and transmitted, especially those influenced by the family, and the cohesiveness and organization of communities. Investing in communities through special programs, which are derived from a diagnosis made by the city coalition, constitute the main response.

Special programs targeted at socially disadvantaged groups, some of which may be particularly susceptible to violence (street children, unemployed youth in trouble, waste pickers, young people with no fixed address, and drug addicts) are crucial for long-term prevention. Crime prevention and social action are inseparable. To do nothing is to automatically create a large group of people excluded from many aspects of society, or potential criminals.

Finally, cities need the support of central government in particular, for observation, research into, and analysis of, information on the causes of criminality, evaluation, coordination of the various players, and policies that require financial backing.

Investing in Communities

Mobilizing the inhabitants of a neighborhood against crime means appealing to behavior and norms rooted in the culture of the neighborhood. The informal resolution of conflicts, mediation, conciliation, and other forms of arbitration, facilitate the maintenance of peace. The ways of achieving this vary from city to city and range from "peace agreements" between ethnic groups to defensible space, better security within homes, programs for cleaning and maintaining residential or commercial areas, action against vandalism, neighborhood watch, community policing and the direct participation of tenants in the management of their homes (Marcus 1995). The key is to generate a sense of community identity (which is rarely spontaneous) focused on a collective space and project.

Solutions to the many problems facing low-income groups in gaining access to city services and land are the main way of reinforcing community feeling in Third World countries. Meanwhile, the fight against crime requires specific actions that focus, on the one hand, on stopping fragmentation into small groups and, on the other, on preventing the isolation of individuals who are paralyzed by fear. In these same areas, the struggle against domestic violence does not merely educate but also strengthens women's organizations. Such organizations usually have a significant role in poor neighborhoods in a great range of community activity, such as health promotion and care, and education. A variety of initiatives by NGOs and grassroots groups contribute to this neighborhood mobilization. Uganda's Resistance Councils, born from the popular struggle for peace, are an example of the institutionalization of community identity (see Box 2.5).

Cooperation with the Police

If neighborhoods are to be effectively mobilized to ensure security, cooperation with the police is essential. The protection of those who are vulnerable to crime, campaigns against vandalism, and mechanisms for assisting the victims of domestic violence, all require police support. This presupposes a police force that is close to the people and not excessively repressive; in effect, a police force that is ready to resolve residents' problems with them.

There are various examples of close cooperation between the police and communities. Such cooperation tends to lead to a more visible police presence, closely linked to cooperation with their counterparts in security councils, and to the diversification of the police, who bring indispensable expertise to preventive action: "The expertise of police services is absolutely essential for the development and implementation of situational prevention methods (those that aim to reduce the opportunities for crime). These services must cooperate with local communities. The police are in fact the best placed to notice the emergence of certain problems of a criminal nature and alert the community. Moreover, they have data vital to the analysis of difficult situations and, as a result of their training, are able to propose effective solutions" (ICPC 1994).

One development that deserves special attention is the process of diversifying police functions in Brazil, Argentina, and Chile with the

---

Box 2.5.   Uganda's Resistance Councils

The Resistance Councils emerged during the war in Uganda in the late 1980s. They are grassroots organizations with responsibilities within defined areas, both urban and rural. They were legalized in 1988, and nine leaders are elected democratically every four years.

Their main objectives are: to guarantee security and respect for the law within their jurisdiction; to be a link with government initiatives; and to promote the development of their area and mutual assistance within the community. They have a role in crime prevention and control, and in legal aid for the poor. They may intervene in civil law cases—for instance, in cases of debt, contracts, damage to property, fraud, common law, and land problems. They also intervene in criminal cases that involve sums up to a certain figure. They deliver justice quickly, free of charge, and in a way that residents can understand.

They are the first institution to whom people turn in cases involving theft, violent disputes or accidents, and the Resistance Councils in turn report to the police or the law courts. If there is an arrest, the police do not enter the neighborhood or the victim's house without the agreement and presence of the head of the Resistance Council.

Evaluations show that, apart from their contribution to the social and economic development of the neighborhood, Resistance Councils have improved security, facilitated cooperation with the police, avoided the abuse of power by the military, and practiced effective forms of mediation and conciliation. They have also contributed to the creation of neighborhood identity among residents (Nsibambi 1991).

---

creation of female police units that specialize in the problems of domestic violence. Another is in the Philippines, where an NGO and the police work together in addressing domestic violence in Cebu City (Banaynal-Fernandez 1994). Close cooperation between police and the community has to be developed over time, and requires a clear statement of policy from the authorities and from the force itself, in addition to a clear methodology that is well thought out.

Urban Justice: Local Justice

The criminal justice system plays a key role in crime prevention, in the protection of victims and in the education of city dwellers, as well as in reducing crime. It must also be accessible. New forms of justice have appeared in various countries and they include, among other things, penal mediation, local justice and conciliation. Penal mediation consists of finding a negotiated solution to a conflict and making offenders face their victims. If the perpetrator makes restitution, he or she is not sent to court. Mediation requires the consent of both parties and is led by a mediator who may or may not be a lawyer. It is a fast and informal form of justice that resolves the majority of cases promptly and responds to the need to limit the number of cases that are not dealt with, or are dropped by the conventional judicial systems.

A set of mediation experiences has been put into practice in many cities or even in schools. In St Denis de la Réunion, with the support of the municipality and judicial system, more than 15,000 cases of mediation have been dealt with. This is a large number compared with overall judicial activity. In Finland, mediators form an active group within their communities in 110 municipalities. In Abidjan, ethnic or religious leaders mediate in local conflicts.

Other experiences of conflict resolution through mediation are exemplified in Lisbon, Portugal, where neighborhood conflicts in a public housing area are resolved by Promoters (mediators) employed by the municipal housing agency to improve the well-being of the residents. Cultural mediators in Turin, Italy, facilitate relations between existing services and foreign immigrants, providing a response to the problems experienced by newly arrived foreigners. Social mediators in the Department of Saône et Loire, France, intervene in cases of absenteeism from school, shoplifting etc. Street mediators in Perpignan, France, work with homeless people in public areas and in "squatter" areas and refer them to care services, shelters and soup kitchens.

Another kind of mediation, led by an ombudsman, aims to protect individuals against administrative or judiciary action, or those arising from public or semi-public organizations. In Dakar, for example, "the reports of the mediator who deals with more than 4,000 complaints per year concerning the administration of justice, about slowness or refusal to act, provide an excellent source of information on shortcomings and obstacles, on the problems of access to justice for the poor. A large number of claims relate to citizens reduced to poverty. Litigation involves public services, private enterprises, retirement and social protection organizations and the users of abusive, monopolistic public utilities whose arbitrary procedures are questioned (Diagne 1995).

A third model, inspired by the concept of local justice, comes in the form of Justices of the Peace (England, Spain), *Maisons de justice* (France) and neighborhood tribunals (the Barangay courts in the Philippines or neighborhood courts in Latin America). These may function with or without professional judges (Philippines, England). This approach has the advantage of being physically close to inhabitants, accessible, inexpensive, fast, using oral communication and dealing with people's everyday problems. The Ugandan Resistance Councils described in Box 2.5 have also adopted this form of justice. Their competence is generally limited to civil or criminal matters of minor or moderate importance. Unlike mediation, the judge may impose a sanction without the agreement of the two parties, and may use public force to impose a punishment. In the rural areas of Peru, where this form of justice is institutionalized, it tends to widen its field of competence, sometimes in conflict with the authorities and the regular judicial system, for it is so popular that people prefer to use it rather than other judicial options. Like penal mediation, this model is often criticized by professional magistrates, who label it as second-class justice. The principal obstacle to the institutionalization of this form of justice is the corporate interest of magistrates (Correa and Jimenez 1995).

Finally, the forms of general conciliation that are analogous to penal mediation may have the same role in all judicial domains, for instance, in civil or family cases. They presuppose the agreement of the parties in conflict, and may be administered by a conciliator who is not a lawyer. The most interesting example comes from China, where two million of these popular tribunals for reconciliation are scattered throughout towns and villages, and deal with an average six million cases per month.

The interesting aspect of these forms of justice is that they are fast and accessible. They also have an educational value, for they build morale based on informal means of regulation and grounded in local tradition. Another benefit is their low cost, especially when the conciliator and mediator are not professional judges. Above all, they eradicate feelings of impunity, and demonstrate that justice does exist.

Two final examples of ways of making justice accessible emerge from the practices of governments, NGOs or cities. The first example is provided by the centers of legal education or advice aimed particularly at the most disadvantaged. Assistance is available for women, ethnic groups, victims of domestic violence, and others; this works through the dissemination of knowledge and the provision of legal advice on children's rights, human rights or other legal rights. The vast majority of NGOs working in the legal sector devote their energies to this kind of education. Familiarity with their rights makes citizens feel more a part of society and leads to a reduction in conflicts. One significant instance is the mobile legal information centers set up in Chile; these involve a specially equipped bus touring all the neighborhoods, with lawyers giving free advice to the inhabitants of poor areas who have legal problems.

The second example is the center that specializes in one type of problem: the Latin American *comisarias de familia* that deal with domestic violence, NGOs specializing in defending land rights in squatter settlements, drug treatment centers and those that specialize in providing

---

Box 2.6.   Community Justice for Minors in Portugal

The Commissions for the Protection of Minors are official non-judiciary institutions. With the consent of parents and cooperation of the family, they are competent to deal with abandoned minors and with children whose security, health or education is at risk. They include a magistrate, a doctor, a psychologist, representatives of the community, the education service, the police, private bodies with a social mission, and social action and parents' groups. They stress the measures that can be realized within a family and neighborhood, and appeal to local forces. They carry out studies on the security of young people, make recommendations to the authorities, and cooperate with local organizations to seek out joint solutions (ICPC 1995).

---

legal aid to the informal sector. Not all deal with some kind of crime, but they contribute to prevention. The community justice system for minors in Portugal is a good example of this practice (see Box 2.6).

The *boutiques de droit* (law shops) that bring together a number of specialized legal services are one way of serving the most disadvantaged. They are signposts for the judicial systems of the future: multifunctional, close to local people, working in partnership with the community and police, fast and effective. Indeed, this type of city-based partnership is the most effective way of making the prevention of violence everybody's business.

References

Banaynal-Fernandez, Tessie. 1994. "Fighting Violence against Women: The Experience of the Lihok-Pilipina Foundation in Cebu." *Environment and Urbanization* 6 (2): 31–56.

Clarke, Ronald.1995. "Situational Crime Prevention in Building a Safer Society." In Michael Tonry and David Farrington, eds., *Crime and Justice: A Review of Research*, Vol. 19, pp. 91–150. Chicago: University of Chicago Press.

Correa, Jorge, and Maria Angelica Jimenez. 1995. "Acceso de los pobres a la justicia en Argentina, Chile, Peru y Venezuela." In Franz Vanderschueren and Enrique Oviedo, eds., *Acceso de los pobres a la justicia en paises de América Latina*, pp.21–48; 111–61; 163–84; 185–220. Santiago, Program de Gestión Urbana and Ed. SUR.

Diagne, Pathé. 1995. "Accès à la justice dans les quartiers urbains pauvres." In Alioune Badiane and Franz Vanderschueren, eds., *Pauvreté urbaine et accès à la justice: Impasses et alternatives*, pp. 27–116. Paris: L'Harmattan.

Dryden Witte, Ann. 1995. "Urban Crime: Issues and Policies." *Housing Policy Debate* 7(4): 731–48.

Hagiwara, Yasuo. 1995. "Urban Criminality and its Countermeasures in Asian Countries." Paper prepared for the Japan College of Social Work, Tokyo.

ICPC (International Center for the Prevention of Crime). 1994. "Report of the Round Table of the Prevention of Criminality, Quebec, 1994." Montreal: ICPC.

ICPC. 1995. "Urban Policies and Crime Prevention (Montreal)." Paper presented to the Ninth UN Congress for the Prevention of Crime, Cairo.

ICPC. 1998. "European and North American Conference on Urban Safety and Crime Prevention, Montreal 1989. Final Declaration." In *Reference Document for International Forum of Mayors for Safer Cities*. ICPC–UNCHS.

International Prison Observatory. 1995. *Annual Report*. Paris: International Prison Observatory.

Latin American Weekly Report. 1995. Issue of 8 June.

Marcus, Michel. 1995. "Les modes de régulation des conflits urbains." In Alioune Badiane and Franz Vanderschueren, eds., *Pauvreté urbaine et accès à la justice*. Paris: L'Harmattan.

Moncayo, Hector Léon. 1995. "Acceso de los pobres a la justicia en Colombia." In Franz Vanderschueren and Enrique Oviedo, eds., *Acceso de los pobres a la justicia en paises de América Latina*, pp.279–96. Santiago, Program de Gestión Urbana and Ed. SUR.

Nsibambi, Apolo. 1991. "Resistance Councils and Committees: A Case Study from Makerere." In H.B. Hansen and M. Twaddle, eds., *Changing Uganda: The Dilemmas of Structural Adjustment and Revolutionary Change*, pp. 279–96. Nairobi: Heinemann Kenya.

Wikstrom, Per-Olof H. 1991. *Urban Crime, Criminals and Victims: The Swedish Experiment in an Anglo-American Comparative Perspective*. New York: Springer-Verlag.

Zaluar, Alba. 1995. "La drogua, el crimen, el diablo." In Albert Concha, Fernando Carrion and German Cobo, eds., *Ciudad y Violencia en America Latina*. UMP Series Gestión Urbana. Quito: UMP.

3

Municipal and Subnational Financial Management

Editor's Introduction
Richard Stren

Local—and municipal—governments are occupying an increasingly important role in the management of public finance. To some extent, this is a function of decentralization, as more and more national governments devolve both important powers and functions, as well as resources (or the ability to raise revenues), to local governments. We will discuss the revenue side of this development more fully in the next chapter. But the financial management role is also growing because cities are becoming the centers for a much wider range of economic initiatives.

The proportion of public-sector expenditure accounted for by local (or, in most cases, municipal) government has always been relatively low in developing countries. Unfortunately, we do not have good statistical information on local finance because most countries do not supply consistent and reliable data. For example, the *Government Finance Statistics Yearbook* published by the International Monetary Fund, the primary source for international data on government finance, gives information on local government finance for only 52 out of its 114 listed countries in its 1998 edition, with time series, detailed data for only 12 developing countries (IMF 1998). Figures published by UNCHS in 1996 covering a sample of 18 wealthy countries, 4 transition countries and 16 countries from Asia, Africa, and Latin America show the average proportion of local government to total governmental expenditure is 22 percent in the first group, 20 percent in the second group, and only 9 percent in the third (or "southern") group (UNCHS 1996, p. 174). Unfortunately, many of these figures are over a decade old. Under Bolivia's *Ley de Participación Popular* (implementation of which began in 1994) municipal governments will automatically receive 20 percent of all central government revenues through fiscal transfer. Comparing the percentage of municipal to total public-sector spending between the 1970s and the early 1990s for Colombia, Argentina, Chile, and Peru, we see that the proportions increased respectively from 10.5 to 15.7 percent, from 5.4 to 8.6 percent, from 4.7 to 12.7 percent, and from 2.2 to 9.2 percent (UNCHS 1996, p. 167). There are good reasons to believe that these proportions—and therefore the overall financial importance of local and municipal governments—will have risen further by the end of the 1990s.

Although municipal budgets may be increasing as an element in the larger public finance picture, they are still very modest. The municipal budget is a major tool of financial management, to allow effective planning for maximum benefits to the city's people. Budgets can be conceived in a number of different ways.[1] For example, a budget may be considered a prediction, or as intended behavior. The budget document contains words and figures indicating expenditures for certain items and purposes which it is assumed will be carried out when the indicated funds are spent. Alternatively, the budget may be considered as a means of making choices—between alternatives with greater or lesser value, in the most efficient and effective fashion in order to achieve certain objectives. Finally, the budget may be considered as a contract, or as a set of mutual obligations among actors and agencies that certain actions will be carried out at certain costs. But behind such a contract is a set of relationships supporting the agreements reached in the document. While all of these interpretations of budgets can be simultaneously valid, the budget is also a very political document—in which the resources of the community are brought to bear on public purposes which, in specific cases, enjoy predominant political support. In short, the budget is not just a printed document, it is the culmination of a political, social, and economic process which expresses the most important values and objectives of the community. Moreover, once the budget has been "passed," its implementation will almost certainly bring more political activity to the surface.

For many years the budgeting process was a closed technical exercise controlled by planners and other experts. But during the 1970s and 1980s,

---

1. For a general interpretation of the purposes and politics of budgeting, see the classic monograph by Aaron Wildavsky (1964).

local budgeting began to be understood as a central element in strategic planning, as communities attempted to maximize their competitive advantage in an increasingly globalizing world. By the 1990s, budgeting became a much more open and transparent process. As Paul Singer—an economist and secretary for planning in the São Paulo city government from 1989 to 1992—puts it, budgeting has become "a vehicle for popular participation in the allocation of public funds among a large number of competing objectives. The improvement of budgeting, making it more transparent, meaningful, understandable, and analyzable, has increased the possibility that rational choice of means will be made and, at the same time, that common citizens may take part in the definition of priorities and the evaluation of competing demands for public assistance" (Singer 1996, p. 101).

The three readings in this chapter deal with the technical, the participatory, and the political sides of municipal financial management. The economist Richard Bird "sets the stage" by introducing some of the larger issues in municipal and intergovernmental finance. Three basic "givens" are important to understand: local governments are chronically short of money; there is extreme inequality in the resource base between local governments (even in the same country); and local governments have limited tax powers. In spite of these limitations, he argues, some local governments are more successful than others even when their resources appear roughly similar. Local initiative does make a difference. Sometimes these differences are purely local, but sometimes they involve local governments coming to imaginative agreements with both national governments and local quasi-public associations (as in Colombia) in order to supply a high level of local services. If decentralization is to be effective, good information and even public discussion of intergovernmental fiscal relations is needed, Bird argues.

Some keys to successful management of local government finances include ensuring accountability for decisions made, and the systematic collection and reporting of information that can be used to verify compliance. Local authorities should have access to lucrative taxes (such as the income tax), and not be restricted (as is the case in most countries) to fees for particular services and the property tax. For large urban areas, Bird favors supplementary, or "piggybacked," local income taxes constructed as an attachment to national taxes, as an addition to more traditional taxation sources. Whatever the solutions arrived at, however, transfers from central to local governments will remain. For transfers to be effective, they should be transparent, predictable, and subject to an agreed formula that is not negotiable.

As for the budgeting system, Bird argues that local budgets must be comprehensive, accurate, periodic, authoritative, timely, and transparent. Of course, for this to happen budget officers must be well trained, information must be available, and intergovermental transfers need to be predictable. At the other end, there needs to be regular monitoring and measuring of outputs, so that future budgetary decisions will be based on information about past experience. In the specific example of financing infrastructure—a major responsibility for large urban governments—Bird offers some suggestions in the area of borrowing, user finance, private-sector finance, special districts or local associations, the earmarking of in-tergovernmental transfers, and the financing of recurrent costs of projects. Perhaps his main suggestion is that beneficiaries of services and infrastructure should be involved or at least taken into account wherever possible in the financial planning exercise.

The second article in this chapter is an account of one of the most inno-vative budgetary processes in the developing world: the so-called "partici-patory budget" of Porto Alegre, Brazil. Since 1989, the municipal regime in this city of 1.3 million has worked with decisionmaking forums of citizens at the local level to decide on the annual investment budget. As the article by Rebecca Abers describes the system, it is based on the work of 16 forums based on local regions of the city; there are in addition five thematic forums (created in 1994) involving education, health and social services, transpor-tation, city organization, and economic development; and a municipal bud-get council with representatives from the regional and thematic forums. The system was originated by the Union of Neighborhood Associations, eventually resulting in some 400 people participating in 16 assemblies around the city. By 1995, some 7,000 people were participating in the regional as-semblies, and 14,000 more in further meetings to negotiate compromises be-tween the demands of one region and another. The system is complex, and continues virtually throughout the year. The regional forums even micro-manage the actual implementation of capital projects. The Porto Alegre sys-tem has been blessed by the UNCHS as one of the "best practices" for oth-ers to emulate. According to the municipality, more than 70 cities elsewhere in Brazil and throughout the world (including Buenos Aires, Barcelona and Saint Denis) have adapted this system to their own needs (Porto Alegre 1998, p. 10). According to Abers, the process serves the valuable purpose of teaching people how to negotiate with each other and with the administra-tion, while at the same time raising the understanding of many about the needs of the poorest and most deprived sections of the population. The author's final point about participatory budgeting is that it would not have been possible without the active, time-consuming and persistent efforts of local government officials to work with neighborhood groups.

As a counterpoint to the academic account of the Porto Alegre case by Abers, the final document in this chapter is a recorded conversation with Raul Pont, the mayor of Porto Alegre from 1996 to 2000. In this discussion, the mayor explains how important the participatory budget process has been to his party, the PT (Workers Party). Effectively, the success of this process in Porto Alegre resulted in the election of a PT government at the state level in the 1996 elections. While Pont was not directly involved in the development of the system, he supports the system strongly because it is immensely popular with the people (especially the most needy groups in the population), and also because it has raised the credibility of the municipal government, permitting them to triple their revenue from local sources. If some groups reject this system, others are very supportive. But keeping the process going over the last 11 years has involved an alliance with various neighborhood groups and an NGO, named Cidade ("City") that publicizes the process and teaches the people some of the basics about municipal finance and budgeting. The city does not have a formal strategic plan as such, but in the process of discussing and debating the budget in an open, public fashion every year, the larger issues of development and a common vision for the city appear to coalesce in a relatively spontaneous fashion.

References

IMF (International Monetary Fund). 1998. *Government Finance Statistics Yearbook.* Washington, DC: IMF.

Porto Alegre. 1998. *Porto Alegre: Socioeconomics.* Porto Alegre: Porto Alegre City Hall.

Singer, Paul. 1996. "Budgeting and Democracy." In Robert H. Wilson and Reid Cramer, eds., *International Workshop on Local Governance: Second Annual Proceedings,* pp. 101–22. Austin, TX: Lyndon B. Johnson School of Public Affairs, University of Texas at Austin.

UNCHS. 1996. *An Urbanizing World: Global Report on Human Settlements 1996.* New York: Oxford University Press.

Wildavsky, Aaron. 1964. *The Politics of the Budgetary Process.* Boston: Little, Brown.

Setting the Stage: Municipal and Intergovernmental Finance

Richard M. Bird

The fundamental imbalance between expenditure needs and revenue possibilities makes it critically important that cities spend what they have as effectively and efficiently as possible. At the same time, however, the pervasive uncertainty and instability of revenues—not least those coming from other levels of government—makes effective budgeting and expenditure management difficult. There are no quick solutions or easy fixes, but experience in various countries has demonstrated that particular strategies and institutional arrangements—some within local control, some dependent on central government action—may be of considerable help to hard-pressed urban managers.

Patterns and Problems of Local Finance

The structure of local government finance in any country is invariably unique, but certain broad patterns recur.

Local Governments are Short of Money

Since "own resources" are almost always insufficient, local governments are usually dependent upon transfers. Even with transfers, resources are often inadequate to provide even the most minimal level of many of the services with which such governments are charged. In 1991, for example, local governments in the United States spent, on average, over $2,000 per capita; in contrast, per capita local expenditures ranged from $153 in Brazil to as little as $4 in Paraguay (UNCHS 1996, p. 176).

Not All Local Governments are Equal

There are large and small cities, heavily urbanized and rural municipalities, rich and poor areas. The resulting unevenness in access to local public resources can be marked. In 1990, per capita local expenditures in the United States varied from 43 to 327 percent of the national average, while in Chile the ratio of per capita municipal revenues in the lowest "zone" was 44 percent of that in the highest, and in Indonesia the comparable ratio was only 7 percent (UNCHS 1996, pp. 178–79). Striking differences between big cities and other local governments may be found in most countries, reflecting both the fact that big cities are richer and that they tend to carry out a wider range of functions.

Local Governments Have Limited Tax Powers

Despite the generally greater revenues in larger cities, a third common pattern found around the world is that few countries permit local governments to levy taxes capable of yielding sufficient revenue to meet expanding local needs. In 18 developed countries, for example, only 62 percent of local expenditure was financed out of local revenue in 1989. A study of 18 developing countries found that own-source revenue provided as little as 30 percent of local revenue in some countries but more than 90 percent in others (World Bank 1988, p. 155). Another study found that the median share of city expenditures financed by local revenues was 78 percent, ranging from 30 percent in Kingston, Jamaica, to over 100 percent (owing to negative borrowing) in Dhaka, Bangladesh (Bahl and Linn 1992, pp. 34–5).

Like the other patterns noted, for the most part these facts reflect conscious choices made by central governments. Countries can and do exercise considerable discretion in deciding the size of local governments, the extent to which local activities are financed from local revenues, and the types of taxes levied by local governments.

The property tax is the most important source of local revenue. The other major source is some crude form of business tax, such as the industry and commerce tax found in a number of countries of Latin America. Such taxes have been generally more successful than property taxes in providing revenues that expand with economic activity and expenditure needs. Unfortunately, they are also economically distorting and, to some extent, conducive to political irresponsibility owing to the ease of "exporting" part of the tax burden to non-residents.

The size and nature of local government own-source revenues matter. To quote perhaps the most thorough study yet made of city finance in developing countries: "[C]hanges in locally raised resources determine the ability of an urban government to expand its services. Where locally raised revenues fare badly, urban government expenditure suffers; where they do well, urban expenditure thrives" (Bahl and Linn 1992, p. 43). If central governments want local governments to play an active and expanding role in the provision of public services, they must both provide them access to adequate revenue sources and permit and encourage them (for instance, through the design of intergovernmental fiscal transfers and the adoption of an appropriate framework for managing public expenditures, as discussed below) to make efficient use of the resources thus provided.

There are No Simple Solutions

The solutions to the three basic financial problems just mentioned seem simple: give local governments more money; give even more money to the poorest local governments; and give them access to growing revenue sources. Such simplistic responses are misleading, however. Alternative solutions may prove more appealing. Why not reduce local government functions to levels they can afford? Should they be given money in the form of increased transfers, or greater opportunity to raise taxes of their own? The rationales and implications of these two approaches to closing the financial gap may be quite different. Should poorer areas be given greater transfers than richer localities, or should they finance fewer functions? Although each country must strike its own balance with respect to such questions, the considerations set out in the balance of this paper should be relevant to all.

The Central Role of the Central Government

Each country gets the local government it wants. Local government officials and politicians respond to the incentives with which they are faced. If these discourage initiative and reward inefficiency and even corruption, then it is no surprise to find corrupt and inefficient local governments. The solution is to alter the incentive structure to make it possible and attractive for honest, well-trained people to make a career in local government. Similarly, if local governments make decisions the central government does not like, the latter can establish an incentive structure to lead local governments, acting in their own interests, to make the "right" decisions.

An important condition for successful decentralization is thus the existence of an adequate and appropriate set of incentives. In their absence, decentralization may not only fail to improve local service delivery, but it may carry risks up to the level of national destabilization. If more expenditure responsibilities than revenue resources are decentralized, service levels will likely fall. If more revenues than expenditures are decentralized, local revenue mobilization may decline. Even if both sides of the budget are decentralized in a balanced fashion, local governments may not have adequate administrative or technical capacity to carry out their new functions in a satisfactory fashion.

Even when the incentives facing local government are wrong-headed, local policies can sometimes make a real difference. In Brazil, for example, some cities are well run and efficiently provided with services. Others, superficially similar in character and resources, are badly run and poorly equipped. In Colombia, some departments provide superior health services than others with similar resources. Such differences may arise owing to historical developments, a caring and charismatic local leader, or some other chance circumstance.

Whatever the cause, such experiences emphasize two important points: first, even in the perverse situations in which local governments are often placed by inappropriate central policies, there is usually some scope for local initiative; and second, local initiative can make a real difference in the lives of local people. What is needed to improve local government in many countries is both to provide an appropriate institutional environment and to encourage the emulation of good examples.

Recognizing Diversity

The diversity of local government reality is seldom matched by equal diversity in central government rules. Successful decentralization must recognize in some way the diversity and heterogeneity of the local government universe and permit an equally diverse and heterogeneous set of responses to particular decentralization initiatives, up to and including accommodating "home-brewed" informal-sector solutions to particular local problems, rather than imposing inappropriately centrally determined and rigid models.

One approach is to make "contracts," or specific agreements, with different areas in accordance with their capacities and interests. For example, education and health are departmental responsibilities in Colombia, although most of the financing comes from the national budget. Exactly how these responsibilities are carried out varies widely from department to department. In the coffee-growing region, for example, the quasi-public Federation of Coffee Growers plays an important role in shaping (and financing) rural development policy in terms of building roads, schools, and so on. Although many problems remain in Colombia, the recent decentralization of some key services has largely followed this tradition of flexibly accommodating a wide range of local conditions—of focusing pragmatically on what may work rather than attempting to fit everyone into the same centrally determined box.

The Need for Information

A common problem is the lack of an appropriate central government structure to monitor and support local governments. Central governments have to monitor and assess the finances of subnational governments, both in total and individually, in order to understand the existing situation of local governments and the likely effects of any proposed changes in local finance. Regular and detailed financial data must be maintained on local governments.

Uniform financial reporting (and budgeting) systems should be established—perhaps with different degrees of complexity for different categories of local governments. In addition, an appropriate agency—preferably one with a certain degree of political separation from the central government—should be made responsible for collecting and processing these data in a timely fashion. Developing such institutional "infrastructure" is neither quick nor cheap, but it is essential if countries want to decentralize substantial and important public-sector activities successfully.

More informed and open public discussion of intergovernmental fiscal relations is needed. Regular publication of relevant data would help. A small nongovernmental research institute focusing on local government problems might be established. Implementing such suggestions may require additional central government support to develop and maintain an appropriate reporting system and to train and support local government officials. If decentralization is to be effective, support is often needed to upgrade the technical capacity of local governments to carry out their expenditure functions efficiently and effectively. Each functional area has different needs, problems, and possibilities, and may have to be treated differently.

Establishing the Right Institutional Framework

Central governments must provide an appropriate institutional framework for effective local government. Two main conditions required for successful decentralization are, first, that the local decision process should be democratic; and, second, that the costs of local decisions should be fully borne by those who make them. When these conditions are fully satisfied, devolution of functions is sensible. Even if they are not, the delegation of implementation responsibilities to local bodies may still make instrumental sense, provided that incentives are properly structured.

For incentives to be conducive to good decisions, those who make decisions must bear the consequences. Politically, this means that political leaders at all levels should be responsive and responsible to their constituents, and those constituents should be as fully informed as possible about the consequences of their (and their leaders') decisions. Economically, local residents should not be able to shift costs to nonresidents who do not receive benefits; and local decisionmakers should be fully accountable to their citizens for the use made of revenues collected from the citizens (through local taxes), to users of local public services for the use made of the revenues they contribute (through user charges of various sorts), and to taxpayers in general for the use made of any transfers (or subsidized loans) received. Administratively, a clear set of framework laws is required (on local budgeting, financial reporting, taxation, contracting, dispute settlement, rules to be followed in designing user charges, and so on), as well as adequate institutional support to enable local governments to operate effectively in this environment.

It is of course easier to lay down such general prescriptions than to satisfy them. Nonetheless, if these conditions are not met, the perverse incentives that too often already exist in many countries may well be exacerbated by decentralization. Decentralization should in principle yield a more efficient and equitable pattern of public services than the overcentralized and unresponsive public sector currently found in many developing countries. But in practice it will do so only if it is properly implemented (Litvack, Ahmad, and Bird 1998).

If decentralization is to work, those charged with providing local infrastructure and services must thus be accountable both to those who pay for the services and to those who benefit from them. Ensuring accountability at the local level requires not only clear incentives from above but also the provision of adequate information to local constituents, as well as the opportunity for them to exercise some real influence or control over the service delivery system. "Informal" organizations almost by definition must be structured like this or they cannot continue to exist. But introducing a similar degree of responsiveness into formal governmental organizations can be a considerable challenge in the political and social circumstances of many developing countries.

If accountability is the key to improved public sector performance, information is the key to accountability. The systematic collection, analysis, and reporting of information that can be used to verify compliance with goals and to assist future decisions is a critical element in any decentralization program. Such information is essential to informed public participation through the political process. Unless local "publics" are made aware of what is done, how well it is done, how much it cost, and who paid for it, no local constituency for effective government can be created.

The Benefit Model of Local Finance

Local governments understandably are often concerned about the distributional effects of their policies. They are right to be concerned. The lives of the urban poor may in some instances be much affected by local revenue and expenditure policies (Bird and Miller 1989). Nonetheless, painful experience in many countries suggests that all too often attempts to help the poor through, for example, providing particular urban services free or below cost have in the end done little good and, in some instances, much harm to both the efficiency and the effectiveness with which local governments make use of their scarce resources. In general, therefore, it seems best to tackle poverty alleviation as directly as possible rather than distorting urban price structures in an attempt to do so (Bird and Rodriguez 1999). The basic requirement for efficient and effective local government is the "matching principle." Expenditure responsibilities should be matched with revenue resources. Revenue capacities should be matched with political accountability. And benefit areas should be matched with financing areas. This may be called "the benefit model of local finance."

The basic rule of efficient expenditure assignment is to assign each function to the lowest level of government consistent with its efficient performance. So long as there are local variations in tastes and costs, there are clearly efficiency gains from carrying out public sector activities in as decentralized a fashion as possible.

Leaving aside the important distributive question, almost all public services (except national defense, foreign policy, and surprisingly few others) should in principle be delivered at the local level, with local decisionmakers deciding which services are provided, to whom, and in what quantity and quality, and with local taxpayers paying for them. The essential economic role of local government is to provide to local residents those public services for which they are willing to pay, and local governments should be accountable to their citizens for the actions they undertake to the extent those citizens finance those actions. Consequently, (a) local governments should, whenever possible, charge for the services they provide; (b) where charging is impracticable, local governments should finance such services from taxes borne by local residents, except to the extent that the central government is willing to pay for them; and (c) where the central government does pay, careful consideration should be given to how local governments are accountable to the central government. Public-sector activities are unlikely to be provided efficiently unless the lines of responsibility and accountability are clearly established.

User charges. The first rule of local finance should be: "Wherever possible, charge." For efficiency, charges should be levied on the direct recipients of benefits, whether residents, businesses, or "things" (real property). The appropriate policy is to charge the correct (roughly, the marginal cost) price. Only thus will the right amounts and types of service be provided to the right people—that is, those willing to pay for them. Experience with such charges in most countries is not very encouraging, however. User charge finance remains more potential than reality.

Choosing local taxes. Since central governments set the rules and generally take the best-yielding taxes for their own use, local governments do not have sufficient access to tax sources to free them from dependence on transfers. Nonetheless, unless local governments have some degree of freedom to alter the level and composition of their revenues, neither "local autonomy" nor local accountability is a meaningful concept. In particular, local governments should be able to set tax rates, albeit perhaps within limits. Such rate flexibility is essential if a tax is to be adequately responsive to local needs and decisions, while remaining politically accountable.

Local governments should not only have access to those revenue sources that they are best equipped to exploit —such as residential property taxes and user charges for local services—but they should also be both encouraged and permitted to exploit these sources.

A possible problem is that local governments may attempt to extract revenues from sources for which they are not accountable, thus obviating the basic efficiency argument for their existence. Although limited local taxation of business may be warranted on "benefit" grounds, it may be desirable to limit local government access to taxes that fall mainly on nonresidents— such as most natural resource levies, pre-retail stage sales taxes and even nonresidential real property taxes. One approach may be to establish a uniform set of tax bases for local governments (perhaps different ones for such categories as big cities, small towns, and rural areas), with a limited amount of rate flexibility permitted in order to provide room for local effort while restraining unproductive competition and unwarranted exploitation.

In practice, the property tax remains the main source of revenue for local governments in most developing countries. Experience suggests, however, that there are at least two substantial constraints on its use. First, it is inherently difficult to administer in a horizontally equitable fashion, particularly when prices are changing rapidly. It is therefore difficult to impose very heavy taxes on this base. Second, the temptation to indulge in politically painless but economically inefficient "tax exporting" means that constraints should be placed on local taxation of nonresidential property.

The principal alternative (or supplement) to property taxes found in developed countries is some form of local income tax, generally levied as a supplement to national income taxes. If more local revenue is desired, there is much to be said for supplementary ("piggybacked") local income taxes, particularly in large urban areas. If a country wants its local governments to be both large spenders and less dependent on grants, it must provide them with access to national tax. Piggybacking is the only viable way to do this while retaining an important element of accountability. This prescription is, of course, difficult to implement in developing countries, for much the same reasons that national income taxes work less well in them. The greater importance of the small (and often "informal") enterprises that are so hard to tax in any country, like the inevitably lesser administrative capacity in developing countries, means that in this, as in so many other respects, poor countries end up trying to do more with less.

DESIGNING INTERGOVERNMENTAL TRANSFERS. Transfers from central to local governments will undoubtedly continue to constitute an important feature of the public finances of many countries. A well-designed system of intergovernmental transfers is thus essential to any decentralization strategy.

What is critical about intergovernmental transfers is not who gives them, or who gets them, or what the details of program design are, but solely their *effects* on policy objectives. As with user charges, the idea is to "get the prices right" in the public sector—or, to put it another way, to impose a "hard budget constraint" in the sense of making local governments accountable. Good transfers should in principle be transparent, predictable, and not subject to negotiation (Bird 1999).

Managing Public Expenditures

The scarce public funds available should be used as effectively as possible. Both financial honesty and political accountability require that budgeting and financial procedures are properly established and implemented—that budgeting, financial reporting, and auditing are comprehensive, comprehensible, comparable, verifiable, and public. But it is equally important to ensure that budgeted resources are applied efficiently and effectively. Proper public expenditure management must (a) adequately control the total level of revenue and expenditure; (b) appropriately allocate public resources among sectors and programs; and (c) ensure that governmental institutions operate as efficiently as possible (World Bank 1998).

Local budgeting should take place within the structure of a medium-term expenditure framework, both to ensure the proper financing of investment projects, and to reduce the scope for short-term political manipulation of budgets (for instance, to expand public employment in an unsustainable fashion). An essential first step is to put sound budgetary and financial procedures into place, especially in the more important local governments, such as states and large cities. Local budgets must be comprehensive, accurate, periodic, authoritative, timely, and transparent. The budget law must be clear, and it must be enforced. Moreover, what is done must be subject to external audit to ensure that the law is followed. A strong budgeting and financial system along these lines satisfies two essential requirements of good government: it establishes the basis for financial control; and it provides reasonably accurate, uniform, and timely financial information.

Institutional safeguards should be in place to ensure fiscal discipline and allocative and operational efficiency. For example, it is critical to local fiscal discipline that the amount of revenue from intergovernmental transfers be predetermined, and not subject to political re-negotiation during the budgetary year; local governments must not be able to depend on central government "bail-outs" of imprudent financial decisions, such as unsustainable borrowing or expenditure increases.

Allocative efficiency requires that managers receive adequate and accurate information on the effectiveness and social outcomes of the programs for which they are responsible. Operational efficiency may be achieved by allowing line managers significant discretion, within budgetary cash limits, to reallocate funds among inputs, or even across budgetary periods, subject to attaining predefined operational (performance) goals and to complying with appropriate internal and external financial control and audit systems. The emphasis is thus shifted from input controls (hiring so many persons at such and such a wage, or renting so many square meters of space) to output controls (providing health care of a determined quality to so many persons within a specified time period, or issuing so many marriage licenses). But, of course, there must still be full accountability by clearly identifiable decisionmakers on all expenditure decisions to reduce the possibility of fraud.

Shifting the emphasis in public finance from inputs to outputs is an essential step in improving policy outcomes, but this involves some risks; furthermore, it is not yet clear how best, or to what extent, the shift can be accomplished in the difficult circumstances facing local public sectors in most developing countries. Prudence suggests that a sound system of financial control and accounting should be in place before managers move too far in these new directions.

Financing Infrastructure

Three approaches to infrastructure finance are: to borrow the money; for users to finance the infrastructure; or for the investment to be financed by the central government, with the local government being responsible only for financing the recurrent costs of operation.

Borrowing

When the benefits from infrastructure projects are enjoyed over a considerable period of time, it may be both fair and efficient to finance such projects in part or in whole by borrowing. Moreover, borrowing may be the only practical way to finance large capital projects without large and undesirable fluctuations in local tax rates from year to year.

In most developing countries, however, local government access to capital markets is limited, both because capital markets are poorly developed and because central governments are seldom keen to allow any but very restricted access by local governments. When local borrowing is permitted, it often requires central approval and is heavily restricted. In many cases, local capital finance through borrowing takes place mainly from government-sponsored and financed agencies, such as municipal development funds. Unfortunately, the record of such agencies in most countries is poor, with many loans not being repaid and local governments having few incentives to repay (Davey 1990).

Some countries have given local governments virtually unlimited authority to borrow. This, too, is likely to prove a mistake. Unrestrained local access to credit in a situation in which financial markets are not well regulated, and local governments are desperate to expand local economic activity, may result in disaster. A better approach, despite the problems mentioned in the preceding paragraph, might be to develop more appropriate modalities for local government capital financing and borrowing, in the first instance through centrally controlled sources. Any such borrowing, however, should be at close to commercial terms, since operating redistributive policy through loan finance is even less appropriate than through matching grants.

User Finance

An attractive and feasible way to finance local infrastructure in some instances may be through some variant of benefit taxation. In some countries
of Latin America, for example, street improvements, water supply, and other
local public services have been financed by a system of taxation known as
"valorization," in which the cost of the public works is allocated to affected
properties in proportion to the benefits estimated to be conferred.

Studies in Colombia, where valorization has been most used, suggest
that several factors are critical to its success: careful planning and execution of projects; participation of beneficiaries in both planning and managing projects; an effective collection system; and, often, significant initial
financing of the valorization fund from general government revenues (so
that works can be started in a timely fashion, without requiring prospec-
tive beneficiaries to put up all the funds in advance). Similar lessons have
emerged from experience with an alternative approach called "land readjustment" in Korea, in which large land parcels are consolidated and developed by the local government, and part of the property is then returned
to the original owners in proportion to their ownership, while the balance
is sold by the government at market prices in order to recoup development
costs. Although careful planning and fairly sophisticated management are
required for success, these experiences demonstrate that local governments
can in some circumstances develop urban infrastructure, in effect by playing the role of a developer.

Another way in which beneficiaries may finance local infrastructure
has recently been developed extensively in North America through the use
of so-called "exactions," "lot levies," "development charges," and similar
systems, under which governments impose levies on would-be property
developers in proportion to the estimated costs that the development will
impose on the urban infrastructure. For example, if new residences are to
be erected, and the average cost of adding them to the urban water and
sewerage system is $100, the development charge—to be paid up front
before the project is authorized—would be $100 (or possibly some dis-
counted equivalent). Such schemes may sometimes help financially pressed
urban governments accommodate population expansion.

Private-Sector Finance

Some countries have experimented with "mixed" public-private financing
of urban infrastructure, such as roads and transit systems. Such schemes
have potential and deserve careful consideration where they seem

appropriate; but care must be taken to ensure that certain conditions are satisfied in order for such "mixed" financing to produce beneficial results. This approach is most likely to prove successful when projects are carefully designed and implemented, and when the responsible public agencies are technically and financially able to hold up their end of the deal. Weak governments cannot rely on private agents to overcome their weaknesses and still expect to make the best possible bargains for the public they represent.

Governments must be careful that they do not end up assuming the "downside" risk of projects, while allowing their private partners to reap any "upside" gains. Similarly, care must be exerted to ensure that what occurs is not simply the replacement of public-sector borrowing by (often more expensive) private-sector borrowing. "Privatizing" the design, construction, and operation of urban infrastructure may have many merits; but it is not a panacea, nor is it free.

Matching Grants

The boundaries of local governments seldom coincide neatly with the benefit areas of their activities. One way to deal with interlocality benefit spillovers is through the use of matching grants. The basic problem with matching grants as a way of dealing with spillovers is that no one, anywhere, has a good idea of the magnitude of spillovers associated with particular services. In practice, the spillover argument thus provides at most a rationale for central government support of some local expenditures; it almost never indicates *how much* support is needed—though a priori the required matching ratios found in many countries (for example, 10–20 percent) as a rule seem likely to be far too low for allocative efficiency.

Special Districts

In some instances the best approach to providing local infrastructure may be to create a single-purpose local or regional government, or to form an association of different general-purpose local governments. Yet another approach is through the creation of "clubs" or associations of affected municipalities. Two-tier local governments exist in many countries, with the higher tier being responsible for infrastructure in whole or in part. Even when such formal levels do not exist, lower-level localities should often be encouraged to work together when they have shared interests.

An important role may sometimes be played by "sub-local clubs," such as community associations. When local residents have a common interest in the provision of a particular service that is different from the interests of members of the wider community, they should be encouraged and facilitated in working out a solution. The economic advantages of such community solutions are often obvious, as is the general desirability of the increased local participation in the political process that results. On the other hand, the more "governments" there are, the higher transaction costs will be—and, all too often, the more obscure the lines of accountability. Single-purpose jurisdictions (such as water districts and school boards) may, for example, be efficient providers of the specific service with which they are concerned. At the same time, however, they may undesirably weaken general-purpose local governments, both in terms of competition for resources and reduced political accountability, and hence hamper the efficient provision of other public services. A recent examination of Canadian experience with special-purpose districts concludes that they make government more difficult for citizens to understand; they reduce the degree of citizens' control over government; they reduce accountability and hence, probably, the overall efficiency of resource allocation in the public sector; and they appropriate significant proportions of revenue that would otherwise accrue to local governments (Kitchen 1993).

Earmarking

A pervasive feature of local-government finance in developing countries is the prevalence of earmarking. In many Latin American countries, substantial parts of intergovernmental transfers are earmarked to local infrastructure investment. Although such earmarking is seldom fully effective—there is usually some substitution of transfers for own-source revenues—the result of this practice may be to expand capital spending to some extent, while exacerbating the already difficult problem of funding operating and maintenance expenditures.

Such earmarking may distort local preferences, exacerbate perverse incentives already found in the local finance system, and connect revenue sources with expenditures in totally illogical ways. Earmarking sometimes makes sense, however. When there is a strong benefit link between the payment of an earmarked tax (or fee) and the use of the tax to finance additional expenditures, not only is the source of financing eminently sensible in equity and political terms, but it may also serve the important efficiency purpose of signaling local preferences. Such well-designed earmarked benefit taxes are, in effect, surrogate prices and, when set appropriately, may provide useful guidance both to the more efficient utilization of existing infrastructure and to better investment decisions. In the conditions of many developing countries, however, to establish such prices may seem a counsel of perfection.

Financing Recurrent Costs

Even when capital projects get built, they are often inadequately maintained. Even when (as is often the case) local governments have not been involved in the selection or execution of projects, they are often assumed to be willing and able to look after the subsequent costs required to keep the infrastructure operating and in good condition. This assumption is often mistaken: not only may local governments not have the financial resources or technical capacity to undertake this task, but the incentives facing them seldom encourage them to do so. Indeed, these incentives may sometimes be perverse in the sense that the less a local government does to maintain its infrastructure the more likely it is to be rescued from above.

In some instances ingenious solutions have been found to the problem of financing recurrent costs. A study of rural road maintenance in Indonesia, for example, found that in one instance, a private firm was willing to maintain a road it needed to get its product to the main highway, and, in another, a group of farmers who clearly benefited from road improvements were similarly willing to carry out routine maintenance tasks. Although these examples are of well-defined projects with clear beneficiary groups who have no good alternative, many small infrastructure projects fit this prescription—and even some larger projects have sufficiently clear beneficiaries to make some variant of user-charge financing the preferred alternative.

Conclusion

Financing infrastructure is a serious problem when the resources available for local capital expenditure are as scarce as they are in many developing countries. Nevertheless, the situation is seldom completely hopeless. In some instances, borrowing may offer one means of capital finance. In others, users can and should be called upon to pay a substantial fraction of the cost of infrastructure, either up-front (as with valorization), or after the fact (through appropriately earmarked user charges). Properly designed matching grants, mixed public-private financial arrangements, and imaginative and flexible institutional structures may all prove helpful. As with local finance in general, the problem is not that nothing can be done. It is rather that little useful is likely to be done unless countries incorporate into their local-government system institutions that encourage the exercise of forethought, imagination, effort, and prudence—the key ingredients of good governance anywhere.

References

Bahl, R.W., and J. Linn. 1992. *Urban Public Finance in Developing Countries.* New York: Oxford University Press.

Bird, R.M. 1999. "Transfers and Incentives in Intergovernmental Fiscal Relations." Paper prepared for the World Bank ABCD-LAC Conference, Valdivia, Chile, 20–22 June.

Bird, R.M., and B.D. Miller. 1989. "Taxation, Pricing, and the Urban Poor." In R.M. Bird and S. Horton, eds., *Government Policy and the Poor in Developing Countries,* pp. 49–80. Toronto: University of Toronto Press.

Bird, R.M., and E. Rodriguez. 1999. "Decentralization and Poverty Alleviation: International Experience and the Case of the Philippines." *Public Administration and Development* 19: 299–319.

Davey, K. 1990. *Municipal Development Funds and Intermediaries.* Working Paper No. 32. Washington, DC: World Bank.

Kitchen, H. 1993. *Efficient Delivery of Local Government Services.* Discussion Paper 93–15. Kingston, Canada: School of Policy Studies, Queen's University.

Litvack, J., J. Ahmad, and R.M. Bird. 1998. *Rethinking Decentralization in Developing Countries.* Washington, DC: World Bank.

UNCHS. 1996. *An Urbanizing World: Global Report on Human Settlements, 1996.* New York: Oxford University Press.

World Bank. 1988. *World Development Report 1988.* New York: Oxford University Press.

World Bank. 1998. *Public Expenditure Management Handbook.* Washington, DC: World Bank.

Learning Democratic Practice: Distributing Government Resources through Popular Participation in Porto Alegre, Brazil

Rebecca Abers

The practical process of fostering cooperation between government and civil associations raises some questions, especially with respect to "empowering" the poor. Those who do not have access to, or who have been unable to form, civil associations are often the poorest, who live in the neighborhoods that have been most deprived of basic services. Thus, government policies that favor such associations are likely to continue excluding those who have always been the most excluded. And this seems to counter the very aims of "empowerment"—which may on the one hand seek to empower civil organizations, but on the other hand seeks to help people gain the tools necessary to be able to form such organizations.

This paper[2] looks at one highly acclaimed experiment in which ordinary citizens are given control over the distribution of public resources, the participatory budget policy in Porto Alegre. Since the *Partido dos Trabalhadores*, or Workers' Party (PT), came to power in Porto Alegre in 1989, the municipal administration has worked with local neighborhood organizations to develop a policy through which citizens can decide how best to distribute capital expenditures throughout the city. Regular decisionmaking forums made up of elected representatives have been created at a number of levels: sixteen regional forums bring together neighborhood representatives in different parts of the city; five thematic forums incorporate activists from throughout the city; and a municipal budget council houses representatives from each of the regional and thematic forums. The result has been an extraordinary reversal of traditional modes of spending that typically focus on highly visible investment in overpriced tunnels, bridges, and soccer stadiums. Since 1989, when the PT came to power in the city, the majority of investments have been directed to small-scale urbanization and infrastructure projects throughout the city's periphery. The "black box" of the budget has been opened, with more than 14,000 people now participating each year to

---

2. Excerpted from Chapter 4 in Mike Douglass and John Friedmann, eds., *Cities for Citizens: Planning and the Rise of Civil Society in a Global Age*. Chichester: John Wiley, 1998. Reproduced by permission of John Wiley & Sons Limited.

determine how the city should invest in their neighborhoods, and with the formation of an elected municipal budget council that has deliberative powers over all city expenditures.

Recognizing these impressive advances, this paper examines the extent to which the participatory budget policy has actually led to the empowerment of groups normally excluded from public influence. The specific character of participatory budgeting raises particular challenges with respect to what I will henceforth refer to as the "inequality problem." Many experiments with popular participation—such as self-help housing projects, creches, and rural village economic development efforts—involve making decisions affecting relatively small communities. In this case, however, the decisions involve resource distribution among neighborhoods and regions throughout an entire city. A number of authors have suggested that poor communities function on a logic of solidarity and reciprocity, through which the poor frequently make substantial sacrifices to protect the very poor. Such a logic seems less likely to operate where everyday social ties, such as those linking individuals within small communities, do not exist. The participatory budget also involves making hard decisions about limited resources. The problems of inequality and of exacerbating existing inequalities seem likely to be even stronger in a process, such as this one, that involves competition among a variety of distinct communities where preexisting solidarity ties are weak.

In this paper I suggest that the state can play an important role in counteracting these problems of inequality, both by creating a context favorable to the emergence of new civil associations, and by helping participants with self-interested goals to integrate ethical questions of distributional justice into their decisionmaking. Contrary to perspectives that see participation as a mode of "limiting government," this paper suggests that the successes of this policy have grown out of a great deal of involvement by state actors on a day-to-day basis, in ways that have had both direct and indirect influences over the organization of civil society.

Local Government and Democratization in Brazil

In the late 1970s, the military dictatorship that was installed in Brazil in 1964 began to weaken. In the context of an increasingly free press and the beginnings of a return of the rule of law, the late 1970s and early 1980s emerged as a "golden era" of popular mobilization in Brazil. Urban community movements demanding the provision of basic services made substantial gains, and a radical union movement peaked in 1979 with more than 3 million workers on strike throughout the country. These grassroots campaigns were widely supported by a growing number of opposition intellectuals and politicians, and a series of issue-based social movements, such as the Amnesty Campaign and the reinvigorated student movement. They gained organizational coherence and political legitimacy by tying into a network of Christian Base Communities associated with the Liberation Theology Catholic Church. It is out of this network of mobilizations that the PT was born. A coalition of radical unionists, social movements, church groups, and left-wing intellectuals and politicians formally established the party in 1981 (Gadotti and Pereira 1989; Keck 1992).

After a long period of austerity, democratization and substantially increased municipal financial autonomy[3] have made it possible for local governments to become more responsive to the needs of the poor. But decentralization has also bolstered the power of conservative local elites, who—with more resources at their disposal—have engaged in intensified clientelistic relations and corruption. Clientelist relationships exist at two levels. At the first level, neighborhood leaders—typically, the presidents of resident associations—make deals with politicians in which material benefits, such as the construction of a community center or the provision of sports equipment, are exchanged for the votes which the leaders mobilize (Gay 1990). While this system does provide some goods for those neighborhoods with "connected" leadership, promises come more often than results. The second level of clientelism represents much more capital investment and political influence, as it involves local business groups, particularly those that are engaged in real-estate development and that provide the means of collective consumption to the city, such as construction companies, hospitals, and transportation enterprises (Daniel 1988). While much "honest" contracting does go on, civil construction companies are particularly notorious in Brazil for engaging in clientelist exchanges that dig deep into government revenues. All this fits into a system of local

---

3. Over the course of the 1980s, the Brazilian federal government gave increasing powers to state and local government. This process culminated in 1988, when a new constitution was ratified, raising municipal revenues and increasing local decisionmaking autonomy. In addition to increased government transfers from both the state and federal levels, municipalities gained the right to levy two new taxes—a fuel tax and a property transfer tax. These and other measures dramatically raised the revenue potential of larger cities.

governance in which decisionmaking continues to be made behind closed doors, with little accountability to the (poor) majority of the population.

Since the early 1980s, the PT has campaigned at local, state, and national levels to challenge this status quo. Although it includes many traditional left-wing activists among its founding members, the PT has taken care to distance itself from the centralism of earlier socialist parties. The party is organized into "nuclei"—small groups in neighborhoods, schools and work-places, which meet, make decisions and elect delegates to zonal, municipal, and regional party conferences. The idea behind this "pyramidal" system is to insure bottom-up decisionmaking in which a large party base rooted in popular movements has direct contact with the top leadership. A culture of democratization has informed party platforms in which "democratization of decisionmaking" and *inversão de prioridades* (reversal of priorities) are the most hailed mottos. Particular emphasis has been given to the idea of participation. Many assumed that, if the PT obtained power and opened up participatory channels, civil society would organize itself into decisionmaking bodies that could effectively control the government "from below." By thus rearranging the power hierarchy, such "popular council" governing would eliminate clientelism and the social injustices it implied.

Although the PT won several municipalities in 1982 and 1985, it was not until 1988 that a significant number of cities elected PT mayors. Partici-patory policies of all kinds were then implemented on a large scale in big cities such as São Paulo and Porto Alegre, as well as in the numerous small and medium-sized cities (many in the São Paulo region) where the PT ran the mayor's office (see Abers 1996). Immediately, administrators saw that merely providing participatory spaces was not enough—civil society was not necessarily up to the prospect. In many cities, popular movements were only weakly organized and unevenly spread. Only a small portion of the population participated, and those who did were not necessarily represen-tative of the most disadvantaged groups. All this countered the second PT motto, *inversão de prioridades*, which implied funneling benefits to the tra-ditionally excluded. Out of this confrontation with experience, the concep-tion of participation defined by the PT governments matured significantly.

The Porto Alegre Administration and Participatory Budgeting

In the limelight of the PT's participatory efforts, the budget policy in Porto Alegre grew up under special conditions, and has had an unusually long lifespan. In the early 1980s, in several parts of Porto Alegre, groups of neigh-borhood leaders began to form "regional" organizations linking adjacent neighborhood associations. Neighborhood coalitions soon followed in other regions of the city, often promoted by leaders of these first two councils, most of whom were associated either with the left-populist *Partido Democratico Trabahista* (Democratic Labor Party, PDT) or with the emerging PT. In the same years, these activists created a city-wide umbrella organization with the objective of articulating neighborhood associations throughout Porto Alegre. This *Unido de Associaciones de Moradores de Porto Alegre* (Union of Neighborhood Associations of Porto Alegre, UAMPA) gained power in the early 1980s and rallied support for the PDT candidate in the first post-dictatorship elections for mayor that took place in 1985. The PDT candidate won the election and came to power with great expectations on the part of local movements, who now hoped that their demands would finally be attended to.

During the PDT administration, the UAMPA leadership, at this time controlled by activists affiliated with the PT, began to conceive the idea of participatory budgeting. For years, neighborhood movements had waged numerous struggles with the local government over specific and isolated demands. Whether or not the government responded was related less to the demand's importance than to the political success of particular neighborhood groups in pressuring the government.

Now, the leaders wanted to raise the level of this demand-making. They called on the first democratically elected mayor to hold a city-wide debate on priorities for investment and to open up the "black box" of the budget, revealing how the city government used its revenues. The PDT mayor repeatedly promised to do this, both in his campaign and over the course of his term, but never followed through. He ended his term amid accusations of rampant corruption, with the administrative structure of city hall in shambles.

It is in this context of disappointment that the PT came to power in 1989 in Porto Alegre. It was quite clear that the *Administração Popular* (popular administration) would have to take participatory budgeting seriously. But the initial financial situation of the government was chaotic—in the first year, 98 percent of the city's revenues went to pay salaries (Campello 1994, p. 71). Over a year went by before the government had funds available for even minimal capital spending. Nevertheless, over the course of 1989, neighborhood leaders from the various regional organizations met with the administration to begin to discuss how a participatory budget process might occur, and to draw up an initial plan of investment.

In a city of 1.3 million people, the process had to be decentralized. Assemblies had to be small enough to be manageable and the participants familiar with the needs of the area they were discussing. In the first meetings, the administration proposed to follow the division of four administrative regions defined in the city's master plan. But the movement leadership argued that those regions were too large and had no correspondence to the structure of neighborhood organizations in the city. By the end of the year, the movements and the administration had agreed on 16 regions. Open assemblies were held in each one, where citizens presented their demands for investment. About 400 people participated in the 16 assemblies, electing the first "budget delegates" in a proportion of 1 to 5 people present. Since this group still seemed too large to negotiate effectively with the administration, a commission was formed that worked closely with the secretariat of planning—then responsible for the budget process—to come up with an investment plan for the following year. This commission was the first formulation of what later became the municipal budget council.

The method of defining regional boundaries involved a loose negotiation among participants and the administration. The boundaries of 7 of the 16 regions were fairly easy to define. They simply followed the neighborhood membership of existing regional articulations of neighborhood associations. The remainder came almost by elimination, filling the empty spaces. In the case of the Central region, the negotiators attempted to bring together the large cluster of middle-class neighborhoods around the downtown. More peripheral regions were divided up according to major physical divisions. Over the years, numerous adjustments have been made in the borders of these regions, as neighborhood associations suggested that they "belonged" more in one region than another, either because of physical proximity or because of organizational affinities.

Many describe the investment plan that participants and the planning secretariat drew up in the first year as no more than a colossal wish list that avoided making any hard decisions favoring some communities over others. Nearly every demand that participants considered "high priority" was included in an investment plan that would have required several annual revenues to implement. Only in 1990, however, did administrative and tax reforms begin to produce receipts for capital expenditure. Under pressure from popular movements, the administration then started to invest in the poor periphery. But, since the investment plan developed the year before presented no clear order of priorities to follow, the agencies investing in public infrastructure ultimately decided which demands to implement first according to their own political and technical considerations. Convinced that a more streamlined process of defining priorities was necessary, the administration decided totally to restructure participatory budgeting in mid-1990. A new planning office, directly subordinated

Figure 3.1.   Schematic Diagram of the Participatory Budget Process in Porto Alegre

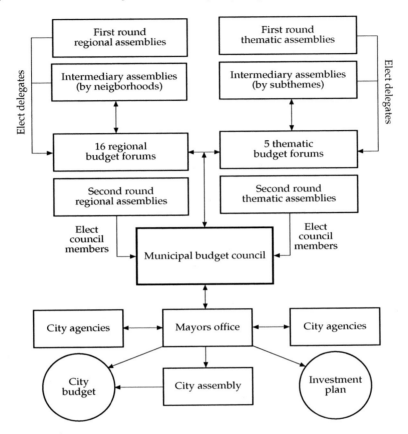

Source: Authors.

to the mayor's office, was created to coordinate the budget process, and
an ambitious team specialized in "strategic planning" began to redesign
the process. It is this group that developed the basic shape of the participatory budget that still exists today.

The budget discussions are formally launched in April of each year with
the calling of open, general assemblies in each region of the city. These assemblies have a mobilizational and almost theatrical character, more designed to
attract new individuals to the process than actually to make specific decisions.
Videos are shown describing the process, explaining the basic components of
a budget, and presenting the major investments that the administration carried out in the previous year. Time slots are available for a certain number of

participants to speak. For about 45 minutes, participants compliment and criticize the administration, and make a variety of appeals to the participants.

In the weeks following this first assembly, intermediary meetings at the neighborhood or "micro-regional" level take place to draw up actual priorities that are formally presented to the administration at a second round of regional assemblies during June. Since they are close to home, and since important priority decisions are made in them, the largest mobilizations of participants take place for these intermediary meetings. For example, in 1995, while about 7,000 people participated in the first set of large regional assemblies, 14,000 people participated in intermediary meetings. At these assemblies, participants negotiate a "hierarchy" of investment categories, ranging from healthcare to sanitation to street paving. In some neighborhoods, consensus is easily reached about which type of investment is the most important. In others, complicated voting methods are used to place the seven main categories in order. Then, within each category, participants propose specific projects and place them in priority order.

The more complex negotiations about investment decisions occur in the regional budget forums and the municipal budget council, whose members are elected during the two rounds of open regional assemblies. "Delegates" are elected to the regional budget forums as a percentage of those present in the first assembly and in the intermediary neighborhood meetings. At the end of the first regional assembly, the general body of participants determines how the delegates will be elected. Usually each neighborhood is allowed to elect the number of delegates corresponding to the number of participants it mobilized. At the second set of regional assemblies, participants vote for two representatives and two alternates per region to sit on the city-wide municipal budget council.

After the intermediary meetings, the regional budget forums begin to coordinate the priority lists of the numerous neighborhood assemblies into a single list of priorities for the region as a whole. The delegates, who most often are the principal leaders of each neighborhood, use a variety of methods to combine all of the neighborhood priorities into regional priorities. In some regions, this distribution is decided by a direct vote, thus depending on how many delegates each neighborhood has been able to mobilize and on how the negotiations among delegates evolve. In others, participants employ complex methods of criteria to rate priorities according to relative needs. The results of this negotiation are constructed over the course of many forum meetings and generally involve both the use of "distributional criteria" and direct negotiation among neighborhood representatives.

The work of the forum of delegates continues all year long. Most of the monthly or bimonthly meetings involve negotiations with city agencies. A common dispute concerns the agencies' definitions of "technical" restraints limiting the implementation of prioritized projects. Since "economic feasibility" is an elastic concept, whether or not an agency's evaluation stands often depends on the negotiating power and persistence of the delegates. Or an agency might suggest that an order of priority be changed. For example, the storm drainage department may argue that jumping over a costly first priority in the drainage category might make it possible to attend to the second, third and fourth priorities, thereby benefiting more people.

The administration also brings "institutional demands" to the forums—investments that it thinks ought to be made, but that do not emerge from the neighborhood assemblies. The forums have ultimate decisionmaking power over whether such investments should be made. They are also important for putting pressure on the administration to fulfill its promises. Delegates regularly call in agency representatives for explanations about projects that have been slow to get off the ground or that were implemented improperly. Finally, the members of the municipal budget council are expected to keep their region's delegates up to date about what happens at council meetings and to get their approval on important council decisions. Delegates often complain that this articulation does not occur to their satisfaction.

Another important role of the forums is to micro-manage the actual implementation of capital projects. The delegates organize "monitoring commissions" of neighborhood residents to follow the progress of the projects, keeping watch on the companies contracted by the administration to ensure that funds are not wasted, that construction is prompt, and that their intentions are respected. They also spearhead important negotiations within the community. For example, in hillside shanty-towns where streets are ill defined, building a paved avenue that cars and buses can pass through might require some residents to pull back their fences, or even relocate altogether. The delegates contact residents and attempt to convince them to do so, a process that is often very complicated and time-consuming.

The municipal budget council is the other center of the budget process. While the regional forums negotiate with the administration about how resources will be allocated within the regions, the municipal council focuses on the distribution of investments among the regions, on investments affecting more than one region, and on the overall distribution of resources among agencies. After each region has presented its priorities, in early September, the government presents the council with its proposal for distribution of expenditure among the agencies, divided into gross figures for personnel, maintenance and capital expenditures. While in the first year that I followed the council meetings the government's proposal was left unchallenged, in the second year council members negotiated millions of dollars of changes. According to the city charter, the basic budget proposal must be submitted to the *Câmara de Vereadores* (city assembly) by 30 September.

The budget council then discusses and debates the specifics of the investment plans of each agency. Meeting two or three times a week from October through December, each agency presents its investment plan—which must reflect the priorities presented in the regional assemblies. The main job of the council is to determine whether or not the distribution of funds among regions that each agency proposes is acceptable. While the order of priorities determined by each regional forum is rigorously followed, it is the municipal council that decides how much funding each agency will have to invest in each region. At the end of this period, the administration publishes and widely distributes an annual investment plan, itemized by region. This plan is treated as the formal contract of the investments that the administration promises to carry out.

From January through June, when the next municipal budget council takes office, the rhythm of council activities slows down. It is during this period that the general rules of the process are discussed. One central debate each year concerns the types of criteria that the council will use in the following year to mediate conflicts over how investments will be distributed among regions. Councilors also discuss the electoral procedures used in the regional assemblies, and raise questions about the technical criteria employed by the various agencies. Policy has changed substantially over the years as a result of these discussions between administration and council members.

One of the most important such changes, which made the decision-making process all the more complicated, was the creation in 1994 of five thematic forums to provide a space in which spending issues not relevant to any specific region, such as the city-wide transportation system or economic development proposals, could be discussed. The hope was also to bring into the participatory process a spectrum of citizens whose activism is not linked to neighborhood organizations, such as labor unions, professional groups, business organizations, cooperatives, non-governmental organizations and environmental movements. The thematic forums created were: education, health and social services, transportation, organization of the city, and economic development. Each one functions in a similar way to the regional forums, with two big assemblies, a lengthy

Municipal and Subnational Financial Management **139**

intermediary negotiation process, and the election of delegates and two representatives each to the municipal council. The existence of these forums has provided an important space for participants who wish to go beyond the localized level of discussion. But it has also further challenged the capacity of the administration to be responsive to assembly-made priorities, because the thematic forums sometimes call for changes in the basic policy orientation of the administration, and suggest highly expensive and multiple-year investments.

Learning Democratic Practice

In many ways, the participatory budget is a small policy with small objectives bringing ordinary people into the discussion of how to distribute basic investments among their neighborhoods. Yet the policy has gone far beyond most efforts at government reform that make efficiency and cost reduction their main objectives. The result—I think—is more than an isolated "successful" government effort. Significant transformations in the way civil society functions in Porto Alegre have taken place on a level that it is difficult to believe would simply disappear should the PT be voted out of office and the policy eliminated. Even where movement corporatism and self-interested action are the rule, the practice of participation involves a learning process through which some of the contradictions of democratization can be overcome and through which organized civil society can expand. Or, as democratic theorists such as Pateman (1970) and Macpherson (1977) have proposed, participation is developmental: its practice can have a "cascade" effect which both improves the participatory process itself and transforms public life more generally.

Qualitative and survey research among participants[4] showed that in Porto Alegre, the Participatory Budget Policy generated a mobilization effect that countered the problem of inequality in several ways. Mobilization grew out of the confidence that people had that participating would bring meaningful returns to their everyday lives. Each year, thousands of new participants were integrated into the process, in many cases representing neighborhoods and communities that had had little previous experience

---

4. The research involved extensive interviews with participants and government employees over a two-year period, observations of over one hundred meetings, and a survey of particpants at Regional and Thematic assemblies. See Abers 2000 for a detailed analysis of the results.

with collective action. Likewise, clientelist neighborhood leaders and their personal connections lost their clout. The budget policy served as a direct and convincing incentive for neighborhood organizations to democratize, calling residents to assemblies, holding elections and mobilizing for action. This "mobilization factor" alone was very important for balancing out organizational inequalities among participating groups over time.

Along the way, participants have developed a series of democratic skills. The most elementary are the basic habits of collective decisionmaking—holding coherent meetings, allowing all to speak, and learning how to debate and vote on complex issues where choices are multiple. Participants have also gained critical skills in negotiating with the administration. They pressure agencies to produce information about government actions and to demystify technical rules. They often successfully force administration officials to talk in ordinary people's terms and, in doing so, unmask attempts to veil in technical complexity the real reasons for rejecting or changing the demands prioritized.

The participants I studied also showed a marked capacity to learn how to combine efforts at mobilization "to get the goods" with a comprehension of the needs of others. The dynamic of priority-setting under conditions where no single group monopolizes decisionmaking seems to promote that comprehension, as cooperative actions evolve out of the negotiations. As people gain experience with participatory decisionmaking, they learn that often selfishness can backfire, and concern for other's needs does not necessarily diminish one's own benefits. All this is bolstered by the fact that most neighborhood activists are far from indifferent to moral arguments about the need to help the poorest. While most argue that those who participate should be privileged, most are also sympathetic to the idea that "objective" criteria reflecting the relative needs of neighborhoods should influence distribution. In some regions, very complex calculations are utilized that combine the amount of participation each neighborhood presents with data about infrastructure deficiencies and needs. This suggests that disputes among neighborhoods to distribute resources are not necessarily a "dog-eat-dog" story where the strongest movements take all the goods. To some extent, participants can be trusted to make distributive decisions, although efforts by the state to pressure them to incorporate issues of relative needs into their discussions have proved worthwhile.

Indeed, in these times of glorifying "limited" government action, it is important to note that all this was possible only because the administration put considerable effort and investment into the process. From the beginning of the first PT term, participatory budgeting was considered a priority policy, and all city agencies were expected to cooperate. The administration had to make clear to participants why attending the assemblies would be beneficial to them, and then had to follow through with the promises. The importance of "demonstration effects" for mobilizing people poses challenges for translating this participatory success to other areas of decisionmaking. All too often policies do not draw participant interest because their meaning to everyday life is unclear. Identifying and publicizing the effect of government policies on people's lives can be critical to participatory success. That success also depends on the capacity of state programs to nurture participation on the street and on a day-to-day level. In Porto Alegre, community organizers with origins in popular movements worked as hard as they ever did as activists, contacting citizens, organizing meetings, and promoting alternative ways of making distributional decisions. Directors and high officials of the various agencies also gave huge portions of their time to making the participatory process work, spending most evenings and weekends attending assemblies all over town to discuss neighborhood and regional needs. This suggests that a good participatory policy does not necessarily diminish the involvement of government in decisionmaking. On the contrary, in order for citizen participation to be feasible, a great deal of active support on the part of the state is necessary.

Observers concerned with "participant autonomy" might argue that government involvement in participant decisionmaking necessarily amounts to a manipulation of results and an attempt to control civil society. I argue, however, that we need to begin to distinguish between the "good" and "bad" ways that the ties between state officials and "private" citizens can form. This has been noted by a number of students of "good government" who argue that what Evans (1996) calls "embeddedness"—the networks of relations that cross the boundaries of state and civil society—can result in both personalistic uses of government resources and in greater accountability and effectiveness. Conversely, Tendler (1996) has noted that good government policy can in certain cases promote the emergence of stronger and more effective civil associations. This parallels my conclusion that where governments provide returns to participation, new civic associations will flourish. But I have also gone further, suggesting that the influence of government officials in the day-to-day workings of participatory decisionmaking can promote more cooperative attitudes and more systematic ways of distributing resources fairly. In doing so, that influence can counter some of the chronic vices of participatory decisionmaking.

A final point concerns the importance of time. Many participatory policies are declared failures and shelved only a few years after they are initiated. All of the processes I describe here took several years to develop, as both administration and citizens gained experience with participating. It took several years before the administration had sufficient revenues to invest. But only after the policy could offer returns to participation did a large number of new participants begin to mobilize. This initial mobilization also took some time and the complex processes of developing cooperative attitudes among recent participants took even more time. Today, not only is participatory budgeting considered successful by most political groups in the city (with oppositional candidates for mayor promising to maintain the policy), but also it is being copied throughout Brazil, even by municipal administrations held by other parties.

Time also reveals new challenges, however. For example, in recent years, the administration has sought to go beyond the small, local scale of the regional budget forums, to create general policy-oriented thematic forums and a number of other councils in areas such as housing, transportation and culture. The objective of these councils is to open broader policy arenas to an increasingly qualified participatory populace. But as I have noted here, merely opening participatory channels is not enough. This is demonstrated by the fact that these forums have often struggled to recruit enough new activists to carry out the enormously time-consuming tasks that participation requires. To be sure, there may be limits to how much time and commitment ordinary people will give to public life. But there may also be new and creative ways that the government can encourage people to do so, even in areas that are more general and less immediate than the current version of the participatory budget policy.

References

Abers, Rebecca. 1996. "The Workers' Party and Participatory Planning in Brazil: From Ideas to Practice in Emerging Democracy." *Latin American Perspectives* 23(4): 35–53.

Abers, Rebecca. 2000. *Inventing Local Democracy: Grassroots Politics in Brazil.* Boulder, CO: Lynne Reinner.

Campello, Tereza. 1994. "A política salarial dos servidores públicos de Porto Alegre no Governo Olívio Dutra." In Carlos Henrique Horn, ed., *Porto Alegre: O Desafio da Mudança,* pp. 69–82. Porto Alegre: Ortiz.

Daniel, Celso. 1988. "Poder local no Brasil urbano," *Espaço e Debate* 8(24): 26–39.

Durham, Eunice Ribeiro. 1984. "Movimentos Sociais: A Construção da Cidadania," *Novos Estudos Cebrap* 10 (October): 24–30.

Evans, Peter. 1996. "Introduction: Development Strategies across the Public-Private Divide." *World Development* 24(6): 1033–37.

Gadotti, Moacir, and Otavanio Pereira. 1989. *Pra Que PT: Origem, Projeto e Consolidaçao do Partido dos Trabalhadores*. São Paulo: Cortez.

Gay, Robert. 1990. "Community Organization and Clientelist Politics in Contemporary Brazil." *International Journal of Urban and Regional Research* 14(4): 648–66.

Keck, Margaret E. 1992. *The Workers' Party and Democratization in Brazil*. New Haven, CT: Yale University Press.

Macpherson, C.B. 1977. *The Life and Times of Liberal Democracy*. Oxford: Oxford University Press.

Pateman, Carole. 1970. *Participation and Democratic Theory*. Cambridge: Cambridge University Press.

Scheper-Hughes, Nancy. 1992. *Death without Weeping: The Violence of Everyday Life in Brazil*. Berkeley, CA: University of California Press.

Tendler, Judith. 1996. *Good Government in the Tropics*. Baltimore, MD: Johns Hopkins University Press.

A Conversation with Raul Pont, Mayor of Porto Alegre

Claudia Marcondes (CM): Could you explain to us how you got into politics in the first place?[5]

Raul Pont (RP): My political trajectory began when I got involved with the student movement and worker's unions. In a way, my political participation started with the military coup in Brazil [in 1964] but in opposition to the coup. For many years I did not get involved with either of the two political parties that were allowed in Brazil [during that time], the ARENA and the MDB. My activities were mainly through the student movement, until the beginning of the 1970s, and then through the workers' union. I am a history teacher by profession. Later I pursued graduate studies in political science. It was through the foundation of the Workers Party (PT) at the end of the 1970s that I went on to contest my first election... I was first elected in 1982, when the party went through its first election experience.

...In 1985, I stood as a candidate for mayor of Porto Alegre, in another election when we did not have much of a chance, but it was also an opportunity to construct the party. The result was very good, and in the following year I was elected as a state deputy in Rio Grande do Sul. The party was able to elect four state deputies and two federal deputies in that year. Then in 1988 there was a new election for mayor, and the man who is the present governor of Rio Grande do Sul, Olivio Dutra, won the election for the PT. The mandate was for four years. In 1990, I was elected as a federal deputy, but in 1992 I renounced the mandate to go back to Porto Alegre, to be a vice-mayor with Tarcio... At that time in Brazil, re-election was not permitted. So when Olivio finished his mandate in 1992 he was substituted by Tarcio, who is a lawyer, who also has a background of involvement with the student movement and worker's unions. I was the vice-mayor again, then in 1996 I was elected as the mayor, in a mandate that will be over next year... Now that there is the possibility of re-election, we haven't decided whether I will continue. The decision is a collective one—

---

5. This conversation, which took place in Portuguese, was recorded in Toronto over lunch on 23 August 1999. The recorded transcript of the conversation was translated, and edited for this book. Except for passages that have been removed because of considerations of length and/or relevance for the present purposes, the text of this document is a direct translation of the spoken conversation. Claudia Marcondes (CM) is an architect/planner of Brazilian origin was at the time the Director of UTUI, the University of Toronto Urban International.

it belongs to the party—but we intend to win and elect a mayor in our party's fourth mandate.

CM: Has your success with the participatory budget played a role in your party's electoral success?

RP: ...In fact, in the last election, we really guaranteed Olivio's victory [at the state level] with a huge landslide in Porto Alegre. Rio Grande do Sul has a population of almost 10 million; there are about 7 million voters, and the victory was by 80,000 votes. It was a very tight contest overall, but in the capital we won with a very large margin. So we can say that it was the voters in the capital (Porto Alegre) who guaranteed the victory. The difference in votes in the capital was 250,000 votes, so although we lost the election in the rest of the state, the victory in the capital was enough to guarantee the election. This year Olivio Dutra has already initiated the participatory budget as a statewide project. This is much more difficult and much more complex [than in Porto Alegre] but assemblies have already been established in 467 municipalities throughout the state.

...In other municipalities of the state, this is an experience that still does not have the level of complexity that it does in Porto Alegre.

CM: How well established is the participatory budget in Porto Alegre?

RP: In Porto Alegre the participatory budget has been going on for 11 years as a regular, systematic experience. There, it is already consolidated; a very large number of people, in fact, several thousand people participate on a regular basis. This year, in the large meetings, we were able to count the number of people involved, but it is often impossible to follow the whole process. In the smaller communities, the micro-regions, the Town Hall cannot keep track of everything that is going on, but in those meetings where we're able to count the people who attend, there were over 20,000 people present, participating in two large cycles of regional plenary meetings, organized by themes.

CM: What would you say are the most important lessons that can be taken from the experience of participatory budgeting in Porto Alegre?

RP: Our experience with democratic participation, which lies behind participatory budgeting, is that it is an instrument, which presupposes the presence of a certain crisis, a certain failure of representative democracies.

These are incapable of involving the citizen, involving a more direct participation in a system of political parties, such as the current system in Brazil... There is no respect for the decisions of the voters, candidates change parties during their mandate, the party says one thing and then takes an altogether different course of action during the course of government.

So in our government, we wanted to do something where the people would have a larger degree of control of what was taking place, have more power of decision over the application of public sources, establish other priorities—coming directly from the public and not from technical experts. The experience has been very positive, not only because it has proved that people participate when the avenues and instruments are available—they participate with grace and in a completely voluntary fashion—but also in the sense that it destroyed the idea that planning or technical knowledge are decisive when making a budget. People know how to make a budget from their own necessities and demands. You also remove that mysterious and technical aura from the budget.

CM: Before the people get involved in the budgeting process, do you prepare them for some of the technical aspects of budgeting that they will encounter?

RP: Parallel to the budget experience, we have courses that are available to the population... These are annual, and they unite delegates and counselors. Those taking these courses go through a minimum curriculum which includes the main lines and rules of financing, of investing, the legal implications, our obligations to a payroll with debts from previous financing, and so on. Now, we also have an NGO in Porto Alegre called Cidade, which is dedicated exclusively to the following up of the participatory budget. They have a newspaper, a periodical, and they also operate an informational course. But they are not from the City Hall; they are independent. They establish a relationship with the delegates and their leaders, and promote courses about the city. But the City Hall also does the same. And sometimes we do it through a common agreement with Cidade. In many regions of the city, we provide courses during the budgetary process and even outside the process. Cidade is funded by an outside organization, perhaps American or European, I am not sure. But they have publications, a newspaper and a magazine of a didactic nature.

One part of our budgetary process is regional, and another is thematic...we have five large plenary meetings by themes, which are Education, Leisure and Culture; Health; Social Assistance; Movement and

Transportation; and Economic Development and Revenue (*tributos*). In the economic development and revenue meetings, for example, people give their opinions and make proposals regarding the types of fees and taxes that relate to the municipality... In the thematic plenary meetings they decide on policies, but their decisions have to be implemented through the budget. So they organize the people, and then go to the budget meeting, and point out, for instance, that a day care is in demand in a certain area, or that there is one that wants to make an agreement, and we are aware that it is a good day care center ... and then if the local inhabitants of the area approve, then the money goes towards another agreement... In our second mandate, we had no agreements involving children six years and under, but today, there are 120.

...So, in this case these thematic councils struggled to get organized with several groups that work with children-related issues, then went to the budget meetings and determined the budget policy that needed to be implemented. The same goes for groups that work with the unemployed, and go to the budget meetings and ask for a place where a coop could be started... They can also make economic proposals at the economic development and revenue meetings.

CM: What is the role of political parties with respect to participatory budgeting? Are members of opposition parties excluded from the process?

RP: The most conservative parties do not participate, and they direct their followers and associates not to go to the municipal councils. They are against this method, arguing that the existing system of democratic representation, through the house of representatives, the state legislative assembly, or the national congress, is sufficient. That is as far as democracy needs to go. There is no need for other forms of participation. On the other hand, there are other parties (in addition to the one in power), that do participate in the participatory councils. But the main point is that the majority of the people involved in the budget, are not affiliated to any party. They are voters, they are citizens, and that is all. What gives the Porto Alegre budget so much credibility—and this is an important point which we insist upon— is that any citizen can go and express him or herself, to speak, to become a candidate, to be elected, to become a delegate or member of a council. This credibility is what guarantees the success of the overall project. Our party does not manipulate the process. There are no direct manifestations of the party. Still, to be honest, the identification of the party takes place whenever we are able to meet the people's demands. For example, who are the people who decide? Even in the city centers...or in the wealthiest neighborhoods, the members of the population that participate are those who are the most needy. In the central areas of the city there are still ghettoes of irregular occupation, slums where as many as 80 families might live. These are the people who participate in meetings of those central neighborhoods, and there they form the majority, rather than the middle-class people who also live there. The largest business associations do not participate; the small ones do. The association of local (small) businesses in a certain neighborhood will participate, as will some unions of the "medium" sectors. Large industry does not get involved. Rather, they try to exert their influence directly through a mayor, or … they do not go. But there is room for their participation, that is guaranteed.

Richard Stren (RS): Is there a strategic plan for Porto Alegre?

RP: No, we do not have a strategic plan as such. But there is a lot of publicity and information about the budget, so perhaps it serves the same purpose. [Shows a document] This is a periodical which always publishes the participatory budget in the last page. It carries very specific news;…here is something about the technological incubator, here the construction of a highway overpass, this is about health. Here there is an opinion about taxes, this is a tribute to a renowned sculptor of our city, one of the greatest sculptors we have, who has just celebrated his 80th birthday; here is an avenue that will gain another lane. These pages are news, but as you can see by the color code, the last page is dedicated to the budget: the projects that are being carried out, the agenda for the participatory council, news about participation in the march of the landless, and other stories like this. This paper is issued in 50,000 copies, every two weeks. It is distributed at bus stops, and in front of the university, where there are great concentrations of workers. We try to keep the people informed, and we also provide a calendar of the meetings. This calendar is also published in other newspapers of the city, and it is aired on television. But to have them aired, we have to pay. The television does not provide this service free of charge.

CM: Do you use the internet?

RP: Yes, as a municipal government we have a homepage. There is an entire section about all the metropolitan regions—these are all on the internet.

CM: Could you give us an idea of how the people work with civil servants in this process?

RP: Between the works and the services, the population has been involved in a large number of decisions; ... in the last year, 325 work projects were decided by the community. These also include services. For the City Hall to go through with 300 projects in a year...it changes—and this is important—the work of the civil servants... There are 21,000 [public] servants in Porto Alegre. And half of them are in health and education. But this is a small network, relatively speaking. State-wide it is much bigger... Social assistance has also grown significantly, because of the unemployment crisis in these last years. Proportionally, this was the budget that grew the most, the area of social assistance, in these last years...

CM: What about the economy of Porto Alegre? Did the participatory budget have any impact on it?

RP: In 10 years we have practically tripled the municipal revenue... As we see it, this means that the city has attracted investment. It is not because we have adopted a tough taxation policy—we have not increased taxation, and there has been no increase in fees and charges. But because of the credibility we have gained over the budget, we have been much better able to enforce the collection of the revenues owing.

CM: Thank you so much for agreeing to discuss your experiences with us.

4

Financial Management—Revenue Raising

Editor's Introduction

Richard Stren

As a respected World Bank researcher pointed out in 1994, of the 75 developing and transitional economies with populations of over 5 million, all but 12 claimed to have embarked on some form of transfer of power from central to local units of government (Dillinger 1994). Indeed, the latter part of the 1980s, and the 1990s, saw an almost unprecedented "wave" of decentralization initiatives in developing countries, to the point that, as James Manor points out:

> Decentralization has quietly become a fashion of our time. It is being considered or attempted in an astonishing diversity of developing and transitional countries ... by solvent and insolvent regimes, by democracies (both mature and emergent) and autocracies, by regimes making the transition to democracy and by others seeking to avoid that transition, by regimes with various colonial inheritances and by those with none. It is being attempted where civil society is strong, and where it is weak. It appeals to people of the left, the center and the right, and to groups which disagree with each other on a number of other issues (Manor 1999, p. 1).

The nature of these decentralization policies varies tremendously—from incremental changes in protocols of intergovernmental relations on the one hand, to major constitutional amendments or even new constitutional forms on the other. Three large countries gave new constitutional powers to municipalities during this period. In Brazil, a new constitution in 1988 considerably increased the power of municipalities in relation to the states, assigning to them control of intra-city transport, preschool and elementary education, land use, preventive health care, and historical and cultural preservation. In India, an important constitutional amendment in 1992 provided an illustrative list of functions that are henceforth considered appropriate for municipal government; among these functions are planning for economic and social development, urban poverty alleviation, and even urban forestry. The amendment also limited the degree to which state governments are able to suspend democratic local government, and provided for a revision of state-local fiscal relations. The new South African constitution of 1996 devotes a whole chapter (Chapter 7, containing 14 separate articles) to local government. Among other things this chapter of the constitution states that the objects of local government (including municipal government) are "(a) to provide democratic and accountable government for local communities; (b) to ensure the provision of services to communities in a sustainable manner; (c) to promote social and economic development; (d) to promote a safe and healthy environment; and (e) to encourage the involvement of communities and community organisations in the matters of local government" (Section 152). The clear import of these and other decentralization initiatives is that local governments—and in particular large municipalities—are expected to undertake *and to finance* a much wider and more inclusive range of responsibilities for both services and other economic and social activities.

If decentralization to local authorities (including municipalities) is to be effective, it needs to be real decentralization, in the sense of devolution rather than deconcentration or delegation, as Robert Ebel and François Vaillancourt point out. Decentralized subnational governments must be accountable to their citizens, and must be "in a legal and financially viable position to make spending decisions." The reasons for decentralization in the first place may be partly economic (i.e., to respond more effectively to community preferences for services, to access local tax and revenue bases, and to coincide in scale with the area over which the service is offered), but they may be partly political, and even personal in the case of some leaders. Generally, local authorities are not permitted the most lucrative and collectible taxes (such as payroll taxes on salaries), so that when their powers increase, they have difficulty in finding the revenue to discharge their new responsibilities. In such a case, as Jerry Jenkins and Richard Bird (1993) once argued, the fiscal gap (i.e., between new powers and inadequate revenue sources) can become a fiscal trap (i.e., when local governments must rely on other levels of government to provide them with the resources they need, thus losing their autonomy). In their article in this chapter, Ebel and Vaillancourt consider a wide range of revenue sources for local governments—such as user charges and fees, business levies, personal income taxes, real property tax, sales taxes, tax sharing with the national government, and borrowing—noting that the eventual choices should arise from an overall debate on local financing based on research, and at the same time should be part of a broader understanding of how local and national governments can best coordinate their respective revenue-earning systems for the public benefit.

To complete this section, we present two articles dealing with more particular aspects of local authority finance. From a wide-angle view, we switch our lens to examine some specific approaches in detail. In his article on user fees for local services, Richard Bird states that "whenever possible and desirable, public services should clearly be charged for rather than given away." Aside from raising the necessary revenue, this approach to service provision provides important information about the effectiveness and popularity of public services, although (as in the case of parks, roads, and some other public goods) the approach cannot be applied in all cases. Bird argues that, depending on the facility in question, different pricing regimes should be applied; examples are short-run marginal cost pricing (SRMC), long-run marginal cost pricing, average cost pricing, average incremental cost pricing, multi-part tariff pricing, and declining block pricing. Pricing decisions are very important for local governments, but in addition to technical calculations, urban managers must know the product, they must know the data on which prices are being charged, they must be ready to adjust the data as necessary, they must try to set the prices as closely as possible to SRMC levels, they must justify any subsidy, and they must consider carefully how to promote and to implement the tax proposal. As charges and fees are becoming an increasingly important part of the municipal revenue portfolio, good pricing decisions are both politically and economically essential.

The article by Sumila Gulyani deals with the new World Bank demand-driven approach to water supply. This is an example of the kinds of user fees that can be applied to new infrastructure, thus strengthening the local government's capacity to collect revenue. The earlier supply-side approach to urban water supply, whereby the costing of facilities was based on an assumption of the approximate proportion of their income that people would be willing to pay, has failed in many countries because people do not pay the estimated charges, with the result that the network cannot either maintain itself or expand into new areas. The new, more demand-driven approach relies on careful project selection (based on detailed household surveys of the level and type of service people want, and how much they are prepared to pay), and the provision in the completed schemes of different levels of service for people with different needs and resources. This new approach involves, of course, obligatory metering, user fees for everyone using the service, and the design of a tariff structure ensuring that the full capital and operational costs can be recovered. Although some might argue that the poor will pay more for water under such a regime, the author argues that, in fact, in the absence of an adequate water distribution infrastructure in the first place (caused by costly supply-based planning) the poor are already paying much more than the rich for privately supplied water. While the demand-driven approach needs to incorporate good institutional planning for effective distribution and management, it should provide a better basis for investment in water projects than previous schemes.

References

Dillinger, William. 1994. *Decentralization and its Implications for Urban Services Delivery.* Washington, DC: World Bank for the Urban Management Program.

Jenkins, Jerry, and Richard Bird. 1993. "Expanding Consent in the Finance and Delivery of Urban Services." In Jerry Jenkins and David E. Sisk, eds., *Development by Consent: The Voluntary Supply of Public Goods and Services*, pp. 145–74. San Francisco: ICS Press.

Manor, James. 1999. *The Political Economy of Democratic Decentralization.* Washington, DC: World Bank.

Fiscal Decentralization and Financing Urban Governments: Framing the Problem

Robert D. Ebel and François Vaillancourt

Of the 75 developing and transition countries with populations of over 5 million, all but 12 claim to have embarked on some form of transfer of fiscal power from central to subnational governments (Dillinger 1994). Each decentralizing country faces issues that are at the same time very different and very similar. Differences arise from the diversity in national economic and demographic structures, institutions, traditions, geography, and access to new technologies. Similarities tend to set the broad policy framework, and allow countries all over the world to compare and learn from each other's experiences.

The fundamentals of the open economy serve as the underpinning of the policy similarities. The open subnational[1] jurisdiction cannot restrict the flow of goods and services across its borders by erecting economic barriers such as tariffs, quotas, or import licenses; nor can it effectively control cross-border movements of labor and capital. This high degree of product and factor mobility makes the character of subnational fiscal policy different from that of structurally similar national policies.

Fiscal decentralization is thus associated worldwide with issues ranging from the broad one of achieving a desired degree of both vertical and horizontal balance between jurisdictions, to narrower (but not less important) concerns about expenditure impacts of unfunded mandates imposed by "higher" levels of government, and restrictions on the choice of local revenue sources.

There are also political similarities between countries. Chief among these are the reaction "from below" to long years of extensive central control, and the fiscal expediency of central governments easing their own strained finances by reducing transfers and shifting responsibilities "downward."

Within this context, three themes emerge with respect to intergovernmental policy in decentralizing economies: first, a well-functioning

---

1. The term "subnational" refers here to all levels of government below the national; the term "local" excludes the intermediate levels (such as regional, provincial or state).

intergovernmental system is key to the accomplishment of broader reform objectives; second, new subnational governments must be allowed to build institutional capacities in a way that makes them accountable for their fiscal decisions; and, third, many of the required reforms will entail sweeping changes, making reform an often politically difficult process.

Models of Fiscal Decentralization

Decentralization is a broad term encompassing several arrangements of intergovernmental affairs. There are three basic variants:

Devolution is the most complete form: independently established subnational and local governments are given the responsibility for delivery of a set of public services, along with the authority to impose fees and taxes to finance them. Devolved governments have considerable flexibility to select the mix and level of services, and may receive some financial support in the form of transfers from the center. The essence of decentralization is that these governments must be accountable to their citizens, *and* must be in a legal and financially viable position to make spending decisions. A political corollary is that the tax and spending decision process be structured to represent the views of all citizens. This is why the concepts of democracy, fiscal decentralization, and public sector efficiency are closely related.

Deconcentration refers to the decentralization of central government ministries. Deconcentration with authority means that regional branches of central offices are created with some ability to make independent decisions. Deconcentration without authority occurs when regional offices are created with no independent capacity from the center.

Delegation is intermediate between devolution and deconcentration. Subnational or local governments (not branches of government) are given responsibility for delivering certain services, but are subject to some supervision by the central government (which may provide some form of finance for the service).

In practice, all governmental systems are likely to have some elements of all three variants; centralization/decentralization is a continuum rather than a dichotomy. Table 4.1 provides quantitative evidence on the importance of devolution for 46 countries for which data were available in 1999. Local governments vary in importance from less than one percent to more than 50 percent of government revenues, and on average are more important than the intermediate subnational entities because of their greater prevalence.

Table 4.1.   The Importance of Three Levels of Government, 46 Countries, 1993-96

Country	Year	Own revenues as percent of total government revenues		
		Percent central	Percent subnational	Percent local
Albania	1995	98.02	—	1.98
Australia	1996	68.09	26.70	5.21
Austria	1995	72.84	9.73	17.43
Belgium	1995	93.67	—	6.33
Bolivia	1996	79.36	5.82	14.82
Botswana	1994	99.42	—	0.58
Brazil	1993	72.42	23.27	4.31
Bulgaria	1996	88.60	—	11.40
Canada	1993	48.78	39.07	12.15
Croatia	1996	88.39	—	11.61
Czech Republic	1996	83.97	—	16.03
Denmark	1995	67.79	—	32.21
Estonia	1993	75.74	—	24.26
Finland	1995	63.60	—	36.40
France	1996	86.38	—	13.62
Germany	1993	65.76	20.82	13.42
Guatemala	1993	96.29	—	3.71
Iceland	1993	78.18	—	21.82
Ireland	1994	91.28	—	8.72
Israel	1994	90.48	—	9.52
Italy	1996	99.99	—	0.01
Kenya	1994	94.03	—	5.97
Latvia	1995	80.42	—	19.58
Lithuania	1995	75.70	—	24.30
Luxembourg	1995	89.60	—	10.40
Malaysia	1996	86.97	9.74	3.29
Mexico	1994	79.56	14.86	5.58
Mongolia	1996	77.29	—	22.71
Netherlands	1996	88.96	—	11.04
Neth. Antilles	1994	48.26	—	51.74
New Zealand	1996	91.39	—	8.61
Nicaragua	1995	90.64	—	9.36
Norway	1995	78.35	—	21.65
Paraguay	1993	97.73	—	2.27
Peru	1996	94.67	0.89	4.44
Poland	1996	85.44	—	14.56
Portugal	1994	94.90	—	5.10
Romania	1994	93.29	—	6.71
Russia	1995	99.94	—	0.06
South Africa	1995	86.04	3.40	10.55
Spain	1994	83.85	5.53	10.61
Sweden	1996	68.46	—	31.54

(table continues on following page)

Table 4.1 *(continued)*

Country	Year	Own revenues as percent of total government revenues		
		Percent central	*Percent subnational*	*Percent local*
Switzerland	1995	56.19	23.10	20.72
Thailand	1996	93.74	—	6.26
United Kingdom	1995	91.96	—	8.04
United States	1995	58.68	25.45	15.87
Averages				
OECD		78.03	7.16	14.80
South and Central America		87.24	6.40	6.36
Eastern Europe		86.95	0.00	13.05
Africa/Asia		84.53	1.64	13.83
Total		**82.50**	**4.53**	**12.97**

Note: Averages are arithmetic means. Data represent central, subnational, and local government own revenues only. Transfers between levels of government and from outside the country (e.g., European Union) are excluded.

Source: International Monetary Fund. 1997. *Government Finance Statistics Yearbook 1997*, Country Tables.

Why Decentralize?

An important argument in favor of maintaining centralized control is to maintain stability. In countries that are less economically diversified and, therefore, more "exposed" to fluctuations in commodity process, natural disasters, wars, debt burdens, and chronic inflation, central government control of the main tax and borrowing instruments argues against extensive decentralization—though it should be noted that the exposure problem may well be an outcome of excessive centralization. Also, the local governments of many countries have very weak administrative capacities—again, possibly a result of the centralization policy itself.

The fact that much of the world is undergoing some form of decentralization, however, attests to its importance. There are at least three economic explanations for this trend:

- To enhance a nation's economic efficiency. An efficient solution is one that maximizes social welfare, subject to a given flow of land, labor, and capital resources. That set of governments closest to the citizens can adjust budgets (costs) to local preferences in a manner that best leads to the delivery of a bundle of public services that is responsive to community preferences. Subnational/local governments become agencies that provide services to identifiable recipients up to the point where the value placed on the last (marginal) amount of services that recipients are willing to pay for is just equal to the benefit they receive (Bird 1995).[2]

- Revenue mobilization. Well-functioning subnational/local governments are able to access some tax bases more readily than a central government can (e.g., certain user charges, rudimentary sales taxes, and real property taxes).[3] Local governments have the greatest comparative advantage in the property tax, especially in identification of the tax roll and collection. Where central governments have levied the property tax, it tends to be no more than a minor source of revenue.
- Size of jurisdictions. As subnational/local governments price appropriately those services that flow to their citizens, a more efficient jurisdiction results. Efficient pricing will also provide an incentive for experimentation in favor of various forms of intergovernmental (e.g., inter-local) cooperation in service delivery.

Frameworks of Multi-Level Finance

The traditional analysis of public finance examines the fiscal functions of subnational/local and central governments in terms of their respective (and

---

2. The notion that moving service provision closer to the people will lead to gains in local welfare is derived from median voter theories of public expenditure determination. These models come out of developed countries and are heavily influenced by the democratic processes of budget making. The model predicts, for example, that the level of tax effort and expenditure mix in local areas are responsive to (i) changes in the relative prices of public services; (ii) community income; and (iii) local preferences. Moreover, not only are people likely to get what they want and are willing to pay for, but they are more likely to hold elected representatives accountable for the quality of services delivered. Research in the United States demonstrates that as the cost of services go up, local governments purchase less. If local income rises, communities spend more on local services; and, if the structure of the population changes, so does the mix of public services (Bahl 1991).

3. An argument can be made for various forms of automobile taxation (Bahl and Linn 1992; Bird, Ebel, and Wallich 1995).

largely separate) roles and responsibilities for allocation, stabilization, and income distribution. The general conclusion is that, for the efficiency reasons stated above, the allocation function is largely a subnational/local responsibility. The traditional approach then assigns the stabilization and distribution roles to the center.

The Need For a Broader Model

The application of this framework to the transition/developing country case shows that it must be broadened. In nearly all countries, subnational finances critically influence the nation's ability to achieve goals of economic efficiency, privatization, macrostablility, and provision of the social safety net (distribution). And, in countries with a limited tradition of self-government, developing effective local and political institutions may be key to nation building. Here is where a key theme emerges: establishment of a well-functioning intergovernmental system is critical to the accomplishment of the reform objectives (efficiency, privatization, macrostability, income support, and nation-building) of most economies. The efficiency objective has already been mentioned; to summarize the other four:

PRIVATIZATION. If there has been a transfer of large parts of the stock of state enterprises from central to local governments, the latter have inherited a pivotal role in promoting or inhibiting privatization.

MACROSTABILITY. Local finance must be viewed in conjunction with the general objective of macroeconomic policies. With the need to reduce the overall public-sector deficit, it is essential that municipalities not be used as a vehicle for "soft budget constraints," whereby transferred responsibilities are financed by negotiations over the size of transfer payments.

INCOME SUPPORT. Important parts of the social safety net have also been delegated to subnational/local governments, even though this may violate the criteria for effective service delivery—a local government cannot be expected to deliver such services if, as is true generally, local government is chronically underfunded.

NATION BUILDING. Finally, some countries are explicitly "nation building" in the sense of designing an intergovernmental system that will serve as the fiscal "glue" for addressing their heterogeneous internal economic and demographic interests.

Once the problems of subnational/local responsibility in privatization, and the tendency for a "soft budget" constraint are addressed (in reforming countries, presumably a short- to medium-term problem), the transition/developed economy model will begin to conform to the traditional approach. However, the intergovernmental nature of the safety net responsibility will probably remain in flux for a very long time; and, where it matters, nation building will always be heavily intergovernmental.

A Review of Research Issues

Issues can be identified in five major areas in connection with launching the fiscal decentralization initiative, with many specific topics for research emerging under each of the five as the process unfolds.

Assignment of Expenditure Functions

Under the command economy, subnational/local governments had few, if any, autonomous spending responsibilities. Beginning in 1990, in Poland, several transition governments in Eastern Europe enacted "local self-government" laws, patterned after the Council of Europe's European Charter on Local Self-Government (Council of Europe 1985); a key feature of these laws is the assignment of various expenditure responsibilities ("competencies") among governments. Their implementation, however, varies greatly as, in some countries, the intent has been supplanted by the reality of central preemption of proposed subnational authority, or by the lack of institutional readiness of subnational governments. The fiscal decentralization process is one of on-going adjustment and experimentation (Bird and Vaillancourt 1998). As a nation's economy and demographics change, so must its institutions change—including its fiscal ones. Law-making and bureaucratic regulation is often just too cumbersome and imprecise a process for dealing with the complexity and subtlety of intergovernmental change (Hegedus and Tosics 1993; Bird, Ebel, and Wallich 1995).

The first question is whether an assigned activity is an appropriate governmental function. As technologies and group bargaining processes change, some activities that were once viewed as "public" may be accruing to the private sector—even major highways have become candidates for private-sector activity. Once an activity has been determined to be public, then assignment criteria (among which tradeoffs must then be identified and weighed) can be applied. In brief, functions should be assigned to the government that (i) has adequate legal authority and management capability; (ii) encompasses a geographical area commensurate with its functional responsibilities; and (iii) is willing to pursue intergovernmental policies for promoting inter-jurisdictional cooperation.

IMPLEMENTATION. Once agreement is secured regarding the merits of fiscal decentralization and the criteria for expenditure assignment best satisfied by central, regional or local governments, three related questions of government structure arise. First, should there be a general purpose intermediate government, such as a provincial level, between the central and the local? Second, are special-function districts desirable? (These are agencies established to finance and deliver a single type of service, such as water supply; they offer both an economically efficient and a politically viable option.) Third, is the size of local government efficient? (In some countries, the political imperative to create more local government units has led to fragmentation, and some form of consolidation should be considered.)

BEYOND ASSIGNMENT—ACCOUNTABILITY. If fiscal decentralization is to achieve its intended efficiency goals, it must be accompanied by policies that will ensure local budget discretion and fiscal accountability—the explicit linking of legislative decisions to decisionmakers (Bird, Ebel, and Wallich 1995). There are at least four barriers to accountability: (i) central hiring of personnel to perform services that are locally provided and managed (as with school teachers); (ii) unfunded mandates and preemptions of local authority (e.g., central orders to local governments to perform services for which they are not cost-reimbursed);[4] (iii) lack of local budgetary certainty (e.g., central withholding of agreed central transfers); and (iv) centrally set local expenditure norms (e.g., a mandate whereby the central government details cost and capacity specifications to be used in local service provision).[5]

Strengthening Subnational Finances

The system of subnational finance in many countries is characterized by subnational government dependence on transfers and shared taxes from the central government, and an almost complete lack of robust

---

4. The mandate question can be tricky. For example, a central mandate to protect the rights of ethnic minorities, and to provide for civil liberties, is essentially different from the unfunded fiscal mandate contemplated here.

5. The center's dictation of minimum service standards can be accomplished through the grant system.

own-revenue sources. As long as this situation prevails, it will not be possible for local governments to contribute to their nation's fiscal health by increasing their own tax effort. Table 4.2 presents the importance of transfers and own revenues for local governments in 46 countries. It shows a one-third/two-thirds split between grants and own revenues; taxes are the most important source of own revenues, accounting for two-thirds of them.

Because subnational governments must remain dependent on sharing central tax revenues, national tax policy will significantly affect the subnational revenue base—national tax policy becomes subnational tax policy. The key point of discussion focuses on "which taxes" should be assigned centrally rather than locally:

USER CHARGES AND FEES. A general rule in public finance is to charge for services whenever direct beneficiaries can be identified. When the consumption of a service benefits not only the direct users but also others (for example, consuming clean water reduces contagious diseases) then some subsidization may be appropriate. User charges and fees have a particularly appropriate role in infrastructure financing (new construction as well as upgrading and maintenance).

BROAD-BASED BUSINESS LEVIES. Business taxes are less well suited to subnational government. In order to minimize potential distortions in the flow of factors and goods within a nation, a high degree of national uniformity is desirable for levies such as the corporate income tax and the value added tax (VAT); the latter also has certain institutional characteristics, such as border adjustments, that make it an inappropriate local tax source.

PERSONAL INCOME TAX. Often a national tax, this can be also be effectively utilized locally, even for small units of government, especially by allowing for some form of "piggybacking" on the centrally defined and administered system (Davey and Peteri 1995).

REAL PROPERTY TAX. The role of property taxes is a major unanswered question in many economies. As noted above, they are ideally suited as benefits levies. In some countries progress is being made to take the first and necessary steps of setting up the required institutional mechanisms (e.g., cadastre, tax billing and collection systems). The importance of these steps should not be minimized, as setting up a property-tax system that does not work is probably a worse policy than not having one and relying on transfers funded by central taxes.

Table 4.2. Revenues of Local Governments, 46 Countries, 1993–96
(percent)

Country	Year	Grants	Own revenues	Total taxes[a]	Income taxes[b]	Property taxes	G&S[c]	FF&S[d]
Albania	1995	94.31	5.69	2.03	0.02	0.02	1.88	2.32
Australia	1996	17.06	82.94	43.45	—	43.45	—	26.35
Austria	1995	14.27	85.73	50.93	19.03	4.57	16.92	28.54
Belgium	1995	54.18	45.82	37.68	31.43	—	5.22	—
Bolivia	1996	9.88	90.12	79.37	2.45	7.14	45.34	7.28
Botswana	1994	83.19	16.81	9.79	0.07	8.47	0.73	2.32
Brazil	1993	64.59	35.41	13.35	—	4.30	8.03	4.02
Bulgaria	1996	33.87	66.13	53.80	48.36	3.66	1.75	7.16
Canada	1993	45.90	54.10	38.82	—	33.05	0.52	11.34
Croatia	1996	8.54	91.46	51.43	43.51	5.55	2.32	24.22
Czech Republic	1996	37.54	62.46	44.03	39.65	2.46	0.48	9.78
Denmark	1995	43.13	56.87	46.87	43.77	3.04	0.07	6.10
Estonia	1993	24.09	75.91	69.98	68.88	0.63	0.47	3.52
Finland	1995	28.34	71.66	38.91	—	—	—	0.09
France	1996	34.59	65.41	46.43	7.17	15.89	5.38	14.40
Germany	1993	34.57	65.43	27.90	24.18	3.46	0.25	—
Guatemala	1993	66.95	33.05	13.21	0.57	1.14	3.47	3.25
Iceland	1993	9.86	90.14	70.59	41.65	12.41	—	13.20
Ireland	1994	74.09	25.91	6.20	—	6.20	—	9.98
Israel	1994	42.02	57.98	32.40	—	30.70	—	9.35
Italy	1996	64.81	35.19	23.47	—	—	—	5.19
Kenya	1994	—	100.00	32.01	—	21.95	10.01	1.67

Table 4.2 (continued)

Country	Year	Grants	Own revenues	Total taxes[a]	Income taxes[b]	Property taxes	G&S[c]	FF&S[d]
Latvia	1995	24.91	75.09	73.16	59.42	11.61	2.13	0.79
Lithuania	1995	27.17	72.83	67.83	61.54	6.28	–	4.25
Luxembourg	1995	37.31	62.69	33.72	33.45	–	0.27	24.41
Malaysia	1996	26.47	73.53	–	–	–	–	–
Mexico	1994	2.12	97.88	76.90	0.09	18.22	1.29	14.52
Mongolia	1996	42.21	57.79	46.27	24.78	0.07	21.00	7.96
Netherlands	1996	64.79	35.21	11.47	–	3.95	1.01	10.05
Neth. Antilles	1994	3.03	96.97	90.06	84.59	1.66	3.80	2.36
New Zealand	1996	9.14	90.86	55.39	–	46.71	4.43	–
Nicaragua	1995	8.07	91.93	73.98	0.14	4.41	60.19	–
Norway	1995	38.64	61.36	43.95	39.37	4.34	0.25	13.91
Paraguay	1993	–	100.00	57.62	9.16	31.43	15.97	7.44
Peru	1996	53.23	46.77	15.11	–	–	–	–
Poland	1996	33.11	66.89	36.12	20.66	11.90	3.24	22.55
Portugal	1994	49.43	50.57	29.22	4.09	19.53	5.59	3.25
Romania	1994	41.79	58.21	49.27	3.18	6.26	0.41	5.13
Russia	1995	14.79	85.21	80.67	46.58	8.14	18.09	0.25
South Africa	1995	13.05	86.95	39.23	–	39.23	–	27.55
Spain	1994	34.76	65.24	46.18	9.23	12.89	21.42	8.91
Sweden	1996	13.88	86.12	77.08	77.08	–	–	–
Switzerland	1995	16.90	83.10	48.34	40.94	7.21	0.19	26.25
Thailand	1996	30.62	69.38	55.03	–	8.05	46.98	7.56
United Kingdom	1995	72.86	27.14	10.81	–	0.16	–	5.40

165

Table 4.2 (continued)

Country	Year	Grants	Own revenues	Total taxes[a]	Income taxes[b]	Property taxes	G&S[c]	FF&S[d]
United States	1995	38.81	61.19	40.86	2.36	30.15	8.34	11.60
Averages								
OECD		37.97	62.03	39.44	17.80	11.76	3.33	10.43
South and Central America		29.26	70.74	47.08	1.77	9.52	19.19	5.22
Eastern Europe		34.01	65.99	52.83	39.18	5.65	3.08	8.00
Africa/Asia		30.07	69.93	38.10	13.68	13.77	10.32	7.35
Total		34.41	65.59	43.28	19.29	10.44	6.90	8.57

a. Taxes (total and each item) as a percent of own revenue. Percentages shown in the Income, Property, and G&S taxes columns may not add to the figure shown in this ("Total taxes") column, since "other" local taxes (including social security contributions and other tax items) are not included in this table.

b. Income (personal/corporate) taxes.

c. G&S: Goods and services taxes (VAT, sales, etc.).

d. FF&S: Fees, fines, and sales of services. These are part of non-tax revenues which also include enterprise and property income, other non-tax income and capital income; they are thus not included as a component of the "Total taxes" column. Thus "Total taxes" and "FF&S" do not always add to "Own revenues."

Note: Averages are arithmetic means.

Source: International Monetary Fund, 1997. *Government Finance Statistics Yearbook 1997*, Country Tables L.

Sales taxes. Excise and single-stage retail taxes should be prime candidates for local use, especially if a taxing region is large enough to avoid revenue loss from customers crossing borders into lower-tax regions.

Tax sharing. Tax revenues can also be shared between central and subnational/local governments, with the center collecting the taxes. The system has the advantage of administrative simplicity and feasibility, an important consideration in most countries in which localities have yet to develop their own administrative capabilities. There are, however, some important disadvantages: it maintains the old regime's system of local fiscal dependence and thus undermines central as well as local fiscal accountability; it is incompatible with the efficient provision of local public services, which requires a system of intergovernmental transfers firm enough to serve as a basis for budget certainty, and flexible enough to be compatible with structural reform; and, to the extent that sharing is on an "origin" or "derivation" basis, as it almost always is, it may exacerbate local fiscal disparities by undercutting the equalization attributes of formula-based transfers.

Intergovernmental Transfers

Since a subnational government's ability to raise revenues rarely permits it to meet its expenditure needs, transfers are required to close the gaps. A key to making central-to-local transfers "work" is often to develop objective, formula-driven systems, whereby transfers are regularized and, at the margin, the costs and benefits of local decisions are borne locally. Within this context there are numerous issues that require the attention of policy analysts. They include the degree to which grants can be used to promote vertical balance among governments; the use of categorical or matching grants to correct for interjurisdictional spillovers; and the need to mitigate the impact on local jurisdictions and their residents of unequal fiscal resources and needs (Bird, Ebel, and Wallich 1995).

Borrowing and Debt

Borrowing is usually a minor source of finance for local governments in most developing market economies (Wallich 1992). This reflects both the generally conservative position of most local governments, and the limited sources of finance. While in principle there is no reason that local governments should not borrow, their access to credit should be constrained to prevent overextension. Many countries only permit borrowing that is limited to agreed and defined purposes and amounts. Furthermore, the amount of debt any city may incur must be related to its potential to repay; this may be based on revenues from the investment itself (for example, if user charges are imposed) or from general taxes. Indeed, borrowing, unless at subsidized rates—which is usually inappropriate—is only a way of bringing forward in time future tax revenues, and does not add new resources directly. Its relevance is that public investments thus financed may provide infrastructures that increase private output and, thus, the tax base.

Sources of borrowing include: bond finance (once local fiscal integrity is established and capital markets develop); the commercial banking system; a central government loan fund operated by ministries of local government; and a municipal development bank, usually capitalized by the center. In most countries where capital markets are not well developed, the central government limits and controls credit and borrowing. One reason for imposing such discipline is that public-sector borrowing may crowd out private-sector credit demands and, from a macro-economic point of view, it is generally desirable to constrain overall public-sector borrowing (Wallich 1992; Ebel, Fox, and Melhem 1995).

Managing State-Owned Enterprises

The potential for misuse of locally owned state enterprises is already apparent in some transition economies. Initially, the mass transfer of assets was expected to provide a one-time financial windfall that would be a source of start-up funds, while giving time to set up own-source revenue systems. The result has been mixed at best. Indeed, in some cases, rather than giving local governments a head start, large blocks of transferred state-owned enterprises with a negative net worth are inhibiting the development of financially viable subnational government. In these circumstances, the issue is not so much one of how to use the proceeds from privatization, but rather of how to manage the assets in order to build viable public institutions (e.g., utility monopolies), or to restructure enterprises so that they can be privatized in the future, or to prepare the enterprise for shutdown.

A Final Comment

What is—or should be—readily apparent from this brief review is the critical need to develop a body of research that will lay out, in a systematic and evenhanded manner, options for policy reform in a way that will make clear to policymakers the nature of their choices, and the tradeoffs among competing reform proposals. This is true even where the reform process is lagging. The point that matters is whether, when a country is ready to act politically, there will be a readily available set of research to frame the policy debate and choices among competing policy alternatives.

References

Bahl, Roy W. 1991. *Fiscal Decentralization: A Report Prepared for the Local Fiscal Management Study.* Washington, DC: U.S. Agency for International Development.

Bahl, Roy W., and Johannes F. Linn. 1992. *Urban Finance in Developing Countries.* Oxford: Oxford University Press.

Bird, Richard M. 1995. *Financing Local Services: Patterns, Problems and Possibilities.* Major Report 31. Toronto: Centre for Urban and Community Studies, University of Toronto.

Bird, Richard M., Robert D. Ebel, and Christine I. Wallich, eds. 1995. *Decentralization of the Socialist State.* Washington, DC: World Bank.

Bird, Richard M., and François Vaillancourt. 1998. "Fiscal Decentralization in Developing Countries: An Overview." In Richard M. Bird and François Vaillancourt, eds., *Fiscal Decentralization in Developing Countries*, pp. 1–48. Cambridge: Cambridge University Press.

Council of Europe. 1985. *European Charter of Local Self Government.* Strasbourg: Council of Europe.

Davey, Kenneth, and Gabor Peteri. 1995. *Local Tax Reform In Hungary.* Report prepared for the Hungarian Ministry of Finance.

Dillinger, William. 1994. *Decentralization and its Implications for Urban Service Delivery.* Washington, DC: World Bank.

Ebel, Robert D., William F. Fox, and Rita M. Melhem. 1995. *The Hashemite Kingdom of Jordan: Intergovernmental Fiscal Relations and Municipal Financial Management.* Sector Study. Washington, DC: World Bank.

Ehdaie, Jaber. 1994. *Fiscal Decentralization and the Size of Government.* Policy Research Working Paper 1387, Public Economics Division. Washington, DC: World Bank.

Hegedus, Jozsef, and Ivan Tosics. 1993. *The Structure and Problems of Local Government Budgets in Budapest and the Agglomeration Settlements.* Budapest: Metropolitan Research Institute.

Wallich, Christine. 1992. *Local Finance and Intergovernmental Fiscal Relations in Developing and Transition Economies.* Report prepared for the Economic Development Institute of the World Bank Urban Policy Seminar, Hanoi, Vietnam.

Wolman, Harold. 1990. "Decentralization: What Is It and Why We Should Care?" In Robert J. Bennett, ed., *Decentralization, Local Governments and Markets: Towards a Post-Welfare Agenda,* pp. 29–42. Oxford: Clarendon Press.

User Charges in Local Government Finance

Richard M. Bird

In some important respects, a local government is analogous to a business. It provides services to its customers—residents. In turn residents must pay for the services they receive. Of course, unlike a business, a government can impose taxes to finance its activities. Taxes, however, are "unrequited transfers" that bear no specific relation to the services that taxpayers receive. Taxes provide revenue to local governments, but that is all they do. In contrast, financing local services through user fees or charges not only provides funds with which to supply such services but also provides invaluable information on which services should be provided, in what quantity and quality, and to whom.

The Rationale for User Charges

To many people the very idea of charging for public services seems ridiculous; in a democracy, if an activity is carried out by the public sector, then presumably the market has been rejected as a means of obtaining the service in question. Attempts by governments to charge for services traditionally provided for free (like most parks) or to raise prices for services provided below cost (like roads) are thus likely to be viewed by the public at large, let alone by those more directly affected, as little more than a "revenue grab." Such views seem widespread in many countries, but they are often misconceived. Governments are engaged in a vast array of programs, some of which cannot and should not be priced in any meaningful way. For many government services, however, prices of various sorts are already charged, and for many others there are good reasons why they too should be priced. Moreover, some prices already charged (e.g., for roads) should be changed significantly. As a rule, what is now priced by government in most countries, and how it is priced, reflects historical accident and administrative convenience more than rational policy.

Those who benefit directly from the unpriced (or underpriced) provision of public services will be unhappy if proper charging policies are adopted. Most citizens, however, should welcome the adoption of a well-designed policy of cost recovery and user charges in the public sector—one which will lead to the best possible use of scarce public resources. Maximizing the efficiency with which scarce public resources are used is not the whim of an ideologically driven economist. It is simply common sense. Scarce public resources should surely be used to provide as large a bundle as possible of desired services, and that is all that is meant by efficient resource use.

The main economic rationale of user charges is thus *not* to produce revenue but to promote economic efficiency. Well-designed charges achieve this goal *both* by providing information to public-sector suppliers as to how much clients actually are willing to pay for particular services *and* by ensuring that what the public sector supplies is valued at least at (marginal) cost by citizens. If government expenditure is financed through general taxes, rational consumers will choose to consume it to the point at which the marginal costs *to them* just equal the marginal benefits they receive. When consumers are not explicitly charged for consuming a service, this means that the value they attach to the last unit they use is approximately zero. In reality, however, nothing in life is free, and there are real costs in providing any service. The result is that when no charge is imposed for a service, more of it will be consumed than society as a whole would really be willing to pay if the real costs were taken into account. "Under-pricing"—the free (or subsidized) provision of services—thus results in "over-consumption." As it were, resources are poured into a "black hole"; something goes in—the resources used in producing the "excess" services—but nothing of equal value to society comes out. The pernicious effects of this situation on both rational resource allocation and government finance may be accentuated if, as often occurs with respect to public infrastructure such as roads and airports, the resulting crowding is taken as a signal that there should be even more of the under-priced service provided. Good user charges can avoid such waste.

Designing User Charges

Unfortunately, determining the proper domain and design of user charges may sometimes be challenging. In principle, the economically efficient price for *any* good or service is the price that would be charged in a perfectly competitive market. Such a market is one in which there are many buyers and many sellers, all of whom have full information not only about the price and cost of the item in question but also about all possible substitute and complementary products. To be socially efficient, the goods in question must have no public goods characteristics, or, to put it another way, the prices of all products must fully reflect all external costs and benefits.

Moreover, any distributional issues must be assumed to be dealt with in other ways (for instance, by lump-sum transfers). Almost by definition, not all these conditions are likely to be satisfied when it comes to publicly provided goods and services. Of course, some of them—such as the competitiveness of markets—may not be fully satisfied with respect to the private sector either. But the problem is more serious in the public sector. Indeed, the economic rationale for public-sector activities arises largely because some or all of the conditions required to achieve market efficiency are violated: "publicness" matters; excludability is not feasible; scale and sunk cost factors result in monopoly provision; non-priced externalities are significant; or distributional concerns are important. Nonetheless, although these factors are important, their mere existence does not preclude charging for public services. Rather, such problems imply simply that care is needed in designing appropriate user charges. It is important not only to impose user charges where appropriate but also to "get the prices right" and to impose the *correct* charges.

Marginal Cost Pricing

Efficient public-sector user charges are marginal cost prices. Implementing this simple principle may prove difficult for two major reasons. First, it may be hard to define costs properly in the case of many public-sector activities. Second, even if such costs can be clearly defined, it may be difficult to estimate them in the quantitative terms needed to determine appropriate user charges.

The costs relevant to marginal cost pricing are quite different from the costs with which public sector managers, even those operating activities already structured as cost centers, are likely to be familiar. The notion of cost in financial accounting refers to identifiable monetary outlays incurred in the process of carrying out a particular activity. Such costs include, for example, wages, rent, utilities, transportation, and supplies. The figures reporting such costs reflect actual financial outlays made in some particular time period. However, *economic* costs are not accounting costs. The fundamental economic concept of cost is opportunity cost—the value of the benefits that could have been obtained had the inputs been used for some alternative purpose. From this perspective, the cost of, say, a park does not simply consist of any tangible construction and operation costs that might be recorded in some financial accounts. Instead, the relevant cost is the (highest) value that the land could have realized had it been used for some other purpose, such as logging or residential development.

Effective application of the marginal cost pricing principle requires estimation of such social or opportunity costs. This may be a difficult task. Moreover, estimating the *marginal* cost of providing another unit of a particular service requires the identification of all the additional costs arising as a result of this incremental expansion. Congestion in transport facilities clearly gives rise to real social costs, for example, but it may be hard to convert such costs of waiting into monetary values, as must be done to add them to other relevant costs in order to determine efficient prices. Even when there are no conceptual problems in measuring the relevant marginal costs, there may be problems of measurability. Often, for example, some relevant market price can be found—for example, the value of land used for a park if it were to be logged, or built on. But such prices can be used to measure socially relevant marginal costs only if it can be assumed that market prices are good approximations to marginal cost prices.

Apart from defining and identifying costs appropriately, several additional basic issues must be decided in determining efficient marginal cost prices. One of the most important concerns the question of whether fixed costs (investment costs) are to be included. In principle, in order to ensure the efficient allocation of resources, it is clearly *short-run* marginal cost (SRMC) prices that should be imposed. Only when such charges are imposed will existing facilities be efficiently used. To achieve this result, however, it must be assumed that the size of the facility is optimal to begin with—a most unlikely eventuality given the way in which most public sector investment decisions have been made in the past. For SRMC prices to be appropriate for existing capital facilities, the prices must be altered as usage changes. That is, when there is excess capacity, no charge will be imposed, but as usage levels rise, user charges will also rise to reflect increasing congestion costs—so that when the time comes to replace the facility, the funds will be available to do so. The problem with this solution is twofold. First, as noted earlier, congestion costs are in any case difficult to estimate accurately. Second, even if such costs can be estimated, user charges, once set, tend often to be "sticky," that is, difficult to alter significantly without major political and administrative efforts. Such efforts are particularly unlikely to prove rewarding when the task is to raise prices to pay for a deteriorating level of service.

If instead, fixed costs are included in the initial pricing calculation—that is, *long-run* marginal costs (LRMC) are used as the basis for setting user charges—overbuilt facilities will be even more underutilized than would otherwise be the case. Moreover, managers will not be able to benefit from the demand information signaled by observed reactions to SRMC prices. A wide range of public-sector activities, particularly those involving large capital investments in infrastructure, may be characterized as facing decreasing average costs. Facilities with large sunk costs and high economies of scale, such as hydroelectric plants and telecommunication networks, are examples. As output expands in such cases the cost per unit falls, at least up to some point. But if average costs are decreasing, then marginal costs—the cost of providing an additional unit of service—must, by definition, be below average costs. Applying marginal cost pricing in such cases thus means that the user charge will be less than average cost, which in turn means that efficient charges will result in financial deficits.

Average Cost Pricing

How can such deficits be financed? One obvious solution is by general taxes. But why should the beneficiaries of the service in question be subsidized by taxpayers in general? An alternative solution might be to set prices at average costs rather than marginal costs. All costs would then be recovered, but of course with higher prices presumably the use of the facility would decline below the socially desirable level. Nonetheless, this obviously inefficient practice is often followed in practice simply because such prices are easier to calculate (especially if only financial costs are considered, as is usually the case). As usually applied, the average cost pricing approach estimates the total financial cost of providing a particular service and divides by the number of units currently provided to obtain the appropriate user charge.

There are two major problems with this approach. First, as already stressed, the result will not be efficient. If costs decline as output increases, the price will be too high and the output less than society really wants. If costs increase as output expands, the price will be too low, too much of the service in question will be demanded, and resources will again be misallocated—especially if the excess demand at the unduly low price is taken as an indication that output should be increased by new investment. Only if unit costs are constant, so that marginal and average costs are equal, does average cost pricing make efficiency sense. Secondly, setting average cost prices to recover operating costs requires not only information about how unit costs change as the number of users change but also information on how the number of users will change as prices change. Such information is not easy to obtain. Even if it is available, the resulting prices are unlikely to result in either an efficient allocation of resources (because of the difference between average and marginal costs) or in any useful information as to whether the facility should be extended or eliminated (because the fixed cost aspect has not been factored into the calculation).

Average Incremental Cost Pricing

A compromise approach that may sometimes be useful is average incremental cost (AIC) pricing. Essentially, this approach attempts to calculate the costs incurred as a result of an additional user—like marginal cost pricing—but it does so in a way designed not only to result in full cost-recovery (as in some versions of average cost pricing) but also to be computationally feasible in the real world of public-sector managers. The idea is simply to allocate each element of costs, fixed and variable, financial and (to the extent readily measurable) social, to a particular incremental decision with respect to providing a service, and then to assign to each additional user the incremental cost attributable, on average, to his or her usage.

For example, when a vehicle enters a highway at a particular time, the costs attributable to this decision may be broken down into those arising from the addition of one person at this time at this place (e.g., congestion), those attributable to the place (e.g., building the highway to its particular dimensions), and those attributable to the trip (e.g., wear and tear on the road). An approximation to efficient pricing in this case might be some combination of a time penalty at peak times, appropriate charges for cost recovery for road use (e.g., wear and tear, which is exponentially related to vehicle axle-weight, as well as accidents, which are related to driving records), and perhaps some sort of access charge (vehicle license) to recover the fixed cost of highways. Such charges could be levied in part on vehicles (vehicle licenses), in part on vehicle use (gasoline taxes; tolls), and in part on drivers (drivers' licenses). In each of these cases, the appropriate user charge could be calculated on the basis of available accounting information, supplemented by additional information as needed to take into account important social costs not accounted for in this way (noise, pollution, congestion), and the resulting charges imposed on users as a class on an average basis. Such a system does not by any means amount to marginal cost pricing in the strict sense, but it may be about as close as one can get in practice.

Multi-Part Tariffs

A somewhat similar approach to pricing is through the use of what is called a multi-part tariff. In their simplest form, such tariffs impose a fixed access charge—for example, for connecting to the network—and then an additional charge related directly to the amount of use made of the system. When it is easy to identify the characteristics of the users of a public service, multi-part tariffs may be useful in achieving efficiency. Suppose, for example, that the responsiveness to price change by two distinct groups of users (say, sport and commercial fishing boats) is known, and is different. The less elastic (responsive) the demand, the higher the price that should be charged on efficiency grounds. Those with more choices, who can more easily switch to other services, will reduce demand more for a given increase in prices. Although it may not always seem "fair," the way to maximize efficiency (and in this case also revenue) is to charge more to those who have fewer choices.

Variable Block Pricing

Another common form of price discrimination is declining block pricing, a practice common in some public utilities. Such pricing is closely related to the common practice of imposing lower unit charges on more frequent users (commuters, park visitors, etc.). The basic idea is that the more you use, the less—per unit—you pay. Such a pricing strategy may make sense for a facility with substantial excess capacity, but even then care must be used to ensure that the extra consumption thus encouraged does not cluster and create a peak-load problem. To illustrate, in the case of a transit system, if the system is underutilized except at peak times it may make sense to offer discounts for off-peak travelers, perhaps with the unit price declining the more such travel takes place. But it *never* makes sense to offer similar reductions to the regular commuters who are already straining the system's capacity at peak periods.

As this example suggests, the distributional effects of such pricing may be considered good—the poor, the old, and students who travel off-peak benefit. Or it may be considered bad—the poor commuters who must be at work by 8.30 a.m. are penalized. Sometimes public utilities have for distributional reasons introduced what are called "lifeline" block pricing systems, under which an initial small block of service (e.g., so many kilowatt/hours of power) is priced much below cost. This approach is more logical than declining block pricing, but, as noted below, such distributional considerations should not in the first instance be taken into account in deciding the appropriate level and structure of public sector prices.

Pricing Externalities

Many public services provide not only "private" benefits to direct recipients but also some "public" benefit in the form of an externality. Education, for example, is easy to price. A large guard could be stationed at the classroom door to keep out those who did not pay. But this does not mean that it necessarily makes sense to charge the entire cost to the presumed direct beneficiaries—the students. All citizens gain to some extent from raising the general level of education. This external benefit should be taken into account in setting the price that should be charged for education, as for many other services provided by the public sector at all levels. Indeed, as noted earlier, unless there is some element of general public purpose or externality, it is not clear why an activity should be provided by a public agency in the first place.

The obvious way to take external benefits into account in setting user charges is to estimate the size of the marginal benefit provided to an additional user by the service in question, and then to set the price equal to marginal cost less this external benefit. The resulting financial deficit could then be funded from general revenues. Unfortunately, it is almost always difficult to measure external social benefits in any convincing way. Discussions on this issue tend to reduce to little more than assertions about individual preferences and perceptions. The few attempted studies of external benefits (e.g., of education) suggest that in most cases they are substantially less (say, 10 to 30 percent) than the share often financed from general sources, such as through intergovernmental transfers (say, 50 to 90 percent). In the absence of better information, the best way to deal with this question is probably to put the burden of proof on those subsidies. The appropriate initial position in formulating sound public policy is that any public service with an easily identifiable direct beneficiary should be paid for by that beneficiary, *unless* sound and convincing arguments in favor of a particular degree of explicit public subsidy can be produced. This starting point is in complete opposition to that which many countries seem to have adopted, namely, that whatever subsidies now exist are right, so that the onus of proof for any change lies with the proponents of change.

If there is to be a subsidy, it should be paid in the most efficient way. One approach much used in the public sector (for instance, in education and health) is to pay a *supply* subsidy in order to induce providers to lower their charges to direct users. This approach may be administratively convenient, but it has serious problems. For example, if the subsidy paid depends upon the number of users, inefficient overexpansion may be encouraged. Similarly, the subsidy may go to the wrong people from the point of view of public policy—for instance, to the rich (whose demand for the service is more likely to be elastic) rather than the poor (whose demand is inelastic). Supply subsidies may also result in the provision of "gold-plated" services, that is, services that cost more to produce than society would really be willing to pay if it explicitly had to do so. If such concerns are thought to be significant, shifting from a supply subsidy to a *demand* subsidy is an obvious possible alternative approach. For example, a tax credit or a transfer payment related to the consumption of the service in question might be directed to (the chosen) consumers. Although potentially important, this possible line of approach is not further discussed here. If supply subsidies are to be continued, they should to the extent possible be pre-determined in the budget process, and hence less subject to manipulation by suppliers.

Pricing Local Services More Effectively

Local governments already charge fees and prices for many services. But existing fees are often defective. Water rates, for example, are frequently applied as fixed charges, independent of the volume of water consumed. Consequently, the marginal cost of consumption is zero, leading to over-consumption of water and over-investment in water capacity. Even when metering of water consumption is applied but declining block rates are used, prices may be less than marginal cost for large water consumers, favoring those with big lawns and backyard swimming pools. The fact that sewer charges are usually pro-rated on the amount of the water bill only compounds such pricing errors.

Distance from the source of supply, for example, should matter in setting an appropriate user fee, as should the time of use when there are peaks in demand. The "postage stamp pricing" approach (uniform everywhere) almost never makes economic sense (although it may sometimes be warranted when administration and enforcement costs are taken into account). User fees should correspond to the marginal costs of providing service to each consumer. To cover capital or fixed costs, a connection (or admission) fee should be charged. Such a two-part pricing policy is a more efficient pricing instrument than a user fee set at the level of average total cost. Local governments should be encouraged to adopt an appropriate fee-for-services approach to program delivery wherever possible. Many waste-management facilities and parking lots, for example, are seriously under-priced in most countries.

The Costs and Process of User Charges

The information required to design appropriate user charges is often hard to obtain. Even if the costs of a public-sector activity—for example, the cost of admitting a person to a park in the off season—may readily be calculated, the cost of collecting such a charge may exceed its amount. If so, no charge should be levied. Every road could be a toll road. But the cost of collecting all those tolls—both the administrative and compliance cost and the related social cost of added congestion—means that such charging makes no sense.

An additional factor that should be taken into account in determining user charges is the cost of changing public prices once they have been set. The prices set by public agencies inevitably reflect the outcome of a political and administrative process. User charges are thus inevitably political to some extent and hence, like all political institutions, inherently hard to change. Once set, they tend to prevail until circumstances permit changes. In part for this reason, it is particularly important to set initial prices as close as practicable to economically efficient prices. An initial mistake can last a long time.

Since user charges are inevitably to some extent politically determined, it is important to provide an adequate process both of consultation with affected groups and of review by the public (and perhaps also by an appropriate central government agency) in order to ensure both that the prices set are reasonable and acceptable, and that subsequent adjustments can and will be made as appropriate. The details of just how this might done of course need to be worked out with care for each particular area, but a few general principles may be stated here.

First, it is important to set out clearly the parameters within which individual public sector managers can determine prices. Political processes are distinguished from market processes primarily by emphasis on perceived procedural fairness. It is therefore imperative to set out clearly exactly what this means and how it is to be attained in user charge policy.

Second, it is important to provide clear and strong incentives for managers to impose efficient user charges. Unless they have something to gain from the difficult task of designing and implementing such charges, it is unclear what their incentive would be. This problem may be especially important when, as may sometimes be the case, the result of adopting proper pricing policies would likely be to reduce the demand for the service, and hence to shrink the size of the agency budget.

Third, if the prices set by a particular agency are subject to central review, the principles that will guide the review should be clearly stated and their application demonstrated clearly to the affected managers and the concerned public. Public-sector managers, by definition, cannot and should not be expected to respond solely to the "bottom line" in any financial sense. If they could be, the activity in question should not be in the public sector. But they cannot be expected to act efficiently in pursuit of public policy objectives if the lines and rationale of accountability are not made crystal clear.

Fourth, the relevant public interest is that of the population as a whole. This point must be emphasized to offset an inevitable tendency: the only public voice to be heard on charging policy is that of the direct beneficiaries of the previous policy, who are clear losers. Of course, efforts must also be made to persuade affected groups that the pricing policy adopted is reasonable. To achieve this, the policy must not only *be* reasonable, but it must be persuasively presented as such to a group of people whose natural interests are generally diametrically opposed to user charges. One way to do this may be to persuade the directly affected users that if they do not pay a price reasonably related to the benefits they personally receive, the service will not be provided.

Finally, experience suggests that the major area of general public concern with user charges is that they are "unfair" and "regressive." Such concerns will, of course, often be raised by directly affected users in pursuit of their own interests; but they may nonetheless be quite real. In reality, however, appropriately designed user charges may be fair and even progressive. If taxpayers pay for identifiable public services that they consume, and no one either receives a service without paying for it or pays without receiving a service, this outcome would probably be perceived by many to be perfectly fair. The rich, as a rule, pay no more or no less for bread or milk than the poor. Why should they pay more or less for a fishing license? Nonetheless, the public sector makes less use of charges than seems warranted, in part because of their perceived adverse distributional effects. If, for example, a service that was previously provided free of charge to everyone will now extract the same payment from everyone who uses it, how can the new user charges not hurt low-income households? On closer examination, such arguments are less convincing than may first appear. What would happen in the absence of adequate user charges? Who really benefits from a zero-price policy? The answers to such questions need to be carefully examined before the "fairness" of imposing user charges for any particular program can be appraised.

The income profile of consumers of a large range of government services suggests that upper-income households may sometimes benefit disproportionately from the consumption of free, or low-cost, public services. For example, low storage and landing fees at local public docks disproportionately benefit the few households that own private yachts, and most of the benefits from subsidized higher education accrue to upper-income families. There is certainly no presumption that zero-priced public services are necessarily either effective or efficient means of redistributing income, assuming that is what society wishes to do. Moreover, if charges sufficient to cover marginal costs are introduced, fewer general taxes—a significant share of which are paid by the poor, and which carry their own economic costs—would have to be collected. Indeed, if properly designed and applied, such user charges might even extract proportionately more from the rich than from the poor.

In such instances—and there may be more of them than seems commonly to be recognized—the introduction of correct user charges should improve both the efficiency *and* the equity of public-sector operations.

Two alternative strategies may perhaps be utilized to alleviate such distributional concerns. The first is to present a detailed and convincing study of the expected distributional effects of imposing user charges. If such effects are not serious, this should be demonstrated convincingly. If, however, there may indeed be some adverse distributional effects, a second approach of admitting their existence and demonstrating what will be done to offset them should be followed. Among the possible offsets might be devices such as "lifeline" pricing schemes (access to an initial basic quantity of the service for everyone at low prices) or compensating changes in general transfer payments. Alternatively, for certain services, some variant of a "smart-card" scheme might be appropriate; all users would access the service using a card, but low-income users would be given a certain initial credit on their cards, thus simultaneously achieving universality (everyone has the same card) and targeting (those who need it have free or subsidized access).

Similar approaches should be taken in other areas of legitimate public concern for the possible adverse effects of user charges on the achievement of relevant public policy goals. *Either* people have to be persuaded that such effects will not in fact occur, or will be so small that they will not matter; *or* they have to be convinced that the goals in question can and will be more efficiently and effectively achieved by explicit budgetary subsidies, or in some other way. Close attention to such political-economy issues is often the key to public acceptance of more rational policies on user charges.

For Further Reading

Bailey, S. 1988. *Practical Charging Policies for Local Government.* Discussion Paper 20. London: Public Finance Foundation.

Bird, R.M., and T. Tsiopoulos. 1997. "User Charges for Public Services: Potentials and Problems." *Canadian Tax Journal* 45: 25–86.

Kitchen, H. 1993. *Efficient Delivery of Local Government Services.* Discussion Paper 93–15. Kingston, Canada: School of Policy Studies, Queen's University.

Meier, G.M. 1983. *Pricing Policy for Development Management.* Baltimore: Johns Hopkins University Press for the World Bank Economic Development Institute.

Mushkin, S., ed. 1972. *Public Prices for Public Products.* Washington, DC: The Urban Institute.

The Demand-Side Approach to Planning Water Supply

Sumila Gulyani

Proponents of the demand-side approach present it as the "new" and alternative way to plan and provide water and sanitation services in developing countries. In its simplest form, the new approach argues that utilities should "provide services that people want and for which they are willing to pay"—a notion that has existed in public finance theory and literature for a long time (for example, Milliman 1972; Gramlich 1994).

There are, however, few precedents in either the developed or the developing world of water utilities that: (a) provide service only to those households willing to pay the full cost; and (b) consciously plan to provide a lower level of service, or no service at all, because a particular community has a lower willingness to pay. The latter point is normatively different from a situation where a utility *de facto* provides no service, or poorer service, for instance, to a squatter settlement; the new approach argues that it is actually legitimate for the utility not to provide service to a neighborhood that is not willing to pay. The two points are the distinguishing features of the new—and World Bank-led—demand-driven approach to water supply.

This articles presents an analytical overview of the demand-side approach, its key features, and central arguments. It also discusses how the proponents of the demand-driven approach perceive the problem with water supply, their interpretation of why supply-side approaches do not work, and the evidence that has influenced them. The final section discusses the contributions and weaknesses of this approach.

The Water Problem and the Inadequacy of Supply-Side Solutions

The *World Development Report 1992* (World Bank 1992) estimates that about a billion people do not have access to adequate water supply; specifically, 170 million urban residents lack a source of potable water near their home, and 855 million rural residents are without safe water. Traditional supply-side projects are unlikely to solve this problem, however, since they have not worked well in the past. A World Bank evaluation of water projects found that an estimated one in four water systems are not working at any one time, and the number of systems being abandoned is approximately equal to the number of systems being commissioned (Briscoe et al. 1990). Further, even when the improved systems do function they are often not used—for example, surveys in Kenya and Côte d'Ivoire show that only one-third of the population reported to have access to improved facilities actually use them (Briscoe et al. 1990).

The World Bank's Water Demand Research Team (1993) argues that project failure and lack of maintenance can be directly ascribed to a focus on supply-side issues in water provision, and a lack of understanding of demand for water. The Team notes, for example, that the supply-side rule of thumb that people will pay about 3 to 5 percent of their income has no basis. Similarly, the notion that rural households cannot afford to pay for water is often a mistake. These incorrect understandings have led to massive and poorly targeted subsidization of service, that has helped the rich but not the poor, has hurt the financial viability of utilities, and has led to deterioration in service reliability and, consequently, to low willingness to pay by users—most communities are now caught in a low-level equilibrium trap.

The Bases for the New Demand-Driven Paradigm

Even as evidence of problems with supply approaches was mounting, micro-studies were documenting widespread use of water vending in developing countries. These studies have found that a majority of the population in cities as different as Jakarta, Indonesia; Onitsha, Nigeria; and Port-au-Prince, Haiti relies on private water vendors, and that they are paying exorbitant prices—several times those charged by the government utility—for these services. In Onitsha, for example, of a population of roughly 100,000 households, only 8 percent, or 8,000 households, have access to working water connections, and the vast majority relies on the vending system (Whittington, Lauria, and Mu 1991). During the dry season, the vending system collects about 24 times as much revenue as the public water utility. On an annual basis, households in Onitsha pay water vendors twice the operation and maintenance cost of a piped distribution system. In contrast to the rule of thumb that people will pay a maximum of 3 to 5 percent of their income, the poorest households are paying the most for water—as much as 18 percent of their income during the dry season, versus 2 to 3 percent for upper-income households. The conclusion is clear—even in this relatively poor and small town in Nigeria, household expenditures on water are sufficient to make a piped-water system feasible and allow full cost recovery.

The results from Onitsha are consistent with findings elsewhere. Even in an affluent city like Jakarta, only 20 percent of the population has access to piped water (Crane 1994), and in Port-au-Prince, Fass (1988) finds that the poorest households sometimes spend as much as 20 percent of their income on water.

Key Features of the Demand-Driven Approach

There are three arguments that lie at the center of the demand-side approach. First, water subsidies meant for the poor benefit only the rich, bankrupt the utilities, and lock communities into a low-price low-quality trap. Second, the poor do pay for water, and all types of communities are willing to pay a lot for higher quality services. Together these arguments lead to the conclusion that utilities can and should charge full costs for water and use the revenues to improve service and expand coverage—that is, utilities should aim to move from a low-price, low-quality service for all households to a high-price, high-quality service for those that are willing to pay for it.

The goal of the new approach is to select projects that have a higher chance of success—projects that are economically justifiable and financially sustainable. For this, supply needs to be matched to demand. The intent is to give customers better service, and also choice of service level based on their willingness to pay; and to give utilities revenues, and incentives to perform. While there is little literature that explicitly articulates the "official" or standard position on planning and implementing demand-driven projects, the following is what that literature appears to suggest.

Project selection must be economically justifiable. While this might sound like a standard rule, a review of World Bank water projects has revealed that economic benefits had not been estimated (quantified) in most projects—that is, good economic analysis was not a criterion for selection. The new approach appears to suggests two rules: (a) maximize net benefits (the sum of the producer and consumer surplus)—this requires relatively accurate estimates of demand and supply/cost curves; and (b) select only those projects for which there can be full cost recovery.

Typically, this involves household-level surveys (with appropriate sampling techniques) for each of the communities that a project intends to cover. The surveys need to identify, for example, alternative water sources, perceived quality, current levels of water use, and expenditures on water. More important, the surveys estimate users' willingness to pay. Surveys in one community usually cannot be used to predict household behavior even in a neighboring community; studies have found water demand to be extremely site-specific (Griffin et al. 1995).

As concerns selection of level of service and alternatives, given that project planners have studied and understand local demand and practices, they are in a better position to assess which systems the community prefers, which of various technical alternatives is likely to work, and which alternatives are economically and financially viable. Further, customers can choose a higher or different level of service if they pay for it. Proponents of demand-driven planning argue that this is a key difference from supply-side planning, which has tended to focus on identifying one best technical solution within the bounds of arbitrarily established constraints or rules of thumb, and has not offered alternatives.

User fees are, of course, a central piece of the new approach. These are critical because they will help to reduce wasteful consumption and curtail excess demand that arises when a valued good is provided free. Further, user fees help to ensure that utilities have adequate revenues which they can use to improve service quality and reliability, and to expand service to cover a greater number of people, in particular the poor.

Metering is necessary to levy appropriate user charges. Each water connection must be metered; per capita charges or flat monthly fees are not really tenable because they compromise the key goal of economic efficiency. Metering also provides the utility with valuable information on consumption that can be used to design an appropriate tariff structure.

Tariff structure and rates need to be designed to ensure that the full capital, operation, and maintenance costs can be recovered. To be efficient, the volumetric tariff should be set equal to the marginal cost of service provision. However, this may result in the utility losing money because average costs tend to be higher than the marginal cost of production. To solve the problem, the tariff could be designed as a two-part charge—for example, the monthly bill would consist of a fixed fee, plus a variable charge with the tariff or rate per unit of consumption being set equal to the marginal cost of production.

Apart from the tariff rate the utility also needs to decide on the tariff structure—that is, whether to use block tariffs or uniform tariffs and whether to cross-subsidize among user groups. In contrast to existing practice in most developing countries, the demand-side approach recommends neither increasing nor decreasing blocks, but a uniform tariff structure.[6] The approach also argues for an elimination of cross-subsidies among user groups and, in particular, from industry and commercial establishments to residential users.

---

6. Developing countries have often opted for an increasing block tariff structure based on the understanding that the rich consume more and can afford to pay more. Recent studies show, however, that this may be a highly inappropriate structure. This

The only exception that may be required for poor households is, perhaps, an amortization of connection charges (World Bank 1992); in rare cases, free public taps and subsidized connection charges may be justifiable.

Proponents of the new demand-driven approach emphasize that it needs to be implemented as a whole, internally consistent "package," and they do not leave much room for alternative interpretations. Thus far, however, the approach has not been implemented anywhere as a package; it is likely that governments may chose to implement only certain aspects of it, or to rely on demand-side studies only to tailor their usual supply-side approaches.

Although there is no evidence on whether the recommendations suggested by demand-side planners would work, there is one case where the power of the demand-side approach as a planning tool has been tested. In Kerala, India, a willingness-to-pay survey was conducted before a water project was implemented; three years later, a follow-up study checked the accuracy of people's stated intentions (Griffin et al. 1995). The surveys showed accurate prediction of the proportion of households that would connect (91 percent accuracy), and surprising accuracy in assessing individual household behavior—71 percent of the households did as they intended (i.e., to connect or not connect to the system).

Policy Implications

The World Bank (1992, 1994) argues that developing countries need to adopt the policy of providing, at full cost, private services that people want (water and collection of waste water) and allocating scarce public funds only for services with wider communal benefits (treatment and disposal of waste water). Willingness-to-pay studies are, for the Bank, an appropriate tool for assessing the services and service levels that people want.

The implications of this approach are best illustrated by the Bank's approach to rural water provision. The Bank has developed a typology of villages based on their demand for water, and suggests how one might begin designing programs for these rural communities (see World Bank 1992, 1994; World Bank Water Demand Research Team 1993). In this

---

is because poor households tend not to have individual connections. Often, several poor households share a connection, or buy from other households and kiosks; consequently, the poor frequently end up paying a significantly higher average price than richer households with individual connections (Whittington 1992; Crane 1994).

approach, villages where households have a high willingness-to-pay are provided with piped water connections and the tariffs are set to recover full costs. In villages where the willingness-to-pay is somewhat lower, the recommended strategy is to provide public water points or kiosks that charge for water. In villages where willingness-to-pay for any kind of improved service is low, the recommended strategy is to do nothing (unless a willingness-to-pay emerges).

Overall, the decision on what level of service to provide to a community as a whole—private piped connections, metered yard taps, public taps, water kiosks, or boreholes—depends primarily on one factor: the amount that the community is willing to pay. However, the top level of service—piped water and metered private connections—should be made available to households who are willing to pay for it, even in communities where the majority will be offered access only to lower-level systems such as public taps. Whether this approach will lead to a system that is much different from the current situation—where only the rich have piped water connections—remains unclear. A key benefit, however, is that the rich and "connected" will be required to pay substantially more for their water.

Contributions of the "Demand" Literature

Micro-level demand studies and the broader literature on demand-side approaches have made a valuable contribution to our understanding of household demand for water, and household-level decisions on source choice. These studies provide important hints as to why people may or may not connect to a new system, and the variables that planners need to consider. Five insights appear to be particularly significant.

First, the literature emphasizes the "jointness" of various independent variables in determining demand and source choice (World Bank Water Demand Research Team 1993). Previous studies have tended to focus on individual variables such as income or distance, while the new studies emphasize that income is not the sole determinant and, often, not even the most important determinant of demand. Rather, three sets of characteristics—socioeconomic characteristics of the household, characteristics of existing water sources, and household attitudes towards public provision—jointly influence a household's willingness to pay for, or use, an improved water source.

Second, water projects may result not only in health benefits, but also in savings in time and energy spent in collection, and in substantial reductions in the price that previously unserved households now need to pay for water. If, indeed, a water project provides piped connections or yard taps to households, and eliminates the need to buy water from vendors at exorbitant prices, it is likely to result in substantial savings for poor households, even if the charges are based on a principle of full cost recovery. Such projects can thus directly contribute to poverty alleviation (Whittington and Swarna 1994).

A third, related, contribution is the finding that poor households pay high prices for water, prices that are substantially higher than those paid by better-off households served by public utilities. The studies also show how well-intentioned policies such as increasing block tariffs can hurt the poor, and how projects might be better tailored to meet the needs of the poor.

Fourth, the finding that demand is very location-specific has serious implications for the design of projects. Finally, if one case—that of Kerala—can be counted as evidence, the demand-driven approach does appear to have developed analytical techniques and planning tools that have reasonable predictive power.

Weaknesses of the Demand-Driven Approach

Demand-side proponents admit that, thus far, a majority of the work has focused on shedding light on "levels of service and financing arrangements that will emerge from a demand-driven approach," and that it has not addressed critical institutional questions (World Bank Water Demand Research Team 1993, p. 65). Further, as the package of recommendations has not been implemented anywhere, there is no empirical evidence to support the notion that this approach is likely to work better than the previous one. The following outlines some of its weaknesses.

Proponents highlight the contrast between their perception of the user/ household with that of the supply-side planners. They argue, for example, that supply-side planners have assumed that rural households cannot afford to pay for expensive systems, and should be provided the cheapest and most durable technical solution. Demand-driven planning assumes that users are rational decisionmakers (in economic terms), they fully understand the value of clean water, and their decision on whether to connect or not reflects economic trade-offs. Hence, understanding household behavior and decisionmaking is sufficient to guide policy. Although the two approaches place themselves at opposite ends of the spectrum on household behavior, the reality and better approach is more likely to lie somewhere in between. As many health experts working on developing countries would argue, they are in the business of changing peoples' attitudes and behavior, not of accepting them as demand-driven planners suggest they do (cf. Cheo, Whittington, and Lauria 1996).

A second criticism is that the methodology on which these studies are based is fraught with problems that can lead to serious errors. Willingness-to-pay studies suffer from various kinds of bias—hypothetical, strategic, and compliance bias (for example, see Griffin et al. 1995)—and the methodology may be too prone to error in the context of the human resource constraints of many developing countries.

Third, while the demand-driven approach itself emphasizes the jointness and complexity of predicting demand for water, it selects but one variable—the price that people are willing to pay—to assess whether they would switch to a new source. Users may be willing, for example, to pay for piped water, but if they do not like the taste, they may still choose not to use the source; despite a perfectly valid willingness-to-pay assessment, the "improved" water source may not be used.

Fourth is the lack of attention to institutional factors: (a) the capacity required to implement the approach; and (b) the way in which the new approach interprets institutional problems such as non-performance of utilities. The first is an important pragmatic concern. The demand-driven approach requires that the problems of each community or village be independently identified and that the solutions be tailored accordingly. However, a World Bank water demand study in the Punjab itself admits: "the institutional capacity does not currently exist on the part of the government to undertake the kind of technical assistance required to address the needs and conditions of villages on a community-by-community basis" (Altaf et al. 1993). The second—perhaps the greatest weakness—is that the new approach does not really acknowledge a key lesson of experience: it is the lack of institutional capacity, combined with inappropriate institutional arrangements that have been the key causes of failure, not only of water projects but of development projects in general (Israel 1987; Therkildsen 1988; Ostrom, Schroeder, and Wynne 1993). In other words, it is not just prices or user charges that have been "incorrect." By contrast, the demand-driven approach assumes—rather simplistically—that one of the key problems is the lack of appropriate charges; that these charges can be designed, implemented, and enforced by the utilities; and that, once they have revenues, water utilities will (automatically) have the incentive to improve service and will actually expand service to cover the poor. However, the new approach may not necessarily move people from a low-price, low-quality service to a high-price, high-quality service.

It may well result in high-price, low-quality services that characterize utilities in other infrastructure sectors—such as electricity and telecommunications—in developing countries.

In conclusion, the new demand-driven approach has contributed significantly to our understanding of the "problem" with water supply and the nature of demand for water; and it deserves attention as an analytical technique and planning tool. The lack of attention to the institutional determinants of success and failure is, perhaps, the Achilles' heel of the new paradigm.

References

Altaf, Anjum, Dale Whittington, Haroon Jamal, and V. Kerry Smith. 1993. "Rethinking Rural Water Supply Policy in the Punjab, Pakistan." *Water Resources Research* 27(7): 1943–54.

Briscoe, John, Paulo Furtado de Castro, Charles Griffin, James North, and Orjan Olsen. 1990. "Toward Equitable and Sustainable Rural Water Supplies: A Contingent Valuation Study in Brazil." *World Bank Economic Review* 4(2): 115–34.

Cheo, Kyeong Ae, Dale Whittington, and Donald T. Lauria. 1996. "The Economic Benefits of Surface Water Quality Improvements in Developing Countries: A Case Study of Davao, Philippines," *Land Economics* 72(4): 519–49.

Crane, Randall. 1994. "Water Markets, Market Reform, and the Urban Poor: Results from Jakarta, Indonesia." *World Development* 22(1): 71–83.

Fass, Simon. 1988. *Political Economy in Haiti: The Drama of Survival.* New Brunswick, NJ: Transaction.

Gramlich, E.M. 1994. "Infrastructure Investment: A Review Essay." *Journal of Economic Literature* 32 (September): 1176–96.

Griffin, Charles et al. 1995. "Contingent Valuation and Actual Behavior: Predicting Connections to New Water Systems in the State of Kerala, India." *World Bank Economic Review* 9 (September): 373–95.

Israel, Arturo. 1987. *Institutional Development: Incentives to Perform.* Baltimore: Johns Hopkins University Press.

Milliman, Jerome M. 1972. "Beneficiary Charges: Towards a Unified Theory." In Selma Mushkin, ed., *Public Prices for Public Product,* pp. 27–51. Washington, DC: Urban Institute.

Ostrom, Elinor, Larry Schroeder, and Susan Wynne. 1993. *Institutional Incentives and Sustainable Development: Infrastructure Policies in Perspective.* Boulder, CO: Westview.

Therkildsen, Ole. 1988. *Watering White Elephants: Lessons from Donor-Funded Planning and Implementation of Rural Water Supplies in Tanzania.* Uppsala: Scandinavian Institute of African Studies.

Whittington, Dale. 1992. "Possible Adverse Effects of Increasing Block Tariffs in Developing Countries." *Economic Development and Cultural Change (U.S.)* 41: 75–87.

Whittington, Dale, and Venkateswarlu Swarna. 1994. *The Economic Benefits of Potable Water Supply Projects to Households in Developing Countries.* Economic Staff Paper No. 53. Manila: Asian Development Bank.

Whittington, Dale, Donald T. Lauria, and Xinming Mu. 1991. "A Study of Water Vending and Willingness to Pay for Water in Onitsha, Nigeria." *World Development* 19(2/3): 179–98.

World Bank. 1992. *World Development Report 1992.* Oxford: Oxford University Press.

World Bank. 1994. *World Development Report 1994: Infrastructure for Development.* New York: Oxford University Press.

World Bank Water Demand Research Team. 1993. "The Demand for Water in Rural Areas: Determinants and Policy Implications," *World Bank Research Observer* 8(1): 47–70.

5

Private Involvement in the Provision of Public Services

Editor's Introduction

Richard Stren

When Margaret Thatcher came to office as Prime Minister of the United Kingdom in 1979, she almost immediately set out to reform the governmental system. A year later, similar attempts at reform began in the United States under the Presidency of Ronald Reagan. Although some of these reforms were not themselves new, the intensity and commitment with which they were pursued was almost unprecedented in recent history. As Donald Savoie (1994) has convincingly argued, the two leaders shared many common concerns (partially related to their conservative political orientation), and central among these was a disdain for the civil service, which both felt to be too large, too costly, inefficient in many areas, and not sufficiently innovative. Aside from reducing the size of the civil service at all levels and deregulating important areas of the economy, both leaders felt that many public functions could be performed better, and more cheaply and efficiently, either by the private sector, or at least by the public sector using private-sector methods.

In Britain and the United States, the decade of the 1980s was a period of major reforms in government. Changes occurred in local government as a response to these national leadership initiatives. In the United States, for example, state and local governments were under intense pressure to revise their approach to management and service delivery, as a reaction to severe reductions in funding from higher levels of government. The result in many cases, argue David Osborne and Ted Gaebler in their best-selling book, *Reinventing Government* (1992), was *entrepreneurial government*—a new form of government that shared many qualities of business organization, but was still responsible to its local electors and concerned with assuring social cohesion, equity, and effective policy management. Osborne and Gaebler describe a range of initiatives taken by local governments to improve service delivery, expand tax collection, enhance management efficiency, and improve labor-management cooperation. One of their key proposals is to encourage local governments to think of their voters and citizens as customers, and to treat them in a more responsive fashion.[1] Where possible and feasible, they promote subcontracting services to private firms, charging for services where demand justifies, and forming partnerships with the private sector to undertake development projects. The balance between public and private involvement in any sector is justified by the comparative efficiencies that each can bring, while safeguarding principles of justice and equity.

By the 1980s, the language of "reinventing government," and of applying private-sector experiences and culture to local government—in particular municipal government—began to cohere in a new approach to local administration in the developing world. From the control-oriented approach which characterized local government in the 1960s and 1970s, local administrators (with the support of international agencies such as the Urban Management Programme, UNCHS, UNDP and the World Bank) began to call themselves "urban managers," and the administration of their local authorities began to be identified as "urban management." While urban management as a concept was never precisely defined (Stren 1993), it refers in general "to the political and administrative structures of cities and the major challenges that they face to provide both social and physical infrastructure services. These include managing urban economic resources, particularly land and the assets of the built environment, creating

---

1. In a subsequent book (Osborne and Plastrik 1997), one of the original authors and another colleague propose more detailed strategies for "reinventing government." The five main strategies they discuss are: "The Core Strategy: Creating Clarity of Purpose; the Consequences Strategy: Creating Consequences for Performance; the Customer Strategy: Putting the Customer in the Driver's Seat; the Control Strategy: Shifting Control Away from the Top and Center; and the Culture Strategy: Creating an Entrepreneurial Culture." While the subject of this book is largely local governments around the world, the language has much in common with a business management text.

employment, and attracting investment in order to improve the quality and quantity of goods and services available" (Wekwete 1997, pp. 528–9). The shift from "local government" to "urban management" carried with it a whole new vocabulary and understanding of administration—from control and supply-side initiatives, to "enabling" or "steering" (rather than "rowing"), based on a more demand-driven and service-oriented approach.

The articles in this section illustrate, in different ways, the application of these new ideas to perhaps the most important functional area of municipal government: the provision of public services and infrastructure. In his paper on public-private relationships and performance in municipal service provision, Richard Batley presents a systematic discussion of the arguments both for and against privatization in developing countries. His central concern is to examine the arguments for private-sector involvement in urban service supply, and to evaluate the evidence that private participation improves efficiency. From experience in the three major areas where evaluation has been carried out in the area of service provision—waste collection, water, and electricity supply—one can conclude that the introduction of competition has had a more significant effect on performance than has change of ownership as such. Indeed, in most cases the public role "changes but does not disappear." In most developing countries, formal privatization has in fact been less significant than "informal" privatization—where the failure of public services leads small firms, communities or households to step in to make up for the deficiency. This is particularly the case in poorer countries. Although neoclassical economic theory would argue that public intervention in service delivery is inefficient, Batley shows that there are many feasible combinations of public and private responsibility for service delivery, depending on the good or service being provided. He then attempts to classify public services in order to compare the theoretical feasibility of their privatization, against practice in a number of countries. (The services discussed are piped sewerage, water supply, infrastructural development, slum upgrading, solid waste collection, waste disposal, and primary education.) Many different arrangements for managing and delivering these services are possible, depending on the service and the organizational capability of the municipality. In general, certain services (such as water supply and refuse collection) seem to be better managed than others (such as refuse disposal), perhaps because they attract political attention. At the same time, some towns and cities manage services better than others, regardless of the service in question. But the general proposition that involving the private sector in provision of services is always successful in terms of performance is only partially

validated by the research—which points to a range of factors such as existence of competition, operational autonomy, political support for management, and the local politico-institutional environment. Thus, privatization
may indeed convey benefits, but it must be planned carefully for each service, within the local institutional context.

The next article in this section, by World Bank environmental specialist
Carl Bartone, focuses on the role of the private sector in a particular service—
solid waste management. At the outset, the author indicates some of the
problems faced by many countries in operating their solid waste disposal
systems. "Typical solid waste services" he says, "are subject to pervasive
political interference, which adversely affects operational decisions on investment, pricing, labor, and technological choices. Through well-
designed management or service contracts or concessions, basic conditions
for improved efficiency can be met." But which activities are most appropriate to be carried out by private operators, and what conditions need to
be in place before the private sector is brought in? A study of four Latin
American cities in which the private sector was involved yields a number
of interesting conclusions about particular benefits that can be obtained by
municipalities. Other evidence also shows that the cost of contracted services is generally less than when undertaken by the municipality, and further, that contracting for exclusive collection zones is more efficient than
an open competition among private contractors for a single common collection route. What accounts for success in outsourcing this service? Bartone
suggests six basic factors: competition must be possible (and can include
municipal departments competing with private contractors); there must
be political support for the process; the public sector must have the technical capacity to specify, negotiate, and supervise the private contractors;
medium-size to small firms must be permitted to enter the competition;
consolidation is required for adequate disposal facilities; and there must
be effective monitoring of performance. Overall, he argues that there are
many positive advantages to be obtained from the privatization of waste
disposal services, but that techniques for supervision of these new relationships must be carefully developed by each municipality.

The final paper in the section, written by Usha P. Raghupathi and Om
Prakash Mathur, explains the case of an Indian town—Tirrupur, with a
population of some 300,000—that developed a private-sector plan for a
major water supply and sewerage project. Two elements of this case are
particularly interesting in the present context. The first is that the initiative
to undertake the scheme came from the private sector. In view of the extreme importance of an improved water supply system to the town's

garment industry, the Tirrupur Exporters Association first made the argument that a major scheme was necessary to maintain the town's competitive position. Once it was established that public funds at the necessary level would not be available, a private company prepared the feasibility report. To carry out the plan proposed, a decision was taken to create a special purpose joint venture company. The company included the various levels of governments, a private financing company, parastatal agencies, and the exporters' association—the principal user for the project. Equity participation came from both public and private sources, and the company decided to issue bonds as well. The project, which will include intra-city roads as well as water infrastructure, has not yet been completed, although at the time of writing the paper, tenders for construction were being reviewed. The principle of full cost recovery was central. The authors conclude that a mixture of public and private support can be put together for municipal infrastructural projects, but in this case, leadership from the private sector was the catalyst in getting the scheme underway.

References

Osborne, David, and Ted Gaebler. 1992. *Reinventing Government: How the Entrepreneurial Spirit is Transforming the Public Sector.* Harmondsworth: Penguin.

Osborne, David, and Peter Plastrik. 1997. *Banishing Bureaucracy: The Five Strategies for Reinventing Government.* Reading, MA: Addison-Wesley.

Savoie, Donald J. 1994. *Thatcher, Reagan, Mulroney: In Search of a New Bureaucracy.* Pittsburgh: University of Pittsburgh Press.

Stren, Richard. 1993. "'Urban Management' in Development Assistance: An Elusive Concept." *Cities* 10(2): 125–38.

Wekwete, Kadmiel. 1997. "Urban Management: The Recent Experience." In Carole Rakodi, ed., *The Urban Challenge in Africa: Growth and Management of its Large Cities*, pp. 527–52. Tokyo: United Nations University Press.

Public-Private Partnerships for Urban Services

Richard Batley

The Issues

Developing countries are experiencing a push for privatization from several sources, partly from their own experience of the fiscal difficulty of sustaining services but also under pressure of donor influence, particularly through structural adjustment programs, and of the example of those advanced countries which have gone down this path. Where privatization or commercialization has taken place in developing countries, it has usually first been of smaller, potentially competitive state-owned enterprises producing tradable goods (Cook and Kirkpatrick 1988; Kikeri, Nellis, and Shirley 1992; Adam, Cavendish, and Mistry 1993; Odle 1993). The introduction of private involvement in large strategic enterprises and in public services has been slower and raises more difficult issues, at least of public interest and acceptability (Cook and Minogue 1990). The fundamental claim is that increased efficiencies should follow from the replacement of public monopoly by private competition or even, given the rigidities of public administration and the tendency to "government failure," by private monopoly (Wolf 1988). This article examines the arguments for private-sector involvement in urban service supply, considers alternative forms of public-private partnership, and queries the evidence that private participation makes for greater efficiency.

The service sectors that have received most comprehensive evaluation are solid waste collection, water, and electricity supply (Ascher 1987; Vickers and Yarrow 1990, p. 40; Walsh 1995, p. 231). A widespread conclusion is that the introduction of competition has a more significant effect on performance than a change of ownership, especially if privatized bodies continue to come under detailed regulation (Cook and Kirkpatrick 1988, p. 22; Vickers and Yarrow 1988, pp. 40–1; Shapiro and Willig 1990, p. 58).

It is clear that "privatization" takes many forms (Cook and Kirkpatrick 1988). Most often, the public role changes but does not disappear. Rather than a simple transfer of assets from public to private sectors, we are usually talking about changing their roles and relationships with regard to ownership, operation, control, and regulation (Foster 1992, p. 2). The capacity of governments to perform these new roles and to manage new relationships with the private sector is an important policy issue that has so far been given little attention in research on developing countries (Batley 1994, 1996).

Rolling Back the State

The question whether the public or the private sectors should deliver particular urban services is resolved differently in different countries, but most are under some pressure to move towards greater private involvement. Three processes can be identified:

- *Programmed privatization,* where governments make policy decisions to sell assets, to franchise the whole operation or to contract out particular aspects of it;
- *Pragmatic privatization,* where an initial decision to involve the private sector is made, due to necessity or to management convenience, and leads to a growing commitment;
- *Informal or unintended privatization,* where the failure of public services leads private firms, communities or households to step in to make up the deficiency.

In most developing countries, there has probably been faster "progress" in informal than in programmed privatization. Formal programs of privatization have been modest, except in the more obviously "productive" activities previously undertaken by state-owned enterprises (commerce, industry, agricultural marketing), and in infrastructural services (telecommunications, electricity generation and, to a much more limited extent, gas distribution, ports, railways, and water supply) (World Bank 1994, p. 64). These programs have often been imposed by fiscal crisis, debt, donor pressure, and political last resort, and have often been ill-prepared (Cook and Kirkpatrick 1988; Edwards and Baer 1992; Pirez 1994). "Informal privatization," where households and enterprises find their own solutions in response to the failure of public services, may be more common in the poorer countries, especially in the sphere of essential personal services (transport, health, education) and basic infrastructure (water and power) (Moser, Herbert, and Makonnen 1993; Batley 1994).

Where there has been movement from public-sector supply to the involvement of the private and community sectors, it has often been for purely pragmatic reasons. Most developing countries are under pressure to privatize, due to the scarcity of government resources or the influence of aid donors. Zimbabwe, for example, is embarking on widespread contracting out of municipal services, partly on the initiative of central government in response to structural adjustment. What begins as a pragmatic step often leads to a more wholehearted commitment to privatization: for example, in the contracting of solid waste collection in Penang, Malaysia and Recife, Brazil (Batley 1996).

The Limited Case for Government Intervention

Neoclassical economic theory and recent theories of state failure advocate competitive market mechanisms essentially on the grounds of efficiency. It is argued that, by comparison, non-competitive provision leads to (a) allocative inefficiency: services allocated do not correspond to consumers' preferences and/or are charged at prices (excessive or subsidized) that do not reflect producers' real costs; and (b) productive (sometimes known as internal or technical) inefficiency: resources are not used economically to produce a given output, or the given level of resources is not used optimally to maximize outputs.

In this view, the case for public intervention therefore has to be exceptional, resting on the argument that there are situations where the market will fail to perform efficiently or at all (World Bank 1997). A simple classification of such situations follows:

- *Private firms have no incentive to provide goods or services for which it is not feasible to charge in proportion to consumption.* This will arise where users cannot be excluded from consumption and/or where their consumption is not rivalrous (in competition) with that of other consumers of the same service. Such "public goods" would include, for example, street lighting or police services.
- *Private firms will not provide efficiently where markets are incomplete or non-competitive;* for example, where there is natural monopoly (e.g., piped water), where the investment is so large as to restrict competition, where consumers are ill-informed to judge between alternatives (e.g., medical or legal services).
- *Private firms on their own will ignore the costs and benefits of consumption by those who lie beyond the reach of the market.* The wider society may benefit from the extension of a service even though the direct consumers may be unable or unwilling to pay for it; an example of such a "positive externality" is vaccination. Conversely, a "negative externality" is industrial pollution where non-consumers may pay the price of other people's consumption.
- *Markets may not achieve socially acceptable levels of equity.* "Merit goods" are those that are defined in any society as basic conditions of citizenship, regardless of ability to pay. Primary health and education typically come into this category.

These concepts provide a set of considerations against which to consider the case for government intervention, but they should be treated with caution. There are few services that fall neatly and wholly into any category, and where they do belong depends partly on local circumstances and judgements (Malkin and Wildavsky 1991). The theoretical approach does, however, have the virtue of bringing these considerations into the open, forcing us to identify the reasons for intervention. By identifying the specific case for intervention, those who argue for restricting the role of government can pin it down to specific activities. Thus, even where there is a case for intervention, government does not necessarily have to assume the entire responsibility for the provision of a service.

Government's responsibility can be restricted by narrowing it down to its strictly necessary functions. One way is to "unbundle" services into their component parts so that only those elements that really require direct public-sector involvement are subjected to it (World Bank 1997, p. 54). For example, electricity generation can be put onto a competitive basis, while its distribution to homes may be monopolistic and therefore kept in the public sector. Alternatively, there may be scope for "horizontal unbundling" in which a monopoly service may be broken up geographically, as in the case of British water supply. This allows performance comparison between district monopolies and promotes "contestability" by reducing the costs of entry to, and therefore of competing for, a place in the market (Vining and Weimer 1990).

The other way is by separating responsibility for arranging for a service to be delivered from the actual production of the service (Savas 1987, p. 61). According to this argument, governments could, in principle, usually achieve their objectives without getting involved in the direct production or delivery of services. Several writers (Kolderie 1986; Wunsch 1991; Ostrom, Schroeder, and Wynne 1993) distinguish between the responsibility for "provision," which might be governments' concern, and "production," which might be done by private or community actors. I think a clearer distinction is between (a) "direct provision," which is the act of physically producing (constructing, creating, maintaining) and delivering a service; and (b) "indirect provision," that is ensuring that a service is available by setting policy and service standards, coordinating, financing, enabling, and regulating producers.

A Classification of Public Services

Using these concepts, we can analyze the characteristics of some particular services to compare the theoretical case for private-sector involvement. The following briefly analyzes (a) two forms of urban infrastructural service—water supply and sewerage; (b) two aspects of infrastructural development—

infrastructure installation and slum improvement; and (c) two personal or household services—primary education and solid waste management. The analysis is for illustration; a proper analysis of particular cases would have to take into account particular local circumstances. Goods and services do not have fixed characteristics: the tendency to monopoly, informational problems, the significance of scale and of "externalities" will vary by location, prevailing institutions, and level of technology. For example, when water is brought from the river via piped connections to households, it is turned from a "public good" into a "private good" for which it is feasible to charge consumers and exclude non-payers.

Piped Sewerage Systems: These are at the "public goods" end of the spectrum (excludable but non-rivalrous); they are monopolistic, large-scale, and with both high positive externalities (health benefits), and negative externalities (neighborhood pollution). These are likely to be cases for direct public provision, although private firms could be contracted for specific works.

Water Supply: Piped water could be operated as a fully commercial enterprise, being excludable and rivalrous. However, its characteristics as a natural monopoly, the scale of necessary investment, its significant externalities and its essential "merit goods" nature lead to the case for government involvement at least in ensuring and regulating provision. These considerations may also suggest direct provision by public agencies, especially in the case of wells and street standposts, where difficulties of charging indicate the need for direct community control.

Infrastructural Development: This area can be considered in four respects: the assembly of land, the installation of infrastructure at primary (city) and secondary (neighborhood) levels, and the making of tertiary (household) connections. The state has a necessary role only in the sense of ensuring, facilitating, and regulating primary and secondary infrastructure (indirect provision). It may also adopt such a role in the assembly of land, but the arguments for its doing so are less convincing: there are no great problems of scale for private developers, and the external impacts on wider society are more modest than in the case of basic infrastructure. Also, private owners may well be more successful than government in excluding non-payers from land invasion. If there is an argument for an involvement of the state in the direct provision of developed land, it may rest principally on its powers of compulsory purchase, and on the desire to ensure planned, rather than market-led, development. Public agencies may need to be involved in the direct installation of city-wide primary infrastructure where there are no firms of sufficient scale to bear the investment costs, long-term returns, and associated risks, or in order to avoid private monopoly.

Slum Upgrading: Improvement of slums has the qualities of a public good: it is not possible to exclude non-payers from the benefits, and the benefits can be shared without rivalry across the community. It has a potentially high positive impact on surrounding areas, indicating a strong case for public-sector involvement, but it is sufficiently small-scale for community to substitute for government in aspects of provision.

Solid Waste Collection: This does not have public good attributes: it is, in principle, possible to charge users and to exclude non-payers. A fully commercial operation might apply most readily in the case of the collection of business waste. However, the high negative impact of uncollected waste on surrounding areas indicates the need for public-sector involvement, at least in ensuring provision, although the operation of the service could be contracted out to firms or communities. The case for public-sector involvement, charged to the general tax revenue, is particularly strong in the case of poor residential neighborhoods, producing low volumes in difficult terrain and with low willingness to pay by direct beneficiaries.

Waste Disposal: The disposal of waste approximates a public good: it is difficult though not impossible to exclude non-payers, and one customer's use of disposal space hardly restricts that of others. The service has some of the features of a monopoly—once established, the cost of extending it to additional users is low. Disposal sites are likely to be difficult for private firms to acquire without recourse to state powers of compulsory purchase. There are considerable negative external effects on those living near disposal sites; these can only be compensated by some government intervention in charges and re-allocation of benefits. These are arguments for direct public control of the provision of the service.

Primary Education: This does not have public good characteristics; it is moderately rivalrous (to the extent that classroom space and teachers are in short supply) and it is possible to charge and to exclude non-payers. Its scale is sufficiently small for private and community involvement in its delivery. However, there are benefits for society as a whole and there are also clear equity considerations, both of which indicate the necessity for a governmental role at least in ensuring that there is adequate provision and in subsidizing access for the poor. Difficulties of identifying the necessitous who are to receive subsidies argue for the existence of open access public schools.

From this analysis we can see that the most likely candidates for private involvement are solid waste collection, land assembly, infrastructure installation at the local level, contracted-out public works, and education. Similar analysis might add: housing, markets, curative health, public transport, electricity generation, telecommunications (Roth 1987, 1990). However, all these activities are likely to need some oversight, regulation or financial support by the state to ensure their provision. Water supply, sewerage, solid waste disposal, and city-scale infrastructure systems are most likely to require direct government involvement in the actual production or delivery of the service.

Organizational Arrangements for Service Provision

Recognizing that there are different functions in the supply of a service allows us to see that there will rarely be a straight and simple choice between public versus private provision. Rather, there are different ways of combining the public and private sectors in various organizational arrangements depending on how the direct (production and delivery) and indirect (policy, standards, finance, coordination) roles are split. The World Bank (1994) describes these as ways of allocating responsibilities for *operation and maintenance* (direct functions) and *ownership and financing* (indirect functions) between the public sector, the private sector, communities, and users.

This section describes some of the possible organizational arrangements for service provision, considering some of the circumstances under which each might be the appropriate choice. In practice, "appropriateness" is a complicated issue which has to be considered in relation to particular country circumstances. At least three factors come into play: the reasons or motives for government intervention in the service sector (as outlined above), the capacity of government to perform the roles required of it, and the organizational traditions of particular places and services.

Pure Public-Sector Provision

"Pure" public provision arrangements are those in which government or communities take full responsibility for all (direct and indirect) aspects of a service from its ownership, planning, financing, and installation, to its management and delivery. Public provision without any private involvement is difficult to justify on the technical grounds of the characteristics of goods and services, but it is most defensible in the case of public goods with tendencies to monopoly, need for large-scale investment, and with important positive or negative external effects on wider society. Among the services considered here, the most likely candidates are sewerage and solid waste disposal. Similarly, on theoretical grounds, pure community provision may apply to public goods or services of small scale and few external effects beyond the neighborhood. Slum improvement, local wells, drainage, and paths are examples. However, government is likely to claim involvement in the indirect provider role as funder and regulator.

In spite of its limited justification, pure public provision has been the aim of many governments for most urban services until recently. Government responsibility is, however, rarely as complete as it would claim. Public services rarely achieve comprehensive coverage. Households and communities are forced or choose to make their own arrangements for housing, water, sanitation, and refuse disposal in large areas of most rapidly growing cities. Where, as in much of Africa, public systems have gone into decline with the increasing impoverishment of governments, the need for self-provision becomes even more prevalent. Uganda is one case where communities of all classes have had to step in to deliver alternative services in the fields of education, health, and solid waste (Batley 1996). We have seen a situation where, under the cover of comprehensive public provision, informal or unintended privatization has, in fact, taken place.

Contracting Out Service Production and Delivery

Various arrangements exist by which governmental bodies retain indirect responsibility for the provision of a service while contracting all or some aspects of its production or delivery to private firms or other non-governmental organizations. Under a first set of arrangements, the public authority bears the full financial risk, remains responsible for setting standards, and retains full ownership of facilities. Private contractors usually receive payment according to contract and not to their own operational efficiency. Examples are: contracting of construction work to the private sector; "service contracts" in which particular aspects of the operation or maintenance of a service are contracted to a private body for a fixed period (usually around five years); and "management contracts" in which the entire operation and maintenance of a publicly owned service is transferred to a private body for a fixed period.

These arrangements are ways of involving the private sector even in the case of "public goods," where it is difficult to charge to recover costs and where there is market failure. The public authority, and not the consumer, pays the contractor. Such contracts, being short term and specific, also safeguard the interest of the public authority: to a high degree it retains its control even of the delivery of the service. They are therefore likely to be appropriate where there is a strong public interest and government does not wish to cede its responsibility: for example, in situations of monopoly, or where there are strong equity considerations or wider social effects.

On the other hand, piecemeal contracts may have the disadvantage of creating problems of fragmentation and difficulties of coordination. These arrangements are therefore most easily manageable where tasks are naturally divisible and discrete: for example, construction and maintenance works, vehicle maintenance, neighborhood services, and aspects of internal administration such as billing and salary payments.

Lease, Concession, or License of Monopolies

There is a second set of contractual arrangements that give private firms a longer-term involvement in the production or delivery of a service, and a stake in its ownership and financing. The following three arrangements offer a gradation of increasing private participation in the provider role:

- Lease contracts, under which a public system (for example, water) is transferred for a fixed period (up to around 10 years) to a lease-holder who has to finance working capital but not investment in the fixed assets. The lessee retains a proportion of tariff revenue.
- Concessions or franchises, in which the concessionaire must also finance investment in the fixed assets making up the system itself, and is therefore likely to retain a higher proportion of tariff revenue over a longer period (around 15 years). Such arrangements are typical of the French public utilities and are increasingly being adopted for public utility management in middle- and high-income countries.
- Licensed private monopoly ownership, in which the licensee owns the assets as well as being responsible for their financing. However, the operation of the system is conditional on compliance with contractual obligations laid down by government and supervised by public regulation. This is the arrangement now typical of British public utilities.

These terms can only apply in situations where leaseholders, concessionaires or licensees can earn a return by charging for the delivery of the service. Sufficient political support also needs to exist to allow profitable charging to be effected and to be guaranteed in the long term. At the same time, given that responsibility is substantially transferred to the private sector, government has to have the capacity to make cast-iron contracts and to police them effectively. This is especially the case with licensing, where government gives up the control implied by ownership and relies for supervision on the technical competence and neutrality of an independent regulatory body.

Capacity must also exist on the part of the private sector. There must be enough firms capable of competing for the contract or license, and they must have sufficient financial capacity to take on commitments to long-term investment. In many developing countries this may imply the entry of foreign companies, but long-term investment may be difficult to attract when it involves the installation of fixed assets in uncertain political situations for the supply of services to poor populations.

With these considerable qualifications about their feasibility, leasing, franchising, and licensing are ways of managing natural monopolies whilst avoiding the concentration of power in the public sector. They all achieve this end by separating the direct and indirect aspects of provision, and subjecting the private producer to public contractual control or regulation. They are most clearly applicable to non-public goods with a monopoly tendency, and where there is sufficient public interest (on grounds of welfare or external effects) to justify continued public control—for example, the public utilities (water, electricity, gas) and collective services such as refuse incineration, bus terminals, and municipal market management.

Licensed Competition between Producers

A minimum level of government involvement in managing the provision of a service is in the licensing of competing private (or private and public) direct providers. Unlike the case for the regulation of monopoly, here market conditions exist and government seeks to regulate the outcome of competition. Within the framework of their license to operate, the direct providers take almost all responsibility for the service.

Licensed competition is appropriate to "private goods," that is those which it is possible to charge for and which individuals compete to consume. There must be some case for government intervention, resting either on the need to promote equitable access or to mitigate the effects of unrestrained competition on society at large. An example of the first sort would be the management of bus transport to ensure that an entire city is covered at similar tariffs; of the second, that market-stall holders fulfill basic health requirements or that builders comply with building regulations. On the other hand, the arguments are not so strong as to demand direct public-sector entry into the production or delivery of the service.

Partnership between Public and Private Providers

Several sorts of joint arrangement can be identified where state agencies and private bodies act in a mutual endeavor, working in parallel rather than dividing roles hierarchically: joint ownership; "mixed economy" companies, in which governments, municipalities, and private companies have shareholdings; joint investments in which public and private organizations focus their different sources of investment finance on a joint purpose, perhaps through the formation of a trust; and joint ventures in which the different powers and capacities of the public and private sectors are harnessed to a shared purpose.

Partnership in joint schemes is most likely to occur where there is a strong possibility that opportunities for private investors will be generated by government involvement. The public sector's contribution might be either to undertake necessary investments which private firms are unable to perform (due to their large scale, high risk, or difficulty of charging to consumers) or to facilitate private action (through finance or the use of the coercive powers of the state). There should be an equal conviction on the governmental side that there will be public gains from the private investment. In the urban sector, these conditions seem most likely to exist in the case of the acquisition of land and the installation of infrastructure for housing and commercial development.

Joint Ventures with Beneficiaries

Apart from the normal processes of influence on decisionmaking through political representation, the beneficiaries or users may be involved directly in the administration of public services. This may take place at the level of the formulation of broad policy about provision or in the management of implementation. The objective is to break the bureaucratic-professional control thought to be intrinsic to public monopolies, exposing them to the choice of the consumer in a direct way which representative politics cannot achieve.

Direct user participation in the design and management of public services is most likely to apply in the case of local "public goods," that is, goods and services which the private sector cannot supply and which are sufficiently small in scale to be managed locally. Moreover, the case for participation seems to be stronger where the benefits are collective and there is no great rivalry between users or beneficiaries. Otherwise, there is the risk of domination or the exploitation of scarcity by sectional interests. Likely examples are neighborhood improvement schemes, community water, drainage and cleaning, local roads, and schools. At the wider policymaking level, some municipalities in Zimbabwe and Brazil involve citizens as a whole in formulation of town budgets and policy priorities through neighborhood consultations.

Public Support for Private Consumption and Provision

Need may be transformed into market demand by government support to the users or purchasers of private goods and services. The most obvious way in which this may be done is through financial support in the form of cash payments, vouchers, and loans to consumers, or subsidies to providers; an alternative is to facilitate choice and strengthen competition by improving the market information available to consumers. The advantage to the public authority is that supporting private provision may be cheaper than the costs of establishing an alternative public service, whilst guarding the virtues of competitive efficiency and individual choice.

A policy of supporting private provision assumes the existence of competitive market conditions: that services are consumed individually, that there are competing providers, that purchasers possess adequate market information on alternatives and that there is excess capacity among service providers. Otherwise choice will not exist and prices are likely to be forced up by public intervention. In practice, it is the experience of the diversion of government financial support into the wrong hands, in situations of extreme scarcity and inequality, which has often led governments to provide services directly, bypassing the private sector. Government support for the purchase of private goods may therefore apply where, on the one hand, competitive conditions exist and, on the other, there are reasons for only limited government intervention to give equity of access or to secure wider social benefits. Such examples exist in education, social insurance, transport, housing, and basic food rations (Batley 1996; World Bank 1997, Chapter 3).

The Experience of Private Participation

The introduction of private providers and market principles into the provision of public services is intended to increase efficiency through competition, to increase responsiveness to consumer choice, and to bring in private resources. The test is whether these benefits are realized in practice. A survey of research undertaken for the United Nations Urban Management Program (UMP) assembled some of the available evidence for urban services in developing countries (Batley 1996). Some broad conclusions are indicated below.

The presumption that involving the private sector makes for higher levels of efficiency received only cautious endorsement. Where direct comparison could be made between parallel services in one city, particularly in the case of education and solid waste collection, there was generally better private performance. However, it is not possible to generalize to the conclusion that privatization must mean greater efficiency and effectiveness overall. In those cases where there were competing public and private operators, the "better performance" of the private entrepreneurs was often at least partly due to the fact that they were awarded the easier sectors of the market. Moreover, there were often knock-on effects of privatization that actually *increased* the costs of the public sector: the need to manage the private contractors and to retain a reserve capacity, and the inability to shed staff in spite of privatization. A key conclusion of the research was that the effects of privatization must be considered "in the round'; that is, taking into account not just the possibly greater efficiency of the private part of a service but the gross effects on the total cost of providing the service.

In those cases where there was no private involvement, often a fully public service performed at least as well as a mixed one in another country. For example, public refuse collection systems in Mexico and Zimbabwe, and education systems in Malaysia and Mexico, were among the best performers in cross-national comparisons.

Factors other than ownership may be more important in determining performance. First, some services perform better than others, regardless of whether they are in public or private ownership. The evidence is that services that are more publicly visible attract higher levels of political attention and investment funds: water versus sewerage, refuse collection versus disposal, infrastructure installation versus maintenance, and almost everything by comparison with primary education. This suggests the case for increasing the public "visibility" of deprived services through the publication of comparative information. Second, it is also clear that some countries and some towns generally perform better than others, regardless of who operates the service. The evidence is that there are local institutional factors that provide an enabling environment to public *or* private providers. Key among these were sustained political strategy, political support for the technical autonomy of service managers, access to investment finance, and strong private enterprise involvement in local policy and politics. Public-private partnership needs to be considered at the level of political participation and not just of service operation.

Conclusion

This has been a technical analysis of the motives and options for private involvement in the delivery of urban services. In practice, many factors beyond the technical determine how services are organized and delivered in particular countries. In spite of the pressures towards privatization, most governments have proven very conservative in the steps they have taken in this direction; history, vested interests and institutional traditions are important. Often it is only crisis that has driven change. The survey of technical options can be a useful way of challenging established orthodoxy, by raising the question why government needs to be involved in service delivery and finding the best organizational means of addressing that need.

While encouraging exploration of alternative ways of delivering services, this article has cautioned against a naive belief in privatization. The gains in efficiency are uncertain; and government does not simply shed roles but takes on new ones.

References

Adam, C., W. Cavendish, and P. Mistry. 1992. *Adjusting Privatization: Case Studies from Developing Countries.* London: James Currey.

Ascher, K. 1987. *The Politics of Privatization: Contracting Out and Public Service.* London: Macmillan.

Bartone, C. 1991 "Keys to Success: Private Delivery of Municipal Solid Waste Services." *Infrastructure Notes.* Infrastructure and Urban Development Department, World Bank. Washington, DC.

Batley, R. 1994. "The Consolidation of Adjustment: Implications for Public Administration." *Public Administration and Development* 14: 489–505.

Batley, R. 1996. "Public-Private Relationships and Performance in Service Provision." *Urban Studies* 33(4/5): 723–51.

Bendor, J. 1990. "Formal Models of Bureaucracy: A Review." In N. B. Lynn and A. Wildavsky, eds., *Public Administration: The State of the Discipline*, pp. 373–417. Chatham, NJ: Chatham House.

Chan, H. S., and D. H. Rosenbloom. 1994. "Legal Control of Public Administration: A Principal-Agent Perspective." *International Review of Administrative Sciences* 60(4): 559–74.

Cook, P., and C. Kirkpatrick, eds. 1988. *Privatisation in Less Developed Countries.* Brighton: Wheatsheaf.

Cook, P., and M. Minogue. 1990. "Waiting for Privatisation in Developing Countries—Towards the Integration of Economic and Non-Economic Explanations." *Public Administration and Development* 10(4): 389–403.

Donahue, J. 1989. *The Privatization Decision: Public Ends, Private Means.* New York: Basic Books.

Edwards, S., and W. Baer. 1992. "The State and Private Sector in Latin America: Reflections on the Past, the Present and the Future." *Texas Papers on Latin America.* Houston: University of Texas.

Foster, C.D. 1992. *Privatization, Public Ownership and Natural Monopoly.* Oxford: Blackwell.

Gidman, P., with I. Blore, J. Lorentzen, and P. Schuttenbelt. 1995. *Public-Private Partnerships in Urban Infrastructure Services.* Urban Management Program Working Paper Series 4. Nairobi: UNDP/UNCHS/World Bank.

Kikeri S., J. Nellis, and M. Shirley. 1992. *Privatization: The Lessons of Experience.* Washington, DC: World Bank.

Kolderie, T. l986. "Two Different Concepts of Privatisation." *Public Administration Review* 46: 285–9l.

Malkin, J., and A. Wildavsky. 1991. "Why the Traditional Distinction between Public and Private Goods Should Be Abandoned." *Journal of Theoretical Politics* 3(4): 355–78.

Moser, C., A. Herbert, and R. Makonnen. 1993. *Urban Poverty in the Context of Structural Adjustment: Recent Evidence and Policy Responses.* Urban Development Division Discussion Paper. Washington, DC: World Bank.

Odle, M. 1993. "Towards a Stages Theory Approach to Privatization." *Public Administration and Development* 13: 17–35.

Organization for Economic Cooperation and Development (OECD). 1987. *Managing and Financing Urban Services.* Paris: OECD.

Ostrom, E., L. Schroeder, and S. Wynne. 1993. *Institutional Incentives and Sustainable Development: Infrastructure Policies in Perspective.* Boulder, CO: Westview.

Pirez, P. 1994. "Privatization and the City: The Case of Buenos Aires." Buenos Aires: Centre for Social and Environmental Studies (CENTRO).

Roth, G. 1987. *The Private Provision of Public Services in Developing Countries.* Oxford: Oxford University Press.

Savas, E.S. 1987. *Privatization: The Key to Better Government.* Chatham, NJ: Chatham House.

Shapiro, C., and R. Willig. 1990. "Economic Rationales for the Scope of Privatization." In E. Suleiman and J. Waterbury, eds., *The Political Economy of Public Sector Reform and Privatization,* pp. 55–82. Boulder, CO: Westview.

Triche, T. 1990. "Private Participation in the Delivery of Guinea's Water Supply," Policy Research Working Paper 477, Transport, Water and Urban Development Division. Washington, DC: World Bank.

Vickers, J., and G. Yarrow. 1988. *Privatization: An Economic Analysis.* Cambridge, MA: MIT Press.

Vining, A., and D. Weimer. 1990. "Government Supply and Government Production Failures: A Framework Based on Contestability." *Journal of Public Policy* 10(1): 1–22.

Walsh, K. 1995. *Public Services and Market Mechanisms: Competition,Contracting and the New Public Management.* London: Macmillan.

Williamson, O.E. 1975. *Markets and Hierarchies: Analysis and Anti-Trust Implications.* New York: Free Press.

Williamson, O.E. 1985. *The Economic Institutions of Capitalism.* New York: Free Press.

Wolf, M. 1988. *Markets or Government: Choosing between Imperfect Alternatives.* Cambridge, MA: MIT Press.

World Bank. 1994. *World Development Report 1994: Infrastructure for Development.* New York: Oxford University Press for the World Bank.

World Bank. 1997. *World Development Report 1997: The State in a Changing World.* New York: Oxford University Press for the World Bank.

Wunsch, J.S. 1991. "Institutional Analysis and Decentralisation: Developing an Analytical Framework for Effective Third World Administrative Reform." *Public Administration and Development* 11(5): 431–52.

The Role of the Private Sector in Municipal Solid Waste Service Delivery in Developing Countries: Keys to Success

Carl R. Bartone

The provision of municipal solid waste services[2] is a costly and vexing problem for local authorities in most developing countries. Service coverage is low, resources are insufficient, and uncontrolled dumping is widespread, with resulting environmental problems. Moreover, substantial inefficiencies are often observed in publicly operated services. One solution commonly proposed is to contract service provision with the private sector in the belief that service efficiency and coverage can be improved; evidence in support of this claim has emerged from several developing countries. Nonetheless, private sector participation should be viewed only as a possible opportunity, not a panacea, and there are important questions on whether, and how, to involve the private sector in the provision of municipal solid waste services.

Roles for the Private Sector

There are three important roles for the private sector in the solid waste management field. First, where existing public service delivery is either too costly or inadequate, participation of the private sector offers a means of enhancing efficiency and lowering costs. Second, in situations where local public funds for investment are in chronically short supply, the private sector may be able to mobilize funds. Third, the private sector is well situated to draw on international experience, and to introduce proven and cost-effective technologies.

Greater efficiency in service delivery is normally achieved through the introduction of commercial principles and by paying greater attention to customer satisfaction (World Bank 1994). Many local government departments suffer from multiple and conflicting objectives and inadequate accounting for costs or financial risk, and put too little emphasis on revenues collected and the quality of service delivered. Managers have

---

2. The views expressed are solely those of the author and do not necessarily represent the opinion of the World Bank or its affiliates.

little incentive to satisfy customers, or to achieve a reasonable return on assets through efficient operation and adequate maintenance. Typical solid waste services are subject to pervasive political interference, which adversely affects operational decisions on investment, pricing, labor, and technological choices. Through well-designed management or service contracts or concessions, basic conditions for improved efficiency can be met, such as introducing limited and well-focused performance objectives, financial and managerial autonomy (with a hard budget constraint), and clear accountability, both to customers and to providers of capital. Moreover, the private sector can provide specific skills or expertise that may be lacking in the public sector. At a minimum, the private sector can provide performance benchmarks for public-sector entities. Note also that many cities have improved public service delivery efficiency by introducing competition and commercial principles (see subsection "Competition Counts," below).

Private-sector participation is also a way to secure investment finance from private companies for solid waste equipment and facilities, in return for contracts or concessions to provide service (Cointreau-Levine 1994). Participating firms bring to bear not only their management expertise and technical skills, but also their credit standing and ability to finance investments. However, for this opportunity to materialize, there must be a reasonable level of assurance that the investments made can be recovered. Where local governments do not have the funds to provide for the renewal and expansion of existing equipment, can they be reliably expected to meet their payments to suppliers and contractors? If the risks are too great, it may be difficult to attract private operators into the sector without adequate guarantees.

How the private sector participates is also an important consideration. Municipal solid waste services fall into the category of public goods, meaning that competition *in* the market is not always feasible. It is, however, possible and advisable to create competition *for* the market. This can be accomplished by the unbundling of activities—separating activities in which economies of scale are not important from those in which they are. Because of the characteristics of solid waste services, they can be separated by markets—either geographically or by service categories. The possibility of unbundling creates numerous opportunities for private-sector participation in a competitive environment. Efficiency can be increased by means of competition, managed through simple contracts for specific services all the way up to long-term concessions that require operation, maintenance, and facility expansion.

Lessons from Experience

The Experience of Latin American Cities

To verify the claims that the private sector can improve efficiency and service coverage, a cross-sectional analysis was conducted in 1989 in four Latin American cities that were reported to have competitive private operations—Buenos Aires, Caracas, Santiago, and São Paulo. For comparison, a similar study was carried out in Rio de Janeiro, where there is a public solid waste company. Also, in Buenos Aires operations were carried out by both the public and the private sector, allowing for further comparisons. Findings indicate that the private sector is more efficient in providing solid waste services and should play an expanded role in solid waste management (Bartone et al. 1991).

In each of the four cities that contract for services, private delivery involved competitive bidding for exclusive service provision in well-defined urban districts. Except for São Paulo, the profile of firms working with solid waste was fairly uniform; medium or small construction or transport companies operated their own fleets, equipment, workshops, and facilities to provide garbage collection, street sweeping, and, sometimes, transfer and disposal operations. In São Paulo, several large firms provided these services. The contractual arrangements were also similar in all cities; the duration of the contracts was usually between four and eight years, sufficient to recover investments in fleets and equipment.

Except in the case of Santiago, where payment was on a lump-sum basis, performance was a key criterion on which compensation was based. Cost recovery, through a user tax, generated a significant part of city revenues for paying private operators. In Caracas, the refuse tax was billed together with electricity charges; the remaining cities levied it with the property tax. The self-financing ratios were high; in Santiago, where inflation was low, cost recovery was 100 percent. In Caracas and São Paulo, the self-financing ratio was respectively 66 percent and 70 percent; but in Rio de Janeiro, it was only 10 percent.

According to these case studies, the private sector can operate more efficiently than the public sector in the delivery of municipal solid waste services. Privately provided services are also more cost effective. In São Paulo, for example, the cost of providing services was approximately half that in Rio de Janeiro. In addition, where direct comparisons of labor and vehicle efficiency could be made, the private sector performed more efficiently. For comparable service areas, vehicle efficiency was 71 percent higher in São Paulo than in Rio, and labor efficiency 13 percent higher.[3] In Buenos Aires, public collectors (which serve about 30 percent of the city) used 7.5 times more workers per 1,000 population served, and 4.5 times as many workers per vehicle, than the private collectors.

The private-sector landfill operations observed in all four cities were also well run, and provided a reasonable degree of environmental protection, much higher than normally observed in developing countries.

Evidence from Other Cities

The results of the Latin American study have been corroborated by observations in other cities in such diverse developing countries as Botswana, Colombia, the Czech Republic, Indonesia, and Malaysia. In the last country, for example, prior to 1996[4] most local authorities contracted out up to 80 percent of solid waste collection services to between one and nine contractors, through a well-defined competitive tendering process (Sinha 1993). The cost of contractor services in Malaysia average 23 percent lower (after taxes!) than the cost of service provided by the local authorities. In the words of Kazal Sinha: "The competitive atmosphere created by farsighted local authorities contracting with private companies results in more efficient, thorough, productive services at a lower cost. Moreover, it frees the local authorities from the difficulties of operations, and allows them to devote their energies to supervising, managing and establishing policies—the true challenges of governing" (Sinha 1993).

Rigorous studies conducted in industrialized countries also support these findings. Research from the United States, Canada, and the United Kingdom, that surveyed more than 2,000 cities, showed that services

---

3. At the time of the study, the municipal solid waste company in Rio de Janeiro was at a significant disadvantage, resulting from political interference in business decisions. For example, although the collection fleet was 12 years old and, as a result, operations and maintenance were costly and difficult, the municipal company was not allowed by local government to invest in new compactor vehicles. Shortly after this study was concluded, the restriction was lifted and new trucks were procured— leading to greater operational efficiency (Luiz Leite, personal communication).

4. In 1996 the Malaysian government took over solid waste services from municipalities and moved to large-scale private concessions. This article only reports the pre-1996 private sector experience of cities.

provided by public monopolies typically cost 25 to 41 percent more than competitively contracted services (Donahue 1989). The same surveys revealed that contracting for exclusive collection zones is much more efficient than having open private competition along common collection routes.

Keys to Success

Based on the observed experiences from cities around the world, six key messages emerge that can contribute to the success of public-private partnerships in the field of municipal solid waste management.

Competition Counts

The private sector can operate more efficiently than the public sector in providing municipal solid waste services, so long as the requirements for contestable markets are met—that is, the establishment of exclusive service districts and competitive bidding (Baumol and Lee 1991). This assertion is consistent with the Latin American and Malaysian experiences summarized above, and with the results of rigorous studies conducted in several industrialized countries. In the absence of competition, however, there is no reason to expect greater efficiency and cost-effectiveness from the private sector. Conversely, municipal departments can also compete for contracts, thus improving competitiveness and bringing down overall costs. This approach, known as "managed competition," has proven successful in several U.S. cities such as Charlotte, Indianapolis, Phoenix, Oklahoma City, and San Diego, and is practiced widely in the United Kingdom (*World Wastes* 1993; ERM 1998). It has also been practiced in Malaysia, and in the Latin American cities of Buenos Aires and Bogotá.

Political Will is Critical

Participation of the private sector as municipal contractors depends mainly on political decisionmaking. Though contracts are awarded after competitive bidding, true competition depends on government attitudes, as expressed in bidding conditions and the behavior of the officials in charge of the bidding process. Equally important are required changes in the laws and regulations governing contracts, as well as aspects such as environment, labor, trade, access to finance, risk sharing (that is, allocating commercial and sovereign risk between private and public partners), property transfer, and entry and exit conditions. The importance of regulatory transparency and judicial predictability in creating a favorable infrastructure investment environment cannot be overemphasized. Promotion of private-sector involvement also depends on government support. Incentives such as credit schemes, payment-guarantee bonds and trade policies, can promote the market and enhance efficiency. Political will is also important for achieving a greater degree of self-financing by means of applying appropriate user charges, in turn reducing the perceived risks of private contractors.

Build Local Technical Capacity

In developing-country cities, an important step in achieving effective private sector involvement is, paradoxically, to strengthen the technical capability of the public sector so that it is better able to exercise proper contract control, inspection, and supervision. The existence of public agencies that are capable of specifying, negotiating, and monitoring contracts efficiently, without unnecessary burdens on private operators, is important. In São Paulo, for example, the threat of large operators forming a cartel is averted by the strong technical capacity of the city agency (LIMPURB) and its ability to negotiate with firms, in addition to its decentralized contract supervision and payment (Bartone et al. 1991). Also, technical capacity in cost accounting and municipal tax administration is vital for solid waste services, as for all municipal services. Better knowledge of real service costs is fundamental for contract negotiations. An additional consideration is that capable municipal departments will be better placed to compete with the private sector for contracts.

To Collect—Divide and Conquer

There are few barriers to entry for local private firms, given that economies of scale are very limited in collection operations, while economies of contiguity are large. The operations are relatively simple, and the investment requirements are moderate. This is borne out by the number of small and medium-size construction and transport companies engaged in collection operations in the four Latin American cities studied (Bartone et al. 1991). In Santiago, for example, there are seven small to medium-size firms contracted by 21 of the 23 communes for collection and street sweeping.

Collection districts in Santiago are also small (an average size of 170,000 population), which enhances contestability.

Consolidate for Enviromentally Safe Disposal

Disposal operations benefit from centralized solutions because they have significant economies of scale and major environmental spillover effects (or "externalities," as they are called by economists), as well as greater investment and skill requirements. These characteristics offer opportunities for private-sector involvement through comprehensive management contracts, lease contracts, or concession arrangements to build and operate disposal and recycling facilities. In all four Latin American cities studied, private firms successfully built and operated a variety of disposal facilities, including transfer stations, composting plants, incinerators, and sanitary landfills. Another advantage of transferring disposal operations to the private sector is that local authorities are relieved of the conflicting responsibilities of being both operator and regulator, and can focus on setting and enforcing environmental standards. In addition, privatization often leads to technology transfer linkages with foreign companies and experts, that can be important in achieving improved disposal practice. Both private participation and foreign expertise can also play major roles in improving industrial and hazardous waste management. In Latin America, the privately run landfills studied were among the best observed in the region, in terms of meeting environmental protection objectives.

Accountability—Emphasize Performance Measures

Both the award of contracts and payment for the contractual services provided should be based on clearly defined operational standards, regulatory requirements, and specific performance measures; for example, price per ton collected, per kilometer of road swept, per ton/kilometer hauled, or per ton disposed. But the choice of specific technology options should mostly be left to the private sector, so that it can optimize operations while meeting performance requirements. Performance monitoring can include both inspection and direct measures, such as the use of weighbridges or landfill-monitoring wells, as well as mechanisms for receiving and dealing with customer complaints. With regard to the latter, the creation of a Complaints Bureau can be an extremely effective measure for involving the public in monitoring the performance of private contractors.

Postscript

The subject of public-private partnerships for improving municipal solid waste management is being given priority attention by a collaborative donor program established through an initiative of the Swiss Development Cooperation (SDC), the Urban Management Program (UMP), and the World Bank. The program is a partnership that also involves an extended group of external support agencies such as the World Health Organization (WHO) and the United Nations Center for Human Settlements (UNCHS), several bilateral donors, professional associations and specialized NGOs, and a network of developing-country experts. Efforts are focused on promoting effective public-private partnerships, developing guides for the preparation of contract and bidding documents, and understanding and developing the role of informal private-sector groups (waste pickers, microenterprises, and community groups) in waste collection and recycling activities.

This work builds on a discussion paper prepared for the UMP by Sandra Cointreau-Levine (1994), that sets out a framework for decisionmaking on private-public partnerships for the provision of solid waste services. Different forms of private involvement are analyzed, along with issues affecting choice; and criteria are proposed for choosing between public or private provision. Recently, a "toolkit" has been produced for preparing bidding documents and contracts to engage the private sector in solid waste service delivery (Cointreau-Levine and Coad, in press). In the simplest terms, these papers reiterate the need to give maximum attention to competitiveness, transparency, and accountability.

References

Bartone, Carl R., Luiz Leite, Thelma Triche, and Roland Schertenleib. 1991. "Private Sector Participation in Municipal Solid Waste Service: Experiences in Latin America." *Waste Management and Research* 9: 495–509.

Baumol, William J., and Kyu Sik Lee. 1991. "Contestable Markets, Trade, and Development." *World Bank Research Observer* 6:1–17.

Cointreau-Levine, Sandra. 1994. *Private Sector Participation in Municipal Solid Waste Services in Developing Countries: Vol. 1. The Formal Sector.* UMP Discussion Paper No. 13. Washington, DC: World Bank.

Cointreau-Levine, Sandra, and Adrian Coad. In press. *Guidance Pack: Private Sector Participation in Municipal Solid Waste Management.* St. Gallen,

Switzerland: Swiss Center for Development Cooperation in Technology and Management.

Donahue, John D. 1989. *The Privatization Decision: Public Ends, Private Means.* New York: Basic Books.

ERM (Environmental Resources Management). 1998. *Planning Guide for Strategic Municipal Solid Waste Management in Major Cities.* Draft report prepared for the World Bank, Washington, DC. Processed.

Sinha, Kazal. 1993. "Partnerships in Solid Waste Collection: Malaysian Experience." *Regional Development Dialogue* 14(3): 40–49.

World Bank. 1994. *World Development Report 1994: Infrastructure for Development.* New York: Oxford University Press.

World Wastes. 1993. "Public Collectors Inject Competition into Operations." *World Wastes* (May): 10.

Public-Private Participation in the Provision of Infrastructure to Tirrupur, India

Usha P. Raghupathi and Om Prakash Mathur

This study[5] identifies an example of governance through fiscal innovation in the area of public-private sector participation in water supply (Raghupathi 1999). The location is a small town called Tirrupur, in southern India, where the government has taken a major initiative in involving the private sector in the provision of infrastructure for the city's industrial estate, as well as for the city itself. Tirrupur will be the first town in the country to have a water-supply project that will be developed and implemented through a public-private partnership arrangement—in this case, by a joint venture company. The initiative will improve both the economic and social life of the residents of the town.

The provision and financing of municipal and urban infrastructure and services in India have historically been a responsibility of the state and local governments. Special-purpose public undertakings have also invested substantially in the financing of infrastructure such as water supply and sewerage and, on a smaller scale, citywide roads. The underlying rationale in public-sector financing is that many of these infrastructural services are in the nature of "natural monopolies," or characterized by "externalities," "non-excludability," and "low price elasticity of demand," and have, as a result, been financed from public resources.

Recent years have witnessed a major shift in thinking in the country about these financing modes. For one thing, it is increasingly recognized that public-sector resources may not be sufficient to meet the infrastructure investment requirements of cities and towns. The India Infrastructure Report, for instance, has estimated such requirements to be anywhere between Rs. 800 billion to Rs. 940 billion for the period 1996–2001 (Government of India 1996). Given the demands on public resources from other sectors, this scale of funding is unlikely to be available for urban infrastructure, thus opening it to

---

5. The study was prepared as part of the research conducted under the Global Urban Research Initiative (GURI) Phase 3 activities, 1996–97. GURI was coordinated by the Centre for Urban and Community Studies of the University of Toronto until 1998.

other financing modes and alternatives. Second, the last few years have generated within India a debate on the role of governments, including that of local governments, and what they should be concerned with. This debate has resulted in two related strands of policy: privatization, and the trend to an enabling role for the government. In a sense, privatization is an extension of the principle of subsidiarity, which requires that the government should undertake functions only to the extent that it can do so better and more efficiently than the private sector. This line of argument has reinforced the need to distinguish between the provision of public goods and services, and their production and delivery.[6] Better understanding and application of such distinctions, or what Rakesh Mohan calls the "unbundling of services," has led to an increasing interest of the private sector in the provision of such services (Government of India 1996).

As distinct from the concept of privatization, the term "enabling government" describes a situation where conditions are created for the participation of the non-governmental sector in the provision of services and infrastructure, at the same time as the non-governmental sector is given the right to compete with the government for the production of these services. These developments have ushered in an era of a pluralistic type of governance in India and, as a consequence, the gradual substitution of government as historically understood by a pluralistic range of governance bodies involving the public, private, and voluntary sectors.

The Need for Reliable Water Supply

It is in the context of this policy shift that Tirrupur, a small but highly specialized town, compelled by the need to survive in a highly competitive global market and actively supported by the different levels of government, took the initiative of involving the private sector in the provision of a good that has historically been viewed as a natural monopoly—water supply. The key factor in the initiative was the economic compulsion: good quality water must be available in adequate quantities for the cotton knitwear industry if this was to remain competitive in the international market. Water was a crucial infrastructure input in garment production for washing, dyeing, bleaching and other processes. The

---

6. One factor that has traditionally influenced the structure of government and the division of functions has been the extent of economies of scale in the production of services. Once provision and production functions are dissociated, these services can be produced by whichever sector is able to achieve the greatest economy.

existing modes of drawing water were becoming unreliable and constrained, leading to negative externalities whose costs were too high for the industry to stay economically viable.

Tirrupur is a special-grade municipal town located 50 kilometers to the north-east of Coimbatore in Tamil Nadu State in southern India. In 1971, the town recorded a population of 113,302, which increased to 235,661 by 1991. Tirrupur has been experiencing an annual population growth rate of between 3.6 and 3.8 percent; by the turn of the century its population is projected to increase to over 300,000. The economic base of the town is almost wholly linked to the manufacture of cotton knitwear. Often referred to as the *banian city* (the vest city), it initially produced vests and undergarments for the domestic market, but later extended its production for global markets. As a consequence, the growth and development of Tirrupur has been phenomenal. It accounts today for over three-quarters of India's cotton knitwear exports. In 1986, exports from the town were a mere Rs. 0.18 billion in value; by 1992 this had reached Rs. 15 billion. It is estimated that the value of exports will be between Rs. 25 billion and Rs. 30 billion in 1997. In 1986, there were only 10 to 15 leading exporters in the town, but the number had risen by 1996 to nearly 400. This spectacular growth has been achieved in spite of the poor levels of infrastructure support, such as water supply, effluent disposal, roads, power, and telecommunications.

The growth of population and industry has widened the gap between the demand for, and supply of, infrastructure and services. A major problem in Tirrupur today is water supply, the main sources of which are rivers and borewells. While the municipality provides water for household consumption, the garment industry uses non-municipal sources, such as privately trucked water and borewells, so the cost is extremely high. The town has no sewerage system and the only river that passes through the town, the Noyil, is, in fact, an open sewer. The industrial units do not have effluent treatment facilities. The bleaching and dyeing industries consume large quantities of water and dispose of it, untreated, into the river. This water is carried to downstream villages, where it has affected agriculture, human habitation, and all forms of life. The haphazard growth of the town, coupled with poor enforcement of environmental regulations by the municipality and the Tamil Nadu Pollution Control Board, have led exporters to discharge effluents consisting of toxic chemicals and colors into the Noyil river. Many dyeing units discharge their effluent into any open water body or even on land. This has brought a phenomenal increase in health risks in the town, and has also affected the supply of potable water.

Tirrupur's Financial Situation

Tirrupur town has a municipal body whose functions and fiscal powers are governed by the Tamil Nadu Municipalities Act, 1965. In 1994–95, it had a total revenue income of Rs. 103.12 million and an expenditure of Rs. 98.26 million on its revenue account. The main sources of revenue for the municipality provided for in the Act are taxes on property, non-tax revenues such as fees and fines, income from municipal properties, and state government transfers on account of shared taxes and grants, and loans on capital account. Property tax is the single largest source of revenue for the municipality, contributing anywhere between 30 and 40 percent of the revenue. The major heads of expenditure—public health and sanitation, and water supply and drainage—accounted in 1994–95 for 33.6 and 39.8 percent respectively of the total municipal revenue expenditure.

Measured in terms of the growth rate of revenue income and other financial ratios, the financial performance of Tirrupur Municipality can be said to be creditable. However, its debt servicing has been far from satisfactory, with the result that it has a large accumulated debt of over Rs. 330 million. With this financial position and the level of revenues that the municipality is able to generate, it is not in a position to undertake any large-scale expansion of the infrastructure and services for which it is responsible.

The Private Sector Organizes

Towards the end of the 1980s, the garment exporters of Tirrupur formed an association, the Tirrupur Exporters Association (TEA), to bring the problems of the industry to the attention of the government. The TEA asked the central government and the state government of Tamil Nadu to accord to Tirrupur the status of an Export Growth Center, and to make special funding arrangements for infrastructural development. The TEA argued that investments in infrastructure were essential, both to enhance the production and productivity of the garment industry, and to improve the quality of exports. Plans were accordingly formulated on the assumption that public-sector financing would become available. Because of the scale of the requirements, however, these plans made no progress; public-sector financing at this scale proved elusive.

The Tamil Nadu Corporation for Industrial Development, which had been set up in 1991 to advance the interests of industry in the state, made a similar assessment, observing that, in view of the non-availability of public funds, other institutional and financial options should be explored.

One option was to involve the private sector in the provision of such services as water supply, sewerage, effluent disposal, and roads. A key question was whether a project could be developed that would cover these components, and still be financially viable and able to pay for itself. Water was the only component that lent itself to direct charging; the cost of the other components could be met only through taxation. Several questions thus arose. In what manner should the private sector be involved in this project? What should be the mode? Should the private sector be encouraged to develop, manage and operate on an ownership or lease basis or on one of BOT? What kinds of concessions will the private sector require in order to undertake such a project? The possibilities of private-sector participation in the provision of such services also presented questions on the sources of financing, determination of a unit price, regulations, accountability, and the like. The entire exercise entailed several interrelated steps:

ESTABLISHING VIABILITY. The first step involved establishment of the feasibility and financial viability of the project covering water supply, sewerage and drainage facilities, industrial effluent collection and treatment system, and improvement and expansion of intra-city roads. Infrastructure Leasing and Financial Services (ILFS), a private company, undertook the task of preparing the feasibility report, and presented what finally came to be known as the Tirrupur Area Development Plan (TADP). The report provided details of costs, pricing, and recovery mechanisms, establishing that the project was financially viable. The Plan entailed an estimated investment of Rs. 5,890 million. It is important to point out that this exercise was preceded by large-scale field surveys, focusing on the willingness and ability of households and industry to pay for the services, and on the environmental impact of the project on the neighboring villages. The surveys constituted a crucial input to the TADP exercise.

DETERMINATION OF INSTITUTIONAL RESPONSIBILITY. A critical issue was the institutional framework that would be able to undertake the project. Considering that the implementation of the TADP would necessarily involve raising resources both in domestic and international capital markets, and would require expertise in entering into complex debt-equity arrangements, a decision was taken to create a special purpose vehicle, a joint venture company called the New Tirrupur Area Development Corporation Ltd. (NTADCL). This was considered to be the most effective option from a strategic, resource-raising and risk-sharing point of view; regulations of various types, as well as internal management capacity of Tirrupur Municipality, prevented it from playing this role. NTADCL was incorporated in 1995 and a memorandum of understanding signed between the state government of Tamil Nadu, TACID, ILFS, and TEA on the broad parameters of project design. It was a unique institutional format of pluralistic governance that included the governments, state-level parastatal agencies, a private-sector financing company, and the exporters' association, the principal user or the beneficiary of the proposed project.

CONSIDERATION OF FINANCING OPTIONS FOR THE TADP. While it was generally understood that public financing of the order envisaged was unlikely to be available, other questions concerning the proportion of debt to equity, and the mechanism for raising debt-financing, confronted such agencies as the ILFS and the state government. A broader equity base was considered both desirable and essential to secure the cooperation of the participating agencies and timely completion of the project. As such, a decision was taken for NTADCL to have equity holders comprising the Government of India, TACID, TEA, ILFS, and the BOT operator. The participation of TEA was significant as the most important beneficiary. Similarly, the equity participation of the BOT operator was viewed as necessary for ensuring its continued attention to the project's operation and maintenance. Debt, it was decided, will be raised from financing institutions such as the World Bank, USAID and ILFS, and from equipment suppliers by issuing what are tentatively called the Water Bonds.[7] The debt-to-equity ratio is envisaged to be 2.6:1. A linked, but critical, decision in this respect was to sell water on the principle of full cost recovery in the aggregate, meaning that the pricing could differentiate between consumer groups according to their ability to pay; this approach alone could ensure the financial viability of the project.

SELECTION OF THE BOT OPERATOR. The key to the success of the project and, indeed, to the larger issue of private-sector participation in such projects as water supply and sewerage, is the operator who is to be responsible not only for creating the infrastructural capital but also for operating and maintaining the project for 30

---

7. Financial closure was anticipated in late October 1999, meaning that all funds required for implementing the project should be committed and mobilized. (In fact, closure was delayed until early in 2000.) Water Bonds were to be issued once financial closure was achieved.

years. The operator has also to secure adequate return on equity within a limited period before transferring the project to NTADCL. In view of the planned financial participation of international and domestic institutions in this project, it was decided to seek global tenders on established BOT patterns and norms. The entire process of reviewing the tenders has since been conducted by experts unconnected with the participating institutions, or other stakeholders, in an open and transparent manner. The selected operator is a consortium composed of Mahindra and Mahindra, an Indian firm; Bechtel, a U.S. firm; and United Utilities International, of the United Kingdom.

The Tirrupur project constitutes a major step in putting into practice the principles underlying privatization and the enabling of government, and is a typical case of government facilitating activity by the private and other sectors. Because of its parameters and scale, the development of this project has taken several years, a period that has seen wide-ranging consultations involving public and private institutions, domestic and international financing companies, and the producers and consumers of services. It has demonstrated that diverse arrangements for financing municipal infrastructure and services are possible, of which the Tirrupur experiment represents only one model. The Tirrupur project is designed on the principle of transparency, i.e., the need to maintain the link between local benefits and local costs in a way that will ensure the awareness of taxpayers.

Observations on the Emerging Connections between Fiscal Innovations and Governance

Sound local finances form an essential component of good governance, and governance can hardly be considered effective if governments—be they central, state or local—are unable to adhere to the canons of fiscal discipline, fiscal efficiency, and fiscal autonomy. The context of the study is significant in that the past few years have witnessed in India, as in several other developing countries, an unprecedented level of interest and debate on local governance, and wide-ranging actions to empower local governments to address their numerous challenges. The central government's initiative to amend the Constitution in order to strengthen the foundations of democratic decentralization at local levels, efforts on the part of at least a few state governments to reform the local tax system, adoption by municipal governments of new modes of financing and resource-raising, and emergence of public-private partnerships in the provision of infrastructure, are but a few examples in this direction.

The case documented here has shed further light on the connections between fiscal innovations and governance. Although it is difficult to generalize, the fiscal innovations provide interesting propositions through which local and state responses can be better understood. For instance, Tirrupur shows that:

- Public financing of infrastructure is only one alternative; given the right price signals, public-private partnerships can be forged in the delivery of even those services that are characterized by "externalities." The Tirrupur case shows that an array of strategies and diverse arrangements exist to make use of the different stakeholders in the provision and delivery of services. It has demonstrated that the government itself can create conditions for the private and voluntary sectors to take up activities which are ideal for market-type pricing regimes, and thereby bring in pluralistic governance.
- Commitment and leadership are critical to initiating changes in local fiscal arrangements. In Tirrupur, it was the Tirrupur Exporters' Association and its economic interest that led to institutional restructuring and public-private enterprise for the delivery of services. It is important to recognize that leadership exists at all levels, and does not necessarily need to emanate from the public sector.

These propositions illustrate how different modes appropriate to local conditions have been used to improve the level, quality, and delivery of urban services. At the same time, citizens' acceptance of higher tax liability and new partnership arrangements in the expectation that they will be the eventual beneficiaries is an important step towards better governance of cities. Mounting pressures on local governments and their acquisition of new roles and responsibilities will have significant implications for local public finances, with emphasis shifting to issues of choice, efficiency, and accountability. The challenge for the local governments will be to provide those services that citizens are prepared to pay for.

Postscript

As of December 1999, inflationary pressures had pushed the project costs to Rs. 12,000 million (the project's financial viability, however, was not at stake). The state government had not provided any guarantee on increased tariffs. Financial closure was delayed because of the equity shortfall, and was expected to take place towards the end of January 2000.

References

Government of India. 1996. *The India Infrastructure Report: Policy Imperatives for Growth and Welfare.* New Delhi: Manager of Publications.

Raghupathi, Usha P. 1999. "Public-Private Participation in the Provision of Infrastructure to Tirrupur: A Governance Perspective." In Om Prakash Mathur, ed., *India: The Challenge of Urban Governance,* pp. 213–29. New Delhi: National Institute of Public Finance and Policy.

6

Land and Real-Estate Markets

Editor's Introduction

Richard Stren

Along with capital and labor, land is one of the three classic elements of production. Paradoxically, land is both the most widespread and one of the most complex features of cities—in both the developed and developing world. When adequate and appropriate land is available for major urban uses—such as residential, infrastructural, commercial, recreational, and industrial—a basic condition for a productive city or urban region has been established. Conversely, when land is scarce or too expensive for certain uses, and well-functioning markets (or submarkets) do not operate, distortions may be created that in turn are likely to reduce the overall productivity of the municipal area.

Both using land for certain public purposes (such as the building of transport networks, community buildings, or recreational areas) and contributing to the maintenance of well-functioning urban land and real-estate markets have become increasingly the responsibility of local governments the world over. The readings in this section deal with a number of aspects of the operation and regulation of these markets.

One of the most important challenges highlighted in the literature on land and housing is the vexing question of land ownership and conveyance. Who has rights over urban land, how these rights are recognized and even protected, and how land is transferred, can have a major impact on the overall availability of land for development. In many cities of the developing world, land rights are ambiguous and multifaceted; a conflict exists between formal and informal markets; formal registration and/or adjudication of land is a very complex, costly, and lengthy affair; and conflicts are legion. A more generalized approach to this traditional question is posed in the paper by Alexandra Ortiz and Alain Bertaud. After a discussion of why governments—particularly local governments—intervene in the urban land market, they elaborate typical planning objectives and some of the policy tools that are used to achieve these objectives. For example, the spatial planning of a city normally involves a zoning map, but to understand the implications of such a desired pattern, the authors recommend studies and analysis of the current distribution of people on the land, a projection of market trends, and the spatial trends (and their costs) implied by zoning plans. The results of applying a model proposed by Bertaud show that in most cases city plans "contradict the incentives implied by market forces and that, more important, the city's plans are internally inconsistent." The second part of the paper looks at the notion of "access to real-estate assets" (i.e., bundles of rights on land and on the structures affixed to it), particularly in relation to improving access by the poor. Using examples of planning tools such as zoning and the floor/area ratio, subdivision restrictions and construction codes, and land titling programs, the authors illustrate some of both the difficulties and the possibilities of improving land access.

In many developing countries, good information on the operation of land and housing markets is at a premium. But both planners and private-sector operators need more information in order to make optimal decisions about the use of urban land in the future. While land and housing markets are neither perfectly competitive nor in equilibrium in developing countries, the establishment of such parameters as rents, prices, and demand and supply for land and housing can be described in a formal way using basic microeconomic theory. The article by Ayse Pamuk introduces a basic equilibrium model and then discusses how city managers and urban planners can identify deviations from the model. As a general rule, housing and land markets will work more effectively to the extent that good information is available; Pamuk's article, using the example of research done in Trinidad, attempts to illustrate what kinds of data might be collected in order to improve public and private sector decisionmaking.

To the extent of the availability of data to the municipal authorities, in most cases they will wish to apply some form of taxation to the land, in order to support municipal services and capital investments. We have discussed the general subject of local taxation elsewhere in this volume, but

Enid Slack's article in this section focuses on the characteristics of the property tax—perhaps the most widely applied form of local taxation the world over. Since property taxes are applied in so many forms, and are so often in the process of being reformed, Slack develops six major principles for the evaluation of property taxes: fairness based on benefits received; fairness based on ability to pay; neutrality; stability; accountability; and ease of administration. She then tracks the process (using the Ontario example) of assessing and taxing real property, concluding with two examples of how to use variable tax rates, depending on the objectives of the exercise.

The final reading in this section is a case study of Portland, Oregon. In this well-known example of a "best practice," Charles Hales explains the application of land-use regulations to improve the economy, strengthen the local government, and provide an improved quality of life for citizens at all income levels. Reflecting on the conditions necessary to achieve success in a North American setting, Hales notes the importance of the community-oriented tradition in Oregon, and the support by a popular governor for a state-level law (Senate Bill 100) which gave citizens access to the planning process. The same Bill required each city and county to adopt a comprehensive land-use plan according to 19 state-wide goals. Each metropolitan area was to draw an urban growth boundary, within which a mix of multi-family and single-family housing would be designated by the city. Within this legislative framework, land-use planning in Portland supported the state's agricultural goals; while a successful grassroots campaign defeated a plan to build a new freeway through residential neighborhoods, leading to the decision of city council to build the city's first light rail line. Hales also points out that Portland's high standards of development requirements in terms of infrastructure, together with mixed-use zoning and the development of public transport, have attracted investment to the city because of the resulting higher quality of life. While the Portland case has been a successful example of land-use planning in its own terms, Hales cautions other cities to find their own recipe, and not to follow the Portland example in an unmitigated fashion.

Land Markets and Urban Management: The Role of Planning Tools

Alexandra Ortiz and Alain Bertaud

Local governments are elected to provide (or to ensure adequate provision of) services to their constituencies. Development objectives, in principle chosen democratically, guide the action plan of those governments. Urban development objectives can be: creating an efficient spatial urban structure; improving the quality of the environment; increasing housing affordability; decreasing commuting time; avoiding congestion in the city center; increasing employment opportunities. To achieve those objectives, planning tools comprise land-use regulations, infrastructure investments, and fiscal policies. City master plans do often contain both the city's objectives and the set of tools to achieve that vision. However, due to over-regulation and lack of quantified analysis, regulations often contradict each other, objectives are inconsistent, and the tools fail to achieve the goals for which they were designed. This article addresses three points concerning the role of planning tools: (i) why and how governments intervene in the urban market; (ii) the need to use quantitative indicators to "audit" government intervention and city master plans; and (iii) how planning tools affect the access of the urban poor to real-estate assets.

Why Do Governments Intervene in the Urban Market?

Economists argue that governments (including local governments) intervene in urban markets to compensate for "market failures," that is, those factors that prevent free private markets from achieving an efficient allocation of resources. Market failures include: the existence of public goods—goods whose consumption by some consumers does not imply non-consumption by others, e.g., streetlighting or fire protection; natural monopoly; large transactions costs; and externalities. Due to the existence of market failures, the social costs (benefits) of producing a given commodity or service are higher (lower) than the private costs. In this context, if the service were left to the discretion of the private sector, it would be produced at levels that would be lower than the social optimum. Public intervention is required to bring production to the point of social equilibrium.

In the case of land markets, externalities can be positive and negative. Negative externalities include: traffic congestion; environmental costs—real-estate development can reduce local supply of green space, affect air quality, increase pressure on local water and solid waste collection; and infrastructure costs, as the neighborhood attempts to deal with the above costs. There are also positive externalities (Malpezzi 1999) such as productivity and employment, racial and economic integration, and benefits associated with homeownership. While few studies have measured the cost of housing-market regulation, the prevalent incentives are consistent with a view that the land market brings about negative externalities. Regulation of land use tends to increase the price and reduce the quantity of land offered, in comparison with an absence of regulation.

The Need to Quantify the Impact of Regulations

Assuming that regulations are needed—to compensate for market failures and to pursue urban development objectives—land-use regulation can occur through the use of several mechanisms, notably zoning regulations; land-use restrictions (for example, on conversion of land from rural to urban uses); road widths, set backs and floor/area ratios; building codes; rent controls; impact fees; and other means affecting the provision of infrastructure and the transport network necessary for real-estate development.

For the urban manager, the first question is whether the urban objectives defined in the political agenda are consistent and feasible. Are the city's development plans consistent with market-oriented development? Does the city's approach to development enable it to exploit the new opportunities confronting the city? Do the proposed public investments and controls on private investments encourage and facilitate growth? How efficiently do the city's public investments deal with the already significant air pollution problems in light of the almost certain increase in demand for automotive transport?

To deal with these questions and to choose the best planning tools, we need to use quantitative indicators. Most of us know the list of problems related to the spatial organization of cities that can presumably be caused by free markets: urban sprawl, strip developments, loss of agricultural land, deterioration of ecologically fragile sites, densities that are too high or too low, and so on. These are the spatial *diseases* that good land-use planning is supposed to cure. The regulatory tools proposed—green belts, zoning, urban growth boundaries—should bring order to the perceived spatial anarchy generated by the market. However, while poor spatial organization is often considered a major urban problem, it has seldom been defined quantitatively; and in the absence of quantification of the problem, measurement of the effectiveness of any proposed remedy will be difficult.

Master Plan Objectives and Planning Tools

Any broad urban objectives branch out into sub-objectives that have direct spatial implications. These spatial implications have to be made explicit before an implementation tool can be designed. For instance, an objective to reduce pollution often leads to a sub-objective to increase the use of public transport and decrease the use of private cars. This sub-objective has a spatial implication. Increasing the use of public transport implies either increasing the number of people and firms located within walking distance of the public transport network, or expanding public transport routes in areas with densities high enough to justify them economically. In spatial terms this means allowing high densities around existing transport corridors, and generally promoting a more compact city. The use of public transport as the main transport mode also implies a monocentric city structure. Other environmental objectives call for the need to protect agricultural areas against "urban encroachments." This would also suggest that—in spatial terms—the regulatory implementation tools contained in the plan should promote a more compact city than the one that would be created by unregulated market forces.

In contrast, some objectives might suggest a more spread out, lower-density city. For instance, a concern with housing affordability might imply increasing the supply of land and consequently letting the city spread. At the same time, improved housing affordability might also require reducing minimum plot size and increasing maximum floor/area ratio. Such changes would imply a greater range of densities between low- and high-income neighborhoods. Depending on the land market, an objective aimed at making housing more affordable might result in either a more widely spread, lower-density city, or a higher-density, more compact city. A concern for the urban environment—as opposed to the natural environment outside the city—might mean higher consumption of land per household and therefore an expansion of the city at lower densities.

Whatever objectives are eventually selected, planners need to develop indicators that can reflect the current and projected urban spatial structure; and they should show in which direction these indicators are expected to move to satisfy the planing objectives. Zoning provides the most widely used regulatory tool to implement the master plan's objectives spatially. Unfortunately, zoning is often seen as an objective per se rather than as a tool. The spatial organization implicit in a zoning plan is often hidden because the plan is the result of a parcel-by-parcel negotiation, and the sum of the parcel-based decisions are seldom added together at the end of the exercise. Because planners initially define the spatial objectives of the plan, it is often taken for granted that the zoning map will be consistent with the plan's objectives. This is not self-evident at all. A zoning map is a complex three-dimensional document that is easy to design but difficult to analyze. In addition, in most cases, planners have not defined the theoretical framework that would permit conducting such a spatial analysis.

To analyze the spatial organization of a city and the implications of a zoning map, we would, first, *analyze the current spatial distribution* of people and compare it to the spatial organization implied by the objectives; second, *analyze the market trends* represented by the spatial pattern of current land prices and building permits, compare market trends to the current spatial organization, and assess whether the market is changing the spatial organization of the city. If the market is changing the spatial organization, then we will examine whether the change is in conformity with or in opposition to the objectives. Third, we would analyze the *spatial organization implied by the zoning plan*—associated with the major objectives—and compare it to: the existing spatial pattern; the trend shown by the market; and the plan's objectives. Finally, we would make an attempt to evaluate the *cost, if any, implied by adopting regulations* that contradict market trends, and we would also identify losers and winners.

Bertaud's model (Malpezzi 1999) has been applied to several countries and cities. The indicators developed to measure a city's spatial structure include: (a) the proportion of land use types; (b) the average consumption of built-up land per person; (c) the density gradient and the density profile; (d) the population dispersion index; (e) the average distance per person to the central business district (CBD); (f) the land dispersion index; (g) the land price and rent gradient; and (h) other sectoral indicators linking spatial structure with the design of infrastructure networks—for instance, square meters of street per person, length of public transport lines, average trip length.

The results indicate that in most cases the city's plans contradict the incentives implied by market forces and that, more important, the city's plans are internally inconsistent. For example, in some ex-socialist cities, the master plan may point the city structure towards becoming a compact, radio-concentric city with few suburbs. The zoning plan, however, with its implicit bias towards reinforcing the land-use patterns developed under socialism and its very specific constraints on density of land use, would prevent this from happening.

Why Access to Real-Estate Assets Is Important for the Poor

Access to real-estate assets[1] is important for all citizens, but particularly for the poor for two reasons. First, real-estate assets are an important form of wealth and socio-economic mobility; second, real-estate assets can be used as collateral for loans. Studies confirm that clear land title increases property values. Jimenez (1984) and Friedman, Jimenez, and Mayo (1988) find a 58 percent increase in property values in Davao (Philippines) and 25 percent in Manila; Dowall and Leaf (1990) find increases of 45 to 60 percent in Jakarta; and Simon (1995) a 21 percent increase in Quito.

On the social side, access to real-estate assets impacts on the sense of pride and citizenship of new owners. In a slum upgrading project in Guatemala City (World Bank 1998b), residents felt the project had changed their lives since "now we live in a *colonia* (formal neighborhood) and not in an *asentamiento* (informal settlement)." While the objective difference between formal and informal neighborhoods is given by the degree of enforceability of the property contracts, the difference between *colonia* and *asentamiento* goes beyond enforceability degrees; it includes a difference of social status.

Most people do own real-estate assets, in one form or another. The urban poor are no exception, particularly those who live in squatter settlements,[2] exerting restricted rights (use and possession, and to some extent disposition and control) over land and its improvements. If quantified, these holdings would account for a significant percentage of the real-estate assets in a city. In fact, large percentages of urban dwellers live in informal settlements. More than 40 percent of the urban population and around 40 percent of the total area in large Latin American cities like Caracas, Bogotá, Lima, and Guatemala City are informal. In most of these settlements

---

1. Real-estate assets are defined as *bundles of rights* on land and on the structures affixed to it. These rights are: use or enjoyment, control (right to alter the property physically), possession (right to occupy and exclude others from occupying), and disposition (allows conveyance of all or part of the bundle of rights). Renters, for instance, have the rights to use the property and to exclude others from enjoying it, but can neither make significant alterations nor dispose of it. Therefore, *real-estate assets do not involve solely real-property ownership, but rather combinations of real-property rights.*

2. The expressions "squatter settlements," "informal settlements," and "slums" are used interchangeably here and mean areas in which the traditional urban development process is reversed: first, families occupy the land, then they build on it, next they install infrastructure, and only at the end do they acquire legal title.

individual structures as well as common spaces are improved over the years. The result is a significant value. In a study undertaken in Lima in 1984, using replacement cost, the average value of an informal dwelling was estimated at 22,038 soles, and the total value of all informal dwellings in the city at 8,319.8 million soles, an amount equivalent to 69 percent of Peru's total long-term external debt at that time (de Soto 1989).

The main problem in the case of the urban poor is the high costs of making these holdings legal and complying with expensive urban regulations. In fact, local planning tools, designed to correct negative externalities, might have adverse effects on access to real-estate assets by the urban poor. While one does not advocate the abolition of planning tools, one stresses the importance of assessing their implications and ascertaining that benefits do outweigh costs.

Effects of Local Planning Tools on Access to Real-Estate Assets

Local planning tools, in particular land-use controls, can be viewed as collective property rights, controlled and exchanged by rational economic agents (Fischel 1985). As such they have the potential to affect the quality of the environment, the provision of public services, and the relative distribution of wealth in a community. The paragraphs below elaborate on access by the urban poor to real-estate assets and on how the local planning tools affect that access. The tools include: (a) zoning, which is the central land-use control in most municipal governments; (b) subdivision restrictions and construction codes; and (c) land titling programs.

Zoning and the Floor/Area Ratio

Zoning determines the land uses allowed in certain areas through—among other measures—minimum lot sizes, maximum construction density, and setbacks. These three can be synthesized in one measure: floor/area ratio (FAR). By controlling the FAR, local governments are controlling consumption of land, the only factor in which poor residents can outbid non-poor residents. As figure 6.1 shows, non-poor residents will always prefer more consumption of land and will be willing to bid for it only after a minimum amount L^*. Poor residents will also prefer more consumption of land, but can only outbid the non-poor below L^*. By imposing a minimum land consumption at L_{min}, municipal governments force the demand of poor residents to the right of L_{min}, where, for the most part, they cannot outbid the non-poor. This explains why large-lot zoning is often labeled exclusionary zoning. The legal options of poor residents to access land are severely curtailed.

Figure 6.1.   Bid Rent for Land: Poor Versus Nonpoor

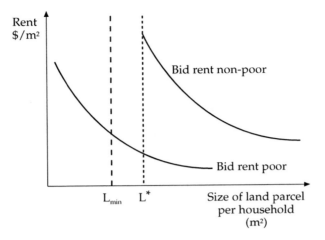

Source: Authors.

During preparation of a slum upgrading project in Caracas (Venezuela), one of the municipalities was found to have established a maximum density of 240–320 inhabitants per hectare, when the observed density in the project area that falls within this jurisdiction is 441 (World Bank 1998a). The same ordinance requires parcel sizes of 250 square meters, when the existing lot areas are 70–100 square meters, and it also limits the number of floors to three. These conditions are identical to those that apply to the highest-density single-family category, R5, and more restrictive than those for multi-family categories R6–R9 (which allow up to 1,200 inhabitants per hectare). The municipal government justifies these restrictions on the following grounds: lack of water and sewerage services; lack of wastewater treatments; unstable soil; steep slopes; and lack of street access. All these are factors which increase the probability of slides, the spreading of fire, and diseases.

By controlling the FAR these conditions will not improve. In fact, in the Caracas slums there are few roads, most of them are paved, and the construction is very tight, leaving few open spaces, resulting in an excellent way of minimizing water infiltration into the soil. This in turn, according to engineering reports, has prevented erosion and landslides. Housing construction is also adapted to the steep topography. To improve the negative conditions identified by the municipality, there is a need to provide access streets to neighborhoods and access to main bulk water and sewerage connections, and to improve the overall physical layout of the districts. On this basis, a more realistic FAR can be established, higher than the one stipulated by the regulation. All these measures are included in the project design. Fortunately for the project the same ordinance provides for an exception to the FAR requirements in the case of special projects as determined by the municipality; without this variance, the project could not proceed as designed because lower FARs would imply: higher plot prices to be paid by beneficiaries (the project contemplates cost recovery); higher property maintenance costs (taxes, services, etc.) that the target population would not be able to afford; and resettlement of a large portion of beneficiaries, which is socially undesirable.

Subdivision Restrictions and Construction Codes

Subdivision restrictions are imposed on developers to ensure that infrastructure services are in place in a newly developed area. The logic behind these restrictions is that the municipal government will eventually assume responsibility for operation and maintenance of the infrastructure, and proper planning of its design is therefore in the municipality's best interests. Construction codes regulate construction, maintenance, and use of structures in order to protect public health and safety. In this situation there is a trade-off between capital costs that are to be paid ultimately by the users, and maintenance costs to be paid by the municipality. As the municipality establishes the rules, it naturally tries to shift the situation to higher capital costs and fewer maintenance costs. The objective of these regulations is laudable but the application can be distorted either by requesting standards that are too high or by specifying certain materials and construction techniques, increasing the price of new development and, in some cases, making it inaccessible to potential low-income buyers. The following case illustrates this point.

In Cali (Colombia) in the early 1990s there was an ambitious project to construct housing and infrastructure for the urban poorest on a 380 hectare tract of land. The project was designed to provide 28,000 lots of 60 square meters each, with basic services, to be developed by self-building. In a second stage 22,500 lots would be serviced in a similar fashion and be developed as multifamily housing. In January 1993, when the mayor presented the *Ciudadela Desepaz* project to the city council, the commercial price of land[3] was 365 pesos per square meter. In August 1993, after subdivision regulations were set and enforced by the municipal government, the

---

3. Based on the price at which lots were actually sold. Prices are in constant pesos as of December 1988.

commercial price increased to 1,580 pesos per square meter, or more than fourfold in a period of seven months. The specific regulations established at that time included: the dedication of 15 percent of the total area to community centers and open space, the development of three deep wells to connect 14,500 units, sewerage connections, electricity connections, installations for public telephones, dedication of 15–20 percent of the area for vehicular streets, dedication of 15–20 percent of the area for sidewalks, provision of parking spaces in the proportion of one for every 10 lots, and dedication of 3 percent of the area as a reserve. According to the cost figures of the private developers, the cost of urbanization oscillated between 32 and 50 percent of their total costs. The land belonged to only seven families who took advantage of the increase in land prices generated by the planning process, and legal complications in the use of municipal eminent domain to acquire the land, and began speculating. Land prices continued to increase as infrastructure was provided; they reached a final peak of 3,600 pesos per square meter. With such an increase in the price of land, the housing units were sold to low- and middle-income families, and not to the poorest as initially targeted.

Land Titling

Municipal governments can sell land to urban squatters (at subsidized values) through land titling programs. These programs can have problems of two types that make access to land by the poor too difficult: eligibility restrictions; and complicated and time-consuming processes.

In terms of eligibility restrictions, Guatemalan law, for instance, requires a beneficiary to be Guatemalan by birth. And although Guatemala has not had a history of foreign immigration it is always possible to find foreigners who, according to this law, even if they have been living on Guatemalan soil for years, cannot receive title. It was found in the ordinance of a Venezuelan municipality that only family groups can be beneficiaries, excluding single men and women without children. These restrictions do not bring about any benefits; in fact they have the potential to encourage violations of the law, as individuals might get false documentation in order to meet the requirements.

In terms of lengthy land titling processes, it has been reported that in urban Peru before 1980 it could take as long as 20 years to issue titles in one neighborhood, with processes involving 200 steps and more than a dozen institutions. In the *La Limonada* neighborhood of Guatemala City the land titling process was reported to take seven years to complete. In contrast, recent studies show (with data available for Caracas, Guatemala City

[Guatemala], Lima [Peru] and San José de Costa Rica), that these processes can be shorter, in the order of 6–10 months and with 10–12 steps if tasks are simplified and coordinated.

The case of Guatemala illustrates the intricacies of the institutional setting for land titling. At present there are five public agencies involved in the process of land regularization: the public owners of land (the National Housing Bank and the municipalities); the National Valuation Agency (NVA); the notaries; the Public Registry; and the National Settlement Directorate. The NVA has information on about 30 percent of the parcels in the country, but the assessments are outdated. Despite its inefficiencies, it is the only institution which by law can perform the land value assessments for regularization of informal settlements. The National Housing Bank is in the process of liquidation and therefore does not have the capacity to handle simultaneously the administration of previous loans, the regularization of new plots, and the preparation of a massive inventory in order to transfer, according to the law, its assets to the newly created Housing Fund and to the municipalities. The role of the National Settlement Directorate is not clear. It is responsible to one of the Presidential Secretariats and its function is to certify that families have been in possession for at least two years of the land that they are in the process of buying. It appears to owe this involvement to having carried out a census of informal settlements some years ago. A better alternative would be to establish legalization committees, with legal assistance and participation of the communities themselves. In that case, proof of possession can be accomplished through the testimony of neighbors and the use of existing documentation; in many informal developments a register of the original distribution of land plots and subsequent transactions is kept for a certain period of time. This mechanism also ensures that new invaders do not pour in, in search of undeserved titles, since it is in the best interest of the existing dwellers to protect their territory.

Implications for Urban Projects

Several recommendations can be considered for urban projects in order to increase access to real-estate assets by the urban poor. These are:

- Audit the existing legislation sufficiently far in advance to find potential problems, such as eligibility restrictions, and zoning and land subdivision regulations, that present unaffordable cost thresholds.
- In land titling programs—within slum upgrading projects or

as stand-alone projects—simplify the processes by reducing the number of agencies involved, contracting out certain activities to the private sector, and letting the interested parties, namely the communities, participate actively.[4] Ensure that titles are registered, otherwise ownership of land is not publicly recognized.

- Look at real estate as a bundle of rights on real property. Under this approach real estate is not necessarily associated with property ownership but with combinations of rights, and this allows for more creative solutions that entail the unbundling and rebundling of rights. One such option is to title land through condominium property. In this case families might have access to ownership of percentages of a lot, which would be so small that they would neither bear any construction costs nor meet even the most lenient zoning regulations. Besides, it would be easier for utility companies to sell services in bulk to the condominium rather than to many small properties. Internal access in the condominium will be determined by the co-owners, exactly as in apartment buildings. In this system both the capital and maintenance costs of infrastructure would be borne by the users, solving the municipality/users conflict of interests.

- Explore alternatives (rather than prohibiting them). In Caracas, for instance, informal real-estate markets are quite active and have achieved some degree of recognition by the municipal governments. Illegal occupiers of land plots have developed a parallel information and registration system by notarizing their ownership of the improvements that they have made (called *bienhechurías*) through documents called *títulos supletorios*. The improvements are sold and the transactions are notarized, allowing the compilation of information on informal real-estate transactions. Notaries, who are part of the formal judiciary system, recognize these limited property rights and their exchange. Some public service agencies do this as well by requesting *títulos supletorios*, among other requirements, for service connections. In effect, these partial titles allow a certain degree of contract enforceability, which is better than

---

4. Particularly suitable activities in which communities can participate are: census of the families, monitoring the compilation of requirements by families, solving minor conflicts, and communication campaigns. This approach has been field tested successfully in the Laos Land Titling Project and in the Indonesia Land Administration Project under different modalities: surveying teams made up of local officials and community members, and communication campaign teams led by an NGO and community members.

none. If this system were recognized more widely, it could be improved to make it more systematic, transparent, efficient, and congruent with land-management policies and land-information systems.

The final issue is the possibility of preventing new land invasions and future growth of informal settlements by allowing demand-driven low-income new developments. In Latin America slums are formed when some families, tired of renting small rooms (one room per family) in tenement houses, get organized, sometimes by a natural leader, sometimes by NGOs, to invade a tract of land that, according to their investigation, is either public land or private land presenting some tenure irregularities (for example, property taxes have not been paid for an extensive period of time). If given the choice, these families would prefer to buy the land as an association and then develop it with technical assistance, rather than squatting illegally. If such an option existed it would constitute a demand-driven urban land reform process. In fact, a similar rationale has been adopted in some cases in Latin America. In Caracas, for instance, some years ago, a community settled informally on a private estate, organized itself, created an association, *Asociación de Vecinos del Barrio Pedro Camejo*, and negotiated directly with the property owner. After an agreement was reached, the association bought the land and awarded individual titles to families. The association created an informal internal regulatory framework to ensure fairness and transparency in the process.

This case illustrates several of the points that a demand-driven low-income development process would entail: (i) organization of the community under a legal entity that can negotiate and trade in the market; (ii) the transaction is between two parties only, making it simpler and faster; and (iii) the transaction is private, with no government intervention. In the case of the Pedro Camejo neighborhood the purchase of the land took place after the invasion and subsequent urbanization. Under the proposal presented here, the land purchase process would take place before settlement and urbanization.

To mimic the demand-driven rural land reform processes, demand-driven low-income developments would need the creation of an agency or a unit within the Ministry of Urban Development or its equivalent. Organized groups of families would present to the agency proposals for development projects. Technical assistance would be offered to the families in the preparation of such proposals. The technical assistance would ideally be contracted out to the private sector and/or NGOs by the public agency. This will ensure independence of technical criteria at the same time as full coverage of the service. The proposals would include possible land tracts to be purchased, progressive master plans for infrastructure and community services, progressive housing construction plans, costs, internal and external contracting arrangements, cash and in-kind contributions, and necessary technical assistance. The agency would evaluate the proposals and select those that yield more economic return and have higher prospects of sustainability. The beneficiaries would proceed to acquire land and initiate its development, and the agency would provide technical assistance throughout the projects.

The parallel between the above proposal and the demand-driven rural land reform processes is, of course, not perfect. The scarcity of urban land and its consequent high costs compared to those of rural land are considerable. This means that the search for a suitable tract of land on which to develop the project might be time consuming and costly. And then, once the land is found, its price might be too high to the point of making the project infeasible. The solution might lie in providing incentives to property owners and using public land management tools like land readjustment, zoning changes, land banks, etc. Proposals of this nature should be seriously considered, but can nevertheless be improved by discussion with both stakeholders and local planners.

References

De Soto, Hernando. 1989. *The Other Path: The Invisible Revolution in the Third World*. New York: Harper and Row.

Dowall, David E., and Michael Leaf. 1990. "The Price of Land for Housing in Jakarta: An Analysis of the Effects of Location, Urban Infrastructure and Tenure on Residential Plot Prices." Report prepared for the Regional Housing and Urban Development Office, U.S. Agency for International Development, Washington, DC.

Fischel, William A. 1985. *The Economics of Zoning Laws: A Property Rights Approach to American Land Use Controls*. Baltimore: Johns Hopkins University Press.

Friedman, Joseph, Emmanuel Jimenez, and Stephen K. Mayo. 1988. "The Demand for Tenure Security in Developing Countries." *Journal of Development Economics* 29(2): 185–99.

Jimenez, Emmanuel. 1984. "Tenure Security and Urban Squatting." *Review of Economics and Statistics* 66(4): 556–62.

Malpezzi, Stephen. 1999. "The Regulation of Urban Development: Lessons from International Experience." Washington, DC, World Bank. Processed.

Simon, Alison. 1995. "Sequencing Infrastructure Development in the *Barrios Marginales* of Quito, Ecuador: Policy Findings of a Hedonic Price Model." Ph.D. dissertation. Department of Urban and Regional Planning, University of Illinois at Urbana-Champaign.

World Bank. 1998a. "Caracas Slum Upgrading Project." Documentation.

World Bank. 1998b. "Guatemala City Low Income Settlements Project." Documentation.

Wurtzebach, Charles, and Mike E. Miles. 1995. *Modern Real Estate.* 5th ed. New York: John Wiley.

Tools for a Land and Housing Market Diagnosis

Ayse Pamuk

The Urban Land and Housing Crisis

Cities in the developing world are growing by 62 million inhabitants each year, requiring the annual addition of some 16 million new dwelling units to their housing stock. As a result, planners in rapidly expanding major cities are faced with the challenge of making their land and housing markets work efficiently and equitably for all households, while striving to finance these efforts with funds generated, for the most part, locally.

Facing increasing population growth and residential density requires knowledge and planning on the part of city managers. Poor planning for new growth and redevelopment often means massive settlements built at substandard quality and without government approvals, resulting not only in lost planning control for city managers, but also foregone municipal revenues and expensive upgrading of poorly built settlements. Informed decisionmaking by public sector agencies, households, and private-sector homebuilders requires sound information on land and housing market operations. Lack of knowledge about demand for housing units and services, and ambiguities in land ownership, often result in poor business decisions by the private sector, and poor decisions on spatial reorganization by urban planners.

In the following sections I introduce a stylized description of land and housing market operations, and discuss how city managers and urban planners can enhance their local management capacity and thereby improve urban policymaking.

Basic Urban Land and Housing Economics

Basic microeconomic theory holds that most economic relationships between consumers and producers in markets are governed by demand and supply fundamentals. Prices are determined under conditions of perfect competition and perfect information, and in the absence of barriers to market participation. Households seek to maximize their well-being (utility) subject to their budget constraints, and producers seek to maximize their profits by combining inputs (land, labor, capital) with available technology. These conditions enable consumers and producers (market actors) to interact in markets that are in equilibrium and where prices are determined competitively.

While the pricing of many products in the market (e.g., automobiles) does fit this model, it cannot be assumed that land and housing prices are determined by perfectly competitive market conditions, especially in developing countries. This is due to several features peculiar to land and housing: (a) they are fixed in space; (b) housing is expensive to build or acquire; (c) both have long lifetimes (housing usually lasts for 50 to 75 years); and (d) accessing land and housing requires households and suppliers to incur significant transaction costs (e.g., to identify available properties for sale or rent; to negotiate sale or rental contracts; to complete land titling; to transfer ownership). Under these conditions, prices are far from being determined under conditions where demand and supply are equal.

These peculiar characteristics, especially locational fixity, lie at the heart of the earliest theories of land rent. The notion of location in relation to place of employment has been the focus of access-space models since the 1820s (Ricardo 1817; Von Thunen 1826), and still serves as a good starting point for our discussion of land and housing prices.

Locational Land Rent

Locational, or Ricardian, rent (named after David Ricardo, who developed an access-space model in 1817), is the price that occupants are willing to pay for a piece of land's unique locational advantages. Citywide, the demand for such locational advantages determines the *relative* value of land and housing at different locations. Their supply, on the other hand, determines the overall *level* of prices in the city. Understanding demand and supply fundamentals for land and housing markets is therefore critical for discovering the spatial pattern of prices.

Briefly, under basic microeconomic model assumptions, demand for land is derived (as a residual) from the demand for the services produced on the land (e.g., agriculture, housing). Thus, demand for residential land is derived from the demand for housing. Demand for land is also affected by the number of people wanting to hold land as an investment, especially as a hedge against inflation. The supply of land is determined by topography and possible housing density, as well as by land-use regulations that specify the density and type of use, and the level of infrastructure, such as roads, municipal water, and sewerage trunk lines.

Substitution of Structure for Land

Real estate is developed at varying densities in metropolitan areas; this is due to the possibility of factor substitution—a substitution that takes place between land and structure. At more central locations, where land is more expensive, residential density is greater. Residential density declines with distance from the central city. This relationship is depicted by the density gradient. A common measure of density is FAR (floor area ratio), expressed as a ratio of building per square footage of land. A FAR of 3:1, for example, means that, for every square foot of land, the landowner may erect three square feet of building. Because of setback and lot coverage requirements, the landowner might have to build a taller building to obtain the square footage. Cost of construction also varies with the FAR, as higher density buildings are more expensive to construct; a developer's profit will thus depend on the construction costs at the FAR permitted.

Land Prices

Land prices are closely linked to demand and supply; when high population growth exceeds the capacity of developers to provide land for housing, land prices rise; or if land-use regulations limit the expansion of supply, price increases should be expected (see Table 6.1).

The absence of strong demand pressures may translate into low land prices in some cases, but regulatory constraints in these contexts should be carefully evaluated. In Trinidad and Tobago, for example, housing demand has been weak because of weak macroeconomic conditions, but cumbersome land transfer processes and highly uncertain building permit approvals are likely to result in land price increases once demand improves (Pamuk and Dowall 1998).

In most countries, local governments regulate land use through zoning and subdivision regulations, and they guide land development through infrastructure provision. Land-use regulations also affect land prices; restrictive regulations (e.g., growth controls) may result in higher land prices, especially if there are no possibilities for population spillover to neighboring jurisdictions, or for infill development in the city's core. Disparity in infrastructure and service extension among neighborhoods may also create price differentials between serviced and unserviced land.

Local governments fund the provision of urban services to their residents through the taxation of real-estate assets. Service delivery variation among localities in a metropolitan area results in a housing price gradient

Table 6.1.   Demand Conditions, Regulatory Constraints, and Land Prices

	Demand conditions	
Regulatory constraints	*If weakened*	*If strengthened*
High	Stable land prices (e.g., Port-of-Spain)	"Skyrocketing" land prices (e.g., Rio de Janeiro, Istanbul)
Low	Low growth in land prices	Medium growth in land prices (e.g., Bangkok, Jakarta)

Source: Pamuk and Dowall 1998, p. 287.

different from the one that is based simply on commuting distance. Poor service delivery in U.S. inner cities, for example, coupled with the flight of wealthier households to the suburbs, has produced pockets of centrally located areas with depressed land prices. When better services can be found at greater distances from the city center, the effect of commuting on land prices diminishes.

Population growth can increase land, and therefore housing, prices significantly, because land absorbs increases in location rent. Since households value proximity to employment, higher land prices near the city center should be expected. In addition, the possibility of substitution of structure for land will result in higher residential densities at the city's core.

Housing Prices

Housing rents or prices compensate for housing attributes, such as size, number of bathrooms, and construction quality, as well as the locational advantages associated with the site. Thus, potential buyers can make implicit valuation of all the attributes of the house, and assign explicit prices for each attribute (e.g., lot size, number of rooms, view). These are not directly observed in housing markets but can be estimated by *hedonic price models*. A hedonic price equation considers the market price paid for a house to be a function of all observable characteristics of that house. Data on housing prices can be obtained by tracking sale transactions (e.g., multiple listing services of real estate agents) or by asking residents directly to estimate the current market value of their house.

Since housing stock adjustment takes time, short-term shifts in demand or supply may result in price changes. Responsiveness of homebuilders to changes in housing demand (e.g., population growth) is determined by land-use regulations. By reducing the supply of land, regulations can cause house prices to rise.

Demand for Housing Units and Services

Two different measures of housing are used in housing market studies: housing units (stock and flow); and housing services. The market for housing units is simply the demand for and supply of dwelling units, and can be relatively easy to measure. The market for housing services considers quality of housing units, with one unit of housing service being the quantity of service yielded by one unit of housing stock per unit of time. The price per unit of housing service is rent (what consumers pay for the flow of services from one standard dwelling per unit of time). Housing services therefore take into account the size of the unit, its structural quality, and locational amenities such as the quality of public schools, local taxes, and access to open space.

Demand for housing units is determined by economic factors, such as household income, economic base of a local area, savings, and interest rates; and by demographic factors, such as rate and level of household formation.

Household income is a strong predictor of housing consumption. Housing demand studies in developing countries show that housing demand is inelastic with respect to income. For renters, income elasticity of demand ranges from 0.3 to 0.6. For owners, it ranges from 0.4 to 0.8 (Malpezzi and Mayo 1985). An income elasticity of demand for housing of 0.8 means that a 10 percent increase in income will result in an 8 percent increase in housing consumption.

Housing demand is also affected by housing prices. When these are high, effective demand for housing decreases. Priced out of the formal housing market, many lower income households in the developing world undertake informal home-building activities.

Demand for the type and quality of housing (rather than simply quantity) is harder to forecast. It is determined by life-cycle and demographic characteristics of households, which in turn influence their tastes and preferences. Housing consumption, for example, increases with age as well as with income. Increases in household size, on the other hand, do not seem to increase housing consumption.

Supply of Housing

Housing is supplied by the private (for-profit and not-for-profit) and public sectors. The percentage of housing built by each varies from country to country. Except in centrally planned economies, most new housing (flow) is supplied by the private sector (with or without plan approvals).

In Trinidad and Tobago, for example, 1,422 building plans (or 1,399 units) were approved by the Town and Country Planning Division in 1989, out of an estimated 6,360 units built that year. In other words, 78 percent of the new housing units in 1989 were constructed without a permit. The amount of housing built without government approvals is significant in the developing world. UNCHS/World Bank Housing Indicators Data, for example, shows that unauthorized housing as a percentage of total housing stock ranged from 8 percent to 54 percent in 1990 in the Latin American cities included in the study (see Table 6.2). The percentage of permanent dwellings in the total housing stock, on the other hand, ranged from 70 percent to 99 percent for the same cities, suggesting that many of these households have made significant investments in their housing, despite lacking building permits.

One can hardly discover housing supply dynamics in developing countries by examining building permit (flow) statistics alone, because these by definition do not recognize unauthorized housing. Unauthorized developments can be estimated and monitored by examining aerial photographs (Bertaud 1989), and interviews with homebuilders and households can provide further detailed information about a range of building activities carried out by different actors.

In Trinidad and Tobago, interviews with developers, brokers and appraisers in 1993 revealed that only three developers were involved in the overall development process of buying, subdividing and servicing the land, and constructing houses for sale. And, in the previous 10-year period, the production volume of these developers averaged 350 units per year. With so few developers, the home-building sector has organized around numerous small-scale contractors, most of whom operate through small home-based offices and rely upon crews of seven to eight workers for small-scale construction projects. The household survey in 1993 found that most households build their houses incrementally over time by themselves or with the help of these small contractors.

The developer interviews revealed a perception of "skyrocketing" land prices between the mid-1970s and the mid-1980s, and stabilization thereafter. The building community thus accurately recognized that land markets were not immune to the contraction caused by the economic recession in the 1980s, and scaled down their activities significantly with expectations of weak housing demand in the late 1980s and early 1990s. Such perceptions, and their likely impact on land and housing markets, can only be discovered by personal interviews with developers and through household surveys.

In summary, detailed case studies show that standard price theory currently does not account for several major factors that affect land and

Table 6.2.   Housing Indicators for Selected Latin American Cities, 1990 (1)
(percent)

City	Unauthorized housing	Permanent dwelling units	Water connection
Quito, Ecuador	54	70	76
Bogota, Colombia	8	97	99
Kingston, Jamaica	50	80	87
Santiago, Chile	20	85	99
Monterrey, Mexico	16	93	91
Caracas, Venezuela	54	90	70
Rio de Janeiro, Brazil	27	99	97

Source: UNCHS/World Bank Housing Indicators Database (1993).

housing prices: transaction costs (including information costs about property titles, information on structural and neighborhood characteristics of units, and negotiation costs in transactions); land-use and building regulations; and ownership structure. The importance of these factors is evident in developing countries where consumers and suppliers undertake transactions without adequate information about market fundamentals, where outdated land-use and building regulations are ignored by most households in home-building, and where a range of claims to land has evolved over time that makes the clarification of ownership a complex endeavor.

Recent extensions to microeconomic theory, recognizing transaction costs in land and housing markets, show that market actors frequently develop a series of arrangements to help them reduce these costs (Pamuk 2000). The emergence and persistence of, and changes in, institutions that respond to these transaction costs require an in-depth understanding of the behavior of market actors.

Land and Housing Market Information Sources

Up-to-date and accurate land and housing market information is central for informed public- and private-sector decisionmaking. For public-sector planners, it is the foundation for evaluating alternative development scenarios. For private-sector developers, it enables rational decisionmaking in the real-estate sector. Reliable and easy-to-use land and housing market information helps consumers make informed decisions about their transactions as well. Data collection, analysis, and reporting are expensive activities, but are necessary for the implementation of government programs.

Table 6.3.   Housing Indicators for Selected Latin American Cities, 1990 (2)

City	Per capita GNP(US$)	New household formation (percent)	House price to income ratio	Land development multiplier
Quito, Ecuador	1,020	6	2.38	4.00
Bogota, Colombia	1,200	3	n.a.	2.87
Kingston, Jamaica	1,260	1	4.94	1.30
Santiago, Chile	1,770	3	2.09	2.80
Monterrey, Mexico	2,010	4	3.74	6.00
Caracas, Venezuela	2,450	2	1.99	n.a.
Rio de Janeiro, Brazil	2,540	2	4.36	10.40

Source: UNCHS/World Bank Housing Indicators Database (1993).

Much of this information, however, is gathered, analyzed, and reported by public agencies in a disjointed fashion.

Secondary Data Sources

National census information on population and housing is usually an excellent secondary data source for urban planners and real-estate investors. With census information on population and housing, simple indicators can be constructed to track the performance of land and housing markets over time, but unfortunately the quality of census reporting varies from country to country. When available, simple calculations can be undertaken from these published tables, such as calculating simple percentage changes over time, comparing ratios over time, and computing percentiles, quintiles, and deciles. National publications based on the decennial census are especially useful for describing population and housing trends in small areas (at the census-tract or enumeration-district level), but are less useful in depicting housing conditions in rapidly changing cities, since decennial census information may quickly become outdated.

Another good source of secondary data is the Housing Indicators Program of the World Bank (UNCHS and World Bank 1992) which identified close to 40 simple indicators to gauge the performance of the housing market (see Tables 6.3 and 6.4). These are especially useful for cross-national comparisons in the region, and cross-city comparisons in each nation. Affordability, for example, is defined as the ratio of median house

Table 6.4.   Selected Land and Housing Indicators

1. House price-to-income ratio: ratio of the median price of a dwelling unit and the median annual household income.
2. New household formation: annual percentage increase in the number of new households.
3. Permanent dwelling units: percentage of dwelling units likely to last 20 years or more given normal maintenance, taking into account locational and environmental hazards.
4. Water connection: percentage of dwelling units with a water connection in the plot they occupy.
5. Unauthorized housing: Percentage of the total housing stock in the urban area not in compliance with current regulations.
6. Persons per room: ratio between the median number of persons and median number of rooms in a dwelling unit.
7. Housing production: net number of units produced (production minus demolition) in both formal and informal sectors per thousand population.
8. Land development multiplier: ratio between the median land price of a developed plot at the urban fringe in a typical subdivision, and the median price of raw, undeveloped land in an area currently being developed.
9. Industrial concentration: percentage of new formal-sector housing units placed on the market by the five largest developers (private or public) last year.
10. Property tax receipts: percentage of property tax receipts in the local government budget.

Source: UNCHS and World Bank 1992.

price to median income. A high value for this indicator (greater than 3) indicates that housing is too expensive for the majority of households. Land development multiplier is another useful indicator that measures the premium for providing infrastructure and converting raw land to residential use on the urban fringe. It is defined as the ratio of the median land price of a developed plot at the urban fringe in a typical subdivision, and the median price of raw, undeveloped land in an area currently being developed. A high value for this indicator would suggest the presence of land-supply restrictions (high regulatory constraints).

Primary Data Sources

When secondary data sources give inadequate answers, primary data should be collected. First-hand information on land and housing markets in developing countries can be gathered by land-price surveys (Dowall

1995), household surveys, aerial photography interpretation, and interviews with developers. Fine-tuned land and housing market research also requires data that can be aggregated at different geographic levels (e.g., neighborhoods, planning areas, real-estate market zones). Greater analytical power can be achieved by using disaggregated data and aggregating it for analysis at larger geographic levels to provide context.

Land Price Surveys

Using the land price survey methodology (for a complete discussion, see Dowall 1995), we designed and implemented a land-price survey in the East-West Corridor of Trinidad in 1993, and examined price changes and land conversion patterns between 1989 and 1993 (Pamuk and Dowall 1998). We found that real (inflation-adjusted) land prices generally remained stable or even declined between 1989 and 1993. Stable (rather than skyrocketing) land prices during this period, however, appear to be more a reflection of weak economic conditions, and should be considered temporary due to the presence of cumbersome land-transfer processes and an uncertain building permit approval process.

Household Surveys

Undertaking any meaningful analysis of residential development processes, predicting future trends, and simulating alternative development scenarios, first requires a sound database, which can best be gathered by surveys. In Trinidad and Tobago, for example, the household survey gathered information on household characteristics, housing conditions, access to land, housing construction and investment, housing finance, community participation, and rental housing. The information gathered was important to understanding housing consumption patterns and the different "paths to housing" used by households.

No comprehensive housing surveys had previously been conducted in Trinidad and Tobago, making the 1993 effort to collect this baseline data even more valuable. With the objective of depicting housing conditions and production processes nationwide, the questionnaire was divided into three main parts: household composition; housing quality; and acquisition and finance of housing by owners and renters. In addition, it contained sections on market intermediaries, sources of information on locating housing, neighborhood characteristics and accessibility, opinions about the house and the neighborhood, and institutional and community support. For an estimate of the costs of carrying out the survey, see Table 6.5.

Table 6.5. Estimation of Household Survey Costs

Steps in the survey process	Person days	Daily rate	Total cost	Estimated percent of cost
Questionnaire design				
Identifying key questions	10	$300	$3,000	
Framing questions	10	$300	$3,000	
Conducting focus meetings	8	$125	$1,000	
Format/layout design	5	$50	$250	
Printing (with CSO assistance)	2	$50	$100	
Sub-total			$7,350	9
Sample selection				
Defining the sample size	1	$300	$300	
Identifying the sample frame	4	$300	$1,200	
Sample stratification	4	$300	$1,200	
Sample selection	4	$300	$1,200	
Sub-total			$3,900	5
Survey administration				
Selecting supervisors	2	$125	$250	
Selecting interviewers	4	$125	$500	
Preparing training and fieldwork manual	8	$125	$1,000	
Training	10	$125	$1,250	
Pretest of questionnaire	50	$65	$3,250	
Revisions based on pre-tests	5	$300	$1,500	
In-person interviewing	750	$25	$18,000	
Monitoring fieldwork by supervisors	125	40	$4,800	
Monitoring supervisors	8	$125	$1,000	
Sub-total			$31,550	40
Data processing and analysis				
Editing and coding	20	$50	$1,000	
Entering data into computer	20	$50	$1,000	
Data verification and cleaning	20	$125	$2,500	
Preparing a codebook	20	$125	$2,500	
Preparing data for analysis	20	$125	$2,500	
Development of an analysis plan	10	$300	$3,000	
Data analysis	10	$300	$3,000	
Presentating preliminary results	5	$300	$1,500	
Preparing final report	20	$300	$6,000	
Sub-total			$23,000	29
Direct costs				
Computer hardware				
Pentium			$1,500	
Laser Printer			$400	

(table continues on following page)

Table 6.5 *(continued)*

Steps in the survey process	Person days	Daily rate	Total cost	Estimated percent of cost
Software				
SPSS Data Ent			$995	
SPSS Windows			$795	
Microsoft Office			$500	
Reproduction of reports			$500	
Local transportation			$500	
Per diems for interviewers and supervisors (102 person days x $20)			$2,040	
Per diem for expatriate professional staff (83 person days x $80)			$6,640	
Telecommunications			$200	
Sub-total			$14,070	18
Total costs			$79,870	100
			per survey: $53.25	

Assumptions:
Sample size: 1,500 households
In-person interviews carried out by 24 interviewers and 4 supervisors in 4 staff weeks
Area population: 1.2 million
Personnel:
   Expatriate professional staff: $300 per day
   Local professional staff: $125 per day
   Local clerical staff: $50 per day
   Interviewers: $25 per day
   Supervisors: $40 per day
Source: Author.

Analysis and Dissemination of Land and Housing Market Information

Information gathered by land price surveys, aerial photographs, and household surveys can be combined to provide an up-to-date, accurate, and detailed profile of land and housing markets. Land-price information from land-price surveys can be combined with household income from household surveys, for example, to assess the affordability of land for households at different income levels. In Trinidad and Tobago such an analysis showed that the 40th percentile of households in the income distribution need to save for more than 20 years to get access to serviced land.

Information gathered on land and housing market operations must also be disseminated to relevant government agencies, private-sector homebuilders, research organizations, and the public. This can be achieved by organizing seminars and workshops that focus on key and topical findings. Resources must also be allocated for dissemination of knowledge through reports, newsletters, and the Internet.

I have touched on a range of land and housing market assessment tools ranging from simple calculations from published census reports and housing indicators databases to detailed land price and household surveys. The level and scope of data gathering will largely depend on several factors: the quality of census data reporting in the country; the availability of land and housing market specialists at the municipality; the computing and information technology resources available; and the quality of previous studies by researchers that can quickly be summarized as a basis for future work. The presence of these factors will greatly enhance the local knowledge management capacity of municipalities and inform urban policymaking.

Policy Implications

I used the tools described here to assist the Ministry of Housing and Human Settlements of Trinidad and Tobago in 1993. I directed and managed the Land and Housing Market Study funded by the Inter-American Development Bank conducted by PADCO, Inc. for the Ministry. Some of the survey results are reported in Pamuk 2000, and Pamuk and Dowall 1998.

The information was used in local discussions to revise two pieces of legislation: (1) the urban and regional planning act; and (2) the regularization of state lands act. The information also provided the analytical basis for the government's national report for the Habitat II conference in Istanbul in 1996.

Key issues identified in the Habitat II report included demand/supply imbalance, low affordability of land and housing in compliance with government regulations, squatting, and cumbersome regulatory approval processes. While these issues might be observed in many other developing countries as well, policymakers in Trinidad and Tobago can now demonstrate their magnitude with hard data rather than based on anecdotal information.

Finally, it must be noted that important urban policy decisions are not made in a vacuum. The extent to which sound land and housing market diagnoses can influence policy decisions will ultimately depend on the political environment within which such decisions are made, a topic which I have not dealt with in this paper.

References and Selected Bibliography

Global Trends and Policy on Urban Land and Housing in Developing Countries:

Pamuk, Ayse. 1991. *Housing in Developing Countries: A Select Bibliography and Field Statement*, CPL Bib. 273. Chicago: Council of Planning Librarians.

UNCHS (Habitat). 1996. *An Urbanizing World: Global Report on Human Settlements 1996*. Oxford: Oxford University Press.

World Bank. 1993. *Housing: Enabling Markets to Work*. Washington, DC: World Bank.

World Bank. 1991. *Urban Policy and Economic Development: An Agenda for the 1990s*. Washington, DC: World Bank.

Urban Land and Housing Economics:

DiPasquale, Denise, and William C. Wheaton. 1996. *Urban Economics and Real Estate Markets*. Englewood Cliffs, NJ: Prentice-Hall.

Muth, Richard F. 1969. *Cities and Housing: The Spatial Pattern of Urban Residential Land Use*. Chicago: University of Chicago Press.

O'Sullivan, Arthur. 1993. *Urban Economics*. Homewood, IL: Irwin.

Pozdena, Randall. 1988. *The Modern Economics of Housing*. New York: Quorem Books.

Survey Research Methods:

Dillman, Don A. 1978. *Mail and Telephone Surveys: The Total Design Method*. New York: John Wiley.

Fowler, Floyd J. 1993. *Survey Research Methods*. Newbury Park, CA: Sage.

Kish, Leslie. 1965. *Survey Sampling*. New York: John Wiley.

Lansing, John B., and James N. Morgan. 1971. *Economic Survey Methods*. Ann Arbor, MI: University of Michigan.

Urban Land Prices: Trends, Measurement, and Monitoring:

Dowall, David E. 1995. *The Land Market Assessment: A New Tool for Urban Management*. Urban Management Programme Tool No.4, Washington, DC: World Bank.

Pamuk, Ayse, and David E. Dowall. 1998. "The Price of Land for Housing in Trinidad: Implications for Affordability" *Urban Studies* 35(2): 285–99.

Urban Housing Markets: Trends, Measurement, and Monitoring:

Bertaud, Marie-Agnes. 1989. *The Use of Satellite Images for Urban Planning*. Report INU 42, Washington, DC: World Bank.

Malpezzi, Stephen, and Stephen K. Mayo. 1985. *Housing Demand in Developing Countries*. World Bank Staff Working Paper No.733, Washington, DC: World Bank.

UNCHS and World Bank. 1992. *The Housing Indicators Program Extensive Survey. Part II: Indicator Modules and Worksheets Update and Revisions*. Washington, DC: World Bank.

Urban Research in Latin America and the Caribbean:

Pamuk, Ayse. 2000. "Informal Institutional Arrangements in Credit, Land Markets, and Infrastructure Delivery in Trinidad." *International Journal of Urban and Regional Research* (forthcoming).

Portes, Alejandro, Carlos Dore-Cabral, and Patricia Landolt. 1997. *The Urban Caribbean: Transition to the New Global Economy*. Baltimore, MD: Johns Hopkins.

Stren, Richard, ed. 1995. *Urban Research in the Developing World: Vol. 3, Latin America*. Toronto: Centre for Urban and Community Studies, University of Toronto.

Property Taxation

Enid Slack

An Overview of Property Taxation

Around the world, almost all local governments rely to some extent on property taxation, and this is the main source of municipal revenue for Canada, the United States, and Australia. In Canada, property taxes provide almost half of total municipal revenues, while property and related taxes account for about 3.9 percent of Gross Domestic Provincial Product (GDPP). This reliance has varied over time, depending on the magnitude of intergovernmental transfers, user fees and other revenues, as well as on changes in the expenditure responsibilities assigned to local governments.

The property tax can be differentiated from other taxes by virtue of two main characteristics: its visibility and the diversity of the local context within which it is implemented. Visibility acts as a constraint on the ability to raise the tax; in contrast to income tax, for instance, the property tax is not withheld at source, so taxpayers tend to be more aware of how much they pay. Furthermore, the property tax also finances services that are very visible, such as roads, garbage collection, snow removal, and neighborhood parks. This visibility makes local governments accountable for the taxes they levy; it also makes reform difficult and, moreover, municipalities face constant pressure not to increase the tax. The second unique characteristic of the property tax is the differing nature of how it is levied by local governments, differences that in turn create different tax structures. The property tax is not a single tax, but rather a complex array of taxes with hundreds of local variations.

Other characteristics include the favorable treatment of residential property; it is common for the property tax to favor residential over commercial and industrial properties. This is done in three ways: the assessment system has deliberately under-assessed residential property relative to commercial and industrial property of comparable value; many jurisdictions have legislated lower tax rates on residential property; property tax relief measures are often provided to residential property owners (and, in some cases, tenants) in the form of tax credits, homeowner grants, or tax deferrals. At the same time, this differential treatment does not necessarily reflect the differential use of services by different property types.

Some authors have argued that the property tax is a benefit tax, a set of user charges for locally provided public goods and services. This means that local differentials in the tax rates simply reflect differentials in the level of services. Others have argued, however, that the property tax is a distortionary tax on capital, borne primarily by owners of capital.

The following six principles can be applied in evaluating the property tax and approaches to its reform in any jurisdiction:

- *Fairness based on benefits received:* Taxes should be related to the benefits received from government expenditures.
- *Fairness based on ability to pay:* Taxes should be similar for those in similar circumstances. For example, people should pay comparable taxes on comparable properties.
- *Neutrality:* The tax should not distort economic behavior, including decisions about where to live and work and what improvements to make to one's property. Negative side effects should be minimized.
- *Stability:* Taxes should not fluctuate dramatically from year to year.
- *Accountability:* Taxes should be designed in ways that are clear to taxpayers so that policymakers can be made accountable to the taxpayers for the cost of government.
- *Ease of administration:* Taxes should be fairly easy to administer. The simpler the system, the easier its administration.

It is often difficult to achieve all these principles at the same time, so choices have to be made. The reform of property taxation in the Canadian province of Ontario—the largest assessment jurisdiction in North America, with 4.2 million separate properties—started out with the goal of bringing equity (based on ability to pay), accountability, and simplicity of administration to the property tax system, but subsequent policies have focussed on tax stability. The result has been to sacrifice equity and simplicity, and to confuse accountability.

The Process of Taxing Real Property

A number of steps are involved in the process of taxing real property: identification of the properties being taxed; preparation of an assessment roll containing a description of the property and the amount of assessment; setting the tax rate or series of rates; issuing tax bills; responding to assessment appeals; collecting taxes; and addressing arrears.

Identification of Properties

The first element in levying a property tax is to identify the property to be taxed. A cadastral survey, carried out by professional land surveyors who must be cognizant of the legal description of the land and any conflicts which may affect it, determines and defines land ownership and boundaries for each property.

In Ontario, there are two systems for people to register interests in land: the registry system and the land titles system. Under the first, any person can register, in a provincial registry office, a document pertaining to title to land. Purchasers generally retain a private lawyer to examine all the registered documents to determine whether a vendor has good and valid title. People can sometimes claim ownership by adverse possession (unchallenged occupation) rather than documents. Under the land titles system, only the property owner can register a document, under the approval of a provincial official. This system is therefore a registry of titles, rather than deeds and instruments. If an owner wishes to divide land, such as by plan of subdivision or condominium, the land must normally be held under land titles. The difference between the two systems has to do with the guarantee of ownership—provided by the land titles system but not by the registry system; the latter being only a system of document registration. Efforts are underway in Canada to convert all properties to the land titles system.[5]

Composition of the Property Tax Base

The base for the property tax is "real property," defined as land and improvements to the land. In some cases, machinery and equipment

---

5. In 1991, the Ontario government delegated responsibility to Teranet Land Information Services Inc. to automate the paper land registry records on ownership held in POLARIS (Province of Ontario Land Registration Information System), a paper-based land registry system that stores and manages ownership data for each property in Ontario. The system had remained virtually unchanged for 200 years. By the beginning of 1999, Teranet had digitally mapped about 2.6 million of the 4.2 million properties in Ontario and put information on these properties into an electronic database. Automation of the entire province is expected to be completed by 2002/03 at a cost of over $300 million. The process includes legal conversion of over 70 percent of the records from a registry system to a land titles system. Teranet has contracts to modernize land-related geographically referenced information systems in other countries as well, such as the Czech Republic, Puerto Rico, and Jamaica.

"affixed" to real property is included. Treatment of minerals, mines, oil and gas wells, pipelines, railways, and public utility distribution systems varies in different jurisdictions.

Other characteristics of the property tax base include exemptions and property valuations. An exemption is an exclusion from the tax base and/or tax liability for certain types of property: for example, churches, cemeteries, aboriginal lands, public hospitals, charitable institutions, and educational institutions. Exemptions violate the principle of neutrality because they favor particular land uses and distort the distribution of the tax burden.

Assessment is the valuation of the tax base and can take different forms. Under *market value assessment*, the market value is defined as the price that would be struck between a willing buyer and a willing seller in an arm's length transaction. Three methods are used to estimate this: (1) The comparable sales approach involves looking at valid sales of properties that are similar to the property being appraised; it is used when the market is active and similar properties are being sold. (2) The depreciated cost approach values the property by estimating the value of the land as if it were vacant, and adding the cost of replacing the buildings and other improvements to that value. The cost approach is used when the property is relatively new, there are no comparable sales and improvements are relatively unique, and is also used to assess industrial properties. (3) Under the income approach, the assessor estimates the potential gross rental income the property could produce, and deducts operating expenditures. The resulting annual net operating income is converted to a capital value using a capitalization rate; this approach is used mainly for income-producing properties.

Under the *rental value assessment* approach, property values are determined according to their current use; the use of rental value eliminates increases in property values due to potential future use and speculation. When a property is put to its highest and best use, and is expected to continue to do so, rental value will bear a predictable relationship to market value—the discounted net stream of rental payments is approximately equal to market value. If current use differs from highest and best use, however, rental value and market value (for example, under the income approach) differ. Taxing potential future income takes into account the wealth of the owner, but not that the owner may lack sufficient cash to pay the tax now.

Unit value assessment is directly related to the size of the property (land and buildings). When the assessment rate per square foot is adjusted to reflect location, quality of the structure or other factors, it is known as unit value assessment. Market value has an indirect influence on the assessment base through the application of adjustment factors. It is generally believed that property taxes based on unit value assessment are less fair in terms of benefits received and ability to pay than are property taxes based on market value assessment. One of the main advantages of unit value assessment, however, is that taxes based on it tend to be less volatile than under market value assessment. Some have also argued that it is easier to understand and cheaper to administer than value-based assessments. Although this may be true for residential properties, it is difficult to use for multi-residential, commercial, and industrial properties that have common areas. Furthermore, to ensure that it is fair in terms of ability to pay, location factors must be included. Once these factors are introduced, a unit value system becomes much more complicated to understand.

Finally, *self-assessments* require property owners to place an assessed value on their own property. To ensure accuracy, they must be prepared to sell their property to the taxing authority for the amount of the assessment. This system of assessment is thus only credible if the government can and will buy the property, and a competent administration is required to ensure that the system works.

Most of the jurisdictions in the world that levy a property tax use some form of value-based assessment. Canadian, American, and British municipalities generally use market value assessment or rental value assessment. Rental value is the basis of taxation in France. Unit value is used in Israel, and has been used until recently in Rotterdam. It is also used in formerly communist countries where the market for real property is not yet well developed. Self-assessment has been used in New Zealand in the past, and is currently used in some Latin American countries.

Whichever assessment method is used, fair property taxes have to be based on assessments that are uniform. Much of the criticism of the property tax stems from a lack of credibility in the fairness of the assessment base. Furthermore, fair and productive property taxes require annual assessments of value. In many countries, a three-to-five-year cycle is used and values are indexed in the intervening years using a consumer price index or a housing price index. Because property values change at a different rate in different neighborhoods, and for different property characteristics, fairness is not achieved when property assessments are merely increased by a common factor on an annual basis.

Property Tax Rates

To set municipal tax rates, a municipality first determines its expenditure requirements. It then subtracts non-property tax sources of revenue available (intergovernmental transfers, user fees, and other revenues) to determine how much it has to raise from property taxes. The property tax requirements are divided by the taxable assessment base to determine the tax rate.

The municipality may levy a series of rates that differ by property class. Variable tax rates are different rates for different classes of property (residential, commercial, and industrial, for example). This system gives local governments the power to manage the distribution of the tax burden across various property classes within their municipality, in addition to determining the size of the overall tax burden on taxpayers.

Variable tax rates may be justified on a number of grounds. First, on the basis of fairness with respect to benefits received, it can be argued that the benefits from local public services are different for different property classes. In particular, a case can be made on benefit grounds for taxing non-residential properties at a lower rate than residential properties.

Second, on efficiency (neutrality) grounds, it has been argued that property taxes should be heavier on those components of the tax base that are least elastic in supply. Since business capital tends to be more mobile than residential capital, efficiency arguments lead to the conclusion that business property should be taxed more lightly than residential property. In reality, however, lower rates are generally applied to residential properties.

Third, variable tax rates can also be used to distort decisions deliberately to achieve certain land-use objectives. Since higher property taxes tend to slow development, and lower taxes speed up development, a municipal policy to develop some neighborhoods instead of others would call for differential taxes in different locations as well as for different property classes.

Fourth, effective tax rates (taxes relative to market value) differ between classes in most municipalities, either because the (nominal) tax rates differ, or because the assessed-to-market value ratios differ. In most countries, effective tax rates are lower on residential property. The reason given is that commercial/industrial property owners can often write off property taxes against income taxes, but residential property taxpayers cannot. The more likely reason for lower tax rates on residential property, however, is that residential property owners represent the core of municipal voters. Taxes are often higher on multi-residential properties than on single-family homes. Although there is no justification for this differential based on benefits received or ability to pay, the practice is widespread. Tenants are often unaware of the property tax they pay because it is included in the rent; levying higher taxes on multi-residential property is therefore expedient.

In some countries, land is taxed relatively more heavily than are improvements (buildings), one of the main advantages being that this does not provide a disincentive to improve one's property. Under a market value tax, any improvement to a property will increase its market value and, by extension, its assessed value. Other things being equal, a property tax discourages improvements. Taxing land does not create a disincentive to improve one's property, but it does, however, provide an incentive to speed up development, and to develop land more fully to realize some income from the property.

Two Examples of How Variable Tax Rates can be Used

Variable tax rates can be determined in different ways, depending on the objectives of the local government. For example, they can be used to counteract changes arising from differential changes in the property tax base of each property class. If residential assessment increases more quickly over time than commercial assessment, local governments can choose tax rates that will stabilize the share of the tax burden borne by each property class. Alternatively, they could use variable tax rates to stabilize tax rates, or to achieve some other tax distribution policy.

The tables illustrate the effects of two different policies on relative tax burdens. In Table 6.6, the objective is to stabilize the share of the tax burden borne by each class; in Table 6.7, the objective is to stabilize tax rates. In this example, there are three property classes: residential, commercial, and industrial; assessed value has increased by 7 percent (from $115 million to $123 million) and property tax requirements have increased by 5 percent (from $2,425,000 to $2,546,250) over the previous year; and residential assessment has increased relatively more than commercial and industrial assessment.

The objective is to maintain the percentage tax shares for the current year as they were in the previous year (bold column 4). The revenue target for the current year ($2,546,250) is apportioned among the property classes according to those percentages. The current tax rate is then calculated by dividing the current revenue yield by the assessed value of property in each class.

Table 6.7 shows the distribution policy required to provide year-to-year stability in terms of the ratios of tax rates levied on each property class (bold column 4). To calculate current tax rates, it is necessary to calculate tax ratios for each class (the ratio of the tax rate for the class divided by the

Table 6.6. Stabilization of Tax Share by Class

Class	Previous assessed value ($,000) (1)	Previous tax rate (percent) (2)	Previous revenue yield (3)	Absolute tax share (% of total revenue by class) (4)	Current revenue yield 2,546,250 × (4) (5)	Current assessed value ($,000) (6)	Current tax rate (percent) (7)
Residential	60,000	1.50	900,000	37.1	944,659	65,000	1.45
Commercial	30,000	3.00	900,000	37.1	944,659	31,000	3.05
Industrial	25,000	2.50	625,000	25.8	656,933	27,000	2.43
Total	115,000		2,425,000	100.0	2,546,250	123,000	

Source: Author.

276

Table 6.7. Stabilization of Effective Tax Rates by Class

Class	Previous assessed value ($,000) (1)	Previous tax rate (percent) (2)	Previous revenue yield (3)	Tax ratios (relative to residential class) (4)	Current assessed value ($,000) (5)	Weighted assessed value (4) × (5) (6)	Current revenue yield (weighted) (7)	Current tax rate (percent) (7)/(5) (8)
Residential	60,000	1.50	900,000	1.00	65,000	65,000	961,742	1.48
Commercial	30,000	3.00	900,000	2.00	31,000	62,000	917,354	2.96
Industrial	25,000	2.50	625,000	1.67	27,000	45,090	667,153	2.47
Total	115,000		2,425,000		123,000	172,090	2,546,250	

Source: Author.

277

residential tax rate). To keep the tax ratios the same from year to year, the prior year's ratios are multiplied by the current year's assessed values to achieve a weighted assessment for each class. The current year's revenue ($2,546,250) is then apportioned to each class in proportion to the weighted assessment for that class. The tax rates are equal to the current revenue yield divided by the assessed value.

Some Lessons for Property Tax Reform

The Province of Ontario recently implemented a new assessment and property tax system which reassessed all properties at market value and permitted municipalities to levy differential tax rates by property class. In response to significant tax shifts projected to occur, subsequent provincial legislation required municipalities to cap tax increases for multi-residential, commercial, and industrial properties for three years. From that experience we can point to some lessons that have more general application. First, the longer tax reform is delayed, the more difficult it will be. Second, annual reassessments will create far fewer shifts in taxes than reassessment after a much longer period. Third, taxpayers need to have confidence in the assessed values, and in the process used to derive them; this means taking the time to do the assessment properly. Fourth, before implementing reform, an impact assessment is necessary to determine shifts in taxation so that policy can be designed before reform, and not in a piecemeal fashion in response to later problems. Fifth, phase-ins and tax deferrals are an essential part of the tax policy design.

A final note from the Ontario experience is that, no matter how economically desirable the long-run outcome of any policy change may be, its transitional effects may be sufficiently undesirable to kill it. From a public choice perspective, the losers from a change in policy tend to be very vocal (even if they are the minority) because they value their losses more than the gainers (even if they are the majority) value their gains. This problem is not unique to property taxation, but it is particularly significant because of the visibility of this tax.

References

Bird, Richard M., and Enid Slack. 1991. "Financing Local Government in OECD Countries: The Role of Local Taxes and User Charges." In J. Owens and G. Panella, *Local Government: An International Perspective*, pp. 83–98. The Hague: Elsevier.

Farrington, Colin, ed. 1993. *Local Government Taxation, International Report 1993.* Proceedings of the Second International Conference of the Institute of Revenues, Rating and Valuation. Budapest, Hungary.

Kelly, R. 1994. "Implementing Property-Tax Reform in Transitional Countries: The Experience of Albania and Poland." *Environment and Planning C: Government and Policy* 12: 319–31.

Youngman, Joan M., and Jane H. Malme. 1994. *An International Survey of Taxes on Land and Buildings.* Derventer, The Netherlands: Kluwer.

The Portland Experience

Charles Hales

Canadian and European cities have much more to teach us about good development than do most American cities, and we in Portland have studied Vancouver and Toronto in particular as models for some of our own development ideas. Although I shall concentrate here on the Portland story itself, our experience demonstrates that land-use regulation can foster, first, a strong economy; second, a fiscally sound local government; and, third, a dynamic and attractive urban environment that provides choices for our citizens at all income levels.

Individualism vs. Communitarianism

Two forces have historically motivated American citizens and have animated our public discussions in Portland and the state of Oregon. One of these forces is individualism, which has to do with the desire of individuals to strike out on their own and stake their claim. This trait is particularly strong in Americans, for whom the pioneer log cabin in the woods is enshrined in the national culture. The other principle is in conflict with this individualism: it is the notion of community, and the desire or even the necessity to come together in common purpose and in mutual obligation. These two forces have shaped Americans, and in turn have shaped our homes, the neighborhoods, and the cities that we have constructed, as well as our political institutions.

Portland has not been immune to this tension but, perhaps because of the particularly inspiring landscape of Oregon, our approach has been more community-based than in other parts of the United States. Our early efforts at land-use regulation include: a 1912 city plan; passage in 1913 of legislation that made all beaches in Oregon public; and the establishment of a planning commission in the city of Portland in 1918. The defining moment for land-use planning in Oregon, and in Portland as the state's principal city, was the passage in 1973 of Senate Bill 100, giving citizens access to the planning process. Senate Bill 100 was not the creation of an autocratic, centralized planning bureaucracy, but rather a proposal by a politician, a flamboyant and often controversial Republican governor named Tom McCall. The Republican Party is well known for its adamant defense of private property rights. At the time, Oregon's economy was heavily dependent on natural resources through farming, logging and fishing, and Governor McCall saw the threat posed to these by the sprawling urbanization of speculative development. He colorfully noted that "sagebrush subdivisions, coastal condomania, and the ravenous rampage of suburbia, all threaten to mock Oregon's model and Oregon's status as an environmental model for the nation."

Urban Growth Boundary

Among the most important elements of Senate Bill 100 are specifications that each city and county within the state must adopt a comprehensive land-use plan and zoning ordinance that conform to 19 state-wide goals. The latter address the planning process, the citizen participation question, resource conservation, development patterns, protection of coastal resources, and so on. Even though Oregon developed its first plan in 1912, the bill adopted in 1980 transformed Portland's policy plans into law.

Each metropolitan area must draw an urban growth boundary, a boundary around the area of the city that may be urbanized. For Portland, this covers the city of Portland and 23 other cities within the metropolitan area, bringing much-needed discipline to Portland's development patterns. Cities must plan for projected population and housing needs. For example, Portland must achieve a goal of 10 housing units per acre on average throughout the city, with a housing mix that is 50 percent multi-family and 50 percent single-family housing. Cities must designate an inventory of land where development can occur as a matter of right, while ensuring that environmentally sensitive lands receive some level of protection.

Governor McCall and his allies in the Oregon legislature were able to put together a broad-based coalition to support state-wide land-use planning. For example, the home-building industry supported the Bill because, although it limited the expansion of land development, it provided greater certainty for developers in that they could build in designated areas without being subject to long-drawn-out legal battles where "Not-In-My-Backyard" fights would turn into expensive disputes over a buildable area; with reduced territorial conflict, they might have less land to use, but more certainty about the land that was available. The Oregon farm bureau also supported the legislation because it ensured that their industry would not be swept away by urbanization. Local governments came to support the Bill because it allowed local jurisdictions to propose locally devised means of meeting state-wide planning goals. In this way, Oregon's land-use system and Portland's implementation of it sought to balance the competing interests of individualism and community by providing a framework for the community to map its future and set the limit for individual use of land.

So what has been accomplished with this land-use planning framework? First, land-use planning supports the state's vibrant economy. Agriculture and the export of grain continue to provide significant contributions to the state's economy. Portland is the second-largest wheat port in the world. The state has a thriving nursery industry, and is a big exporter of grass seed and Christmas trees. Six of Oregon's top ten agricultural counties are in the Willamette Valley, in the shadow of the Portland metropolitan region, which is home to 45 percent of the state's population. As a result of Portland's land-use controls, the farmers can continue to operate their farms without feeling the constant pressure and uncertainty of unplanned urbanization.

The urban areas of the Willamette Valley have a high quality of life and the ability to provide infrastructure—major attractions for new industry. This was not always the case, however. Prior to the 1970s, a four-lane expressway ran along the west bank of the Willamette River, walling off a declining downtown from its principal natural asset. At a time when other cities were building new freeways, the city of Portland tore its freeway down and reclaimed the waterfront. Another grassroots campaign defeated a plan to build a new freeway through residential neighborhoods in the East Side of the city, and the city council instead diverted the money to build Portland's first light rail line. Prior to the 1980s, the heart of the city's downtown was a parking lot. In the 1960s, a proposal for an 11-storey parking structure was made, a proposal that, probably more than any other, motivated citizens' efforts to create a new downtown plan. A design competition was held for a public square, much like the public squares in Europe. Its construction was financed through individual sponsorship of almost 50,000 bricks. Today, Pioneer Courthouse Square is sometimes referred to as the city's living room. The combination of these dramatic actions and infrastructure investments has spurred the success of Portland's downtown as the economic heart of the region.

Public works alone do not create a livable city. Regulations are needed to point private investment in the right direction. For example, downtown office towers built in the 1960s were fortress-like skyscrapers that missed the opportunity to profit from the city's vitality. They occupied the sites but didn't connect to the downtown neighborhood. In the 1970s, the city council instituted design review requirements for buildings to meet the street with storefront retail space. This has become typical of new construction in the central city. By requiring a higher level of development performance, the city created both a market and a public realm far superior to anything provided previously.

The results of our city planning standards can be seen from a 1990 study of business locations. This noted that Portland received high marks from executives for its quality of life, which includes affordable housing, cultural advantages, recreational opportunities, and adequate transportation networks. Portland is attracting more business than ever, not because the city council lowered its standards for land-use regulation, but because it raised them. The city council raised the bar higher than other American cities, and produced a quality of life that is attracting new investment.

Contributing to the Financial Health of the City

The second product of the city council's work is the contribution made by the land-use planning process to Portland's city government's financial health. Land-use planning enables the city to prioritize its infrastructure investments. Moreover, the private sector knows that it can count on the city's plans and is therefore more willing to invest private capital. Over the last several years, Portland drew up a plan to redevelop about 200 acres of under-used industrial parcels and railroad yards immediately adjacent to the central city. The idea is to add 12,000 to 15,000 new residents in the central area to avoid expanding the urban growth boundary onto more farmland. This decision goes beyond merely protecting farmland. City council found that, if growth occurs on the periphery of the Portland region, it would have to add more highway capacity to carry an additional 12,000 commuters into the central city. Adding highway capacity would cost over US$3 billion, and the parking spaces needed to accommodate new commuters would require new garage structures. Light rail can carry the same commuters for under $1 billion. By comparison, the entire total public investment in the area previously mentioned is about $150 million, including $50 million for a streetcar line running through the central district. Instead of spending $3 billion on a freeway expansion and having to find storage space for additional cars, the city is spending a tiny fraction of this sum on a different kind of transport system. Streetcars enable such density to work. Needless to say, this option requires a public cost, but the private investment we expect to see is over $900 million as a result of having chosen this option.[6]

---

6.   National studies corroborate Portland's experience. A study of California Central Valley, comparing two possible development patterns—housing at three or at six units to the acre—concluded that savings of $29 billion in the cost of taxpayer-financed services lay in opting for greater density.

Making a City Livable

More than the benefits of a strong economy and a soundly financed city government, land-use and design controls have made Portland a great place to live. What James Kunstler depicts, in his wonderful book, *The Geography of Nowhere,* are standardized, Americanized, development patterns, which national retail chains are globalizing about as fast as the automobile industry globalized transportation. We say in Portland that we're an exception to that pattern.

Most American zoning regulation has consisted of a lot of "thou shalt nots," "keep your densities low," "separate your uses"—all these provisions have been organized to reduce densities. Kunstler's advice for improving communities is to start with a public ceremony to burn the zoning code, because the zoning code is the genetic code that has caused this sameness in the American geography of cities: single-family subdivisions on *cul-de-sac* streets, big arterial roads, and a plethora of shopping malls. As an alternative, Kunstler points to the European style of mixed-use planning that facilitates greater density of urban space. Portland is, by a complex mixture of public investments, plans, and regulations, making a self-conscious attempt to emulate European urban life. The key ingredients: prioritizing the pedestrian and transit rider over the automobile, higher-density, mixed-use development, and a compact urban area circumscribed by the urban growth boundary. This effort earned a chapter in Kuntsler's book that opened with the question, "Can this be America?"

Our zoning code in Portland, a work in progress, needs to improve in the area of raising the city's minimum densities. We are seeing gradual changes towards promoting a "thou shalt" attitude which advocates, "push your building up to the side walk," "higher floor area ratios," and "mix your uses." We have a mixed-use ordinance that promotes a more intense use of space, rather than just pushing people apart. The recipe for disaster would be an Oregon-style urban growth boundary combined with an American-style zoning ordinance that advocates single-family housing structures in order to maintain low densities. This is simply a method of exclusion that benefits existing property owners at the expense of newcomers, who would not be able to afford to live in the city.

Conclusion: Write Your Own Recipe

In telling the Portland story, we might give you the impression that we think we have the recipe. We have the recipe for Portland. We don't have the recipe for anywhere else. It is each community's responsibility to write that recipe and determine the character that it wants. But there are people who are writing the recipe for you if you don't write it yourself. They are: McDonald's, the International Shopping Center Association, and the highway engineers—large shopping malls over here, low-density single family development over there, and bigger and bigger freeways to connect the two. The only way I believe a city can write its own recipe is to make the transportation plan subordinate to the land-use plan. Otherwise, the automobile will determine your city's destiny and your city will look like everywhere else.

Winston Churchill once said that Americans can be counted on to do the right thing after they have exhausted all the alternatives. Portland is one of the last alternatives, and we think we must do the right thing to provide an example to American cities about how to Europeanize the American development pattern. Land-use planning and regulation are key ingredients in our success. By creating a framework to balance the competing interests of the individual and the community, we have been able to guide our physical development to strengthen our economy, to determine sound public investments, and to create a desirable place for our citizens to live.

Reference

Kunstler, James Howard. 1993. *The Geography of Nowhere: The Rise and Decline of America's Man-Made Landscape.* New York: Simon and Schuster.

7

Urban Poverty

Editor's Introduction

Richard Stren

As the urban population of the developing world increases, both in absolute terms and as a proportion of the total population, a major challenge remains: coping with poverty. In spite of improvements in macro-economic indicators for many countries in the South, the number of urban residents living in extremely precarious conditions is a major provocation to both the imagination and the skill of policymakers. Dealing with poverty is important for many reasons: large numbers of poor people cannot pay taxes or support public services without substantial levels of government funding; the very poor cannot contribute in a productive manner to the development of a pool of skilled human resources necessary to generate goods and services in the modern competitive economy; and the poor cannot easily participate in community activities in order to provide facilities and organizational structures at the neighborhood level, nor can they fully participate in what it means to be a "citizen" of their towns and nations.

For many years, major textbooks and documents on development stressed the overwhelming predominance of rural over urban poverty. The World Bank's *World Development Report* for 1990 highlighted the issue of poverty, concentrating most of its attention on rural, rather than urban, poverty. While it acknowledged that gathering good information on the characteristics of the poor was a continuing challenge, it focused on the income dimension. "Poverty as measured by low income tends to be at its worst in rural areas," the report noted, "even allowing for the often substantial differences in cost of living between town and countryside. The problems of malnutrition, lack of education, low life expectancy and substandard housing are also, as a rule, more severe in rural areas. This is still true in Latin America, despite high urbanization rates. The importance of rural poverty is not always understood, partly because the urban poor are more visible and more vocal than their rural counterparts" (World Bank 1990, p. 29).

The overall incidence of poverty has fallen in many parts of the world since this was written, although major problems remain and new sources of concern have arisen during the 1990s. For example, some groups are socially excluded and have benefited little from the overall growth process in many countries; the impact of new technology has widened the economic distance between skilled workers and the rest; insecurity and violence have become a scourge in some regions, affecting in particular the poor and marginal; and, in some countries, regional pockets of poverty persist. During the 1990s, the concept of "vulnerability" has become important in the analysis of urban and rural poverty, and in the development of policies to alleviate poverty. Vulnerability has an external side (for example, exposure to shocks such as floods or hurricanes, or stress from the gradual erosion of household income through inflation), as well as an internal side (the absence of financial, social, organizational, and personal resources to cope with shock or stress) (Satterthwaite 1995). Clearly, low-income urban groups, however their actual income may be measured, have become more vulnerable to a wide range of stresses and external shocks.

By the end of the 1990s, urban poverty had become increasingly a focus for policy. Not only have the numbers of the urban poor stubbornly refused to decline but, as cities and urban regions become the touchstones for strategic economic planning, the impact of the urban poor on productivity is a more central issue. At the same time, decentralization has become more prominent in its effects on municipal policymaking. Although traditionally they have not concerned themselves with questions of poverty and social policy, municipalities with their new powers and responsibilities are now increasingly concerning themselves with the challenge of poverty reduction (see, for example, Wegelin and Borgman 1995).

The contributions in this section deal with three major policy questions in the general area of poverty alleviation at the municipal level. In the first, on poverty assessment, Jesko Hentschel and Radha Seshagiri explain the reasons for, and the methodologies associated with, what are called "city poverty assessments." The authors say that these assessments are important for two main reasons: because understanding poverty and its incidence will contribute to the design of urban policies that will in turn tend to decrease urban inequality, and thereby social tensions; and because helping the poor through education and gainful employment "will help the city reach its growth and prosperity potential." In all the measures considered, it is important to understand that each city must construct its assessment differently—using common tools and approaches—in order to respond to the problems that local people consider the most pressing and urgent. But these quantitative measures should be supplemented by qualitative and participatory approaches that explore how poor communities understand and experience poverty, and what they themselves think should be done; and how problems differ among different vulnerable groups in the city. On the institutional side, Hentschel and Seshagiri look at anti-poverty programs and their costs and benefits, as well as the overall effectiveness of programs that target the poor. Whatever the particular mix of "tools" for poverty assessment, the process of preparing the assessment can be of major importance "in forming new and more effective partnerships and understanding in city poverty reduction."

The theme of partnerships is taken up by Camilo Granada in a study of two cases of successful poverty reduction in Argentina. He argues that the most direct way of reducing poverty is through employment and income generation. This implies promotion of economic growth in local areas. But, since the promotion of growth does not always result in full benefits for vulnerable groups, it is necessary to work in partnership with the private and NGO sectors—which can work directly with groups of the very poor—when programs are being planned. These partnerships, when initiated by municipalities, "can be broadly defined as joint projects with the active participation and support of mayors' offices, other sub-national and national public agencies, business, and civil society organizations." Granada instances the case of Palpalá, where a number of small-scale projects were initiated by the municipality in the wake of the privatization of the local steel mill which left 4,000 people unemployed. Among the initiatives were a new bus company, a health clinic, and the promotion of small family businesses at the community level. In the second case, San Jorge (on the outskirts of Buenos Aires), an initiative to develop child-care facilities began with an NGO (IIED–America Latina), but spread more broadly into an integrated development program at the level of the whole neighborhood. Eventually, the project included the NGO, the municipality, the recently privatized water company, and the University of Buenos Aires. In two years, the project benefited 350 out of the 450 families living in San Jorge.

The third contribution deals with the important issue of gender in an urban setting. Colleen O'Manique describes a current project in Bolivia—supported by CIDA—in which explicit efforts are being made to integrate gender perspectives into local planning exercises. Given that women suffer disproportionately from the effects of privatization and poor provision of local services in low-income areas, the project ensures that women are equally represented with men in training programs, and that women-led community micro-projects receive support from the project itself, from the municipalities, and from the participating communities. This project is intended to show that, through participatory planning methods, women's interests can be effectively represented at the local level.

As municipalities face up to their responsibilities for the poor and vulnerable within their jurisdictions, new approaches and more complex partnerships and initiatives are bound to emerge throughout the developing world.

References

Satterthwaite, David. 1995. "The Underestimation and Misrepresentation of Urban Poverty." *Environment and Urbanization* 7(1): 3–10.

Wegelin, Emiel A., and Karin M. Borgman. 1995. "Options for Municipal Interventions in Urban Poverty Alleviation." *Environment and Urbanization* 7(2): 131–51.

World Bank. 1990. *World Development Report 1990*. New York: Oxford University Press for the World Bank.

The City Poverty Assessment: An Introduction

Jesko Hentschel and Radha Seshagiri

Yet Another Academic Report on My Overstudied City?

Over the last decades, city managers and activists have faced an urgent need to respond to the plight of the urban poor. Cities all over the world have grown tremendously, and in many regions the locus of poverty has already shifted from rural to urban areas as a result of migration, urban mortality declines, and high overall fertility rates. While poverty at the beginning of the 1970s was still predominantly rural, the turn of the century witnesses cities as the primary loci of poverty in Latin America and Eastern Europe, with East Asia about to perform this transition in the not too distant future. Rapid urbanization itself places enormous pressure on cities to use their limited resources to meet, or facilitate the meeting of, increased demand for water, sanitation, electricity, basic education, health, housing, and transport. With rapid growth in cities has also come the typical urban dimension of poverty: health hazards from air pollution and contaminated water; crowding and traffic congestion; poverty-induced violence; inequality; and the list continues.

Most city managers, as well as the poor themselves, can pinpoint the most pressing problems in their municipalities. City managers know the areas of extreme deprivation in their cities, and where help is most needed. In many places, the help most immediately necessary will be "common knowledge," shared by the poor and policymakers alike—be it in the supply of basic services, nutrition, social assistance programs, or employment creation. Many cities—especially in Latin America—have been subjected to a host of studies, many of which examine in detail deprivation levels or the deficit of service provision in certain locations. And these are only some of the many reports piling up in the offices of city officials almost everywhere.

So why another study? Doesn't much of the important information already exist, such as where the poor live and what they need? Isn't this yet another exercise with little substantial merit? We argue that the City Poverty Assessment (CPA) is not simply "another study." Rather, it is a tool for urban planning, providing crucial and up-to-date information on what city managers (and also many actors in the private and voluntary sectors) need to know when developing city policies and projects against poverty. The CPA provides necessary information to look at poverty from a much broader perspective than simply to ask where the poor are and what they need. It is intended to provide feedback to city managers on diverse topics such as city finances, city employment and growth, the effectiveness of social programs, infrastructure priorities, and so on.

Why Care About the Poor?

Obviously, a comprehensive review of the poverty situation in a city has its costs, in terms of time and financial resources. That is why it is important to question the very necessity for such exercises. The CPA starts from the implicit judgement that poverty is undesirable and bad. Most people will agree with this normative statement, as they view "development" to be closely linked with guaranteeing minimum standards of living for everybody—like freedom from hunger, a healthy and long life, literacy, and so on. Reducing poverty is also important for urban development in other respects. First, the reduction of poverty through purpose-designed city policies will also tend to decrease inequality and thereby social tensions within the city. Second, helping the poor reach their own potential, through education and gainful employment, for example, will help the city reach its growth and prosperity potential.

City policies will impact on different population groups in different ways—establishing these relationships is the task of the CPA. The "poor," although far from being a homogeneous group, will have needs and opportunities distinct from other groups in the city. For example, city investment in education will reach and benefit different groups according to whether this investment takes place in primary schools or in universities. Similarly, increasing local tariffs for electricity or water can have a very different impact on households according to whether they have access to such public utilities. In certain cities in Latin America, the poor might not feel the impact of a rise in prices, as they have no such access. But if they do have access, how hard would it be for them to pay the higher prices? Would they perhaps forego other essential expenditures, such as sending their children to school? It is therefore important to analyze separately the impact of current city policies, or proposed changes to them, on different population groups.

Indicators

Poverty has many faces, and different cities will find that they need to select their own indicators appropriate to their individual circumstances. In most cities, household income or consumption of the most marginalized will be a crucial determinant of poverty levels. This can be accompanied by access to a basic set of services, ranging from water, electricity and sanitation, to school attendance of children. Many cities in Latin America experience increasing levels of violence in the streets; thus, the incidence of violence is also a determinant of well-being. We describe below different types of indicators that cities might find useful. Not all are strictly linked to poverty, but all are important for pro-poor city planning. Also, the combination of many indicators will give the city policymaker an interesting insight into the nature of deprivation.

First would be the most commonly used poverty measures, those based on the per capita *income* or *consumption* of a household. Such monetary indicators aim to assess whether households can afford to buy a very basic basket of goods at a given point in time. There are many ways to define the value of this "basic basket," but in each the basket contains a minimum of goods essential for the household: food (distinguished according to its nutritional contribution), housing, water, clothing, transport, etc.[1] The value of this basic basket of goods is then called the "poverty line," and a large literature exists on how best to define it.[2]

A number of standard indicators are derived by applying poverty lines to data on the income and consumption of households. The most common one is the *poverty rate* (also called poverty incidence, or headcount index) that describes the percentage of the city population whose per capita incomes (or expenditures) are below the poverty line; i.e., the population that cannot afford to buy a basic basket of goods. Second, and also commonly used, is the *poverty gap*. The gap measures the income shortfall of all poor people relative to the poverty line; or, put differently, it characterizes the mean proportionate poverty gap across the whole population (with a zero gap for the non-poor population). Hence, the poverty gap gives a good indication of the depth of poverty. It is a much more powerful measure than the pure headcount rate because it takes into account the distribution of the poor below the poverty line. Third, and also often used, is the *extreme poverty rate*. This measure uses a different poverty line. It compares household (per capita) income against a very austere basket of goods, which

---

1. In most cases, this "basic basket" of goods mirrors the actual consumption pattern of households. In some other cases in Latin America, like Peru for example, it is also determined by a group of experts.

2. For a good explanation and overview, see Ravallion 1994 and Ravallion and Bidani 1996.

in most cases only includes food items. The percentage of the city population not able to afford this is extremely poor. Finally, apart from such absolute measures of poverty, it is also important for city policymakers to assess the distribution of income in the city—a relative measure. Most commonly used here is the *gini coefficient* of inequality, a measure that varies between 0 (complete equality of incomes) to 1 (complete inequality; one person has all the income, all others have none).[3]

We could characterize the second group of indicators as *health and education outcome indicators*. They directly measure the degree of well-being attained by the city's population—to what degree people can lead healthy and long lives, and what level of education they have reached. Several such outcome indicators concentrate on children—the group in society for whom it is of such great importance to be well fed and healthy, because their whole life depends on their first few years.

A widely used indicator is the percentage of all children below the age of five who are malnourished; i.e., children who have not grown sufficiently for their age (chronic malnutrition), or children who do not weigh enough for their height (acute malnutrition).[4] Other outcome measures are the rate of children who die in infancy or childhood, the maternal mortality rate, or the life expectancy of the city population. On education, to track whether educational goals in the city are achieved, indicators could include the percentage of citizens able to read and write, or scores achieved in standardized tests by different age cohorts.

Third, we can think of *access indicators*. Quite different from outcome indicators, these measure access to a set of basic infrastructure and social services. Hence, we should think of them as "inputs," since they do not necessarily tell us whether services achieve the desired impact. While food distribution programs might reach a large proportion of children in the city, malnutrition levels might still be high if contaminated water causes widespread diarrhea for infants. Nevertheless, access indicators are very important since they determine the degree to which city programs are available to different population groups—maybe not a sufficient, but often a necessary, condition for improving the lives of the poor. Access indicators

---

3 See, for example, the inequality website of the World Bank (www.worldbank.org/poverty/inequal/) for an overview paper and references to standard textbooks.

4. The World Health Organization (WHO) maintains a "Global Database on Child Growth and Malnutrition" (www.who.org), containing comparative information, data sources, and analytical information.

are very popular in Latin America since they form the components of the *Unsatisfied Basic Needs Indicator (Necesidades Basicas Insatisfechas)*, used by many national statistical institutes and also the United Nations Economic Commission for Latin America (CEPAL). With variations, the Unsatisfied Basic Needs Indicator includes access of the population to basic services such as water, electricity, sanitation, and education. But access indicators important for CPAs also use social programs such as nutritional aid, and social assistance programs, etc.

Finally, a host of indicators very closely linked with poverty are what we could term *non-income deprivation indicators*. While some of these might be applicable in many cities, others would be very much linked to individual city circumstances. Many will be closely associated with income measures of poverty, but not necessarily so. For example, unemployment might not throw people into poverty if a good unemployment insurance program exists, or if the unemployed can count on some other form of support. But, even if not directly linked to income-poverty, unemployment is undesirable in itself because of its impact on household income, self-esteem, and even health. Other such non-income deprivation indicators could be violence rates (robbery, homicide, domestic violence, etc.), child labor, or discrimination in the city. If, for example, a certain group (distinguished by either ethnic background or gender) is discriminated against in the workplace (as through lower wages), or in public life (as by police treatment or access to institutions such as the justice system), this is a deprivation in itself. Several of these indicators will be more difficult to grasp than the income, outcome, or access indicators discussed above.

Data Sources

These indicators of poverty and social development stem from a variety of different data sources. Some, such as population censuses, are quite standardized and available in every country and city; others are less readily available.

The population census contains basic information on all citizens of a country—its population, demographic structure and where people live. Since the population census is carried out across millions of households, any further information is generally quite limited. Nevertheless, housing and basic service access, education levels, and employment (by sector) are included, which allows city policymakers to gather important information at a very detailed, disaggregate level within the city: descriptive statistics of the housing stock; access of the population to basic services such as water, electricity, and sanitation; and employment patterns in different subsections in the city.

Household surveys are a very important resource for CPAs. While the census covers the whole population in the city, surveys only interview a subset (or sample), generally a quite small fraction, of all city households. This sample is carefully chosen so that the results of the survey nevertheless describe living conditions in the city accurately. As a rule of thumb, cities that have carried out household surveys have used a minimum sample size of 1,500 to 2,000 households. Since these surveys are much smaller in size than a population census—and therefore also less costly—they are important data sources for CPAs and city planning in general.

Many different types of household surveys exist. Almost all Latin American countries have used *employment surveys* to gather information on employment and unemployment patterns and fluctuations. They also include questions on household income, housing features, and demographic information on the household (size, age of members, etc.), and are therefore good sources for income-based poverty indicators and access indicators. *Demographic and health surveys* are special household surveys geared to explore the incidence of diseases and use of health facilities. They often also collect anthropometric data (such as the height, weight and age of children, that can be used to calculate malnutrition rates), and basic data about housing conditions and educational attainment. They do not, however, collect income information.[5]

A household survey specifically geared towards the measurement and analysis of poverty is the *Living Standard Measurement Study Survey* (LSMS). This instrument, piloted in Peru and Côte d'Ivoire in 1985, collects information on household expenditures and income, health, education, employment, agriculture, the ownership of assets such as housing or land, access to services and social programs, and so on.

Finally, another type of household survey that deserves special mention is the *Rapid Service Satisfaction and Needs Survey*. These surveys are geared to go beyond the typical access assessments of "normal" household

---

5. Although demographic and health surveys do not collect income data directly, they do include a large amount of information on household assets. These assets have recently been used to construct a wealth indicator for households which can replace household income in poverty analysis. See Filmer and Pritchett 1998. See also the website of such surveys at www.macroint.com/dhs.

surveys and ask beneficiaries of household services in depth about the quality of the services they receive and their needs. Questions can include: (a) whether households receive the service continuously or with interruptions; (b) whether the service is provided on time and in good quality; (c) whether households think that the service improved over the last year; or (d) which type of service the city should expand or reduce. The last type of question is geared to assess the needs of the population. Often, such needs assessments can be very important planning tools for city policymakers, especially if they show that conflicting priorities exist for different parts of the population. For example, with financial support from the World Bank, a number of small Colombian municipalities conducted such enquiries in 1995.[6] Currently, the cities of Kampala (Uganda) and Cali (Colombia) are fielding such Rapid Service Satisfaction Surveys.[7]

Participatory assessments are indispensable tools for many aspects of the CPA. They can take a number of different forms: certain groups or representatives can discuss city poverty problems and policies in town-hall meetings, communities can rank what they consider to be the causes of poverty, individual interviews can investigate the problems of women or children in households, or citizens can "map out" new streets or infrastructure in actual planning exercises. Participatory assessments can help policymakers determine the type of indicator important for the poor, be it a housing, employment or income dimension. And, an important point, these assessments can get to a certain type of information that other sources normally cannot capture—the incidence and effect of domestic violence, for example.[8]

Table 7.1 summarizes the different data sources that can help assess (and also monitor) city poverty indicators. As can be seen, several indicators can be assessed from a variety of sources, while others depend on unique ones.

---

6. See Fiszbein 1997 for the list of municipalities. Closely linked to such Service Satisfaction Surveys are Beneficiary Assessments which collect information from the participants and beneficiaries in specific programs. For an introduction see Salmen 1995.

7. See the Core Welfare Indicator Questionnaire of the World Bank (1997). Sample questionnaires for the Kampala and Cali City Poverty Assessments can be obtained from Norbert Schady (Nschady@worldbank.org) or Jesko Hentschel (Jhentschel@worldbank.org) at the World Bank.

8. See, for example, Narayan et al. 2000 and Robb 1998.

Table 7.1.   Indicators and Data Sources

Indicators	*Data Sources*
Income poverty indicators Poverty rate (incidence), poverty gap, poverty severity; extreme poverty rate (incidence); income inequality measures	Household surveys such as Living Standard Measurement Surveys, Emloyment Surveys, etc.
Health and education outcome indicators Under-five mortality rate, infant mortality rate, maternal mortality rate, life expectancy	Specialized household surveys such as Demographic and Health Surveys (DHS), some Living Standard Measurement Study Surveys (LSMS)
Malnutrition rate of children	Most Demographic and Health Surveys (DHS), some Living Standard Measurement Study Surveys (LSMS), Nutrition surveys, Height census
Literacy rate, years of schooling	Most surveys and most censuses
Access Indicators Water, electricity, sanitation, garbage collection	Household surveys, population census, rapid surveys
School and health facility	Household surveys, some population census
Social programs (nutrition, social assistance)	Specialized household surveys (LSMS)
Service satisfaction	Specialized household surveys (Rapid Service Satisfaction and Needs Survey)
Non-income deprivation indicators Unemployment	Employment surveys, LSMS
Violence	Violence surveys (only certain types can be measured), participatory appraisals
Child labor	Employment surveys, LSMS
Discrimination	Participatory assessments, household surveys (not directly but through application of models)

Source: Authors.

City Poverty Information Strategy

The foregoing discussion demonstrates the need for an information strategy for cities to assess and monitor the changes in the kind of poverty indicators they choose. While some cities might have such a strategy in place, others may only have very rudimentary and sketchy data on social conditions, that will not allow the development of proper poverty-reduction programs. While data collection will be at the forefront of such an information strategy, it will have to be embedded in an institutional plan to create and maintain a good poverty monitoring unit in the city government. Expense is an issue for data collection, but the cost of data gathering need not necessarily be high as various avenues can be explored:

- *Using existing household surveys and other data sources:* Many countries in Latin America field large employment or LSMS surveys which are very often representative (i.e., give reliable estimates) at the city level. The population census is one, but the many in-depth case studies and beneficiary information that NGOs, public programs and other organizations might possess, are others.
- *Linking a city survey to a national household survey:* Even in cases where representation is achieved at the city level, more detailed information (such as by geographical breakdown within the city) is often desirable. But, rather than conducting a completely new survey from scratch, the city could negotiate that the national statistical institute apply a specific city-module when conducting the national household survey. This will save considerable expense and ensure that the collected data can be linked to some of the other variables routinely collected by the statistical institute (such as income or expenditure data).[9]
- *Conducting Rapid Service Satisfaction Surveys and Participatory Assessments:* Both Rapid Service Satisfaction Surveys and Participatory Assessments can be moderate in cost if designed with a clear purpose and time frame. The rapid surveys generally do not contain income or expenditure information; this reduces costs of fielding the survey significantly. Participatory assessments can use

---

9. Although cost estimates here are very difficult (and depend on the questionnaire and country circumstance), such sub-samples linked to national household surveys should cost in the range of US$25,000 to $40,000.

very effective group methodology which collects opinions quickly and at low cost.

- *Using partnerships with organizations to gather information:* Finally, a large number of organizations are active at the city level in poverty-reduction programs. Several of these may be able to collect data for policymakers through their continuing operations; for example, housing NGOs will frequently have detailed information on the quality of the housing stock in specific areas of the city.

The City Poverty Profile—A Basic Snapshot

The most important first step in the analysis of poverty is to construct a poverty profile. This can have many dimensions; it can include who is poor, where they are in the city, how they earn their living, their access to and use of government services, their living standards with regard to health, education, nutrition and so forth.

Dimension and Geographic Location in the City

The dimension of poverty in the city can be assessed by using some of the indicators mentioned in the previous section. And, since poverty has indeed many faces, it is crucial to get to these different dimensions by describing the welfare of the city's population with, for example, income-poverty indicators, but also the incidence of diseases, violence or malnutrition.

Table 7.2 shows the distribution of income-poverty in Karachi, Pakistan. As can be seen, the poverty rate varies greatly between the different parts of the city, being highest in the rural fringe and lowest in the geographical areas characterized as affluent. However, the table also shows another important dimension of poverty that interests us: while the poverty rate (i.e., the percentage of the population in a specific area that is poor) is important, the other dimension of the geographical location is: *how many of the total poor* live in a certain location. This is shown in column 2, which could also be labeled "contribution to the total poor." As observed, the rural fringe, the area with the highest incidence of poverty, is not the area with the highest share of the total poor, as relatively few people live there.

Information on the spatial distribution of poverty within the city can then be used to construct city *poverty maps*. These can be of considerable value to governments, NGOs and multilateral institutions interested in strengthening the poverty alleviation impact of their spending. For example, they can be used to guide the division of resources among local

Table 7.2.   Poverty Clusters in Karachi, 1990
(percent)

Area	Poverty rate	Poor households in area as percentage of all poor households	Population share
Old city	61	18	12
Old settlements	56	10	7
Korangi	49	12	10
Site	59	27	18
Service areas	54	11	8
Rural fringe	67	7	4
All affluent areas	15	16	41

Source: Altaf et al. 1993.

administrative units within the city as a first step in reaching the poor. Many Latin American countries have constructed poverty maps, most often using an Unsatisfied Basic Needs Indicator as the underlying welfare measure. Recently, some countries have started to construct spatially disaggregated income maps as well, which can then be combined with service deficiency information.[10]

Characteristics of Poor Households

Another major task of the poverty profile is to describe the living circumstances of the poor in the city. This comparison can show how characteristics of poor households can vary within the city—for example, the income-poor in one area might not have access to basic services, while those in other parts of the city do. Again, we use an example from Karachi in Table 7.3. While household size, number of children per household, housing structure, and employment characteristics do not vary much between the extremely poor groups in the Old City and the Old Settlements, education variables do show variation. Hence, this could give city planners a first indication of an educational deficiency in the Old City.

---

10. For information on poverty maps and how they are constructed, see the websites of UNEP at Arendal (www.grida.no), of the World Resources Institute (www.wri.org), and of the World Bank (www.worldbank.org/poverty/inequal/index.htm). See Hentschel et al. 1998 for a description of methods to link survey and census data to obtain spatially disaggregate estimates of income poverty.

Table 7.3.   Characteristics of Very Poor Households Across Poverty Clusters, Karachi

Characteristic	Old City	Old Settlements
Household size	10.2	9.7
Number of children	4.5	4.9
Housing structure (%)		
Permanent	33.0	23.0
Semi-permanent	62.0	74.0
Impermanent	5.0	3.0
Access to services (%)		
Piped water	45.0	63.0
Electricity	91.0	88.0
Gas	52.0	49.0
Employment sector (%)		
Industry	16.0	25.0
Services	73.0	69.0
Education (%)		
Adult males literate	47.0	56.0
Adult females literate	22.0	40.0
Adult males high school	14.0	27.0
Adult females high school	6.0	16.0

Source: Altaf et al. 1993.

Characteristics of Poor Households Compared to Non-Poor Households

The same type of characteristics of living circumstances can now also be used to compare the poor to non-poor groups. Such a comparison will show where the living characteristics of the poor (e.g., the income-poor) are similar and where they differ from better-off groups—for example, the fact that a large part of the poor do not have access to water might not be a distinguishing factor if the whole city population lacks such access. Table 7.4, an example from Cali in 1998, distinguishes five income quintiles in the city's population: 1 is the poorest, 5 is the richest. Such a distinction goes beyond the "poor"–"non-poor" divide imposed by a poverty line and is able to provide a much more complete picture of well-being.

As can be observed in Table 7.4, several characteristics of households do not vary at all by income class, while others do. The employment patterns, the incidence of unemployment, and the access to social programs such as health insurance or a retirement fund are strongly correlated with per capita income of the household. Similarly, secondary school attendance increases with the income quintile. But certain service access (water, electricity) or primary school attendance is close to complete across the income spectrum.

Table 7.4.   Characteristics of Households by Income Quintile, Cali, 1998
(percent)

Characteristic	1 (poorest)	2	3	4	5 (richest)
Employment					
Formal sector	17	31	37	51	54
Informal sector	83	69	63	49	46
Unemployment	43	26	16	13	7
School attendance					
Children 6–12	96	91	89	99	93
Children age 13–18	68	74	67	82	76
Access to services					
Electricity	99	99	99	99	99
Water	99	99	99	99	99
Telephone	50	61	67	84	90
Health insurance	22	38	48	59	65
Retirement fund	13	26	35	46	55

Source: Santamaria 1998.

Important Dimensions of City Life

Characteristics of the life of the poor in different parts of the city, and characteristics across different income classes, are starting points for examining a broad variety of subjects which will have to be tailor-made to individual city circumstances. Some of these could include:

- *Environmental and health conditions of different population groups:* Many assessments of inner-city health conditions suggest that death and disease rates for infants and children are between two and ten times higher in deprived than in non-deprived areas. This situation is closely connected to the poor being much more often affected by pollution than better-off city-dwellers (see Box 7.1). Describing these often-hazardous living conditions is key to understanding the problems of the poor.
- *The income and expenditure patterns of population groups:* Different population groups derive their income from varying sources—and also spend it on different items. Exploring these differences is necessary to assess how changes in the prices of goods will impact on the well-being of the most marginalized groups. For example, if it is found that the poor spend about 10 percent of their income on public transport while the richer groups in the city do not depend on public transport at all, a

---

Box 7.1.   Urban Living Conditions in Rio de Janeiro

By choice of location and by political process directing efforts to clean the environment toward richer areas, the poor are more affected by adverse environmental conditions. More of the poor live in the northern part of the municipality of Rio, which is affected by serious, and health threatening, air pollution. They live closer to heavily polluted water bodies, such as Guanabara Bay, which leads to health risks, for example, for bathing children. Many poor neighborhoods, especially *favelas*, are located on lands exposed to natural hazards (landslides, flooding, etc.). The health costs of pollution particularly affect low-income households, who typically live in more polluted areas and lack the resources for protective expenditures and investments. Environmental improvements will, therefore, often more than proportionately benefit the low-income population. Measures that improve environmental conditions and generate benefits primarily for the poor, such as the extension of basic sanitation, are an obvious top priority. On the other hand, it would be misguided to try to address income inequalities through environmental improvements that would not otherwise be a priority. For example, investments in secondary and tertiary sewage treatment would in many locations not likely be a priority for the poor who might instead prefer faster expansion of sewage collection or better health care and education (World Bank 1998).

---

steep price increase in public transport can cause substantial problems for the poor. The reverse, however, might be true as well: people in the richer parts of the city might be the exclusive users of public transport services while the poor use informal transportation, or simply walk. In this circumstance, the price hike will be borne by the well-off in the city and will not impact on the poor. Similar analyses can be carried out for other public services, and also for food or clothing price increases.

- *Relative poverty risks of different groups within the city:* Different population groups within the city might be at varying risks of being poor (see Box 7.2). Therefore, a poverty profile should also analyze the degree to which poverty and deprivation are linked to certain personal characteristics of its citizens, such as gender, age, or ethnicity. To make comparisons easier, analysts sometimes use the *relative poverty risk,* which sets the likelihood of somebody being poor in relation to all other groups in society that do not have this characteristic. In Peru, for example, a recent poverty analysis showed that a person with an indigenous background was 50 percent more likely to be poor than a person with a non-indigenous background (World Bank 1999).

More than a Snapshot: Changes Over Time

For most urban policymakers, even more important than the "snapshot" of poverty is how city living conditions change over time. This is so for two

---

Box 7.2.   Poverty Risk in Rio de Janeiro, 1998

A breakdown of the poor in Rio shows that certain characteristics of the household head are associated with a higher probability of being poor. In particular, the percentage of poor (compared to the overall poverty rate) is higher for particularly vulnerable groups, including female-headed households (29 percent higher poverty rate); young households, headed by under 25 year olds (105 percent higher); uneducated households, heads without formal schooling (85 percent higher); blacks (55 percent higher) and unemployed (230 percent higher) and informal sector workers (26 percent higher) (World Bank 1998).

---

reasons. First, changes over time give feedback on whether the city is moving in the right direction. While poverty might be extremely low, an increase in poverty has to be of concern. Similarly, even though high poverty levels are a very big concern, a reduction in poverty shows at least that improvements are possible. Second, changes over time can also provide insight into the factors that help people grow out of poverty or fall into it. Such factors can be good "hooks" for the development of city anti-poverty programs.

Poverty Changes over Time

Measuring changes over time requires, first of all, a "rock-solid" definition of the poverty indicators employed. This might seem easier than it actually is in some circumstances. While the measurement of access variables is generally quite straightforward, the most commonly used poverty indicator—an income-based poverty rate or poverty gap—is much more difficult to define in exactly the same way in different years. Household surveys that measure the monetary welfare measure (income or consumption) have to follow the same sampling procedures in different years; they need to ask exactly the same questions, and record the same prices which are then used for adjusting nominal incomes. Often such comparability is not easily achieved.

But if the consistency of indicators is given, comparisons over time can offer many additional insights. For example, poverty, extreme poverty, and inequality levels in Cali in 1998 were not the worst in Colombia and in line with those of Bogotá and Medellín. Table 7.5 reports these same indicators for Cali; however, it records their changes from 1994 to 1998. As can be seen, Colombian cities had very different experiences in these four years: only Bogotá and Barranquilla reduced both extreme poverty and inequality, while extreme poverty and inequality increased in Cali and Bucaramanga. Tracking the different development in

Table 7.5.   Changes in Income Poverty and Inequality of Colombian Cities, 1994-98

City	*Change in extreme poverty rate*	*Change in inequality (gini coefficient)*
Bogotá	−2.5	−0.02
Medellín	+3.8	−0.06
Cali	+0.8	+0.04
Barranquilla	−7.8	−0.19
Bucaramanga	+2.2	+0.01

Source: Santamaria 1999.

Colombian cities was only possible since the Colombian Statistical Institute (DANE) applied its *Encuesta de Hogares* nationwide at different times, using the same income definition, and ensuring representability for various cities.

Factors Associated with Poverty

Time comparisons can also help policymakers to understand better the dynamics of poverty. We discussed above how the poverty profile can provide a "snapshot" of the factors associated with poverty. If such data are now available over time, we can examine if these same factors also change—that is, if they remain strongly associated with poverty or if they lose or increase their importance. For instance, the World Bank (1999) reports that in Peru an indigenous person was 40 percent more likely to be poor than a non-indigenous person in 1994, but almost 50 percent more likely to be poor in 1997. Hence, the indigenous population fell further behind the non-indigenous population. Landless rural households were, as one could expect, more likely to be poor in 1994 than rural households with land. However, in 1997, such rural landless households were about 5 percent *less* likely to be poor—here we have a case where time comparisons can tell us that a certain factor does not appear to be systematically linked to welfare changes. A special case is given if consecutive household surveys interview *identical* households in time and a panel is included in the household survey. Then, more sophisticated methods can be used to link what factors help households grow out of poverty.[11]

---

11. See Deaton 1997 for an explanation of household panels. Examples of panel analysis can be found in Glewwe and Hall 1995 and World Bank 1999.

If cities do not command representative household surveys that contain income information at different points in time, welfare developments can be tracked using other indicators. For example, as one such indicator, Wong (1997) used the share of households that possess certain durable consumer goods (refrigerators, washers, color TV sets) to show welfare developments in Shanghai from 1985 to 1995.

Beyond Indicators and the Profile: Understanding the Meaning of Poverty

While the measurement and description of poverty conditions are important components of the CPA, a variety of other tools can help (and are often necessary) to understand better the meaning and dynamics of poverty. Among others, participatory and qualitative tools can be used to:

- Assess how poor communities understand and experience poverty;
- Explore whether different groups in the community (or individuals in households) face a set of problems in overcoming poverty different from the experience of others;
- Identify vulnerable groups in times of hardship;
- Prioritize poverty indicators among the many that could be employed;
- Learn what poor communities view as the main bottleneck in reducing poverty;
- Understand the living circumstances of the poor and the dynamics and causes of poverty.

In some cases, such in-depth reviews might lead to the adoption of different indicators for poverty monitoring than the ones usually proposed, such as the percentage of households without a plot of land or proper title to their house. In other cases, such "contextualization" of poverty can call for a combination of different indicators (Box 7.3).

Who Pays and Who Benefits from City Expenditures?

One of the central parts of the CPA is the analysis of city finances. Different from municipal finance studies, that look at the appropriateness and level of taxes and expenditures, the emphasis of CPAs is on the distribution and equity aspects.

Responsibility of the City and Central Government

The first step in the analysis of municipal finance from a poverty perspective is to distinguish which functions are performed by different levels of

---

Box 7.3.   Income Poverty and Living Conditions in Bombay

A longitudinal case study in Bombay (i.e., a study that records and observes a community over a period of time), shows that income changes and changes in living conditions need not go hand in hand. Observation of the same families in 1987 and 1992 found income variations to be extremely large in both directions, upward and downward. Such high income mobility went hand-in-hand with very little change in overall living conditions of households, such as the health risks they faced from environmental pollution or their access to basic services. Hence, the study concluded that poverty can be neither understood nor tackled through a simple focus on income. A more comprehensive approach is necessary, one which includes housing and living conditions in addition to the income measure (Swaminathan 1995).

---

government—city, provincial, and central. Programs might work very distinctly in the type of services they fund and how they try to reach beneficiaries. Similarly, taxes might be shared between different levels of government, or cities might have the freedom to levy certain taxes without much central control. This is important background information for understanding how the city can obtain or use its resources in a more pro-poor way.

INCIDENCE ANALYSIS. This is the main tool for assessing the distributional impact of city expenditures and taxes. It aims to quantify the share of total revenues and expenditures that a certain population segment (for example, "the poorest decile," or "population in district 1") pays or receives. There are two dimensions to incidence analysis in the city context: type of household and geographical location. Incidence analysis by type of household requires the availability of a household survey representative at the city level. Using the total expenditure or tax per activity, specific questions of the household survey are then used to distribute total funds (e.g., to the poorest decile of the population). Incidence by geographical location requires good data from the city planning or budget office on where actual expenditures in the city went, and where taxes were raised. The geographic assessment is generally carried out at the level of administrative sub-units.

INCIDENCE OF CITY EXPENDITURES. This generally starts with establishing user patterns of public services and programs, employing the household survey as the main data source (see World Bank 1992). User patterns of services provide information on who in the city obtains what share of services. In Rio de Janeiro, the most frequent users of health services are in income deciles three and four, who—although their share in the population is each only 10 percent—use 15 or 16 percent of total health services provided in the city. The wealthier groups tend to use private instead of public health services, which explains their lower share in total service use.

The second step in calculating the incidence is to distribute actual expenditures according to the user profile. Most often, household surveys will not record the actual benefit received from social programs, so assumptions have to be made. The most common assumption is that benefits for all users, *on average*, are the same. That is, the actual benefit derived from a health visit is independent of the income status of the user.

Data requirements to assess the geographical incidence of program expenditures are more moderate. Detailed city expenditure accounts, that allow for an identification of recurrent and capital expenditures by different sub-units in the city, are generally sufficient, and many cities have good information systems in this regard. The geographical pattern of expenditures can then be compared to the geographical distribution of poverty to establish whether funds flow into the most deprived areas.

INCIDENCE OF CITY TAXES. The other side of expenditure incidence is an assessment of how such expenditures are paid for. While everybody in the city can be asked to contribute to local revenues, it is not desirable to have the less fortunate in the city pay the brunt of total revenues. By the nature of the subject, information on tax payments in most cities is rather scarce, which complicates tax-incidence analysis. In some cases, household surveys do contain important information—for example, if a share of value-added taxes (VAT) goes directly into the account of the municipality, household surveys will provide good estimates of the distribution of these VAT taxes by using information on consumption patterns. But other local taxes, especially the property tax, will not be reported accurately in household surveys (partly because respondents are skeptical about the eventual use of the information they provide). Hence, tax registries at the local level will be the major source of information in most circumstances, and should provide an accurate geographical tax incidence by type of tax. Many inferences can be drawn from a geographical distribution of taxes. For example, if income from property taxes is highest in the poorest areas of town, it is likely that the more wealthy evade such taxes and, consequently, property-tax incidence is likely to be regressive.

City Anti-Poverty Programs

In addition to the assessment of expenditure and tax incidence, CPAs take an in-depth look at the functioning and effectiveness of existing anti-poverty programs.

Institutional Map

A good starting point for such an assessment is the preparation of an institutional map. This records detailed information about the total supply of social programs and services in the city. The map looks beyond the public sector (city and central) and also includes private, community-based, and voluntary organizations. Its purpose is to draw a picture of the total supply of social and productive programs in the city: who does what and where, with how many resources. The outputs can be physical, computerized or both, and they are important information tools for all actors in the city. The preparation of an institutional map can go hand-in-hand with an in-depth review of the functions of the local government and its potential role in poverty reduction.

Institutional maps are key inputs into planning and re-orienting city anti-poverty programs. They identify gaps and overlaps in program provisions between different actors and by geographical area. Combining them with detailed information on the location of poverty and the output of rapid needs assessments, allows for the combination of supply and demand information, and as such can be an important planning tool.

Targeting, Coverage, and Benefit Transfer of Social Programs

Using information from the institutional mapping exercise and also the incidence analysis, the analyst can derive targeting, coverage, and benefit information for social programs. "Targeting" refers to the percentage of total expenditures which go to the poor. "Coverage" describes how many of the poor are reached. These are two distinct dimensions of program performance. For example, a program might be targeted; that is, almost all its expenditures may go to the very poor. However, its coverage rate might be low as well if only very few of the poor are reached. Figure 7.1 brings these two dimensions together: the horizontal axis maps the coverage, i.e., how many of the poor are reached. The vertical axis maps the targeting efficiency, i.e., what percentage of total program expenditures goes to the poor. Programs with large coverage and good targeting would therefore be in the upper right corner of the graph. Most programs in Rio do not show

Figure 7.1.   Program Benefits to the Poor

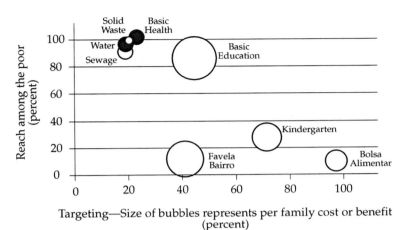

Targeting—Size of bubbles represents per family cost or benefit
(percent)

Source: World Bank (1998).

such characteristics but have *either* good targeting and low coverage (lower right corner) *or* good coverage but weak targeting (upper left corner).

Efficiency of Programs

Measurement problems notwithstanding, an assessment of the economic efficiency of public expenditures is essential.[12] Questions to be answered here include: first, are the expenditures that appear to be directed to the poor directed to high-return activities? Second, are the programs operated efficiently; that is, are administrative and targeting costs justifiable when compared with the benefit derived from the programs? Third, in the broader city expenditure program, is there scope for efficiency-related cuts that would free resources for poverty reduction? Fourth, are public expenditures directed at public goods and services that promote broad-based, efficient growth, or are they captured by special interest groups?

Evaluation and Monitoring of Impact

Social programs—independent of who provides them—need functioning monitoring and evaluation systems to tell city managers and other

---

12. See World Bank 1992 for a review of the efficiency of programs.

policymakers whether the financed programs had the intended impact, such as improving health or reducing poverty. The difficulty here is to develop systems that will distinguish the impact of the specific project from the impact of other developments. For example, to assess the effect of a nutrition project on child malnutrition, it is important to distinguish the direct nutritional impact of the program from the effect of rising incomes on nutrition. The design of appropriate monitoring and evaluation systems is a precondition for designing effective city poverty reduction programs.[13]

City Growth and Poverty Reduction?

Apart from its concern with the evaluation of social and productive programs for poverty reduction, the CPA also assesses how the general economic performance of the city is linked to poverty reduction. Obviously, a city that stagnates economically and has high unemployment rates will find it difficult to reduce poverty signficantly.

The poor's connection with the city's economic development works mainly through the labor market. Hence, there is a need to establish what the main activities of the poor are, in which sectors they work, and what the most likely additional employment sources would be if those were available. In most Latin American cities, the poor's main income source stems from informal sector activities in commerce and construction. With the help of household surveys, it is possible to calculate the impact on employment creation of growth in these (and other) sectors, and to infer the impact on poverty reduction. This will give city managers a basic idea of how—and what type of—growth will be important for poverty reduction.

But employment creation for the poor can also be a function of factors other than city economic performance. Regulations, for instance, can be impediments to establishing their own enterprises. Taxes might deter establishment of enterprises or investment from outsiders. And transport might be a major barrier to getting to places where jobs are. The CPA would analyze all such factors and make appropriate policy recommendations.

Concluding Remarks

We have provided an introduction to the content and tools of CPAs. There is no standard content of such assessments; they need to be adapted to the specific needs of cities. Several aspects of urban poverty touched on here

---

13. See the *Handbook* on impact evaluation by Baker (1999).

will be irrelevant to certain circumstances, while others, not mentioned, will be crucial.

The thrust of CPAs is to provide city policymakers with thorough and good information about the situation of the poor in the city, the functioning of city anti-poverty programs, and the link between poverty and growth. Many of the tools which can be developed are valuable planning tools by themselves, such as poverty maps, institutional maps, the incidence of taxes and expenditures, and rapid service satisfaction surveys. Finally, the *process* of preparing a CPA—which includes collecting information, analyzing it and discussing it with all the different actors, including the poor— will be of major importance in forming new and more effective partnerships and understanding in city poverty reduction.

References

Altaf, M.A. et al. 1993. "Poverty in Karachi: Incidence, Location, Characteristics, and Upward Mobility." *Pakistan Development Review* 32(2): 159–78.

Baker, J. 1999. *Evaluating the Poverty Impact of projects: A Handbook for Practitioners*. Washington, DC: World Bank.

Deaton, A. 1997. *The Analysis of Houshold Surveys*. Baltimore, MD: Johns Hopkins.

Filmer, D., and L. Pritchett. 1998. *Estimating Wealth Effects without Expenditure Data, or Tears: An Application to Educational Enrollments in States of India*. Working Paper 1900. Washington, DC: World Bank.

Fiszbein, A. 1997. "The Emergence of Local Capacity: Lessons from Colombia." *World Development* 25(7): 1029–43.

Glewwe, P., and G. Hall. 1995. "Who Is Most Vulnerable to Macroeconomic Shocks? Hypotheses Tests Using Panel Data from Peru." Living Standard Measurement Study 117. Washington, DC: World Bank.

Grosh, M., and J. Munoz. 1996. "A Manual for Planning and Implementing the Living Standards Measurement Study Survey." LSMS Working Paper 126, Washington, DC: World Bank.

Hentschel, J., J. Lanjouw, P. Lanjouw, and J. Poggi. 1998. "Combining Census and Survey Data to Study the Spatial Dimensions of Poverty." Policy Research Paper 1928. Washington, DC: World Bank.

INEI (Peruvian National Statistical Institute). 1997. *Encuesta Nacional sobre Violencia*. Lima: INEI.

Narayan, D., R. Patel, K. Schafft, A. Rademacher, and S. Koch-Schulte. 2000. *Voices of the Poor: Can Anyone Hear Us?* Vol. 1. New York: Oxford University Press for the World Bank.

Pamuk, A., and P. F. Cavalieri. 1998. "Alleviating Urban Poverty in a Global City: New Trends in Upgrading Rio de Janeiro's Favelas." *Habitat International* 22(4): 449–62.

Ravallion, M. 1994. *Poverty Comparisons: A Guide to Concepts and Methods.* Langhorne, PA: Harwood Academic.

Ravallion, M., and B. Bidani. 1996. "How Robust is a Poverty Profile?" *World Bank Economic Review* 8: 75–102.

Robb, C. 1998. *Can the Poor Influence Policy? Participatory Poverty Assessments in the Developing World.* Washington, DC: Directions in Development.

Salmen, L. 1995. "Beneficiary Assessments: An Approach Described." ESD Discussion Papers 23. Washington, DC: World Bank.

Santamaria, M. 1999. "Poverty in Cali—Basic Comparisons and Developments." Mimeo, Poverty Group, World Bank.

Swaminathan, M. 1995. "Aspects of Urban Poverty in Bombay." *Environment and Urbanization* 7(1): 133–43.

Wong, C. 1997. "How Many Poor People in Shanghai Today? The Question of Poverty and Poverty Measure." *Issues and Studies: A Journal of Chinese Studies and International Affairs (Taiwan)* 33: 32–49.

World Bank. 1992. *Poverty Reduction Handbook.* Washington, DC: World Bank.

World Bank. 1997. "Core Welfare Indicator Questionnaire." Background Documentation. Washington, DC: World Bank.

World Bank. 1998. "Poverty in Rio de Janeiro." Mimeo, World Bank.

World Bank 1999. "Poverty and Social Developments in Peru, 1994 to 1997." Country Report. Washington, DC: World Bank.

Poverty Reduction in Urban Areas: Employment and Income Generation through Partnerships

Camilo Granada

As argued by the World Bank in its *World Development Report 1990*, labor-intensive economic growth is a cornerstone of an effective and long-term poverty reduction strategy. The rationale is straightforward: such growth would create wealth through greater output, and through higher levels of employment that would directly benefit the poor.

Even under the most propitious conditions, economic growth alone does not always lead to reduction of poverty through trickle-down effects. Even when a labor-intensive model is promoted, the most vulnerable groups might not benefit fully from the increased level of activity in the modern/formal sector. This calls for a proactive intervention to provide safety nets and support employment generation that goes beyond traditional labor-market interventions.

The reduction of poverty through employment and income generation addresses not only the income and consumption aspects of poverty, but also key social elements, such as self-esteem and social integration. So the key to alleviating poverty is the creation of sufficient productive employment opportunities for the poor.

In reviewing the issue of employment generation at the municipal level, the first thing to recognize is the limit to what city managers can do. Macroeconomic policy and general growth determinants are usually dealt with at the national level, limiting the scope for municipal initiatives; at the same time, however, addressing unemployment exclusively as a macroeconomic management issue is insufficient. An enabling environment can and should be fostered to increase local competitiveness and the level of economic activity. Special programs should be implemented to help the most disadvantaged groups find employment, or establish their own income-generating initiatives, as an integral part of a strategy to reduce or eradicate poverty.

Even if a consensus is reached on the need to support meaningful jobs for the poor, action in a context of rationalization, reduction of public intervention, and tighter budgetary constraints becomes even more complex and difficult.

Conventional Approaches to Intervention

Traditionally, city governments' main instrument for providing jobs for the disadvantaged has been direct employment. This avenue has become increasingly less open, as pressure from the decentralization process affects the delivery, quality, and cost of services. The need for sound fiscal policies and expenditure accountability are squeezing out the option of using swelling bureaucracies to respond to employment needs.

In the past, public policy has also addressed these issues by creating support mechanisms for the informal sector and micro-enterprises; for the most part, such initiatives have included micro-credit and training programs designed and implemented exclusively by governments. Though it is impossible to generalize, these have mostly led to bureaucratic and inefficient structures, unable to give adequate attention to their constituencies. Budget constraints have also taken their toll on these programs, and the costs of funding and managing micro-finance schemes make them unsustainable in the long run. Finally, they have problems of transparency and equity in their outreach; some have served to strengthen clienteles, while others have failed to reach the most needy, and their resources have benefited the non-poor.

Partnerships: An Innovative Application of an Old Concept

Local leaders and decisionmakers, in both the public and the private sector (including NGOs and CBOs) are finding innovative and creative ways of responding to the challenges posed by poverty. Despite the enormous variety of forms that such initiatives can take, some of the most interesting and successful ones could be grouped under the term "partnerships." These can be broadly defined as joint projects with the active participation and support of mayors' offices, other subnational and national public agencies, business, and civil-society organizations. Partnerships are more complex and sophisticated than simply outsourcing, contracting or privatizing services previously offered by governments, though they can include some of those; an alliance implies an open system of decisionmaking that includes establishing aims, means of implementation, oversight, and evaluation.

The following sections describe two Argentinian examples of partnerships that focus on employment generation or micro-enterprise support.[14]

---

14. The cases were collected as part of a research-training initiative led by the World Bank Institute, called Partnerships for Poverty Reduction. The summaries were published as part of a book, *Working Together for a Change*, by Ariel Fiszbein and Pamela Lowden (1999). Other partnership case studies (not necessarily focused on employment and income generation) can be found on the Latin America Program's website, www.alianzas.org.

Post-Privatization Rehabilitation, Palpalá

The experience of Palpalá represents a comprehensive effort, initiated by municipal authorities, to address the tremendous social shock generated by the privatization of its state-owned steel mill, Altos Hornos Zapla, in 1992. The key to this strategy was to channel resources from the workers' severance payments from Zapla, estimated at US$1 million, into the creation of cooperative micro-enterprises. Some 90 small and medium-size enterprises have since been created with these pooled resources, coupled with the support of the municipal and federal governments, and a professional NGO.

The partnership between the municipal government, private cooperatives, the local school, and the various community groups has allowed Palpalá to avoid the drastic economic and social repercussions often resulting from large-scale privatization. The substantial progress made towards creating an alternative economic base in the locality has averted the extremes of social dislocation and unrest that have been experienced in other provincial areas subjected to similar economic shocks. The initiative is also significant as an example of an emerging new style of local government, whereby the authorities cease merely to be implementers of public programs and become instead the articulators of the local development process. This has also implied a considerable modernization of the working practices of the municipal bureaucracy.

The Partnership

Palpalá is a municipality of about 45,000 inhabitants in the northern Argentine province of Jujuy. Since the mid-1940s, it was home to Altos Hornos Zapla, a government-owned steel mill that employed 5,500 people, or 35 percent of the local labor force. The enterprise ran along highly paternalistic lines; offered health, housing, and other services to a similar percentage of the population; and had a massive impact on the generation of local incomes. With the privatization of the mill in 1992, over 4,000 people lost their jobs, a loss exacerbated by subsequent job reductions in other local companies. Indeed, Palpalá was confronted with an extremely severe economic crisis, with little prospect of resolution within the context of existing institutions.

The municipal government was the catalyst behind the set of initiatives that made the partnership possible. The government's goals included channeling the recently unemployed workers into productive jobs, promoting micro-enterprises, and expanding the methods by which civil society could participate in the decisionmaking process on public issues. The first step involved the pooling of severance payments from Zapla into a common "micro-enterprise" fund. The workers' agreement to contribute their payments was facilitated by the lack of other investment opportunities, coupled with mutual trust and friendship among employees.

The pooling of funds constituted just one component of the development strategy. Further initiatives included: (a) promoting and brokering the creation of the new enterprises among local "investors"; (b) training potential micro-entrepreneurs and municipal staff; (c) raising and channeling additional funds from sources external to the municipality; and (d) facilitating the operation of the new enterprises through a more effective government sector. Partnerships with private, civic, and public entities worked to achieve these goals. The Palpalá experience can be interpreted as one of a network of local partnerships that involves the municipal government, new and old enterprises operating in the area, neighborhood associations and other community organizations, a professional NGO, and several programs funded by the national government.

The partnership approach has yielded tangible benefits on both an economic and a social level. One example involves a new bus company created through an alliance between the municipal government and cooperatives. The mayor brokered its creation by coordinating investors, and by lobbying for the removal of provincial regulations that had permitted a bus-service monopoly. With market flexibility, the new company has grown significantly, and provides greatly needed service from Palpalá to the provincial capital. Another example resulting from the government-cooperative partnership is the health clinic; this provides employment, and also serves an important social function by offering preventive health care and free service to those without insurance. A contract with the provincial government allows the medical staff to use the existing infrastructure free of charge, in exchange for the services provided to the indigent population.

Yet another partnership involves an alliance between the municipal government and neighborhood community organizations, formed with the purpose of increasing the participation of civil society, and disseminating decisionmaking power to the local level. This is a longer-term project, intended to foster small family businesses as well as community participation in the organization of various activities. The Unión Industrial de Palpalá has also emerged through the cooperation of municipal authorities, and serves as a new focal point for local development efforts. Finally, cooperation with community organizations has resulted in systematic efforts to reform the municipal government into a highly trained, effective unit.

Lessons Learned

The Palpalá experience illustrates how an entire local economy can be re-structured, from one marked by mass unemployment and little opportunity for growth, to one in which economic activity is thriving. Moreover, it shows how the private sector can play an integral role in the development process, as well as in poverty reduction. Most communities that experienced similar shocks at this time were unable to deal with the challenge themselves, and waited passively for provincial or federal assistance. Palpalá, in contrast, faced this challenge, starting from recognizing the need to leverage the limited capacity of the municipal government with that of other, non-state, actors.

The collaborative effort of public, private, and community actors succeeded in creating permanent jobs, dozens of small and medium-size businesses, and an efficient and wide-reaching health clinic. Moreover, the benefits of the partnership exceed those that are exclusively economic in nature. Strong ties between cooperatives, the local school, and the municipal administration have created an atmosphere of trust and unity in which individuals are empowered through an increased voice in the government decisionmaking process. These alliances have also led to a positive spill-over effect in which new partnerships are now emerging, not only through the intervention of the mayor, but through the NGOs and private-sector organizations. The Palpalá experience shows how a partnership approach to economic restructuring can overcome significant obstacles in order both to promote growth and to reduce poverty. Without the concerted collaboration of all contributing parties, the experience would simply not have been possible. Its success is also owed, in part, to the close social networks already existing in the city, built around the union organizations of the old steel works.

An Integrated Development Program in a Low-Income Urban Community: San Jorge, Buenos Aires

San Jorge's development program involves a variety of initiatives—child care, infrastructure, job creation—leading to a significant improvement in the living conditions of poor households in a peri-urban neighborhood of Buenos Aires. These initiatives have been made possible through a strategy of partnerships between community organizations, a development NGO (the International Institute for Environment and Development–America Latina [IIED–AL]), several state agencies, and private-sector companies and individuals. In particular, these alliances have been instrumental in overcoming the absence of water and sanitation infrastructure in the San Jorge neighborhood through a partnership involving the newly privatized water company, the NGO, and the municipality.

The Partnership

San Jorge is a very low income community of about 2,700 inhabitants. Extremely poor living conditions affect the majority of the population, 60 percent of which is under the age of 20; 71 percent of the families are under the poverty line; unemployment is as high as 40 percent, while those who work do so mainly in the informal sector. One of the main problems in this kind of settlement is the sanitary conditions. There is no public water or sewerage system, and housing is precarious—conditions facilitating the spread of communicable diseases.

In 1987, a small group of mothers sought to create a child day-care center. With the financial involvement of international agencies and the support of the regional government and NGOs, the first facilities were created, receiving eight children under the age of three. IIED–AL was instrumental in ensuring project implementation and sustainability through community capacity building. Today, the center holds around 100 children, and mothers are part of the staff.

More importantly, that initiative was soon transformed into a broader integrated development program aimed at improving general living conditions; this was based on empowering the community through the inception of a civic organization in the neighborhood. That organization emerged as a reliable partner that could bring the government and the private sector to the table, and thus establish partnerships to achieve their common goals. The San Jorge experience can be interpreted as a process of multiple partnerships, involving different entities.

Perhaps the most noteworthy of those partnerships involves the neighborhood community organization, IIED–AL, the municipality, the recently privatized water company—Aguas Argentinas—and the University of Buenos Aires. The goal was to provide the inhabitants with a proper water and sewage system, where 30 years of governmental initiatives had been unsuccessful; the involvement of a dynamic privately owned utility company made that possible.

Students from the faculty of architecture volunteered to draw the plans for the system. Aguas Argentinas contributed technical assistance, training, and materials. The municipality approved the plans and subsidized part of the costs. The community, through their cooperative, provided labor for the construction. A foreign foundation granted financial resources, while IIED–AL served as coordinator and leader for the entire project. In a two-year period, this project benefited 350 out of 450 families living in San Jorge. Aguas Argentinas, IIED–AL, the municipality, and the provincial government are now collaborating on similar initiatives in other neighborhoods. Not only has the experience been replicated, but new models of how to implement such partnerships have been developed as a result.

A housing improvement credit and technical assistance program was also created through a partnership. Under this, the provincial Secretary of Housing gives financial support and oversees individual projects. IIED–AL trains the people and organizes participatory planning sessions to ensure compliance with the municipality's technical requirements. Private companies provide their expertise, giving technical assistance and brokering materials at lower rates for the program. The communities contribute their work and commit to full repayment of the loans received.

Lessons Learned

The San Jorge experience reveals the critical role that an intermediary NGO can play, both in the promotion of a community organization and in the inception and implementation of tri-sector partnerships. Furthermore, it highlights the importance of the empowerment of the communities as a key factor in the existence of real and sustainable alliances, and in fostering real progress.

This case is also a vivid example of the private companies' contributions to, and benefits from, partnerships. On the one hand, the private sector (Aguas Argentinas, in this case) brings not only the financial means to support poverty-reduction activities, but also, and probably as important, the technical inputs and know-how that will ensure success and sustainability for the project. On the other hand, being part of the partnership allows them to understand and learn how to reach and work with poor communities as clients. In fact, Aguas Argentinas systematized the lessons of this experience and has applied them elsewhere in Argentina as well as worldwide—the company now uses these approaches as part of the services it offers in all the international bids in which it takes part.

Conclusions

The benefits of a partnership-based approach for income and employment generation include, first, the ability of partnerships to bring new resources, both material and nonmaterial. This involves, in part, new kinds of contributors, notably from the business sector, who have resources to offer that are not readily available from traditional sources, including management skills and funds. They leverage more resources from the state but also are an effective way to maximize contributions from poor beneficiary communities, particularly in terms of their commitment to repay loans.

Second, the gains in productivity in the use of those resources, a result of the complementarities and synergies that emerge from the interactions among the sectors working together, represents a further, critical, set of benefits to emerge from the case studies of partnership experiences. With the creation or expansion of income-generating opportunities, challenges seem to increase, because such goals mean putting into place a series of conditions that enable the poor to work and increase their productivity in a sustained manner. In this instance, what emerges is that partnerships are not only helpful but also— probably in all conceivable cases—necessary. This applies to micro-enterprise programs and, still more strikingly, to more integrated approaches that pursue local development in a given region or locality.

Finally, it should be pointed out that, regardless of the type of activity, the interaction among individuals and organizations from different sectors of society tends to create opportunities for creativity and innovation that express themselves in the adoption of new technologies in a variety of fields.

The third crucial area of benefit in a public-private partnership relates to the generation of human, institutional, and social assets that benefit partners, individually and collectively, helping to create the conditions for a more profound impact on poverty reduction. In other words, partnerships build toward both essential components of social capital: actual organizational structures and skills, and the predispositions that underlie them.

A central point in the discussion of poverty reduction and employment generation partnerships concerns the scaling-up of those experiences to become a credible and reliable alternative to traditional schemes of intervention. As the research on partnerships led by Ariel Fiszbein at the World Bank Institute shows, successful cases can be expanded, transferred, and replicated through virtuous circles based on an aspect common to all projects of this kind—the generation and reinforcement of social capital and trust networks. Partnerships can first of all grow by the addition of new activities and areas of development to an initial success. Second, they can also be replicated in other instances or locales by one or several of the initial partners. Finally, effective experiences will serve as models to other actors who may be in different regions but yet face the same type of challenge.

The key element for the scaling-up of partnerships is the dissemination of knowledge and expertise in the dynamics and rationale of the process. An active effort in institutional support, development, and training/learning is therefore needed. Such an effort will only be possible and fruitful with a clear commitment from both public and private actors to work together and trust each other.

References and Further Reading

Arroyo, Daniel, and Maria Elina Estébanez. 1997. *El contexto informal de la vinculaciones entre estado, empresas y sociedad civil en Argentina.* Buenos Aires: FLACSO.

Bigio, Anthony, ed. 1998. *Social Funds and Reaching the Poor: Experiences and Future Directions.* Washington, DC: Economic Development Institute of the World Bank.

Borja, Jordi, Fernando Calderón, Maria Grossi, and Susan Penalva. 1989. *Descentralización y democracia: Gobiernos locales en América Latina.* Santiago, Chile: CLACSO.

Campbell, Tim, George Patterson, and Jose Brakarz. 1991. *Decentralization in Local Government in Latin American Countries: National Strategies in Local Response in Planning, Spending and Management.* Latin American and Caribbean Technical Department, Regional Studies Progress Report no. 5. Washington, DC: World Bank.

Coleman, James S. 1988. "Social Capital in the Creation of Human Capital." *American Journal of Sociology* 94 (Supplement): S95–S120.

De Mattos, C.A. 1989. "La descentralización: una nueva panacea para impulsar el desarrollo local?" *Cuadernos de CLEAH* 51: 57–74.

Evans, Peter. 1996. "Government Action, Social Capital and Development: Reviewing the Evidence on Synergy." *World Development* 24(6): 1119–33.

Fiszbein, Ariel. 1997. "The Emergence of Local Capacity: Lessons from Colombia." *World Development* 20(7): 1029–43.

Fiszbein, Ariel, and Susan Crawford. 1996. *Beyond National Policies: Partnerships for Poverty Reduction.* Annual World Bank Conference on Development Economics–LAC, Bogotá, July.

Fiszbein, Ariel, and Pamela Lowden. 1999. *Working Together for a Change: Government, Business and Civic Partnerships for Poverty Reduction in Latin America and the Caribbean.* Washington, DC: World Bank.

World Bank. 1990. *World Development Report 1990.* New York: Oxford University Press for the World Bank.

Integrating Gender into Urban Development and Poverty Reduction: The Bolivia Sustainable Urban Development Project

Colleen O'Manique

> Attention to gender equality is essential to sound development practice and at the heart of economic and social progress. Development results cannot be maximized and sustained without explicit attention to the different needs and interests of women and men. If the realities and voices of half of the population are not fully recognized, CIDA's objectives "to reduce poverty and to contribute to a more secure, equitable, and prosperous world" (*Canada in the World, Government Statement,* Febuary 1995, 42) will not be met. —*CIDA's Policy on Gender Equality*, Section 2, March 1999.

A four-year CIDA-funded project is underway in Bolivia, executed by the University of Toronto's Urban International unit (UTUI). The Bolivian partners of the Bolivia Sustainable Urban Development Project (BSUDP) are the Ministry of Planning and Sustainable Development, various educational and training institutions, and—most important—the participating municipalities.[15]

The goal is to support sustainable urban development in large urban areas by strengthening the planning and implementation capacity of Bolivian institutions at several levels. BSUDP aims not only to strengthen the technical capacities of municipal governments, but also to make urban decisionmakers and managers more responsive and accountable to the actions, needs and demands of civil society, particularly the most marginalized. The approach is founded on the understanding that critical problems of access to urban services by the poor can only be addressed by building a mutually reinforcing relationship between civil society and governments. The methodology is "hands-on" training and capacity development responsive to the interests and demands of civil society.

In Bolivia's cities, low-paid and insecure forms of employment are the order of the day for most people. In 1995, women accounted for half the workers in the informal sector and about one-quarter of those in the formal sector, and some of the same processes that led them into this situation have also made

---

15. Based on a report prepared for the Economic Development and Poverty Reduction Section, Policy Branch of CIDA, the Canadian International Development Agency, 1999.

their reproductive work more burdensome. Women in poor households, in particular, suffer unequally the consequences of poor provision of services resulting from cutbacks and privatization. Devaluation and inflation have placed a disproportionate burden on women, because deep cuts in household budgets and demand-reducing policies (cuts in public services such as health and education, and in urban infrastructure such as electricity, water supply and sanitation, and public transit) have increased their workload.

For BSUDP, the main challenge with regard to gender lies in reconciling bottom-up, empowerment strategies that originate in the communities with more mainstream efforts in municipal and national bureaucracies, and other institutions involved in the project. This inevitably involves long-term, incremental, and process-oriented change. This particular project can only contribute to starting the process of making Bolivia's cities more egalitarian for all citizens. It adopts a combined strategy of training in gender awareness and planning, consciously involving as many women as possible in the various project activities, "affirmative action" in the form of support for gender-specific projects, and integrating gender analysis into the project activities.

The project initially attempted to involve women NGO leaders in training exercises in the local *Juntas Vecinales* (neighborhood associations), but the knowledge base and capacity in Bolivia to integrate gender perspectives into local planning exercises was found to be thin. Since April 1999, therefore, a specialist in gender and planning has carried out training in Tarija, Santa Cruz, Cochabamba, El Alto, and with the central government, the objective being to increase the indigenous knowledge base in gender and urban planning, so that policymakers can adopt a gender perspective in their planning processes.

In the meantime, a program has been underway to train public servants at the District level in participatory planning techniques. Workshops have been held in Cochabamba and Tarija, the core team consisting of two women and one man; and in all social communication and planning exercises there has been an explicit gender focus. As well, the program has ensured that half of the Bolivian participants from planning departments are women. In the same vein, at least half of urban planning practicum positions go to women. Ensuring women's participation does not *necessarily* mean that agendas leading to sexual equality will be carried forward. However, women are more likely than men to push for policies and programs that will benefit women and break down the current structures of male privilege.

In addition to these "mainstreaming" approaches, BSUDP has put in place projects with an explicit gender focus that are spearheaded by women. Four pilot micro-projects—centers for capacity building for women in productive enterprise—are underway in slum neighborhoods in Tarija. The poor, mostly unemployed women of the peri-urban neighborhoods met together to discuss their priorities and come up with solutions to their poverty. They are now undergoing training in baking, sewing, marketing, literacy, and other skills. Similar projects will be designed and implemented in other Bolivian cities. They are jointly funded, with a contribution from BSUDP, from the municipalities, and from the participating communities. The projects have evolved through a process of consultation with the local NGO *equipo de comunicación alternativa con mujeres* (ECAM), the municipality, and women leaders in poor urban areas—in an effort to strengthen the links between planning, popular participation, and concrete action.

In addition, the project has supported the Women's NGO *Instituto Feminino de Formación Integral* (IFFI) to prepare a participatory strategic urban plan for the city of Cochabamba. Through community meetings with women in different *juntas vecinales* (neighborhood associations) and in different sectors of the economy, IFFI documented women's priorities for urban upgrading and service provision. Other organizations—community groups and NGOs—are tackling some of the issues that have arisen. The overwhelming importance of personal security and issues of domestic violence among women emerged from this particular diagnostic. Plans are underway for neighborhood safety audits, better street lighting, and community policing in Cochabamba, El Alto, and Tarija as a result.

It is this *process* that is central to the overall project, and considered to be as valuable as the benefits that will eventually accrue to the respective communities, in two complementary but different ways. First, from the municipality's point of view, the objective of the institutional learning is to demonstrate that, by working closely with communities, the municipality's resources can be made to go further. Second, from the community's point of view, these projects are intended to show that active participation in planning can lead to a more constructive relationship with the municipality, which helps to show that local development is important and can be achieved.

References

CIDA (Canadian International Development Agency). 1999. *CIDA's Policy on Gender Equality.* [www.acdi-cida.gc.ca].

CIDA. 1999. *CIDA's Policy on Poverty.* [www.acdi-cida.gc.ca].

8

Managing the Urban Environment

Editor's Introduction
Richard Stren

Over the last two decades, we have become increasingly aware of the relationship between cities and their natural environment. This relationship has been a turbulent, and, according to some critics, usually a one-sided affair. Environmentalists have, for many years, either excoriated the city or ignored it. In the first category are such writers as Lester Brown and Herbert Girardet. In an introduction to *The Gaia Atlas of Cities*, Brown writes that "[c]ities are inherently unnatural in that they require enormous concentrations of food, water, and materials in a small area, concentrations far beyond anything nature is capable of providing" (Brown 1992). Later in the same volume, Girardet introduces the subject of urban environment in the following way:

> The history of early cities shows that they often depleted local hinterlands, draining their fertility without replenishing it. They exhausted the forests, watersheds, and farmland that had enabled their existence...The world's large cities now have the whole planet as their hinterland; they draw on resources and dump their wastes all around the globe. How can we avoid turning the planet into a desert, as the majority of our rapidly multiplying humankind becomes urban-based?

> It is the burgeoning cities' huge appetite for the world's resources, and the vast quantities of wastes they discard, that cause the greatest concern about their long-term viability (Girardet 1992, p. 12).

Further, he observes that "cities are giant abusers of Gaia and they have little awareness of the consequences of exploiting her" (Girardet 1992, p. 67), and evokes images of the "city of gluttony," "the city of waste,"[1] and the city as a "parasite." While the author's objective is to promote a more environmentally balanced development of cities, it is clear that he harbors a largely negative and destructive view of the current functioning of cities.

A variation of this argument is the more scientific approach of William Rees, who looks at the "ecological footprint" of cities as involving relationships and exchanges of energy and resources far beyond the city's borders. Because cities require the productive capacity of a land area much greater than that which is included within their own boundaries, their economies are not sustainable in this sense. "However brilliant its economic star, every city is an ecological black hole drawing on the material resources and productivity of a vast and scattered hinterland many times the size of the city itself" (Rees 1992, p. 125).[2] While this provocative argument is valid as far as it goes, there is little discussion in Rees' work of the positive benefits that urban living—in comparison with other possible forms of settlement— may bring to the relationship between humans and their natural environment. Chief among these are the facts that population growth generally correlates negatively with level of urbanization across the world; that dense patterns of urban living save an enormous amount of energy in the form of more efficient transport and heating; that most of the important and creative ideas about environmental improvement come from intellectuals and activists resident in urban areas; and that the social diversity that many cities sustain is often the seedbed of new approaches to political, scientific, and cultural challenges in the wider society.

Because of an underlying distrust of cities, for many years most environmentalists refrained from engaging with urban issues. One of the results for developing countries was the promotion of a "green agenda" in national and international forums, whereas the basic needs of cities in the south could be much better expressed through a "brown agenda." While

---

1. On "waste," Girardet says: "The vast outputs generated by cities in the form of gaseous, liquid, and solid wastes are the result of a lack of understanding of the need to make cities sustainable. Industrial pollution, in particular, can leave environmental legacies that people will have to deal with for generations to come. Cities are bad parasites because at present they have little concern for the health of their host organism, Gaia, the living planet Earth" (Girardet 1992, p. 86).

2. For a more elaborate version of this argument, see Mathis Wackernagel and William Rees 1996.

the "green agenda" of deforestation, global warming, resource depletion, and biodiversity is always a concern, the needs of cities require immediate attention to such "brown" issues as dirty air and water, the absence or inadequacy of public infrastructure (including sewerage systems, roads and public transport, public spaces) and poor waste disposal.

Since the latter half of the 1980s, the attention of the policy community has been drawn increasingly to the problems of the urban environment. A key document in this process of enhancing environmental consciousness has been, without question, the report of the World Commission on Environment and Development—known as the "Brundtland Commission" after its chairperson, Gro Harlem Brundtland—published in 1987. This report elaborated on the important idea of "sustainable development," defined as "development which meets the needs of the present without compromising the ability of future generations to meet their own needs (WCED 1987, p. 43), thereby attempting to find a middle ground between the goals of economic development and those of environmental conservation. But the report also included a ground-breaking chapter entitled "The Urban Challenge," in which the Commission expressed concern over the environmental consequences of rapid urban growth in developing areas, suggesting the importance of local community organizations, the centrality of stronger institutions of local government, and the importance of understanding the link between poverty and environmental degradation.

The growing international interest in the urban environment in developing countries found further expression at the major United Nations Conference on Environment and Development (UNCED) held in Rio de Janeiro in 1992. The "green" agenda tended to obscure the "brown" agenda at this conference, which, however, approved a lengthy document named "Agenda 21." Two chapters are of interest to urban activists—Chapter 7, dealing with the promotion of sustainable human settlements, and Chapter 28, dealing with local authorities. Although the document contains 40 chapters, these two are essential because the whole document depends on the actions of local authorities. "Agenda 21 is essentially a prescription for changes in the way people live. How people live is more a matter of what happens in communities than what happens in countries or continents... It follows that the kinds of changes sought through Agenda 21 must lie with the governments responsible for communities, i.e., local authorities" (Gilbert et al. 1996, p. 16).

Since its publication, many local authorities around the world have undertaken "Agenda 21" projects, bringing their citizens into a consultative process to improve the local environment in specific ways. The key elements of this process, as identified by local practitioners, are: multi-sectoral engagement; consultation with community-based, NGO, business and other groups; participatory assessment of local social, economic, and environmental conditions and needs; participatory target-setting; and monitoring and reporting procedures. A survey carried out by the International Council for Local Environmental Initiatives (ICLEI) in 1996, revealed that 1,812 governments in 64 countries were involved in Local Agenda 21 activities. Active planning was underway in 933 municipalities, and was getting started in an additional 879. Of the 933 already underway, virtually all had established a consultative process with local residents (ICLEI 1997, Chapter 3). Of the total number of local governments involved, 1,631 were located in developed countries, and 181 in developing countries (ICLEI 1997, Chapter 3, Figure 2). While good evaluative studies of most of these cases do not yet exist, even for the European countries that started earliest,[3] a number of successful examples have been reported: Chimbote, Peru; Quezon City, Philippines; Manizales, Colombia. In general, says David Satterthwaite, "many of the more successful case studies [of Agenda 21 initiatives] are rooted in cities with strong local democracies or at least in cities where local democratic moves are not suppressed" (Satterthwaite 1998, p. 4).

The importance of a participatory, democratic framework as a precondition for successful environmental management reforms is clearly underlined in the case of Cubatao, Brazil. Cubatao, on the Atlantic coast to the south of São Paulo, was referred to in the late 1970s as the "valley of death" and the "most polluted city in the world." An industrial city, Cubatao suffered extreme levels of air, water and soil pollution for many years. During the period of military rule in Brazil, little progress was made in dealing with these problems. Once the transition to democracy began to take place in Brazil, a concerned local social movement (organized around the Association of the Victims of Pollution and Bad Living Conditions (AVPM) was able to join forces with progressive planners in the state government in order to carry out significant environmental improvements in the city. From its beginnings in 1983 to 1992, the Cubatao Pollution Control Project was able to control 288 out of 320 primary sources of air, water, and soil pollution in the city. During this period a tragedy occurred, when 700,000 liters of gasoline leaked from a pipeline running under a large slum, leading to a fire which burned 600 shacks to the ground and killed 100 people. This

---

3. For the limitations of evaluation in the context of eight European countries, see William M. Lafferty and Katarina Eckerberg 1998.

accident was widely covered by the local media, leading to a new surge of associational activity, and giving bad publicity to the industrial side. After this accident, the local industries' federation committed its members to compliance with pollution control. Explaining this process in detail, Maria Carmen de Mello Lemos argues that a key element in success was the election of a progressive government at the state level in the elections of 1982, with a governor who gave high priority to pollution control (de Mello Lemos 1998). Media censorship was also eliminated, and civil-society organizations were allowed to operate much more freely. Local democracy and a strong civil society do not guarantee successful environmental management reforms, but they appear to be a necessary condition in the 1990s in many parts of the world.

The articles in this section cover a number of major themes in the urban environment management field. The first, an overview paper by Molly O'Meara, assesses the general problematic of growing cities and shrinking natural resources. The problems of water supply, disposal and recycling of waste, and the planning of neighborhoods in order to conserve energy and resources are essential challenges. A number of governance and economic solutions—such as the examples of Portland, Oregon and Ahmedabad, India—are among the responses the author uses to demonstrate the point that cities can indeed rise above the degrading environmental conditions that they have created. "Efforts to overcome the political and financial barriers to sustainable city planning have one thing in common," says O'Meara, "the dynamism of committed people trading ideas and working together. It is this concentration of human energy that allowed cities to give birth to human civilization, and that may ultimately save it."

An important aspect of the urban environment is its gendered nature. Men and women experience the environment differently in the city. Failure to understand some of these subtle differences may have distressing consequences for poor women, one of the most vulnerable groups in most urban areas. The health-related aspects of this vulnerability are analyzed by Ellen Wasserman, whose article focuses on the maquila system in Mexican cities near the U.S. border. Although women were once the predominant majority of workers in these export processing zones, by 1996 they formed only 47 percent of the total. Nevertheless, as Wasserman explains, the majority of the women who work in the maquiladoras are young, relatively uneducated, and may potentially be exposed to toxic gases and chemicals. Failure to treat waste in the areas around some of the production facilities may lead to elevated concentrations of toxic chemicals in ground water, which may in turn affect the health of the workers and their families living in the informal settlements in border towns. Wasserman details a number of health risks in these areas, concluding that there is a large body of research indicating the connection between poverty and the effects of environmental contamination on the poor. But at the same time, while it seems likely that there are gendered differences, it will be necessary in the future to disaggregate the data according to sex in order to trace the consequences of improper disposal of hazardous materials. Urban managers will have to pay particular attention to the health effects of rapid industrialization in this region.

The final paper in this section consists of three case studies of environmental conditions in cities: one in the United States, and two in India. The connecting thread of these studies is the argument of their writers on the importance of understanding what these conditions mean to the residents of the affected neighborhoods. The residents may be very poor and even illiterate, but they have a well-developed understanding of local hazards and have formed, in many cases, effective strategies to deal with them. When planners work to improve their conditions, they can ill afford to ignore the "local knowledge" of these residents. The first case study deals with East Elizabeth, New Jersey, a neighborhood with major problems of noise, commuter traffic, and waste production. Michael Greenberg argues that the residents themselves understand the complex nature of environmental risk. Solutions to one or even two of these risks will achieve little. The residents themselves, in fact, are better able to set priorities for local action than are national agencies which tend to concentrate on relatively narrow dimensions of environmental pollution. Many forms of pollution and blight, as well as antisocial behavior that derives from these conditions, need to be included in an overall assessment. In the case of Indore, discussed by Aaron Baare and Rajesh Patnaik, the majority of 183 slum areas are subject to regular contact with dirty water and with periodic flooding. In response to these problems, the city built new closed drainage channels. But community members are unhappy with the new system. In contrast to the previous situation when local people could anticipate major floods and move their possessions and family members to higher ground when necessary, the new drainage system gives little warning of an approaching flood and in the end does not drain as effectively. The lesson to be drawn here is that community views on how to manage the flood waters should have been taken into account in the planning. The third study is an account of the work of a local NGO in Delhi, Action for Security Health for All (ASHA). This NGO works with poor residents living in *jhuggie* shelters—temporary shelters of mud, thatch, plastic, and other discarded materials. The health conditions of the residents are generally appalling. When its early efforts to treat patients at a clinic were not succeeding, AHSA determined to pursue a broader approach to health, directing its activities to improving the environment, empowering women, and increasing the understanding of residents about the links between health and their immediate environment. Their experience demonstrated that women play a very important role in managing households and community affairs; this in turn led them to promote community-based women's groups for various improvement activities. They also set up a training program for female community health workers. Overall, ASHA has succeeded in improving the overall health of the *jhuggie* residents. Through an integrated approach and collaborative effort, "child morbidity and malnutrition have decreased," writes Pratibha Mehta, " ...and overall environmental conditions in the slums have improved."

References

Brown, Lester. 1992. "Foreword." In Herbert Girardet, *The Gaia Atlas of Cities: New Directions for Sustainable Urban Living.* New York: Anchor Books.

Gilbert, Richard, Don Stevenson, Herbert Girardet, and Richard Stren, 1996. *Making Cities Work: The Role of Local Authorities in the Urban Environment.* London: Earthscan.

Girardet, Herbert. 1992. *The Gaia Atlas of Cities: New Directions for Sustainable Urban Living.* New York: Anchor Books.

ICLEI (International Council for Local Environmental Initiatives). 1997. Local Agenda 21 Survey: A Study of Responses by Local Authorities and their National and International Associations to Agenda 21. Toronto: ICLEI (www.iclei.org/la21/la21rep.htm).

Lafferty, William M., and Katarina Eckerberg. 1998. *From the Earth Summit to Local Agenda 21: Working Towards Sustainable Development.* London: Earthscan.

De Mello Lemos, Maria Carmen. 1998. "The Politics of Pollution Control in Brazil: State Actors and Social Movements Cleaning Up Cubatao." *World Development* 26(1): 75–87.

Rees, William. 1992. "Ecological Footprints and Everyday Carrying Capacity: What Urban Economics Leaves Out." *Environment and Urbanization* 4(2): 121–30.

Satterthwaite, David. 1998. "Sustainable Cities Revisited." *Environment and Urbanization* 10(2): 3–8.

Wackernagel, Mathis, and William Rees. 1996. *Our Ecological Footprint: Reducing Human Impact on the Earth*. Philadelphia: New Society.

WCED (World Commission on Environment and Development). 1987. *Our Common Future*. New York: Oxford University Press.

Exploring a New Vision for Cities

Molly O'Meara

Twentieth-century cities fail to meet the needs of the present while at the same time compromising the ability of future generations to meet their own needs—the exact opposite of "sustainable development" as defined by the Brundtland Commission's landmark report, *Our Common Future* (WCED 1987).[4] Plato's observation in 400 BC that "any city, however small, is in fact divided into two, one the city of the poor, the other of the rich" holds true today. And the most basic requirements of the urban poor, particularly in the developing world, go unfulfilled. At least 1.1 billion choke on unhealthy levels of air pollution, 220 million lack clean drinking water, 420 million do not have access to the simplest latrines, and 600 million do not have adequate shelter (Hardoy, Cairncross, and Satterthwaite 1990; WRI, UNEP, UNDP, and World Bank 1996).

At the same time, resource use by the rich threatens the security of future generations. Although cities have always relied on their hinterlands, wealthy urbanites today draw more heavily on far-flung resources—quickening the pace of climate change, deforestation, soil erosion, and loss of biological diversity worldwide. London, for example, now requires roughly 58 times its land area just to supply its residents with food and timber; meeting the needs of everyone in the world in the same way would require at least three more Earths (IIED 1995).

Cities take up just 2 percent of the world's surface but consume the bulk of key resources. Roughly 78 percent of carbon emissions from fossil fuel burning and cement manufacturing, and 76 percent of industrial wood use worldwide occur in urban areas. Some 60 percent of the planet's water that is tapped for human use goes to cities in one form or another. (About half of this water irrigates food crops for urban residents, roughly a third is used by city industry, and the remainder is for drinking and sanitation.) Carbon emissions from cities stoke the atmospheric warming that threatens to destabilize global climate, forest cutting to produce urban timber speeds the loss of biological diversity worldwide, and mounting urban

---

4. This article is excerpted, by permission of the author and the publisher, from Molly O'Meara, *Reinventing Cities for People and the Planet*, Worldwatch Paper 147. Washington, DC: Worldwatch Institute, 1999 (www.worldwatch.org).

thirst heightens tensions over water allocation, which threaten to spark conflicts in the next century.

As these links suggest, the struggle to achieve a sustainable balance between the Earth's resource base and its human energy will be largely won or lost in the world's cities. Thus, the challenge for the next century will be to pursue a new urban vision, improving the environmental conditions of cities and at the same time reducing the demands that they make on the Earth's resources.

An Urbanizing World

In 1900, only 160 million people, one tenth of the world's population, were city dwellers. By 2006, in contrast, half the world (3.2 billion people) will live in urban areas—a twenty-fold increase. With North America, Europe, and Japan already highly urbanized, most city growth will continue to occur in developing countries (Table 8.1) Between 1990 and 1995, 263 million people were added to the cities of the developing world—the equivalent of another Los Angeles or Shanghai forming every three months. Indeed, population increase in developing-country cities will be the distinguishing demographic trend of the next century, accounting for nearly 90 percent of the 2.7 billion people due to be added to world population between 1995 and 2030 (U.N. 1998).

Regional variations within the Third World are striking. Some 73 percent of Latin Americans now live in cities, making the region roughly as urbanized as Europe and North America. Thus, the most explosive growth in the future is expected in Africa and Asia, which are still only 30 to 35 percent urbanized (Table 8.2). As urban numbers swell, cities present not only problems but also opportunities, as examples in the next sections will show.

Improving Water Supply and Quality

Most human settlements have been sited to take advantage of water for agriculture and transportation. The world's earliest cities arose in the valleys of great rivers: the Nile, the Tigris-Euphrates, the Indus, and the Yellow. But the rivers and streams that provide drinking water also receive household and industrial wastes, so the flow of water into a city and the flow of wastes out are intimately linked.

Nineteenth-century engineers constructed vast water and sewer systems in industrial countries. The goal was twofold: to meet growing water demand by boosting supplies, and to channel wastewater and rainwater

Table 8.1.   Rate and Scale of Population Growth in Selected Industrial Cities, 1875–1900, and Developing Cities, 1975–2000

City	Annual population growth (%)	Population added (millions)
Industrial cities (1875–1900)		
Chicago	6.0	1.3
New York	3.3	2.3
Tokyo	2.6	0.7
London	1.7	2.2
Paris	1.6	1.1
Developing cities (1975–2000)		
Lagos	5.8	10.2
Bombay	4.0	11.2
São Paolo	2.3	7.7
Mexico City	1.9	6.9
Shanghai	0.9	2.7

Sources: For industrial cities: Chandler 1987; for developing cities: U.N. 1998.

away from people as quickly as possible. These systems were an unquestionable boon to health. With better water and sanitation, life expectancy in French cities, for instance, shot up from 32 years in 1850 to 45 years by 1900. But large, costly projects have failed to reach many rural areas and poor urban districts. Despite gains during the 1980s, the United Nations International Water Supply and Sanitation Decade, 25 percent of the developing world remains without clean water and 66 percent lacks sanitation. Waterborne diarrheal diseases, which arise from poor water and waste management, are the world's leading cause of illness. Each year, 5 million children die from diarrheal ailments; most are from poor urban families (Ridgely 1993; WHO 1998).

Moreover, technologies designed to promote health now contribute to broader environmental ills. The first class of problems occurs in bringing water into cities. The architect Vitruvius wrote in the first century BC that finding water was the first step in planning a new city. But his colleagues today assume water is a secondary consideration, relying instead on engineers to divert rivers or pump water over great distances. Thus, cities have extended their reach for water, destroying fragile ecosystems and reducing the water available for crops. Prime examples include the western United States, where water battles are being waged, and northern China, where 108 cities report shortages. Since the turn of the century, municipal

Table 8.2.   Percentage of Population Living in Urban Areas, by Region, 1950-95, with Projections for 2015

Region	1950	1975	1995	2015
Africa	14.6	25.2	34.9	46.4
Asia[a]	15.3	22.2	33.0	45.6
Latin America	41.4	61.2	73.4	79.9
Industrial countries[b]	54.9	69.9	74.9	80.0
World	29.7	37.8	45.3	54.4

a. Excluding Japan.
b. Europe, Japan, Australia, New Zealand, and North America excluding Mexico.
Source: U.N. 1998.

use of water worldwide has grown 19 times and industrial use 26 times, while agricultural use has increased only 5 times (Shiklomanov 1990).

Another set of damaging effects occurs as water is hurried away from cities. When rainwater is channeled through pipes and gutters, less water infiltrates the soil to recharge underground supplies. Roads also prevent water from seeping into the ground; rain runs off pavement straight into channels, where it speeds into rivers and streams, causing more severe floods than would occur if plants or soil soaked up some of the deluge. Moreover, without enough water to recharge underground supplies, the land may subside, causing rail tracks to buckle, water pipes to burst, and building foundations to crack. In coastal areas, salt water may leak into wells, ruining drinking supplies (Arnold and Gibbons 1996).

Water-short cities in the next century will be pressed to slake their thirst in ways that cause less ecological destruction and require less money. Conservation may be a large part of the solution. Unlike energy, water has yet to become a major target for efficiency gains. Complementary approaches include restricting development near drinking-water sources and using low-cost methods of wastewater treatment (Gleick 1998).

Metropolitan Boston provides an example of successful water conservation. Since 1987, the Massachusetts Water Resources Authority has managed to avoid diverting two large rivers to augment supply, as engineers had initially prescribed. For a third to half the cost of the diversions, the government has reduced total water demand by 24 percent by repairing leaky pipes, installing water-saving fixtures, and educating everyone from schoolchildren to plant managers on water-saving measures (Postel 1997).

Conservation is not only for the rich; developing countries also stand to save money. In the Third World, as much as 60 percent of water is lost through leaky pipes and theft. In Manila, for example, 58 percent of the drinking water is forfeited to leaks or illegal tapping, whereas Singapore, where pipes are better maintained, loses only 8 percent (Serageldin 1994). A key to water conservation is removing incentives for profligate use. Lack of meters, inordinately low prices, and prices that decline as use increases, all encourage wastefulness. As underpricing causes excessive use, the problem feeds on itself. With the cash-strapped water agency unable to maintain its pipes, more water is lost to leaks. This causes the agency to lay claim to additional water supplies, diverting them from agriculture and, as farms fail without irrigation, more people migrate to cities, raising the demand for water. Bogor, Indonesia, took its first steps to break this cycle in 1988, when it installed meters and hiked prices to encourage households to conserve. Demand initially fell by one third, allowing the utility to connect more families to the system (Serageldin 1994, 1995).

Making better use of rainwater is another conservation technique that doubles as a flood-control strategy. Metropolitan Tokyo, with 82 percent of its land surface covered by asphalt or concrete, suffers from torrential runoff that causes floods and depletes underground water supplies. The city has thus turned to rainwater as a supplemental source. Tanks atop 579 city buildings capture this free resource for use in washrooms, gardens, air-conditioning systems, and fire hoses. Now rain that falls on the giant Kokugikan sumo wrestling stadium supplies 70 percent of the water in the building that is not used for drinking (Tokyo Metropolitan Government 1998).

Other forms of water recycling also hold potential to enhance city water supplies. Municipal wastewater can be used instead of high-quality drinking water to flush toilets or to water lawns. If treated, it may be used to irrigate crops or to raise fish. Some 70 percent of Israeli wastewater is recycled in this way. Treatment is made easier if wastewater from industry is kept separate from the residential flow but, in most countries, the flows are combined. As cities in developing countries build sewage infrastructure, they will therefore save money and water if they keep flows separate.

Just as conservation of water can boost supply, conservation of land can protect water quality. A number of cities are finding that cooperating with neighboring regions, industries, and agriculture to protect watersheds is ultimately less costly than trying to make polluted water safe for drinking. New York City, for instance, plans to buy $300 million worth of land upstate to protect the watersheds that deliver the city's drinking water. The tactic is part of a comprehensive watershed protection strategy that, while costly at $1.4 billion, will save the city from having to pay between $3 billion and $8 billion for a new filtration system. In Costa Rica, the city of San Jose has recently embarked on a plan to clean up and protect its water. Waste dumped in the Rio Torres has endangered public health and marine life. The city has set up a watershed agency, the first of its kind in Central America, to help implement the plan to better manage the resource (Gilbert 1996).

Limiting development near important water sources not only preserves water quality, it also prevents floods and provides a connection to nature. In the 1880s, landscape architect Frederick Law Olmsted persuaded Boston that keeping buildings away from floodplains by establishing riverfront parks would ultimately prove cheaper than keeping floods away from buildings through huge public works projects. The result was the verdant Back Bay Fens, a park that protected the neighborhood from flooding.

In addition to improving water supply and quality, cities can also treat wastewater at lower economic and environmental cost. One time-honored biological approach—wetlands treatment—uses more land but is also much less expensive and does not produce toxic sludge. Vegetation in stabilization ponds or modified wetlands extracts contaminants such as nitrates and mercury, while bacteria and other organisms break down toxic compounds (Bastian and Benforado 1983). Phoenix, Arizona, is creating wetlands to clean a portion of its sewage because the option is much cheaper than a $625 million upgrade of its wastewater treatment plant (Rosenbaum 1995).

Where cities have been unable or unwilling to extend sewers to the poorest people, some communities have stepped into the breach with low-cost solutions. The most famous example is in the Orangi district of Karachi, Pakistan, home to nearly a million "squatters." In the early 1980s, Akhter Hameed Khan, a dynamic community organizer, formed a nongovernmental research institute called the Orangi Pilot Project. Between 1981 and 1996, this group helped neighborhoods to organize, collect money, and manage construction of sewers that serve some 90 percent of Orangi's residents (Hasan 1995).

Increasingly, cities are looking to tap the resources of the private sector, as governments alone will be unable to come up with the billions of dollars needed over the next decade for reliable water systems. While only 5 percent of the financing for water worldwide now comes from private sources, privatization, in various degrees, is a growing trend. Still, privatization is not a panacea. Water supply and sanitation are important public services, so some form of public control or regulation will always be needed to make sure that quality and prices are reasonable. Unfortunately, few cities have regulations in place yet to make privatization work fairly.

Mining Urban Waste

Remains from some of the earliest cities suggest that residents at first took a *laissez-faire* approach to waste disposal, simply raising the roofs of their houses as mounting garbage caused street levels to rise. In eighteenth-century Boston, when refuse threatened to impede industrial progress, the city's first "paved" roads were built: wooden planks placed on top of the garbage. A century later, Charles Dickens spoke to both the water and waste problems of nineteenth-century New York when he referred to it as "a city without baths or plumbing, lighted by gas and scavenged by pigs."

Today, garbage is most voluminous in rich countries but most visible in cities of developing countries. In the 1950s, Manila began to dump much of its garbage in a poor neighborhood, laying the foundation for what would become the city's most striking topographical feature—"Mount Smoky." Methane from the rotting refuse burned in an acrid haze, lending the summit its name. Until a newly elected Philippine president razed the garbage mountain in the early 1990s, it towered 40 meters above sea level in Manila Bay and was home to some 20,000 people who made a living from scavenging the refuse (WRI, UNEP, and UNDP 1996).

Like water, waste profoundly affects human health. Hazards are most pronounced in the developing world, where between a third and a half of city trash goes uncollected. Open piles of garbage attract disease-carrying rats and flies, and often wash into drainage channels, where they contribute to floods and waterborne disease. And even the most expensive methods of waste disposal—high-tech "sanitary" landfills and incinerators—are not completely free of health risks. Toxins from landfills can leach into groundwater, and heavy metals, chlorine compounds, and dioxin are among the hazards in incinerator ash (WHO 1995).

City waste has many broader environmental implications. Just as storm drains short-circuit the water cycle, urban waste disposal systems designed to speed wastes away from people actually interrupt the nutrient cycle. Trucks, planes, and trains haul food into cities from great distances, but the nutrients rarely make it back to farmland. They are most often shunted to sewers or trucked to increasingly remote landfills. Not only does this add to the waste disposal burden, it also heightens the demand for manufactured fertilizer, a major source of nitrogen pollution—a growing global threat. Moreover, throwing items away instead of reusing or recycling them increases the demand for new resources obtained by environmentally destructive mining and logging. In the industrial world, waste collection has improved public health, but the problem of waste generation has only worsened. Urbanites in industrial countries generate up to 100 times more refuse per person than their counterparts in developing countries (UNCHS 1996).

But cities have the potential to shift from being repositories of waste to great sources of raw materials. The farms, forests, and mines of the twenty-first century may well be found in our urban centers—in the form of city gardens and recycling plants. Local authorities can spur the transition by providing incentives for composting, recycling, and waste-based industries. Organic waste—paper, food scraps, lawn clippings, and even human waste—is a valuable resource. In industrial countries, food and yard waste alone account for some 36 percent of the municipal waste stream. European cities are leading a trend toward composting, which transforms this organic waste into a product that invigorates agricultural soils. Cities in seven countries—Austria, Belgium, Denmark, Germany, Luxembourg, the Netherlands, and Switzerland—collect these wastes separately, recovering more than 85 percent of them.

Composting can also boost urban food security by enriching city gardens. The UNDP (1996) estimates that 800 million urban farmers harvest 15 percent of the world's food supply. In parts of Africa, urban agriculture is a survival strategy. Some 68 percent of families in Dar es Salaam grow vegetables or raise livestock. City farmers also tend 80,000 gardens in Berlin as well as crops in Buenos Aires that meet one fifth of that city's nutritional needs.

To keep paper and inorganic materials such as metals, glass, and plastics from landfills, a number of cities have found ways to promote recycling and waste-based industries. They can charge a fee for the collection of unsorted garbage, for example, while picking up for free refuse that has been separated for recycling. By adopting "pay-as-you-throw" systems, at least 11 U.S. cities have boosted recycling rates to the 45 to 60 percent range, well above the national average of 27 percent (Beckman 1997). Some cities have gone a step further, to engage the industries that create disposable goods or generate waste. In 1997, Tokyo municipal officials—looking for new waste disposal options in land-short Japan—announced that they would require makers and distributors of plastic bottles to recover and recycle their products.

While the private sector is a newcomer to water supply and sanitation, it has a long history in waste collection and disposal. In some developing-country cities, local authorities have struck recycling deals with private companies and even self-employed wastepickers. In Cairo, the Zabbaleen people have been garbage pickers since they began coming to Cairo in mid-century. With the help of aid agencies, the city and the community launched a program in 1981 to improve city collection service and boost the Zabbaleen's income and standard of living. Today, the Zabbaleen sew rags into quilts and compost animal waste to sell to farmers (Badshah 1996). Similarly, city officials in Bandung, Indonesia, are now working with a local NGO to employ a group of scavenger families. The families receive financial and technical support to separate recyclables more safely and efficiently than they now do, to compost organic wastes, and to create businesses that use the wastes they collect as raw materials. They make money and the city reduces the cost of waste management (Hall 1992).

A handful of cities are moving beyond recycling to "industrial symbiosis," where one company's waste becomes another's input. The first ecoindustrial park began to evolve more than 20 years ago in Kalundborg, Denmark. Today, waste gases from an oil refinery there are burned by a power plant, waste heat from the plant warms commercial fish ponds, and other companies use by-products of combustion to make wallboard and concrete. According to one calculation, Kalundborg's waste-saving approach translates into $120 million in savings and revenues on a $60-million investment over a five-year period.

Building Better Neighborhoods

The layout of neighborhoods goes hand-in-hand with transportation in shaping cities. By building roads, rail lines, or bike paths, cities decide not only how people will move around, but where the accessible and desirable buildings will be and where new services will be needed. By mandating where new buildings can be built and what kind of uses—residential, retail, industrial—are allowed, land-use and zoning laws influence how far people must travel to get to work, buy food, and go about their daily business (Lowe 1991).

Much of the chaotic urban development in developing countries occurs because 30 to 60 percent of city populations live in squatter settlements and 70 to 95 percent of new housing is technically outside the law (Hardoy and Satterthwaite 1989). In Cairo, to cite just one case, informal settlements have grown rapidly, turning a cemetery in the city's eastern section into the "City of the Dead," where poor families squeeze into the small caretakers' rooms in the tombs. At the same time, more than a half-million apartments stand empty because the poor cannot afford the public housing, and because the private sector caters to the upper class (El-Batran and Arandel 1998).

The arrangement of buildings helps determine the livability of a city. Streets come alive with pedestrians when shops, factories, offices, and houses are all within walking distance of each other. And city greenery and parks between buildings cool streets and soothe the spirit. In contrast, public life diminishes when architects design office parks and shopping malls to be enjoyed from the inside, and gaping parking lots to welcome cars but not pedestrians. Crime often plagues fragmented cities that isolate the poor in distinct pockets. Brazilian scholar Raquel Rolnick (1998) has exposed the link between territorial exclusion and violence in cities within the state of São Paulo. On the other hand, urban analyst Jane Jacobs (1961) noted an advantage to diverse street life: many "eyes on the street" deter crime.

Neighborhood layout also influences the resource demands of a city. Changes in the layout can lower energy demands from transportation by a factor of 10 (Newman and Kenworthy 1999). And trees that block buildings from the sun or wind lower the energy the residents need for heating and cooling. Moreover, when neighborhoods are spread out at low density, they require more water, sewer pipes, power lines, and roads. Sprawling cities also use more building materials. Buildings, which consume roughly 40 percent of materials in the global economy, represent a quarter of the demand for wood worldwide (Roodman and Lenssen 1995).

A few cities are beginning to rein in rapacious development, boost parkland, and even improve the quality of buildings that do get constructed. Their tools include regulations or incentives that push developers to build on vacant land within the city rather than outlying green areas, setting aside land for informal settlements, and changing city building codes. To reduce fringe development, a number of older industrial cities are offering incentives to redevelop vacant or abandoned parcels of land within the metropolitan area. Some of the most sought-after new housing in southern England, for instance, is on such "infill" sites. One concern, however, is that a former occupant may have been an industrial polluter who left the land contaminated. By offering tax credits and funds for environmental cleanup, cities and higher forms of government can entice buyers to take the risk—a strategy that benefits the region in the long term.

Increasingly, local authorities in developing countries recognize the truth of a point made a decade ago by Jorge Hardoy and David Satterthwaite (1989): "the unnamed millions who build, organize and plan illegally are the most important organizers, builders and planners of Third World cities." Those who cannot afford a house on the formal market seek out the most precarious slopes and river valleys. Squatters are unlikely to receive an eviction notice—but they probably will never see water pipes and electricity lines either. However, most cities contain places where low-income sites could be developed, at lower cost, because they are already close to transportation and services. In Curitiba, Brazil, the city set aside such tracts for informal settlements (McKibben 1995).

Not only can neighborhoods be laid out better, buildings themselves can be constructed better. Buildings—with their own water, waste, and energy flows—are actually microcosms of the city. They are particularly well suited to use the new decentralized energy technologies such as solar panels and natural gas turbines that generate heat and electricity. Cities can support green construction by setting codes requiring buildings to be energy efficient, and by requiring green design for public construction. The Danish Planning Institute has published a guide to urban ecology in Copenhagen that highlights 45 projects in the city that use much less water and energy than conventional buildings and that contain facilities to compost organic waste (Munkstrup and Lindberg 1996).

In the much less affluent city of Kimberly, South Africa, a private developer teamed up with local residents to replace tin and mud shacks with a low cost "solar neighborhood" for 200 families. Based on that success, the developer is planning a similar project for the smaller town of Ugie, where homes using passive solar design and solar ovens will be clustered in groups of six to share gardens. Household organic waste, composted on-site, will be used in the gardens, as will filtered wastewater. The basic home costs no more than the $3,200 government subsidy for first-time home buyers—a state-assisted "self-help" program designed to address the legacy of apartheid. Costs stay low because residents do the construction themselves (Wilkinson 1998).

Realizing the Vision

At the end of her classic book on the urban environment, *The Granite Garden*, Anne Whiston Spirn (1984) reminds us that "in the present lies not only the nightmare of what the city will become if current trends continue, but also the dream of what the city could be." Taking today's urban problems to an apocalyptic conclusion, Spirn envisions an "infernal city" that has disintegrated following uprisings by city dwellers denied adequate food, water, and work. Social and environmental ills have followed those fleeing cities into a countryside ravaged by suburban development.

Numerous conferences in the last decade have addressed the growing challenges of building and maintaining more sustainable cities, and have helped to reveal two key obstacles to progress in sustainable urban planning: lack of money and lack of political strength (Carlson 1996; United Nations 1996).

Lack of local budgetary control limits the ability of citizens and city officials to make urban environmental concerns a priority. National governments have shifted many responsibilities to city governments in recent years without expanding the ability of local authorities to raise money. Generally, city governments must still rely on the central government to transfer to them a share of the national tax revenue. And in some countries, the amount of the transfer depends upon the size of the local budget deficit, thus encouraging overspending and mismanagement. If and when the transfers come through, local officials—and the citizens who elect them— may have little say in how they are to be spent. World Bank researchers have found the share of locally generated revenue on the decline in most cities of the developing world (Bahl and Linn 1992).

Cities usually have at least two types of tools to raise their own revenue—fees and taxes—although their ability to levy them varies widely. In most industrial countries and a few developing countries, cities are also able to use a third device: municipal bonds. In a sampling of world cities weighted more toward those in the developing world, local taxes were found to be the most important source of revenue (Bahl and Linn 1992). Partnerships with the private sector and communities can also help local authorities achieve their goals. The challenge is to figure out which tools local governments are best equipped to use, and how they can best exploit them to benefit both the environment and their budget.

One of the best ways for cities to close the gap between revenue and expenditure would be to charge adequate fees for the local services they provide. Water provision, waste collection, and transportation have a profound impact on natural resources and quality of life—yet they are usually underpriced. Various fees are effective in meeting both economic and environmental goals. Fees for unsorted household garbage, for example, have bolstered urban recycling efforts in a number of industrial nations. The success of water conservation programs from Bogor, Indonesia, to Boston, Massachusetts, has hinged on charging higher prices. Rather than maintain artificially low prices for all, water authorities or electric utilities can provide targeted subsidies, such as loans or grants to help the poorest families pay for the initial hook-up, which is often the most prohibitive cost. Local authorities can also be far more discriminating in their use of sewer and road subsidies. By taking away support for extension of sewer lines and roads—or by charging fees to install them—local governments can make developers pay the full costs of building on greenfield sites.

As for taxes, central governments generally want to limit competition from local governments for broad-based taxes on personal income and payroll. That cities are denied this taxing power is not necessarily bad news for local officials, because these taxes in effect discourage work and investment and do nothing to improve the environment. The one tax that may yield great benefits for cities—and that cities are uniquely qualified to control—is the tax on land value (Roodman 1998). Shifting property taxes off of buildings and onto land may promote development of vacant lots in central areas.

Municipal bonds, which allow governments to borrow money from the public to finance projects that promote public welfare, may offer local governments an opportunity to obtain more cash up front than they could normally get through fees or taxes. A city can issue two types of bonds that differ in the way that the municipality pays back its debt to investors. Cities repay revenue bondholders by assessing user fees collected from the specific project—for instance, a water or power supply system. But they repay the owners of general obligation bonds for projects such as sewers, where cost recovery is not easily tied to use, by levying taxes. So for bonds to work, a city must have the authority to raise fees and taxes. In addition, governments need access to a financial market where bonds can be exchanged.

A good long-term strategy would be to focus on collecting taxes and fees before resorting to borrowing money. This was demonstrated in Ahmedabad, India, a city with long-standing air and water pollution from a textile industry that suffered a major economic crisis in the 1980s with the closure of several mills. A talented municipal commissioner began a campaign in the early 1990s to balance the city's budget by eliminating costly corruption, raising utility rates, and collecting taxes. As a result, by 1996, the city boasted a substantial surplus, and it used the new funds to initiate a host of projects to improve the local environment and public health. As environmental health rebounded, so too did the climate for investment, which may ultimately attract outside money to solving Ahmedabad's problems. With advice from USAID, the city has floated India's first municipal bond, which will finance improvements in water and sewer infrastructure (Phelps 1997; Mehta 1998).

With insufficient public revenue to meet the rising demand for services, cash-strapped local authorities have increasingly relied on the resourcefulness of local communities and NGOs as well as the profit-making drive of the private sector. Examples of successful public-private partnership range from community-based recycling in Bandung, Indonesia, to private-sector-financed light rail in Portland, Oregon. Such projects have successfully managed to match the need for urban services with the demand for jobs—which mayors worldwide cite as their most pressing concern, according to a recent UNDP survey. UNDP's recently established Public-Private Partnerships for the Urban Environment program aims to help cities in developing countries turn environmental problems into viable business opportunities in water, waste, and energy services (Serageldin, Barrett, and Martin-Brown 1995; UNDP 1998).

Lack of political strength is the second barrier to building sustainable cities. When citizens have insufficient understanding of the causes of local problems, the political process suffers. Many cities lack the basic demographic and environmental data needed to unveil the links between urban trends and environmental problems. In 1993, a Ford Foundation review of urban research in the developing world found that the "urban environment" was listed as a priority area for study in nearly every report they unearthed, but that only 2 to 3 percent of the research actually had an environmental focus (Bartone et al. 1994).

In the hands of the public, information can be a potent political tool. For example, Beijing officials released data on air pollution for the first time in February 1998. By June 1998, according to the *New York Times*, "people who six months ago might have peered out the window and seen fog, or *wu*, now realize that it is pollution, or *wuran*," and they support local government efforts to clean up the air (Rosenthal 1998).

A technology that is well suited to expose the links between urban population and environmental problems is a geographic information system (GIS), which portrays data in a map form. A GIS database, in Quito, Ecuador, integrates epidemiological data from the Department of Health with data on water and waste service provision and data on poverty and employment, thus providing a useful picture of the environmental and social sources of ill health. When maps show people environmental problems in their backyard, they can spur citizen action. By integrating geographic information on polluting factories, major roadways, and air and water quality monitoring, the pollution control agency in Rio de Janeiro State created detailed maps that show the sources of pollution. These maps are available to the public, who can then become actively involved in pollution control by protesting to industries directly (Wheeler 1997).

Another source of useful information is the experience of other cities. For instance, municipal water experts from Nancy, France, who traveled to Costa Rica in 1991, helped design the watershed protection plan in San Jose that was discussed earlier. In recent years, networks for sustainable cities have proliferated, organized by existing municipal associations, NGOs, national governments, and international agencies. The New York-based Mega-Cities Project, one of the most prominent such NGOs, was founded in 1987 to promote exchange between officials from the world's largest cities. For example, it has brought innovations in community-based recycling from Cairo to Bombay and Manila.

A major way that local politics affects the environment relates to the structure of local government itself. Rarely does one government entity correspond to an entire metropolitan region. Often, districts within a metropolis compete with each other for development that will boost tax revenue, and in so doing they push built-up areas out over forests and farmland, pave over watersheds, and invite air pollution from increased car use. The problem is particularly acute in U.S. cities. Portland, Oregon, which has made notable environmental progress, is also the only place in the United States where a city and its suburbs elect a common government that has the power to look out for the interests of the entire metropolitan region.

Proponents of "metropolitanism" are gaining new allies as the economic rationale for united urban regions becomes clearer. David Rusk, former mayor of Albuquerque, New Mexico, has shown that regions with less political division between cities and suburbs are also less segregated along lines of race and class and are economically healthier than politically fragmented regions (Rusk 1993). Thus, inner city boosters and residents of decaying older suburbs seeking to direct investment toward existing infrastructure are allying with environmentalists who are attempting to protect fringe areas from development.

A century ago, those who reflected on life-threatening urban pollution feared that cities might eventually self-destruct. Today, it is not only inhumane living conditions but also unsustainable resource use that pose a threat. Efforts to overcome the political and financial barriers to sustainable city planning have one thing in common: the dynamism of committed people trading ideas and working together. It is this concentration of human energy that allowed cities to give birth to human civilization, and that may ultimately save it.

References

Arnold, Chester, and James Gibbons. 1996. "Impervious Surface Coverage: The Emergence of a Key Environmental Indicator." *Journal of the American Planning Association* 62(2): 243–58.

Badshah, Akhtar. 1996. *Our Urban Future*. London: Zed Books.

Bahl, Roy, and Johannes Linn. 1992. *Urban Public Finance in Developing Countries*. New York: Oxford University Press for the International Bank for Reconstruction and Development.

Bartone, Carl, Janis Bernstein, Josef Leitmann, and Jochen Eigen. 1994. *Toward Environmental Strategies for Cities: Policies for Urban Environmental Management in Developing Countries, UMP Discussion Paper 18* Washington, DC: UNDP/Habitat/World Bank.

Bastian, Robert, and Jay Benforado. 1983. "Doing What Comes Naturally." *Technology Review* (February).

Beckman, Jennifer Ray. 1997. "Recycling-Based Manufacturing Boosts Local Economies in U.S." *Ecological Economics Bulletin* (fourth quarter).

Carlson, Eric. 1996. "The Legacy of Habitat II." *The Urban Age* 4(2): 1, 4–6.

Chandler, Tertius. 1987. *Four Thousand Years of Urban Growth.* Lewiston, NY: Edwin Mellen.

El-Batran, Manal, and Christian Arandel. 1998. "A Shelter of Their Own: Informal Settlement Expansion in Greater Cairo and Government Responses." *Environment and Urbanization* 10(1): 217–32.

Gardner, Gary. 1997. *Recycling Organic Waste: From Urban Pollutant to Farm Resource.* Worldwatch Paper 135. Washington, DC: Worldwatch Institute.

Gilbert, Richard, Don Stevenson, Herbert Girardet, and Richard Stren. 1996. *Making Cities Work: The Role of Local Authorities in the Urban Environment.* London: Earthscan.

Gleick, Peter. 1998. *The World's Water 1998–1999: The Biennial Report on Freshwater Resources.* Washington, DC: Island Press.

Hall, Susan. 1992. "Lessons from a Semi-Private Enterprise in Bandung, Indonesia." In US Agency for International Development, *Privatizing Solid Waste Management Services in Developing Countries.* Proceedings Paper. Washington, DC: International City/County Management Association.

Hardoy, Jorge, and David Satterthwaite. 1989. *Squatter Citizen: Life in the Urban Third World.* London: Earthscan.

Hardoy, Jorge, Sandy Cairncross, and David Satterthwaite. 1990. *The Poor Die Young: Housing and Health in Third World Cities.* London: Earthscan.

Hasan, Arif. 1995. "Replicating the Low-Cost Sanitation Programme Administered by the Orangi Pilot Project in Karachi, Pakistan." In Ismail Serageldin, Michael Cohen, and K.C. Sivaramakrishnan, eds., *The Human Face of the Urban Environment.* Proceedings of the Second Annual World Bank Conference on Environmentally Sustainable Development. Washington, DC: World Bank.

IIED (International Institute for Environment and Development). 1995. *Citizen Action to Lighten Britain's Ecological Footprints*. London: IIED for the U.K. Department of Environment.

Jacobs, Jane. 1961. *The Death and Life of Great American Cities*. New York: Random House.

Lowe, Marcia. 1991. *Shaping Cities: The Environmental and Human Dimensions*. Worldwatch Paper 105. Washington, DC: Worldwatch Institute.

McKibben, Bill. 1995. *Hope: Human and Wild*. Boston: Little, Brown.

Mehta, Dinesh. 1998. "Participatory Urban Environmental Management: A Case of Ahmedabad, India." Paper for the Woodrow Wilson International Center for Scholars' Comparative Urban Studies Project on Urbanization, Population, Security, and the Environment, Washington, DC, 14–15 September.

Mumford, Lewis. 1961. *The City in History*. San Diego, CA: Harcourt Brace.

Munkstrup, Nina, and Jakob Lindberg. 1996. *Urban Ecology Guide—Greater Copenhagen*. Copenhagen: Danish Town Planning Institute.

Newman, Peter, and Jeff Kenworthy. 1999. *Sustainability and Cities: Overcoming Automobile Dependence*. Washington, DC: Island Press.

Phelps, Priscilla, ed. 1997. *Municipal Bond Market Development in Developing Countries: The Experience of the U.S. Agency for International Development*. Finance Working Paper. Washington, DC: USAID.

Postel, Sandra. 1997. *Last Oasis*. Rev. ed. New York: W.W. Norton.

Rabinovitch, Jonas, and Josef Leitmann. 1993. *Environmental Innovation and Management in Curitiba, Brazil, UMP Working Paper No. 1*. Washington, DC: UNDP/Habitat/World Bank.

Ridgely, Mark A. 1993. "Water, Sanitation and Resource Mobilization: Expanding the Range of Choices. In G. Shabbir Cheema, ed., *Urban Management: Policies and Innovations in Developing Countries*, pp. 185–208. Westport, CT: Praeger.

Rolnick, Raquel. 1998. "Territorial Exclusion and Violence: The Case of Sao Paulo, Brazil." Paper for the Woodrow Wilson International Center for Scholars' Comparative Urban Studies Project on Urbanization, Population, Security, and the Environment, Washington, DC, 14–15 September.

Roodman, David Malin. 1998. *The Natural Wealth of Nations*. New York: W.W. Norton.

Roodman, David Malin, and Nicholas Lenssen. 1995. *A Building Revolution: How Ecology and Health Concerns Are Transforming Construction.* Worldwatch Paper no. 124. Washington, DC: Worldwatch Institute.

Rosenbaum, David. 1995. "Wetlands Bloom in the Desert." *Engineering News-Record,* 11 December.

Rosenthal, Elisabeth. 1998. "China Officially Lifts Filter on Staggering Pollution Data." *New York Times,* 14 June.

Rusk, David. 1993. *Cities Without Suburbs.* Washington, DC: Woodrow Wilson Center Press.

Serageldin, Ismail. 1994. *Water Supply, Sanitation, and Environmental Sustainability: The Financing Challenge.* Directions in Development. Washington, DC: World Bank.

Serageldin, Ismail. 1995. *Toward Sustainable Management of Water Resources.* Directions in Development. Washington, DC: World Bank.

Serageldin, Ismail. 1997. "Helping Out with Tiny Loans." *Journal of Commerce,* 2 April.

Serageldin, Ismail, Richard Barrett, and Joan Martin-Brown. 1995. *The Business of Sustainable Cities: Public-Private Partnerships for Creative Technical and Institutional Solutions.* Environmentally Sustainable Development Proceedings Series no. 7. Washington, DC: World Bank.

Shiklomanov, L.A. 1990. "Global Water Resources." *Nature and Resources* 26 (3).

Spirn, Anne Whiston. 1984. *The Granite Garden: Urban Nature and Human Design.* New York: Basic Books.

Tokyo Metropolitan Government. 1998. "Action Program for Creating an Eco-Society." Draft. Tokyo, February.

U.N. 1996. *Report of the United Nations Conference on Human Settlements (Habitat II),* Istanbul, 3–14 June. New York: UN.

U.N. 1998. *World Urbanization Prospects: The 1996 Revision.* New York: United Nations.

UNCHS (Habitat). 1996. *An Urbanizing World: Global Report on Human Settlements, 1996.* Oxford: Oxford University Press.

UNDP. 1996. *Urban Agriculture: Food, Jobs and Sustainable Cities.* New York: UNDP.

UNDP. 1998. "Public-Private Partnerships for the Urban Environment." (www.undp.org).

Wheeler, David. 1997. "Information in Pollution Management: The New Model." In *Brazil: Managing Pollution Problems, The Brown Environmental Agenda*. Washington, DC: World Bank.

Wilkinson, Peter. 1998. "Housing Policy in South Africa." *Habitat International* 22(3): 215–29.

WCED. 1987. *Our Common Future*. Report of the World Commission on Environment and Development. New York: Oxford University Press.

WHO (World Health Organization). 1995. *Solid Waste and Health*. Local Authorities, Health and Environment Briefing Pamphlet No. 5. Geneva: WHO.

WHO. 1996. *The Urban Health Crisis*. Geneva: WHO.

WHO. 1998. *The World Health Report 1998*. Geneva: WHO.

WRI (World Resources Institute), UNEP, UNDP, and World Bank. 1996. *World Resources 1996–97*. New York: Oxford University Press.

Environment, Health, and Gender in Latin America: The Case of the Maquiladoras

Ellen Wasserman

Between the mid-1960s and the early 1990s, Latin America underwent the fastest rate of urbanization in the world.[5] During the latter part of that period, a severe and prolonged economic crisis shook the region, whose recovery is still far from stable (World Bank 1997a, 1997b). The urbanization process was swift and wrenching. During the 1960s and 1970s masses of people fled rural poverty and, often, armed conflict, for the safety, services, and work promised by the cities. However, their numbers were far greater and their skills far less than the swelling megametropoles could accommodate, and vast urban shantytowns grew that today account for 85 percent of the increase in poverty and are a main cause of public health concern (Morley 1994).

Just as rural-urban migration peaked during the 1980s, high external debt burdens, raging inflation, and the collapse of traditional export earnings in many countries impoverished much of the middle class and threw the poor into even more desperate conditions.

In the 1990s, the number of countries reporting food deficits in the region increased, as did the portion of the population that did not earn enough to meet its basic food requirements. Nonetheless, the need to generate export revenues drove many countries to expand intensive agriculture for foreign markets—often in the area known as nontraditional agricultural products—while domestic food crops declined. In 1994, one out of every six households could not have met its food needs even if every cent of its income had been spent for that purpose. Chronic undernutrition, seen in childhood stunting data, affects over 10 percent of children under five and, in Bolivia and Haiti, up to 50 percent (UNICEF 1998).

In the burgeoning urban areas, meanwhile, large numbers of salaried employees lost their jobs during the middle to late 1980s and early 1990s. In 1994, about 40 percent of the urban population was poor or indigent and this was the fastest growing segment of the region's population

(CEPAL 1996a, 1996b). The disparity between the income shares held by the lowest and highest quintiles of the region's population improved somewhat in the first half of the 1990s compared to the three preceding decades, but remained the most pronounced in the world, according to the World Bank (1997a, 1997b).

As part of "structural adjustment," governments sold off state-owned companies (accounting for a large portion of unemployment among salaried workers) and slashed social programs in a restructuring process that continues to this day. Given that the state-owned sector had been one of the most stable sources of employment for urban women, women lost proportionately more jobs as salaried employees than did men (Psacharopoulos and Tzannatos 1992).

The majority of the unemployed of both sexes joined the ranks of the so-called urban informal sector, where employment is often seasonal, unstable, hazardous, and poorly remunerated. Well over half of the region's nonrural work force is estimated to be employed in the informal sector which, in the 1990–95 period, accounted for fully 84 percent of new employment opportunities (ILO 1996). Providing work for everyone seeking full employment would require that an additional 104 million jobs be created by 2010 in Brazil and Mexico alone. Creating those work opportunities will continue to be one of the region's major challenges.

The Case of Export Processing Zones

To reduce foreign debt burdens and alleviate the unemployment crisis of the 1980s, many governments in the region stepped up export programs and increased incentives for foreign companies. They relaxed labor codes (once among the most progressive in the world, at least on the books), eased protectionist trade policies that had been intended to foster import substitution, promoted agriculture for export, and took other measures to attract foreign investment, especially in labor-intensive industries (U.N. 1995a, 1995b).

Export processing zones, or EPZs, also known as in-bond, or "shared production" facilities, became an important part of this strategy in some countries. Appearing on a small scale in the Caribbean in the mid-1960s, EPZs became part of the 1965 United States and Mexico Border Industrialization Program, intended to stem the tide of Mexican migrant laborers who had worked in the United States since the World War II labor shortage, under the "Bracero" program (Schoepfle 1990). Human rights and labor groups have denounced the sweatshop conditions in many of these plants, especially in Central America, for over a decade. Their dense concentration along the

Mexico-U.S. border has given rise to concern about labor and environmental conditions. Its geographic proximity to the United States, the NAFTA accords, and its relative size and relative sophistication where research is concerned make more information available on Mexico than is true for many other countries in the region. For this reason, the article looks at the manufacturing assembly plants along the Mexico-U.S. border in some detail.

The Mexican Maquila System

In 1996 about 1,200 companies were operating in the Mexico-U.S. border assembly, or maquila, system, of which roughly 49 percent were American subsidiaries and the rest were owned by Mexican, Japanese, Korean, German, Taiwanese, and other nationals (CEPAL 1996a, 1996b).

From 1989 to 1997 the average hourly wage in the Mexican maquiladoras was reported to range from $0.84 to $1.59, compared to the $14.31 average for U.S. manufacturing workers in 1989. This average wage includes the substantially higher pay received by managers and administrative staff, however, and many maquila workers are paid far less (Schoepfle 1990; CEPAL 1996a, 1996b). Yet, especially during times of high unemployment, even these low wages may exceed what is earned by many of the 57 percent of the Mexican work force who are employed in the nonagricultural informal sector (ILO 1997a, 1997b).

It is difficult to determine the exact number of those employed by the maquiladoras. Many people—especially women and children working at home or in microenterprises—work for the assembly plants through subcontracting arrangements (Schoepfle 1990). The number of people employed in one way or another by the maquila system may well be nearly double the number working on site in the plants, or some 1.5 million people.

Export processing zones throughout the world are known as the "female industry" and Latin America, where roughly 75 percent of the EPZ work force is female, is no exception. In Mexico, 78 percent of maquila workers were women in 1975. The number of women employed by the maquilas grew from 45,275 to 261,725 (almost fivefold) between 1975 and 1993 and was estimated to have grown another 34 percent, to about 350,000, in 1997. However, the gender patterns in the Mexican assembly plants have undergone a change since then and after their participation soared by 1,300 percent over the same time period, men are now estimated to make up the majority (about 53 percent) of the maquila work force (CEPAL 1996a, 1996b).

Mexican researchers stated in 1994 that the shift toward a stronger male presence in the traditionally female industry was "due to the fact that the supply of work in the maquiladoras had outstripped the supply of female workers." However, this would seem to refer to women workers who meet certain criteria. The vast majority of the women employed in the maquiladoras are 16 to 25 years old, and young, unskilled women are hired preferentially over older women (Schoepfle 1990). The widespread industry practice of requiring pregnancy tests of women job applicants is notorious, as are demands that other forms of proof be given monthly that they have not become pregnant (Jefferson 1996). Industries thereby avoid the expense of complying with legally mandated maternity leave (if enforced, it would entitle women to 100 percent pay for 84 days), with which even non-unionized workers are familiar. Simultaneously, this industry practice may serve to avert legal claims stemming from compromised pregnancies and births (Coalition for Justice in the Maquiladoras 1993a, 1993b).

Health Hazards in the Maquilas

Despite the lack of publicly available inventories of goods imported by the plants, and the paucity of scientific studies, accounts abound regarding unprotected workplace exposure to unidentified chemicals, presumably the solvents, heavy metals, acids, and airborne particles generically known to be used in such industries (Coalition for Justice in the Maquiladoras 1993a, 1993b). Given labor mobility between industries and the economically driven "gender crossing" between traditionally sex-stereotyped industries, it is possible that workers of both sexes are exposed to multiple hazardous substances during the years they work for the maquilas.

The maquiladoras are mostly non-union shops, or workers are assigned affiliation in a "union" sponsored by the companies (Schoepfle 1990). Compulsory overtime is common and those who attempt to organize alternatives or protest are often threatened, fired, and/or blacklisted (Coalition for Justice in the Maquiladoras 1993a, 1993b; interviews with Schoepfle and other U.S. labor representatives). Given their young age, low level of education, limited literacy, and economic hardship, most of the workers are ill-informed about, and powerless to demand enforcement of, labor, occupational, and environmental standards. Nevertheless, some researchers have found that women feel "fortunate'" to have work in the assembly plants (Acosta-Beln 1994).

Both men and women often continue working for the maquila industries through subcontracting arrangements once they leave the plants. Such arrangements usually pay less, entail an irregular flow of work, and are unregulated as to occupational conditions and hazards (Tokman and Klein 1996).

Although some plants, mostly subsidiaries of Fortune 500 companies, are reported to follow "state-of-the-art" industrial hygiene procedures, many are notorious as sweatshops. The plants are off-limits to researchers according to those who have attempted to enter. In 1991 a group of researchers reported that their study was "hampered by the fact that the scientific investigators did not have the right of entry" to the plants, a situation that continues today. As a result, they conducted an indirect study by interviewing workers and collecting environmental spot samples. Workers frequently reported exposure to dust and gases, skin contact with unidentified chemicals during at least part of their shift, poor ergonomics, uninterrupted fast pace, and long working hours (symptoms reported included headache; dizziness; chest pressure; fatigue; pain; numbness; tingling; and eye, ear, nose, and skin irritation). Only one in eight soldering workers had access to a shower. Fifteen percent of the 270 workers surveyed told researchers they were afraid or not allowed to seek medical care when they felt sick at work. Less than half of the workers surveyed reported receiving training from their employers on occupational risks of their jobs. Less than 20 percent reported that the chemical substances they used were properly labeled. Official inspections are rare; funds for such programs are inadequate and inspectors often are themselves not fully trained.

Wastes

More information is available on the volume and content of hazardous waste discharged into the environment by the maquiladora plants than can be obtained on in-plant occupational hazards. The magnitude of the potential in-plant risks may be surmised from figures on dumping, small sets of environmental samples, general knowledge of industry materials, and reports from the people who live and work there. Sampling data available in the public domain are few, but they are consistent with what one would expect given the industries involved. They also indicate that even if workers are not exposed in the plants, they may be in the communities where they live on the outskirts of the industrial "parks."

Most of the maquiladora industries are among those on the EPA's list of "top ten" high-volume potentially hazardous waste generators (U.S. EPA 1994). *Twin Plant News*, an industry journal, reported in 1995 that the maquiladoras were generating about 164 tons of hazardous waste daily, only 54 percent (90 tons) of which was being returned to the United States for treatment, contrary to the North American Free Trade Agreement, or NAFTA, accords (Eaton 1997). Thirty tons was disposed of by Mexican authorities, leaving 44 tons daily, or 14,000 tons a year, unaccounted for (*Twin Plant News* 1995).

Waste disposal capacity, a problem in all of Mexico, is considered particularly acute along the border which "offers the fewest waste treatment and disposal options of any industrially active region in Mexico" (Mignella and Silveira 1997). In 1993, 98 percent of the factories reportedly lacked treatment systems for their waste water. "There is general suspicion that wastes are being dumped at sea, in clandestine inland sites, and into nearby lakes, rivers, and ravines" (Eaton 1997).

The Coalition for Justice in the Maquiladoras, made up of labor, environmental, and human rights groups from Mexico, the United States, and Canada, has worked on these issues for many years. It reports cases where water piped into homes is contaminated with fecal coliforms, agricultural runoff waters contain xylene, chromium, benzene, and lead, and that aquifers, too, are contaminated (Coalition for Justice in the Maquiladoras 1993a, 1993b). It also reports cases of work-site accidents with hazardous substances, including explosions and burns, and one case of discarded toxic material containers being used to store home drinking water.

Spot samples collected in 1990 found that open canals and rivers used for swimming, fishing, and drinking contained raw sewage, volatile solvents, and other chemicals in concentrations "from 20 to 215,000 times in excess" of EPA standards for receiving waters (Lewis, Kaltofen, and Ormsby 1991).

In 1995, well water in communities along the U.S. side of the border known as *colonias*, whose residents are primarily Mexican-Americans or Mexican immigrants, was sampled and found to have elevated sulfate and arsenic concentrations (Haass et al. 1996). The authors of this unique study on water and sanitation improvements in the *colonias* also observed discarded drums being put to use for domestic water storage, as well as the use of "recycled" materials to build shelters. Improper disposal and reuse of empty pesticide containers are common throughout Latin America.

The Coalition for Justice in the Maquiladoras has been among those who have reported clusters of elevated rates of anencephaly and other neural tube defects that, they suspect, may have been caused by prenatal exposure to occupational and environmental toxicants. Low-birth-weight babies are also reported by advocacy groups to be more common among maquiladora workers than among women who work in service-related industries. Under intense pressure from scientists, border communities, and human rights groups, U.S. EPA and Mexican health authorities began a collaboration to study and prevent these diseases along the border, including obtaining the required surveillance data (U.S. EPA 1994).

The dearth or obscurity of studies in border states on both sides could be an indicator of the degree to which the border health situation is not receiving appropriate attention. A team of U.S. researchers "suspect that this relative scarcity of published research on *colonias* is partly due to the very nature of the *colonias*—rapidly growing, unincorporated, underserved, and often politically isolated communities—factors that make even such seemingly straightforward tasks as estimating their populations difficult" (Haass et al. 1996). The population of these sprawling, improvised settlements is predominantly made up of relatively uneducated, Spanish-speaking, underemployed or itinerant workers and their families, who are often so poor that the electricity needed to heat food for their children or operate a fan in the intense heat is run by extension cords from car batteries (personal observation). The supermarkets, pharmacies, and banks taken for granted by most neighborhoods in the United States are nowhere to be found for miles (personal observation). What services exist are provided almost exclusively by church-affiliated or other nonprofit organizations. Political representation is nonexistent because the *colonias* are unincorporated.

Water and Sanitation Problems

Lack of safe drinking water and adequate sanitation services further compounds health risks in the maquila communities and U.S. *colonias*. The influx of people has created large communities along the border, whose population was placed at 9.2 million in 1990. Three and a half million live on the Mexican side, some 5.7 million on the U.S. side, in the 14 sister cities that account for the bulk of the population. The *colonias* on the U.S. side of the border are poor, too, poorer by far than the rest of the country and maquila-related industries in electronics, metals, plastics, and petroleum derivatives and transportation equipment are also sources of employment there.

If for no other reason than the area's rapid rate of growth—43 percent over 10 years—many of the residents lack access to safe drinking water, sewerage services, utilities, and adequate housing. For years, waterways in the area, such as the Tijuana River, into which millions of gallons of raw sewage is dumped daily, have been described as "virtual cesspools" (*Public Citizen* 1996). Health consequences have been documented on both sides of the border, among them hepatitis-A, dengue, amoebiasis, and other water- and sanitation-related diseases. On the U.S. side, in El Paso, researchers found in 1991 that the relative risks for campylobacter enteritis, hepatitis-A, and salmonellosis were 1.35, 1.48, and 1.86 percent, respectively, for residents of low-income *colonias* compared to others (Haass et al. 1996). Prevalence rates for hepatitis-A have been estimated elsewhere to be 35 percent among *colonia* children and 90 percent among adults over 35 years old. The U.S. Center for Disease Control has also reported dengue and elevated TB rates along the American side of the border. Mexican researchers note that, bad as the situation may be in the U.S.-side *colonias*, neonatal infectious mortality in the Mexican sister cities is far worse, although the data are woefully inadequate.

Cause for Concern Regionwide

Rapid urbanization, rural population displacements, urban poverty, changes in the structure and gender make-up of the labor force, lax enforcement of occupational and environmental regulations, and the concomitant inadequacy of water, sewerage, and waste management infrastructures are regionwide concerns. The "epidemiologic transition" observed in the increased reporting of chronic illnesses and the "double burden of disease" (traditional tropical infectious diseases and "modern" chronic ailments) have been the topic of discussion for over a decade (see Murray 1996). There is still a dearth of research that examines these trends from the standpoint of their social etiology, however.

Workplace and residential hazards may be intimated from environmental waste contamination. UNEP (1994) reported that "most developing countries have neither clear waste management policies nor the facilities for treating hazardous wastes" and that reliable data are hard to come by because surveys are not routinely conducted. The report includes no data on contaminated sites or most other waste management indicators for Latin America.

One study conducted in 1993 in Quito, Ecuador, which is smaller and less industrialized than most capital cities in the region but, according to the authors, was "undergoing changes that place it on the threshold," found that the entirety of Quito's wastewater was discharged, untreated, into the nearest river (the Manchángara) (Arcia et al. 1993). A review of official data and spot samples revealed that the river was also contaminated by leachate from toxic waste and heavy metals in garbage dumped on open ground. Fecal bacteria, heavy metals, and other contaminants were detected in vegetables sold in the city, but the source of contamination was believed to be only partly from crop irrigation with water from the river.

As in Mexico, major sources of exposure to hazardous materials in Ecuador occurred in occupational settings and through waste dumping from the two major industrial sectors: textiles and metals. The (female-dominated) textile industry's use of detergents, solvents, volatile glues, bleaching agents, dyes, and sulfites and sulfates and the metal industry's dusts, solvents, acids, cyanides, sulfates and sulfites, carbonates, and nitrates and nitrites were pointed to as likely hazards. However, as noted above, data were "scant and hard to obtain since factory owners are reluctant to acknowledge responsibility" (Arcia et al. 1993).

Even when regulations exist they rarely are enforced, especially in small and mid-size industries. In 1995 it was reported that only 35 percent of the maquilas complied with national regulations requiring records showing how they had disposed of their waste. The same is most likely true for workplace exposures and accidents involving hazardous materials. For the 1986–92 period, UNEP included notification of nine major chemical accidents or incidents in Latin America, of which four required the evacuation of 10,000 to 20,000 people. In the first three months of 1996, 171 accidents involving the transportation of hazardous materials occurred in Mexico alone (INE 1996).

There is no reason to assume that similar conditions do not prevail through much of the region. Numerous small-scale incidents probably escape the attention of authorities and go unreported, or even undetected, throughout the region. As this author noted in 1985, such accidents are likely to occur with increasing frequency given rapid urban growth, especially in the congested settlements of the urban poor that are often sited on undesirable land surrounding factories, refuse disposal areas, and highways and above pipelines and gas storage tanks. The sprawling population density in these areas compounds the risks inherent in lack of regulations and resources to monitor the importation, manufacturing, transportation, storage, and use of hazardous materials.

These acute incidents probably pale in comparison to the chronic accumulation of toxic materials dumped into the environment, and to which occupational exposure may be frequent.

Gender Effects

It is still not possible to determine clear trends in environmental health along gender lines because most countries only recently began to disaggregate reported morbidity and mortality data and, when this is done for employment data, it is often not broken down by branch of industry (ILO 1997a, 1997b). Inadequate as the data are, however, they provide a starting point for what soon may be a significant contribution to understanding the social etiology of multiple environmental exposures. Understanding work in all its forms, paid or not, in or out of the home, is critical to understanding this etiology for women, men, and their children.

Institutional attempts have been made to "include women" in community participation for environmental, water, ecological, and other programs, analyze the etiology of poverty, understand gender effects in the transmission of "pre-epidemiologic transition" infectious diseases such as schistosomiasis and Chagas', and disaggregate some morbidity and mortality data by sex (PAHO/WHO 1993). Although some published studies on industries for export focus on women, they do not apply gender analysis as an etiologic framework to understand the complex interactions of environment and health.

The nascent form of this approach may nevertheless be found in these studies. The heavy presence of women in the export processing zones, especially along the Mexico-U.S. border, has made them acutely visible. Compared to other parts of the region, a sufficient body of information has been published on the border situation to indicate that there is an important relationship between chronic and acute environmental contamination, occupational hazards, especially where the poor and those employed in the informal sector of the economy are concerned, and the lack of regulations or their enforcement. Research there indicates that women and men alike are exposed to multiple hazardous materials in addition to water- and vector-borne pathogens, and they are likely to suffer concurrent nutritional deficiencies as well.

The data also indicate that women are heavily represented in other nontraditional export industries employing agrochemicals and other hazardous substances and are often re-exposed to the same and additional substances when they perform unremunerated, household-related work.

Informal Sector Workers

The information reviewed reveals that a substantial portion of the working population of the region is employed in activities that are informal, and therefore unregulated, unprotected, and have no access to paid medical care. Because of the very nature of the informal sector, information about it is also "informal." That is, it is not reflected in official data. Yet, from the standpoint of potential multiple environmental assaults, workers in this sector may be at the highest risk of all. Even when work may be adequately protected, its instability and low remuneration indicate that many of them do not get enough to eat, lack safe water and sanitation services, and live in settlements that are often themselves hazardous because they are clustered among industrial zones and close to municipal sewage and garbage dump sites. Some of the wastes found in environmental samples have been associated with health problems, including neurological, immune, and reproductive disorders such as cancers. In addition, qualitative reports exist of unprotected workplace use of solvents and chemicals.

Environmental health research is relatively new to Latin America and this review found a dearth of epidemiologic or other health studies on industry-related environmental health hazards, occupational exposures, or related health status analyses, especially where sex-disaggregated data—let alone gender analysis—are concerned. The information reviewed points to trends that have been a long time in the making and are cause for grave concern: the ubiquitous improper use and disposal of hazardous materials and wastes, the lack of knowledge about these materials, and the unprotected multiple assaults to which large portions of the urban population may be exposed. The striking lack of a systematic body of literature also indicates that work-related environmental health research and the formulation of attendant policies are needed in Latin America.

References

Acosta-Beln, E. 1994. *Opening New Paths: Research on Women in Latin America and the Caribbean*. Washington, DC: Woodrow Wilson International Center for Scholars.

Arcia, G., et al. 1993. *Environmental Health Assessment. A Case Study Conducted in the City of Quito and the County of Pedro Moncayo, Pichincha Province, Ecuador*. Environmental Health Project. Field Report No. 401. Washington, DC: U.S. Agency for International Development.

CEPAL (U.N. Economic Commission for Latin America and the Caribbean). 1996a. *Social Panorama of Latin America*. Santiago: CEPAL.

CEPAL. 1996b. *Mexico: La Industria Maquiladora*. Santiago: CEPAL.

Coalition for Justice in the Maquiladoras. 1993a. *The Issue Is Health*. San Antonio.

Coalition for Justice in the Maquiladoras. 1993b. *The Human Face of Work*. San Antonio.

Eaton, D. W. 1997. *Transformación de la industria maquiladora ante el TLC*. Tucson and Monterrey: National Center for Inter-American Free Trade and Centro Jurídico para el Comercio Interamericano (NATLAW/ITESM).

Haass, J. A., et al. 1996. "An Economic Analysis of Water and Sanitation Infra-structure Improvements in the *Colonias* of El Paso County, Texas." *International Journal of Occupational and Environmental Health* 2(3): 211–21.

ILO (International Labor Office). 1997a. *Statistical Yearbook, 1997*. Geneva: ILO.

ILO. 1997b. *World Employment, 1996/97*. Geneva: ILO.

INE (Instituto Nacional de Ecologia). 1996. "Instituto Nacional de Ecologia." *Business Mexico* 6(11): 44.

Jefferson, L. S. 1996. *No Guarantees: Sex Discrimination in Mexico's Maquiladora Sector*. Women's Rights Project. Washington, DC: Human Rights Watch.

Lewis, S., M. Kaltofen, and G. Ormsby. 1991. *Border Trouble: Rivers in Peril. A Report on Water Pollution Due to Industrial Development in Northern Mexico.* Washington, DC: National Toxics Campaign Fund.

Mignella, A., and M. Silveira. 1997. *U.S. and Mexican Hazardous Waste Site Regulations: A Comparison.* Tucson, AZ: NATLAW.

Morley, S. 1994 . *Poverty and Inequality in Latin America: Past Evidence, Future Prospects.* Policy Essay No. 13. Washington, DC: Overseas Development Council.

Murray, C. 1996. *The Global Burden of Disease.* Cambridge, MA: Harvard University Press.

PAHO/WHO. 1993. *Gender, Women and Health in the Americas.* Scientific Publication No. 541. Washington, DC: Pan American Health Organization.

Psacharopoulos, G., and Tzannatos, Z. 1992. *Case Studies on Women's Employment and Pay in Latin America.* Washington, DC: World Bank.

Public Citizen. 1996. "NAFTA's Broken Promises: The Border Betrayed." *Public Citizen*, Washington, DC.

Schoepfle, G. K. 1990. *Labor Standards in Export Assembly Operations in Mexico and the Caribbean.* Washington, DC: Bureau of International Labor Affairs, U.S. Department of Labor.

Tokman, V., and E. Klein. 1996. *Regulation and the Informal Economy: Microenterprises in Chile, Ecuador, and Jamaica.* London: Lynne Rienner.

Twin Plant News. 1995. *The Mexico Option: A History of the Maquiladora Industry.* Flagstaff, AZ.

U.N. 1995a. *Women in a Changing Global Economy. 1994 World Survey on the Role of Women.* New York: United Nations Department for Policy Coordination and Sustainable Development.

U.N. 1995b. *Transnational Corporations and Competitiveness. World Investment Report.* Geneva: United Nations.

UNICEF. 1998. *The State of the World's Children 1998.* New York: United Nations Children's Fund.

UNIDO (U.N. Industrial Development Organization). 1996. *International Yearbook of Industrial Statistics, 1996.* Vienna: UNIDO.

U.S. EPA. 1994. *Workshop on Health and Hazardous Waste Issues Related to the U.S.-Mexico Border. Proceedings.* Tucson, AZ: U.S. Environmental Protection Office.

World Bank. 1997a. *The State in a Changing World: World Development Report 1997.* Washington, DC: World Bank.

World Bank. 1997b. *World Development Indicators 1997.* Washington, DC: World Bank.

Community Experience of Urban Environmental Quality

The three short essays that follow[6] depict environmental conditions in three cities, one in the United States, two in India, and what those conditions mean to the residents of the affected neighborhoods. Together, the essays point to the need to define more clearly the hazards that affect people; to understand in a more sensitive way the effect of attempts to ameliorate conditions; and to intervene in ways that involve the community closely.

Can We Improve Neighborhood Quality in Neglected U.S. Cities?

Michael Greenberg

Webster's New World Dictionary defines the word environment as "all the conditions, circumstances, and influences surrounding and affecting the development of an organism or group of organisms." In other words, everything we see, smell, feel, or hear as soon as we walk outside our home is our neighborhood environment. This includes not only trees and sidewalks but noisy neighbors, litter in the street, abandoned houses, and polluted air.

In policymaking, however, the United States, like many other nations, has a much narrower definition of the environment. In local, state, and national government, environmental problems are equated with air, land, and water pollution. Crime is left to the criminal justice system; blight is the responsibility of housing, community development, police, and firefighting organizations; traffic noise, congestion, and access are left to departments of transportation.

The U.S. Environmental Protection Agency's narrow environmental mandate has not prevented the agency and its state progeny from improving the environment. Nationally, despite substantial increases in population, production, and consumption, emissions into the air, land, and water have decreased (Portney 1992). But this single-agency mandate does not work for inner-city neighborhoods, which face a multitude of hazards.

---

6. The essays are reprinted from *World Resources 1996-97*, Chapter 2, "Urban Environment and Human Health." World Resources is a joint publication of the World Resources Institute, UNEP, UNDP, and the World Bank by Oxford University Press, New York and Oxford, 1996. Essays 1 and 2 appear by permission of the Institute; Essay 3 by permission of the author.

The inner-city neighborhood of East Elizabeth, New Jersey, exemplifies the array of problems facing declining U.S. cities. Residents confront deafening noise from Newark Airport, the tenth-busiest airport in the Unites States, located just 1.6 kilometers away. The New Jersey Turnpike, the most heavily trafficked road in the United States, runs directly through the community.

The largest petrochemical complex on the East Coast, which, according to toxic release inventory data, is the seventh-largest waste-producing site and eighth-largest emitter of toxins in New Jersey, is located on the southwest boundary of the neighborhood. The site of a former hazardous waste incinerator that exploded in 1980 still stands vacant, surrounded by a 2.4 meter-high chain link fence. The neighborhood also contains clusters of abandoned buildings and numerous littered lots. Police warn visitors not to venture into public housing projects located in the center of East Elizabeth because the area is said to be the local epicenter of illegal drug activity.

When surveyed, the citizens of East Elizabeth, as well as local government experts, recognize that there are multiple sources of environmental risk. They also say that solving one or even two of these risks is insufficient to substantially improve neighborhood quality (Greenberg and Schneider 1994, 1996).

At this time, however, the U.S. government does not assess the cumulative risk of living in neighborhoods with crime and other behavioral hazards, severe physical blight, and multiple forms of pollution. Experts well versed in air pollution modeling and epidemiological studies have neither the mandate nor the skills to assess risk from other pollution problems.

Furthermore, crime, uncontrolled dogs and rats, abandoned and unsafe buildings, and various forms of antisocial behavior and physical decay are not included with pollution in risk assessments. As a result, mitigation efforts tend to be piecemeal and uncoordinated, and thus unlikely to reduce markedly the risk these neighborhoods face.

I cannot offer a realistic and simple solution to the multiple environmental problems of the neighborhoods. However, if efforts to rehabilitate our cities are to succeed, we must redefine the concept of environment in a way that matches the realities in multiple-hazard neighborhoods—in a way that is closer to Webster's definition. We cannot set priorities for action unless we understand the full extent of the risks these communities face. For now, those best equipped to set priorities are the residents and local officials who live and work in these neighborhoods.

It is also clear that no single agency can play the heroic knight. The agencies responsible for environment, criminal justice, housing, transportation and other areas must contribute both individually and collectively—along with businesses and communities—to finding ways to improve the environment and quality of life in multiple-hazard neighborhoods.

References

Greenberg, Michael, and Dona Schneider. 1994. "Hazardous Waste Site Remediation, Neighborhood Change, and Neighborhood Quality." *Environmental Health Perspectives* 102(6/7): 542–47.

Greenberg, Michael, and Dona Schneider. 1996. *Environmentally Devastated Neighborhoods: Perceptions, Policies, and Realities.* New Brunswick, NJ: Rutgers University Press.

Portney, Paul, ed. 1992. *Public Policy for Environmental Protection.* Washington, DC: Resources for the Future, pp. 7–25; 275–289.

Community Perceptions of Urban Health Risks

Aaron Baare and Rajesh Patnaik

Understanding how a community perceives health risks such as polluted water, inadequate drainage, or lack of garbage collection is essential to designating effective programs to address those problems. Individuals perceive risks to their health through a lens derived from their cultural, economic, societal, and educational backgrounds, and respond accordingly. For example, a squatter in a slum in Calcutta, India, might happily boil water collected at a public tap rather than move to a house with piped water that was located far from job opportunities; a middle-class family in Los Angeles would probably make a very different choice.

Until recently, these differences in how people view and respond to risks were not part of formal health risk analysis, which has traditionally relied on statistical correlations between exposure to risks and the incidence of various illnesses. Now, health planners are beginning to realize that using such objective measures of risk to design public health projects without accounting for how the affected community itself views the health risk being addressed is a recipe for failure.

Case Study: Indore's Drainage Improvement Project

The importance of incorporating community perceptions into project planning can be seen in the case of a public project designed to relieve flooding in the slums of Indore, India. The majority of Indore's 183 slums are located on the banks of canals and rivers that crisscross the city and on land located in the city's flood plain. Monsoon waters frequently flood these communities, submerging city streets and destroying homes.

Residents of the slums are well aware of the health risks associated with this flooding. Although they might not know the epidemiological details of pollution and contagion, they are all too familiar with the symptoms that they suffer. The names given to different floodwaters illustrate their perception of health risks. Each type of water has its own name. Dirty water that is contaminated with feces is known as *Ganda pani* and is seen as the worst kind of water, containing "small unseen insects" (*kitanuh*) responsible for causing stomach problems and other illnesses. Even wading through such water is recognized to be unhealthful. On the other hand, *Maila pani* (dirty water without excreta) is unpleasant to walk through, but not dangerous. *Pineh ka pani* is water that is clean enough to be used for drinking.

For these poor communities, however, the advantages of their location—close to the city center, with easy access to jobs, low land costs, and strong community ties—far outweigh the health risks associated with flooding and contact with dirty water. In addition, although city planners view the flooding only as a recurring problem, local residents associate flooding with heavy rain and good crop yields, leading to a positive perception of flooding.

In designing a project to improve health conditions in 157 of Indore's squatter settlements, city planners identified flooding as a major health risk and constructed closed drainage channels in an effort to reduce flooding and upgrade sanitary conditions. Despite these improvements, many community members now perceive flooding problems to be worse than before.

One important source of their dissatisfaction is that the new drainage system has reduced the ability of the community to apply its own risk-reduction strategies, thus increasing economic losses from the flooding. Because the drains are closed, residents can no longer predict the severity of the approaching flood. With the previous open drains, community members would adjust their level of flood response depending on rainfall intensity and the volume of water that they see in the open drains.

In light floods, structural adaptations including high internal shelving, raised storage platforms for valuables, and electricity connections at head height were enough to minimize damage. Food supplies, electronics, and mattresses were moved to ceiling-level platforms for safety.

When community members anticipated severe floods, all valuable processions were moved to higher ground. Children, the elderly, and livestock were evacuated first, while clothes and utensils were generally moved last. Unable to implement these coping strategies with the new drainage system, residents fear they many now lose many of the valuables on which they depend for their livelihood.

Residents also believe that the closed system does not drain as effectively as their previous open system. Unlike the open sewers, which were wider, the closed sewers are easily blocked by plastic bags and other trash. Water backups flood the area, in some cases affecting houses that were previously outside the flood-prone area. In addition, because residents can no longer see the water flowing, they do not have confidence that it is draining adequately. Finally, the open drains had the added benefit of washing away rubbish and excreta, which now remain on the streets.

Two lessons emerge from this example. First, for many urban dwellers in developing countries, health is a luxury they cannot afford because their immediate economic survival is at stake. Aware of their limited options, they design innovative ways to try to optimize their conditions. The slum dwellers in Indore, for instance, have developed intricate strategies that attempt to minimize the economic damage done by flooding. These can be very effective in reducing vulnerability to natural and man-made risks.

Second, it is clear that a better understanding of the cultural perceptions of community members can help in the design of local programs that both reduce risks to health and respect the choices of the people living in these cities. The challenge lies in developing a reliable means of ascertaining community views on local health risks and incorporating health into the planning of environmental health interventions.

A Partnership Approach to Improving Health in Delhi

Pratibha Mehta

Many health problems of the urban poor arise from the poverty and the degraded environment in which they live. However, conventional health delivery systems in most cities provide curative services to people, whereas environmental improvements or social services are the responsibility of different government departments. Because these departments tend to work in isolation, they seldom make a coordinated effort to improve the quality of life of the poor. Even existing health care systems are often beyond the reach of the poor because of cost, inconvenient locations, and overcrowded conditions.

In Delhi, India, a local NGO, Action for Securing Health for All (ASHA), has spent the past six years trying to improve the health of poor residents through community-based programs that address both poverty and the environment. The challenge is daunting. More than a million of Delhi's residents live in *jhuggie* shelters, temporary structures made of mud, thatch, plastic, and other discarded objects. *Jhuggies* are small and devoid of ventilation or natural light; many are susceptible to fire, dust, smoke, and noise pollution. The streets *of jhuggie* settlements are heaped with garbage, attracting dogs, pigs, flies, and mosquitos. One study found that although latrines were available in 46 percent of the settlements, most were poorly maintained, and nearly 41 percent of the residents still defecated in the open. *Jhuggies* are often located near garbage dumps, power plants and factories, and roads, exposing residents to risks from chemical residues, toxic wastes, and car exhaust fumes.

Not surprisingly, *jhuggie* residents—particularly women and children— are especially prone to respiratory and waterborne diseases. The infant mortality rate in *jhuggie* settlements is 100 per 1,000 live births, compared with 40 per 1,000 live births for the city as a whole. Roughly 40 percent of children under age 2 have not received all immunizations; 40 percent of women and children suffer severe malnutrition; just 17 percent of pregnant women receive at least three prenatal checkups; and 80 percent of all deliveries are conducted by untrained midwives.

ASHA began in 1988 as an emergency health clinic in a slum in south Delhi to deal with a serious cholera epidemic. During this period, the clinic staff observed that, although treatments were effective in curing patients, the incidence of disease remained unaffected. Indeed, there were repeated recurrences of preventable illnesses. Realizing that the community's health problems were intricately linked to poverty, pollution, and environmental degradation, ASHA began to focus on a broader approach to dealing with health, directing its efforts toward improving the environment, empowering women, increasing the literacy rate, and educating residents about the links between environment and health.

ASHA began by forging a partnership with the public agency responsible for delivering services to squatter settlements. Acting as mediator between the public agency and community members, ASHA managed to get the government to implement on-site slum upgrading projects. ASHA also helped community members form cooperatives. The cooperative objectives were to improve local environmental conditions by acquiring land rights and establishing long-term leases, providing home improvement loans, maintaining and repairing common spaces, and extending coverage of basic services such as water and sanitation facilities and roads.

These initial efforts were marred by difficulties. The on-site slum up-grading schemes had mixed results as news of slum improvement attracted additional settlers and increased land values, displacing the original residents. Local power struggles arose over access to the improved facilities, and the cooperatives ultimately dissolved after ASHA decided to withdraw from the daily tasks of running them.

Through this experience, however, ASHA learned that women play a far greater role than men in managing households and the community. Women's health is a decisive factor in the well-being of their families; thus, they have a much larger stake in improving the living conditions in the community. A clear disadvantage of the first cooperative structure was that it had excluded women from an active role in community decisionmaking.

In response, ASHA helped form *Mahila Mandals*—community based women's groups—within some of the Delhi *jhuggies*. Initially, the *Mahila Mandals* met once a week to talk about community issues and receive health education. However, as the members gained in confidence and capacity, they started representing their community and discussing other concerns such as income-earning activities. A revolving fund was established to provide micro-credit to women to start income generating activities such as vegetable vending, tailoring, small shops, etc. ASHA acts as a facilitator, helping to inform the *Mahila Mandals* about relevant government policies and serving as a communication link to the formal system.

Recognizing that women play a key role as healthcare providers, ASHA set up a training program for female community health workers called *basti sevikas*. Selected through a process of community consultation and aptitude testing, *basti sevikas* are trained to provide basic treatment for colds, fevers, coughs, and diarrhea, and for more serious diseases such as malaria, scabies, and worms. Each *sevika* is responsible for 200 families and charges a small fee for visits. *Basti sevikas* also provide health education about environment-related issues such as handwashing and boiling water, encourage pregnant women to go for prenatal care, and maintain health records for households in the settlements. In exchange, the *basti sevikas* also receive a monthly honorarium.

By approaching health care at the community level and encouraging residents to take charge of their environments, ASHA has helped to improve the overall health of many *jhuggie* residents. Through an integrated approach and the collaborative efforts of public agencies, an NGO (ASHA) and the community, child morbidity and malnutrition have decreased, residents are more likely to seek treatment for minor ailments, and overall environmental conditions in the slums have improved.

9

Transportation and Metropolitan Growth

Editor's Introduction

Richard Stren

In many important respects, transportation and transport planning are to cities what finance and financial planning are to national economies. Just as finance and financial transactions provide a structural basis for the functioning of economies, transport routes and the organization of "trips" by urban populations are among the most essential elements of the form and functioning of all cities. Not only have many cities initially been founded and located on specific sites because of transport connections—such as access to rivers or location at river junctions, proximity to ocean port facilities, relation to railway and/or highway routes—but also the quality and direction of their growth is highly dependent on the character and location of transport routes, both within their borders and regions, and in relation to other cities and jurisdictions. For planners and urban managers, transport decisions are among the most important decisions they and their cities can make. They are important because they affect large numbers of people, because they often involve high levels of capital expenditure (by either the private or the public sectors, or both), and because they affect the operation of the city on an everyday basis. Transport also affects men and women differentially, as we are reminded by Jordi Borja and Manuel Castells. In many cities of the developing world, urban transport is organized around the needs of men in formal employment, who travel from the outskirts of the city to centers of employment in the morning, returning from their work to the outskirts in the evening. By contrast, women have a more diverse trip pattern, especially if they need to work as well as look after children. The traditional American suburban model, according to which the woman was responsible for most of the urban driving, has "entered functional crisis" as the authors put it, now that women have become, in addition, workers. For the city to respond to women's needs, it needs to develop a more flexible, diverse, and dense transport structure.

Failure to deal effectively with urban transport problems can be very costly, as John Flora demonstrates. It is estimated that US$43 billion is lost every year in the United States as a result of traffic congestion; and in Bangkok, close to $4 million is lost every day! Not only do drivers (and others) lose precious time because of less than optimum average speeds in vehicles, but traffic congestion creates more air pollution as well. Pollution from transportation sources in many Latin American cities accounts for around 70 percent of all air pollution, and the health effects of this can be serious; they include increased hypertension and IQ decrements in children, as well as serious respiratory problems, and even chronic respiratory disease. Furthermore, as other studies indicate, road traffic accidents are a leading cause of death in many countries—particularly for adolescents and young adults. While the figures are sketchy, Kenya had a rate of road traffic fatalities some 30 times higher than the United Kingdom and Switzerland in the early 1990s; the number of fatalities from road accidents in India exceeds that in the United States, although the country has less than one-twentieth of the vehicles. In Thailand, one estimate suggests that around half of the 20,000 lives lost each year to accidents are due to traffic mishaps (UNCHS 1996, p. 278).

Bogotá, the capital of Colombia, is perhaps typical of large cities in developing countries in its multitude of transport challenges. Residents of Bogotá perceive transport as the second most important problem in the city (next to personal security). Congestion is a major problem in that city, as the number of motor vehicles of all types almost doubled between 1990 and 1998, while the population rose by 24 percent, and the supply of road space grew by less than 10 percent. Public transport (which conveys 77 percent of motorized journeys) occupied only 27 percent of the limited road space available. But, as Israel Fainboim Yaker explains, Bogotá's congestion is not so much a result of too high a level of car and vehicle ownership, but rather of improper *management* of the transportation system. Fainboim Yaker argues that the city must improve its road network, must discourage the use of private vehicles, must integrate the various modes of a public transportation system (to include a rail system and high-capacity buses), and must introduce regulations that better control vehicle circulation and parking.

As John Flora indicates, a wide range of solutions to traffic congestion and air pollution have been more or less effective in different comparative contexts. Of course, each city must design a system that is appropriate for itself. For cities with populations between 2 and 5 million, there should be a well-designed and well-constructed basic road network, good traffic management, and an effective balance between public and private transportation. One of the best known and successful cases is Curitiba, with dedicated bus lanes connected to an integrated system covering more than 75 percent of the city. The system, which is based on private bus franchises (regulated by government), carries an average of one million passengers per day with no government subsidy. In other cities, traffic congestion can be controlled by the regulation of gasoline prices, the charging of tolls or fees for cars that enter congested areas, or the raising of parking fees in central city areas at peak periods. But both road and rail networks are necessary to manage traffic congestion and to give proper attention to environmental needs.

If transport problems have transport solutions, they also reflect patterns of land use, as Robert Cervero reminds us. With increased motorization in both the developed and developing worlds, average commuting distance everywhere is lengthening, and trips are becoming increasingly dispersed across the physical landscape. Transport modes affect land uses differentially, and new land-use patterns—particularly the extension of large cities in low-rise peripheries—add significantly to the traffic flow. Investing in a light rail line for commuter transit, for example, is likely to encourage new investment in offices and retail shops clustering around the train stations. The same is true for investments in subway systems. By contrast, investment in highways and freeway improvements will lead to more spread-out development from highway interchanges. Overall, says Cervero, transport planning must take place within an overall context of planning within a regional economy, since transport redistributes rather than creates growth. Ideally, major transport investments—as a comparison of Toronto and San Francisco shows—should take place in advance of regional development rather than after it. Cervero's main message is that, for urban economies to function effectively with the lowest level of losses through transport inefficiencies, transport and land-use planning should complement each other. Demand (arising from land-use patterns) and supply (expressed through the construction of new transport infrastructure) must be considered together.

Reference

UNCHS. 1996. *An Urbanizing World: Global Report on Human Settlements, 1996.* New York: Oxford University Press.

Management of Traffic and the Urban Environment

John Flora

Five overriding challenges are evident for transportation policy through-out the world. Two lie in overcoming inherited problems: how to increase access, and how to increase affordability. The remaining three lie in meeting new challenges: adjusting to changing global patterns, increasing responsiveness to consumers, and coping with rapid motorization.

Particularly important is the question of how to deal with rapidly growing motor vehicle traffic (referred to here simply as "traffic"). Surveys have estimated that average vehicle speed for an entire city is currently in the vicinity of 18 kilometers per hour; in many cities, speeds of 4 to 8 kilometers per hour are becoming common throughout the day, not just during rush hour. The economic effects of congestion are very real and obvious in our national economies and our cities—decreased economic activity, unemployment, lack of access to better social and job opportunities, higher prices, and distortions in the allocation of resources.

In the United States, US$43 billion (a low estimate) are lost each year as a result of traffic congestion. In Bangkok, more than a third of the gross development product of the city is lost annually, or close to US$4 million daily. Japan, after implementing a just-in-time delivery system, is now having to scale that back, and revert to the old practice of warehousing and maintaining large stocks. Traffic congestion in the United Kingdom accounts for a loss of approximately US$23 billion per year.

Another result of congestion is atmospheric pollution. In most cities, pollution from transportation sources typically accounts for 40 to 80 percent of the total pollution; in many Latin American cities, the figure fluctuates around 70 percent; in Eastern Europe, it is only 30 percent, while 70 percent comes from industry. While pollution from industry is decreasing, pollution from transportation is increasing in direct proportion. And, of course, this has serious health effects, particularly for the lowest-income segments of the population in cities, who live in greater contact with the street and in more congested areas.

Thus, traffic has components that deserve serious consideration, although not all factors linked to traffic are inevitably bad. Traffic, accessibility, economic growth, and social growth are all part of the same family, but the issues should be handled according to the context and values of each community, with differences in culture and levels of development always being taken into consideration. In short, there is clearly no standard solution that might be applied to every reality.

Sustainability, Synergies, and Trade-Offs

Many past responses appear not to have been sustainable, to the extent that they were of short duration or, in the end, produced more problems than they solved. The implementation of a given policy will produce certain measurable benefits, but there will also be disadvantages; these must be tolerable, and be outweighed by the benefits. In other words, we need to consider trade-offs.

Sustainability has, first and foremost, economic and financial implications; solutions must be affordable to the municipality, the state or province, and the country. Sustainability must also be social: it is not sensible to implement systems that are inaccessible to 40 percent of the citizens, or to implement policies that reduce people's access to their jobs. And sustainability must also be environmentally sound.

Economic and financial sustainability mean different things to different people, but there is a clear need to establish regulatory institutions. The reorganization and restructuring of agencies has been one frequent response in the past, when the state was seen as needing to take over activities directly. The all-importance of the state is no longer desirable, however, and more public-private partnerships need to be created. This does not mean that the state should withdraw from everything; it simply means that public and private roles must be differentiated, identifying areas where each is strongest in order to create partnerships for developing these activities. Costs must be passed along to the users, as this is a highly effective way of recovering the costs directly from the beneficiaries. Appropriate public transportation charges and financing mechanisms can seem at odds with the ability of the poorest to pay; but charges for public transportation must be adopted to finance its operation—where subsidies are needed, another solution must be found.

The private sector is not universally trusted; but this should not inhibit the introduction of commercial elements in the functioning of public agencies and in activities managed by the state, since the fact of state ownership need not prevent public agencies from using commercial approaches. Throughout the world—and Latin America is a leader in this regard—the private operation of transportation fleets is being encouraged. This accumulated experience in the region, which deserves to be exported to the rest of the world, at times is not carried far enough. We need better methods for bidding and concessions. If privatization is to work, people must first of all be protected from unscrupulous and monopolistic activities. Private-sector operators should be encouraged and protected through fair treatment, with contracts that make clear what they are required to do and what they will receive in exchange.

Situations that are economically viable may not necessarily serve the needs of the public effectively. To promote social sustainability, especially in improving physical access to jobs, infrastructure and systems must provide people with mobility, typically an issue in Latin America, where the lowest-income population lives outside the central city where most jobs are. It is therefore necessary to reduce barriers to the informal sector, contrary to the usual practice of keeping the informal sector out. All gender discrimination, although it is often unwitting, must also be eliminated. Women, often the backbone of the family and contributors to household income, frequently do not have access to the services they need.

Greater use of non-motorized transportation must be permitted, something that has not been done as forcefully as it should be in Latin America. Fiscal and financial impediments must be eliminated, with special arrangements for people to purchase bicycles and have access to public transportation. In many areas, a bicycle costs the equivalent of a year's wages, but access to funds to buy one can be ensured in different ways.

The effects of job reduction in the public sector must also be mitigated. For many years, public transportation agencies were a vehicle for granting political favors, "prizes" to be handed out after a successful election; the result was the creation of excessively large organizations. When the Argentine railroads were privatized, it was found that the freight lines could operate with only 25 percent of the former work force. But people cannot simply be ejected from their jobs; a plan for job reduction, retirements and job relocation is needed to help them.

In many of our communities, the charge for public transportation is not affordable to those in the lowest income quintile. We need, rather than charging artificially low fares, to develop a scheme that works—direct subsidy systems, with tickets sold at lower prices in kiosks or other locations, and for which the entrepreneurs are fully reimbursed. Examples of this are the "transportation-voucher" in Brazil and the system in France; both are viable subsidy systems, not simply an artificial implementation of a lower charge.

In terms of land-use planning, our systems have, in practice, segregated the poorest population, to the point where they lose accessibility. It is essential that the planning process emphasize public transportation and non-motorized transport. All too often, the old form of Western planning has been followed, with planning dictated by the automobile, and transportation planning limited to street design. We need an integrated form of planning, emphasizing accessibility and with special attention to public transportation.

There is also a need to develop community participation. The public must be allowed to decide the type and level of service it desires. Sometimes, people do not want a broad boulevard, but a road that can be negotiated in all weathers; they do not want to spend millions, but simply to have dependable access.

Environmental sustainability, above all, must include initiatives for road safety. Accidents and deaths are increasing, and carry a high cost in disruptions to family life, in scarce resources for importing replacement components, and in loss of work.

Promoting ecological and environmental sustainability means developing environmental strategies—at the beginning of a project. It is not necessary to use the most advanced or experimental methodologies. What is needed are cost-effective solutions. If the biggest problem is that of particulates, then the solution is to find the most cost-effective method for eliminating them. Various measures are possible: use of filters in diesel buses, redesigning routes and using alternative fuels such as natural gas. Consideration should also be given to standards for cleaner and lead-free gasoline, and attention should be paid to non-motorized transportation.

There are ample examples of road-building projects in ecologically or otherwise sensitive areas (in Pakistan, for example, a six-lane elevated highway was planned to pass immediately in front of an important mosque). Care must be taken to ensure that all mechanisms for evaluating trade-offs are followed—the process is essential. Figure 9.1 shows that the process is not a one-way street. There are questions of economic and financial, environmental and ecological, and social and distributive viability, all of which must be given equal consideration in any type of program. Satisfying the requirements in one of these areas inevitably has an impact on the other areas; consequently, many of the final decisions will need to be made through a process of balancing the problems against environmental, economic, social or financial viability.

One example follows. Appropriate financial viability dictates that we must always implement charges: if the per-passenger cost of operating a train is 80 cents, then that should be the charge, but many people would be unable to afford it. In many cases, between 20 and 40 percent of family income is spent on transportation, while studies show that spending more

Figure 9.1.   Sustainability, Synergies, and Trade-Offs

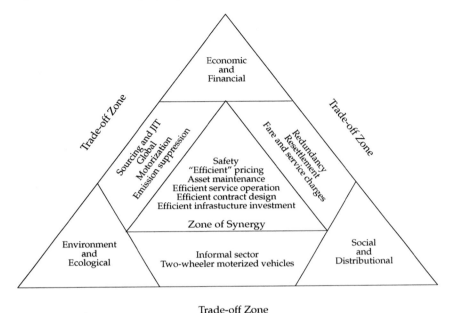

Source: Author.

than 10 to 20 percent represents a heavy and unfair burden. Thus, charges must be kept within an affordable range. This does not mean, however, that the fares must be lowered—it is all too clear what happens to public transportation when this is done. It is essential to find a different way to develop a subsidy scheme and a way of paying for it. One of the most practical ways, and one of the most successful, is the sale of transportation vouchers. If the charge is 25 cents, then that is what the bus company will receive. The tickets, however, may be sold for 10 or 15 cents, with the difference being charged to the government body responsible.

International Experience

Although perhaps no city in the world has had complete success in the management of traffic and the environment, we can draw positive and negative lessons from some of their experience.

   In medium-size cities with populations of between two and five million, three basic elements should always be present to allow for successful management of urban transportation systems. These essential elements form the nucleus of the infrastructure network, broad transportation management programs, and efficient bus systems.

First, there must be a well-designed and well-constructed basic infrastructure network. It is wrong to say that cities do not need more roads, since this is simply not true. Bangkok has many problems, one of the main ones being the lack of a road system. Less than 7 percent of the urban area is taken up by streets, less than half the normal percentage for most cities. Another problem is the lack of road connections; in Bombay, a four-block section of road has lain incomplete for many years that could, if completed, provide a much-needed fourth main corridor in peninsular Bombay, a city of 12 million people; in Guayaquil, there are very few bridges to cross the river that surrounds and traverses the downtown area. This absence of connections creates excessive demand in many parts of the road system. In short, the first thing to analyze in a city is the nucleus of the road network, ensuring that there are appropriate arteries, collector roads, and local feeder roads.

Second, and equally important, is to ensure that the road system functions efficiently, with proper transportation management in place. Santiago, for instance, has an excellent system, with a high level of professional expertise in transportation management. Unfortunately, it has not received the necessary resources and political support. Low-cost improvements can also have a high rate of return: computerized traffic signal systems can reduce time losses by 30 to 40 percent; the system being implemented in São Paulo shows improvements of 40 percent. Restricting turns in Bombay reduced accidents by approximately 60 percent, with time losses in one of the peninsular corridors being reduced by more than 40 percent. Pedestrian crosswalks are also worthy of attention: the construction of medians accomplishes two things: it increases safety for pedestrians who insist on crossing in the middle of the block, and it also serves to divide the traffic. These are familiar measures, but the important point is that a concerted effort must be made, since the central road network will not function without effective traffic management. A common problem, however, is interference with management initiatives, primarily in the form of lack of political will for implementing certain decisions. In addition, the cooperation of the police is needed for supervision and enforcement, key elements for the effective functioning of traffic management.

Latin America is fortunate in its excellent officials and technical experts, but it also has a crucial need to develop training for many more, with updated information covering the latest developments in the field. Without a highly trained team, it will be impossible to make efficient use of the road system, or to convince the political establishment to make good decisions.

It must be said that at times the problem in this area is frequently the inability of the technical experts to lay a clear foundation, rather than the intransigence of politicians; when good, sound reasons are presented and promoted, politicians are inclined to listen.

The third element relates to public transportation and buses. In Brazil, buses are by far the most widely used form of transportation, and are, typically, extremely important in Latin America and throughout the world, with certain notable exceptions, such as China.

One of the most important elements in an effective bus system is the ability to identify the appropriate role of the public and private sectors. It is possible here to separate the government's role as coordinator, planner and regulator from that of the private sector, which is better equipped to serve as operator, and has clear incentives to do so.

It is equally important to give priority to buses through dedicated bus lanes and integrated facilities. Bus corridors can carry between 8,000 and 20,000 passengers per hour, and are highly effective. Dedicated bus lanes are being implemented in Santiago and Buenos Aires. Also worthy of mention (although it is true that this system could not be implemented fully in all cities) is a case familiar to many, precisely because it works well—the Curitiba system.

Curitiba has an integrated system covering more than 75 percent of the city, with dedicated bus corridors (see Figure 9.2 and Box 9.1). This public transportation grid is served by several hundred kilometers of feeder routes, permitting people to avoid passing through the central area when travelling from one part of the city to another. Routes run between districts, with all the routes integrated in a single public transportation system that is one of the most efficient in the world. Cities vary in size and have different problems, but this example offers important lessons.

Bus corridors are used very effectively throughout the world; in Japan and even in the United States, where public transportation is not a strong point, these corridors are highly efficient. But Latin America was the pioneer in this field and, with capacities of up to 20,000 passengers per hour, the system operates effectively and at an appropriate cost.

As cities grow, the road system, traffic management, and buses become inadequate, however, and new thought must be given to moving masses of travelers. A rail system is the logical solution in such a case. The World Bank has historically been considered to be against rail systems, a reputation that—while indeed true for some within the Bank—is not entirely justified. The Bank is not opposed to rail systems, as demonstrated by the financing of the São Paulo Metro, that of Pusan, that of Porto Alegre and,

Figure 9.2.   The Curitiba Integrated Transport System

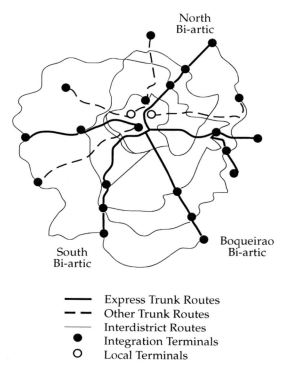

Express Trunk Routes
Other Trunk Routes
Interdistrict Routes
● Integration Terminals
○ Local Terminals

Source: Author.

currently, support for the construction of light-rail systems in a number of countries. Rail systems have their role, but they typically cost between $35 million and $100 million per mile and often serve only 5 to 10 percent of total travel demand.

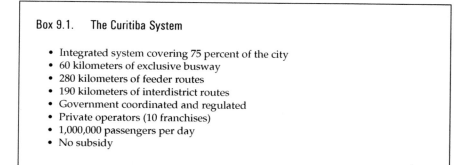

Box 9.1.   The Curitiba System

- Integrated system covering 75 percent of the city
- 60 kilometers of exclusive busway
- 280 kilometers of feeder routes
- 190 kilometers of interdistrict routes
- Government coordinated and regulated
- Private operators (10 franchises)
- 1,000,000 passengers per day
- No subsidy

Metro rail systems are not as flexible as other systems; with buses, for instance, routes can be changed readily. Metros are also large consumers of resources; in Manila, no other infrastructure was authorized for five years during the construction of the light-rail system. Manila provides a good example for discussing the different central activities that are necessary, including rail systems. The Manila system transports nearly 19,000 passengers per hour and covers its operating costs. However, there is still severe congestion in the city, which means that the light-rail system did not solve the problem. There is extensive bus coverage, collective taxis, and a good road system. What is missing, however, is effective traffic management—one of our three essential elements. The publicly owned bus system transports fewer than 10 percent of the people, and its costs are 50 percent subsidized. Private buses have broad coverage and carry the remaining people, without subsidies; however, the regulatory oversight is extremely poor, so the private bus system falls far short of what should be expected.

This situation can be compared to that of Santiago, a city of five million people. Santiago has an extensive rail system, although it needs to be expanded in places. There is effective traffic management of excellent quality, run by a highly skilled technical staff. An efficient bus system operates without subsidies and has broad coverage; new and more environmentally sound buses have now been added. A very efficient Metro is one of the few in the world that operates without subsidies. Those are the good points. Santiago, as have many cities, has tried to deal with congestion by implementing restrictions on vehicle use. Each day, 20 percent of the automobiles were prohibited from operating, as was tried in Mexico City, Athens, and a number of other cities. This measure tends to be highly effective initially, particularly in periods of crisis, when everyone can see and smell the pollution. But after a couple months people begin to adopt alternatives, so the traffic is ultimately reduced by only a small percentage. In the municipality of São Paulo, and in Bogotá, there has been some success with restrictions only applicable during peak periods, but this has required strong enforcement. In general, this type of regulatory control has not produced the desired results.

As cities become larger, therefore, the next important element is the integration of modes of public transportation and the integration of policies and planning. Toronto, Teheran, Athens, Guangzhou, and Holland, Germany, and Brazil are carrying out measures like these. Lack of integration compels people to use two or three modes of transportation to reach their jobs, each one with its separate charge; this becomes difficult to afford.

Consequently, people use cars to the extent possible. The lack of an articulated policy between different agencies creates severe problems. Thus, as the scale of management expands from centralized to more dispersed activities, there must be increasing involvement in policy and management of the systems.

Some comparisons will illustrate this point. Bangkok and Cairo have extensive bus and streetcar systems. Cairo has a rail system; Bangkok has been planning a system of this type. But neither city has a good road system, or effective traffic management, and the biggest problem in both cities is the lack of integrated planning. In Bangkok, it is difficult to determine who is responsible for solving problems: there are at least eleven different agencies, each with an important role that each, unfortunately, believes to be the most important. There is no coordination or working together, problem alleviation does not happen, and the public suffers the consequences. No one can agree on how best to use the private sector.

But in those cities where things appear to be functioning better, such as Paris, Tokyo, and São Paulo, these elements are present: a well-developed rail network, effective traffic management, and extensive facilities for pedestrians. The latter cannot be ignored; when people leave a bus, train or automobile, they must be able to move about without fear for their safety, and they must have good accessibility, for then they will be willing to walk.

Efficient public transportation systems, as demonstrated in recent years in São Paulo, above all with integration between buses, metro and suburban rail, are necessary, as is integrated planning at the metropolitan level. All these factors make a great difference.

New Management Instruments

Measures to promote integration will be inadequate as cities and traffic rates grow. The city of Santiago is presently at that crossroads; while all the right things have been done, traffic keeps increasing and, with it, congestion. The next step is to create fee mechanisms—an appropriate system of prices for services, from fuel to traffic congestion. An obvious one is gasoline. Most gasoline prices in Latin American cities are concentrated at the low end of the scale, while the price of fuel in Europe is high; the latter seems appropriate in view of the costs of congestion and environmental pollution, and it forces people to assess, in an explicit way, their decisions about using an automobile. While this remains a controversial issue, numerous recent studies have demonstrated that gasoline is undervalued in many places, beginning with the United States.

An increase in the price of gasoline does not automatically mean that public transportation fares will rise in the same proportion. Gasoline typically represents from 15 to 18 percent of the cost of operating a bus. There are, however, political problems, and these should be dealt with. First of all, policies on prices should be separated from the social objectives of protecting the lower-income population. To meet this latter objective, subsidy mechanisms must be found that are not an artificially low price for gasoline, since this will only lead to a continuation of the increase in traffic, while the problems of the poorest population will continue to grow. Targeted subsidies can serve as a better way to address these inequalities.

One instrument that makes a long-term difference is a toll for congestion. When people use a large amount of space in the downtown area, they have to pay for that. Similarly, a person driving downtown at rush hour is creating a heavy financial burden on the economy and on the rest of the public, much greater than that created by driving in the country on a Sunday; the two fees can thus be separated.

Tolls for congestion are not easy to implement, but technology has progressed to the point where systems can be introduced without using manual tollbooths or invading people's privacy. Singapore is, perhaps, an overused example, but it is nevertheless important, because it attempts to find explicit solutions to the problem. There is a good system of streets, excellent traffic management, rail systems have been implemented, management is well integrated; but, until appropriate tolls and regulatory mechanisms were implemented, the problems of traffic and congestion were not dealt with effectively.

Unless the problem of congestion is approached realistically from a political and technical point of view, with fees and a proper system of regulation, long-term solutions will not be found. Certainly, large Latin American cities, such as São Paulo, Mexico City, Santiago, and Buenos Aires, must begin to consider charges for congestion.

One thing that is certain, and that applies in all parts of the world, is the need to differentiate appropriately between the role of government and the role of the private sector. Where government runs the entire system, it is not usually cost effective. There are, of course, countries where the government operates the public transportation system efficiently, as in Germany, but few countries can support those costs.

Furthermore, it is unnecessary to do so. France's public transportation system almost meets the requirements that have been defined here. The government is responsible for public transportation, but raises taxes from all commercial activities in order to finance it, and contracts services in the private sector. Latin America has a public transportation service that serves as a prototype, and is probably the most effective in the world from the perspective of cost. The big concern is that this will be lost. For example, Buenos Aires has talked of ending the privatized bus service and transferring it to the municipality. The bus system is excellent; the private sector has operated in route partnerships without government subsidies. The system is beginning to be integrated with the Metro, that is now being operated by the private sector, something that has not happened anywhere in the world. Previously, the Argentine government had been losing $200 million per year—resources not therefore available for social or similar programs—on operating an inefficient system.

The Chilean experience is also interesting. Chile provided a valuable lesson to the world by showing that some degree of regulation of transportation was necessary. Total deregulation led to the emission of particulates in the downtown area, and to buses driving around half empty. After returning to a system of granting concessions for routes and requiring more ecological and environmentally friendly buses, the system has improved. The government is responsible for a certain degree of regulation, but the private sector has shown itself as a more effective operator of services.

To sum up, cities that have dealt most efficiently with management of traffic and the environment have been those that have developed appropriate systems involving a road and rail network. These have been systems with effective traffic management, using skilled and well-trained technical experts, with police who understand what must be done, and who work in close coordination with traffic management staff. These are the cities that have an extensive, cost-effective bus network. Buses are the backbone of the public transportation system, and dedicated bus lanes are a highly effective means of meeting the demand. In corridors with higher demand, there are economically efficient rail transportation systems.

Cities with the more effective systems are those that coordinate planning and investments, that integrate different forms of transportation, and that recognize the appropriate role of the government and the private sector. Finally, systems function best in those cities that have recognized the importance of implementing appropriate prices.

Transportation in Bogotá: Problems and Solutions

Israel Fainboim Yaker

The Problems

The people of Bogotá see transportation as the city's second biggest problem, less serious only than security. Traffic in many areas of the city is congested and, while volumes are extremely heavy, in many cases the congestion is caused or exacerbated by poor infrastructure and traffic management; roads are unpaved or in bad condition, sidewalks are non-existent, traffic lights are out of order or ignored, regulations are violated, and buses block traffic to pick up passengers. All these factors restrict mobility, a situation made worse by inadequate regulation and control of transportation companies and route assignment.

Traffic Outstrips Roads

Bogotá's population has grown rapidly during the last few decades. Average annual population growth between 1973 and 1993 was 4.6 percent, compared to 3.1 percent in Colombia as a whole. In-migration increased again during the second half of the 1990s, as people were displaced by violence and the agricultural crisis. An estimated 130,000 new people settle in Bogotá annually, resulting in a vast expansion of the city and growing mobility pressures. Simultaneously, automobiles grew sharply in number during the 1990s, with currency revaluation and tariff reduction under trade liberalization lowering vehicle prices and opening the market to all types of vehicles. The number of vehicles increased from nearly 404,000 in 1992 to over 617,000 in 1998 (Table 9.1), or about 60,000 new private vehicles a year. In addition, Bogotá has a far greater number of buses and taxis per inhabitant than other capital cities in Latin America.

At the same time, however, the construction of new roads during the last few years has been irregular, to the point where some analysts believe that the city's road plan might be as much as 20 years out of date. Quantitatively, road space has increased at an average of less than 1 percent a year. From fieldwork carried out in 1994 and 1998, Arturo Ardila (1998) has shown how traffic congestion has worsened, with speeds on some roads of under 5 kilometers per hour. Ardila measured the speed on roads into the central business district during the morning rush hour, finding that, in some sections, the average speed was lower than that of a pedestrian.

Table 9.1.   Number of Motor Vehicles in Santafé de Bogotá, 1990–98

Vehicle type	1990	1991	1992	1993	1994	1995	1996	1997	1998
Automobiles	179,878	189,655	208,803	n/a	307,642	330,555	352,123	375,098	399,572
Taxis[a]	38,048	40,380	48,345	n/a	–	–	–	–	–
Jeeps	35,818	38,949	42,611	n/a	49,692	52,936	56,754	60,847	62,235
Vans	48,150	50,055	59,264	n/a	73,666	78,839	85,639	91,861	98,535
Microbuses	1,599	1,930	1,615	n/a	1,509	2,371	2,648	2,957	3,303
Small buses	6,977	7,003	7,065	n/a	7,321	7,542	7,591	7,641	7,691
Buses	11,702	12,549	13,671	n/a	15,327	15,622	16,399	17,214	18,070
Trucks	16,114	16,458	17,132	n/a	18,308	18,647	19,249	19,870	20,511
Dump trucks	1,670	1,678	1,688	n/a	1,694	1,704	1,761	1,819	1,879
Mules	456	462	488	n/a	504	513	531	550	570
Others	3,850	3,855	3,275	n/a	3,573	3,520	2,898	2,387	1,965
Total	344,262	362,974	403,957	n/a	479,236	513,249	545,593	580,244	617,331

a. From 1994, taxis are included in the figure for automobiles. The estimated number of taxis for 1998 is approximately 60,000.
Source: Ministry of Transportation.

Congestion has forced workers to spend 50 percent more time on daily travel than workers in other cities of the same size.

Irrational use of road space makes this situation worse. According to the Master Transportation Plan of Bogotá, a total of 14.9 million journeys per day were completed in 1995, of which 77 percent were by motor vehicle. Of the total motorized journeys, 77 percent were by public transportation, occupying 27 percent of the road space; private vehicles and taxis generated 23 percent of motorized journeys, occupying 73 percent of the road space.

Infrastructure and Management Problems

The main cause of congestion is the weak institutional and administrative capacity of transport authorities, including financial resources; this is reflected in poor planning, maintenance, and operation of the system, reducing its effective capacity and intensifying congestion. This is made worse by specific problems such as badly timed traffic lights, accidents, bottlenecks, and potholes.

A transportation system is properly managed and operated when, among other factors, there is continuous maintenance of its components; an adequate signal system; an efficient traffic police; rapid response to accidents and breakdowns; a synchronized network of traffic lights; and early detection of specific problems in order to solve them effectively (Ardila 1998).

The signal system in Bogotá is deficient: the city has approximately 35,000 intersections; 10,000 kilometers of traffic lanes; 800 traffic lights; and over 100,000 signs, but all signalling is the responsibility of just three professionals (Ardila 1998). In many areas there are no directional signs and, where these do exist, their size and visibility is inadequate, especially at night. It is also common for traffic lights to replace a stop sign, where a more visible sign would be better.

A further problem is that, although police traffic control may have improved with the addition of national police manpower, the total force is still insufficient for the size of the transport system. In addition, accident response time is very slow.

Regulation and control of transportation companies and route assignment are weak. Even though the fare is very low and is not linked to distance traveled, service to the city's popular neighborhoods is poor, largely because of bad road access; at the same time, 90 percent of the bus routes are concentrated in just 14 high-demand corridors, where the infrastructure cannot support the high traffic density. Many areas of the city are therefore poorly served, while the central streets are oversupplied with routes.

The city's financial weakness has severely affected the functioning and development of the transportation system. Although tax reform was introduced in 1993, road maintenance was so poor that Bogotá's road network came close to destruction; a sustained rehabilitation project began only in 1997. New road building was delayed. Complete areas of the city were developed without adequate road infrastructure, overburdening the existing one. Such is the case of the western area of Bogotá, which was urbanized before the Ciudad de Cali and Longitudinal de Occidente avenues were completed. The result was an overload of the Avenida Boyaca, the only available alternative, that resulted in accelerated deterioration of the sidewalks (Ardila 1998). It should be noted that financial resources are still scarce, given the city's enormous needs and the huge demands imposed by the accrued delay of investment in road maintenance.

It is evident, then, that a principal cause of transportation problems in Bogotá is the lack of the government's ability to plan, administer, regulate, and operate the city's transportation system.

Proposed Solutions

The solution to the problems in Bogotá—and cities in general—must include at least four components:

- Constructing and maintaining a road network that meets specified standards;
- Discouraging private vehicle use;
- Building an integrated public transportation system that is coordinated and efficient; and
- Strengthening of the municipal authorities for transportation planning and regulation.

On the first component, it seems neither possible nor desirable to involve cities in costly projects of mass road expansion. For this reason, at the same time that road investment takes place, the indiscriminate use of private automobiles during rush hours and on the most congested roads must be discouraged. To support this goal, better quality public transportation is needed, as is more extensive use of price mechanisms to discourage private transportation and encourage the use of off-street parking. Parking fees in the central city have recently been raised (to increase the profitability of building parking structures); other mechanisms include the definition of exclusive parking zones (known in Bogotá as *Zonas Azules*, or Blue Zones) and, whenever possible, the imposition of urban tolls for cars. Also, as many cities in Colombia have confirmed, a surcharge on gasoline is an efficient instrument to increase the cost of car use and to capture resources for road works. Apart from price mechanisms, physical restrictions can also be adopted, such as prohibiting parking on main roads and public spaces (such as sidewalks, islands and medians, and lawns) with strict control through the use of tow trucks and steep fines.

Recently Adopted Solutions

During the administration of Mayor Mockus (1995–97), maintenance of the road network, previously the responsibility of the Secretary of Public Works, was turned over to a private company. At the same time, good driving behavior and respect for traffic regulations were encouraged through programs promoting the use of crossings and traffic signals, and the mandatory use of safety belts, and helmets and reflective vests for motorcyclists.

In addition, a technical cooperation package was negotiated with the government of Japan, to study the development of a "Master Urban Transportation Plan for Santafé de Bogotá." Carried out by the Japanese International Cooperation Agency, the study was completed in early 1997. A consortium formed by Ingetec (Columbia), Bechtel (United States), and Systra (France) was commissioned to develop a feasibility study for the "Conceptual Design of the Integrated System of Mass Transportation of the Bogotá Sabana–ITM (SITM)."

The SITM will combine integrated and hierarchical mass transportation networks: the Metro rail system will form the backbone, with bus routes on trunk roads, "structuring" bus routes, and flexible feeder routes. The system, to be developed over the next 18 years, includes three Metro rail lines, totaling 79 kilometers in length: Line 1 (1998–2006), 29.3 kilometers; Line 2 (2007–12), 24.7 kilometers; and Line 3 (2013–16), 24.8 kilometers. The other modes would be articulated and organized around these three lines. The plan for the lines and the location of stations would determine the transfer points and a reconfiguration of the bus routes (Mayor's Office of Santafé de Bogotá 1998).

The trunk routes would consist of priority infrastructure for high-capacity buses and transfer points onto the Metro system. The structuring routes would consist of bus stops and adequate signals for the operation of organized collective transportation services on the 120 kilometers of existing infrastructure; these routes would be an intermediate stage between the current system and the eventual operation of bus routes on exclusive lanes, with the Metro rail system. The feeding routes would cover the areas adjacent to Metro stations and the trunk road bus stops, and would supply pick-up and distribution, especially in residential areas. Finally, long-distance routes would provide service in the metropolitan region (Mayor's Office of Santafé de Bogotá 1998).

Three other transportation measures have been adopted. The first is vehicular restriction during rush hours (7:30–9:00 a.m. and 5:30–7:30 p.m., from Monday to Friday) according to license number. The restriction was initially welcomed by the citizens of Bogotá but was later criticized by transportation engineers (Ardila 1998). It penalizes demand, when in fact the problem lies with the inability to manage the system correctly. In the case of Bogotá, a measure of this nature forces people to use their vehicle more extensively during the permitted times. However, the municipal government claims that the measure has increased average vehicle speed from 14 to 30 kilometers per hour, and has reduced pollution levels by 16 percent.

The second measure is a master plan for bicycle routes. These routes are not only environmentally beneficial in not polluting; they also create greater safety for an alternative transportation system that is used by growing numbers of residents. The bicycle routes will be built on existing roads, sharing sidewalk space with pedestrians or sharing road space with cars, according to the area. The current administration of Mayor Penalosa wants to ensure that all new roads incorporate a bicycle route. The municipal government also extended by one hour the availability of "conditioned bicycle routes" on Sundays and holidays, and also expanded them geographically—a scheme strongly approved by citizens; these routes in-volve eliminating vehicular traffic on some of the main streets to allow their use by cyclists and other sports enthusiasts.

Finally, the district authorities developed a program to recover side-walk and road space by installing concrete bollards to prevent vehicles from parking in unauthorized areas; this faced opposition from the commercial sector and informal vendors, who attribute the recent deterio-ration in their sales to these recovery measures rather than to Colombia's economic crisis.

Construction of the Metro Rail System

Although construction of a Metro rail system in Bogotá has been debated con-tinuously since the mid-1970s, the city of Medellín overtook the capital by developing a Metro system that began operation in 1995. High densities in the center of Bogotá, dependence on public transportation, and the city's large proportion of low-income people make the rail system desirable. The first line will join vast poor residential areas to the city's expanded center, with its employment opportunities in the institutional and commercial sectors. The system could certainly have positive economic and social impacts, and it will also strengthen the central city and contribute to consolidating sub-centers.

The major benefits of the project lie in time savings for all transportation system users (not only users of the rail system), estimated at US$214 million a year at the beginning of the operation, and US$400 million a year for the tenth and subsequent years (Mayor's Office of Santafé de Bogotá 1998).

To finance these schemes, in 1996 the national Congress enacted legislation (Law 30) that facilitated the financing of urban public service systems for mass passenger transportation through central government contributions. In February, 1998, an agreement was made between the President of Colombia and the Mayor of Bogotá for building the SITM, and in particular the first Metro line (PLM), with the government committing resources equivalent to 70 percent of the investment cost, over 25 years. Also, the District Council introduced a gasoline surcharge as a mechanism to finance the Metro system, road maintenance, the road plan, and local paving works. The Metro project is now facing an obstacle, however, in the Colombian government's critical financial condition and the unsustainable trend in public finances over the medium term; the government is resisting the commitment of funds for construction of the system before its own fiscal problems are solved.

References

Acevedo, Jorge. 1994. "Bases de una politica de transporte urbano integral en Colombia." In *Politicas e Instruciones para el Desarrollo Urbano Futuro*. Bogotá: Ministry of Development.

Ardila, Arturo. 1998. "El problema del transporte en Bogotá: Diagnostico y perspectivas para el Metro." *Debates de Coyuntura Económica* no. 47, Fedesarrollo.

Mayor's Office of Santafé de Bogotá. 1998. "SITM—primera etapa de desarrollo, 1998–2006," *Debates de Coyuntura Económica* no. 47, Fedesarrollo.

A View of Urban Transport, Infrastructure, and Environment from the Female Condition

Jordi Borja and Manuel Castells

Although women are the primordial agents of linkage between household units and the urban structure, cities are usually developed and planned without taking account of the specific needs raised by such linkage.[1] Urban transport planning, for example, has traditionally focused on organizing patterns of mobility between the home and the workplace, which does not permit reflection of the diversity of journeys which women have to make in taking on their many daily tasks. A study of Belo Horizonte [in Brazil] found that urban transport was organized around the needs of men. Buses ran along routes from the outskirts into the city center at the beginning of the day, and from center to outskirts at the end of the working day, to transport the male workforce in regular employment. But the daily travel needs of women were much more diverse: taking the children to school, shopping, going to health services and, above all, reaching their part-time jobs over a wide spectrum of area and time, at times when there were no longer buses. This resulted in the daily traveling time of the women being three times longer than that of the men (Schmink 1982).

The case of the United States is paradigmatic. Equipped with one of the world's most highly developed transport systems—though one centered on the automobile—mobility in metropolitan areas has reached crisis point since, over the last two decades, women began a generalized taking up of employment (without leaving aside many of their previous responsibilities), coming into contradiction with a transport system organized around the needs of white middle-class males. As in the case of Brazil mentioned above, the urban mobility of the vast majority of men is structured around the journey between home and workplace. Women, on the other hand, must undertake different tasks and fit them all in on the trip to and from work, for which reason they need a much more flexible means of transport which is, nowadays, the car. The incorporation of women into employment has therefore multiplied the number of vehicles on the urban freeways, leading increasingly to their saturation. Transport statistics show that women

1. This excerpt from Jordi Borja and Manuel Castells, *Local and Global: The Management of Cities in the Information Age* (London: Earthscan, 1997, pp. 55–58) is reproduced with permission of Kogan Page Limited.

make many more intermediate stops than men along their routes between home and workplace (McKnight 1994). Furthermore, the traditional suburban model of the American city has entered functional crisis in that it was implicitly based on a full-time driver able to provide mobility for the entire family (taking the husband to the suburban railway station and picking him up after work, taking the children to and from school and their various activities, doing the shopping in large stores, carrying out the necessary paperwork and other procedures for the entire family at various points of the metropolitan structure). Only with this family mobility taken on individually by the housewife could the suburbs extend and ensure the daily life quality today yearned for by the middle-classes of many countries (even those that did not experience it, but contemplated it in the idealized view portrayed in Hollywood productions). But when those housewives became, in addition, workers with set times and places, American women could not continue to provide their services as family driver, and this situation meant a reconversion of the metropolitan transport structure in which connection between the suburbs, and not only the link between center and outskirts, enforced the construction of new freeways and the development of a denser fabric of collective intra-metropolitan transport.

Similar trends have been observed in European countries. A study carried out in France showed the influence of transport on women's work, chosen to cut distance from the home containing the children, to the care of whom mothers still devoted much of their attention. Thus, women with at least one child younger than 14 years had an average weekly traveling time to work of 3 hours and 15 minutes, compared with 4 hours and 5 minutes for women without young children, and 4 hours and 45 minutes for men (Grieco et al. 1989).

In short, the city of women is temporally and spatially diverse, calling for a flexible and dense transport structure, in contradiction with most metropolitan transport systems organized around the regulated working day of traditional male employment. However, as the economy, society and job market become increasingly oriented towards flexibility and diversification of times, spaces, and activities, there would seem to be some convergence between the interests inherent in the female condition and the most likely future outlook for urban transport.

References

Grieco, M., L. Pickup, and R. Whipp, eds. 1989. *Gender, Transport and Employment: The Impact of Travel Constraints.* Aldershot: Avebury.

McKnight, C. 1994. "Transportation with Women in Mind." *Journal of Urban Technology* 2(1).

Schmink, Marianne. 1982. "Women in the Urban Economy in Latin America." In various authors, *Women in Low-Income Households and Urban Services.* Coral Gables: University of Florida.

Integration of Urban Transport and Urban Planning

Robert Cervero

The Co-Dependence of Transport and Cities

Transportation infrastructure is vital to the economic growth and well-being of cities, particularly in developing parts of the world, where transport investments account for as much as 40 percent of public-sector expenditures (Button 1993; Leinbach 1995). Adequate transportation infrastructure is particularly important in the world's megacities, where motorization rates of 10 to 15 percent annually are not uncommon (Midgely 1994). The road capacities of megacities, however, have failed to keep pace with explosive increases in traffic, and worsening congestion threatens economic productivity and the overall quality of urban living. Because cities are often regarded as catalysts to modernization and economic expansion in the developing world, the economic standing of even small towns and rural settlements are hurt to some degree by congestion in big cities. Global levels of motorization are barely 10 percent of what is considered to be market saturation; thus, if the current infrastructure shortfall continues, the economic toll from traffic congestion can only be expected to worsen (International Institute for Energy Conservation 1996).

Transportation and cities are co-dependent, influencing each other in often complex and dynamic ways. It is less the hardware characteristics of roads and transit lines, and more the software characteristics—notably accessibility benefits—that shape urban environments. Opening up a new road to a greenfield spawns growth by making adjacent land parcels more accessible to other places. Transportation is a necessary, though hardly sufficient, prerequisite to new development. However, the relationship works in both directions. Land-use patterns and built environments shape the demand for travel (see reviews by Kelly 1994, Cervero and Seskin 1995, and Newman and Kenworthy 1997), and thoughtful planning can indeed reduce the need for motorized trips. Because of this co-dependency, carefully integrated and coordinated transportation and urban development is essential to a sustainable future—environmentally, and also socially and economically.

A fundamental principle that pervades the field of transport and land-use planning is *derived demand*—we do not travel for its own sake, but rather to reach places. Travel is derived from social and economic needs—to see friends, buy groceries, or go to work. Thus, it is how we arrange physical space and organize urban activities that sets the stage for trip-making. In a normative sense, transportation should be subservient to urban environments, a means to achieving broader personal and societal objectives—earning a living or creating livable communities.

Even though transportation and urbanization co-exist as a "two-way street," my focus here is on one direction of the flow: how transport affects urban development.

Integrating Transport and Land Use in a Diverse World

Increasingly, transportation must serve an urban landscape that is more and more diverse and complex, due to a host of powerful trends and mega-forces, such as economic globalization and technological advances. In the realm of transport and urbanization, these trends get expressed as a msore diverse spatial, temporal, and demographic context. Information technologies, for instance, have not only liberated more and more people from the need to be physically in one place but have also—through spawning just-in-time forms of manufacturing, nurturing new forms of economic production like flexible specialization and outsourcing, and expanding social networks—spread out the temporal distribution of trips. Increasing demographic diversity is seen in the stepped-up role of women in the workplace. Women's greater need to chain trips between work, childcare centers, grocery stores, and home force many to drive. Increasingly, the odds of getting stuck in a traffic jam are as great at midday or weekends as at the traditional morning and evening peak hours. In June of 1996, São Paulo set a new traffic congestion record with 150 miles of clogged roads.

Put another way, the world's cities—led by rising affluence, advancing technologies, and other mega-forces—have been transformed from a predominant monocentric form well suited to point-to-point rail systems, to polycentric forms more conducive to flexible, rubber-tired mass transport, and increasingly to what might be called a cybermetropolis where the alternatives to automobility are few.

One of these changing dimensions, with broad transportation and environmental implications, is suburbanization and exurbanization. Vehicle kilometers of travel (VKT) per capita, what many consider an important benchmark of sustainable transport—land use arrangements, typically increases as growth spreads out and average densities fall, because of longer trips, more motorized trips (e.g., increased auto dependence), and lower average vehicle occupancies (more solo-driving and less transit—"mass" transit requires "mass," or density).

The lengthening of trips has been universal. A study of 11 large European cities found average work trip lengths increased from 8.1 kilometers in 1980 to 9.6 kilometers in 1990, an 18.5 percent rise (Newman, Kenworthy, and Laube 1997). In Shanghai, journeys-to-work lengthened, on average, from 6.2 kilometers in 1981 to 8.1 kilometers 10 years later (Shen 1997). Because longer trips generally induce more private motorization, the environmental repercussions are worrisome. Santiago's steadily worsening air quality (norms are violated roughly half the days of each year) is tied to longer journeys; trip distances are rising by 1.3 percent a year. Longer trips have increased automobile dependence—motorized travel per person in greater Santiago doubled between 1977 and 1991, and the automobile's mode share has risen from 10 percent in 1977 to 25 percent today (Zegras 1998). During the 1980s, Santiago's urbanized area expanded by 20 percent, reducing the amount of productive agricultural land in the metropolitan area by over 60 percent.

Spatially, trips are also becoming increasingly scattered across many origins and destinations, a pattern that is hardly conducive to riding point-to-point systems like mass transit. Increasingly, the geography of travel (tangential) and the geometry of traditional regional transportation infrastructure (radial) do not match, producing trip circuity and giving rise to "suburban gridlock" (Cervero 1986).

There are serious concerns over the long-term sustainability of this pathway. Only an estimated 8 percent of the world's population presently owns a car. If developing countries begin to approach private automobile use in the developed world, the strains placed on natural and social environments will be unprecedented. The spread of German and U.S. automobile ownership rates (respectively 520 and 750 vehicles per 1,000 inhabitants) to the citizens of Poland, Russia, India, Indonesia, and China could wreak havoc on the globe's finite resources.

Of course, rising motorization is rooted in many factors beyond sprawl. Lima's vehicle population soared when the Peruvian government relaxed import restrictions in the early 1990s. From 1992 to 1995, the number of commuter vans jumped from 6,000 to 47,000. In Bogotá, Colombia, the lowering of import tariffs contributed to a 12 percent annual increase in vehicle registration, yet the road system has remained virtually unchanged over the past two decades. A rush-hour cross-town trip in Bogotá can today take up to three hours (Varella 1996). Brazil's anti-inflation plan has allowed many lower-income households to buy a vehicle for the first time, triggering a meteoric rise in car ownership, on the order of 12 to 15 percent annually in São Paulo and Brazilia during the mid-1990s. The need for carefully integrating transport and urbanization has never been greater.

The Transport-Land Use Nexus: What We Expect, What We Find

Infrastructure investment is one of several tools available to the public sector for shaping urban development patterns and controlling growth. Other strategies include regulation (e.g., zoning, growth boundaries), tax policies (e.g., enterprise zones) and land acquisitions. Circumstances vary as to which of these tools most powerfully shapes urbanization; however, among forms of infrastructure, transport is considered to be the strongest city-shaper.

Transportation investments induce growth for one reason only: they improve accessibility—the opportunity to reach places efficiently. A new light-rail station provides a struggling inner-city neighborhood with more customers for its shops, access to job opportunities, friends, etc. Accessible places enjoy locational advantages. It is peoples' desire for locational advantage (and real estate developers' awareness of this preference) that gives rise to urban form. Thus, the outcome of transport investments—enhanced accessibility—rather than the hardware itself is what drives urban development.

Transportation affects physical development in four key ways: *locations; intensities; compositions;* and *values* of land uses and urban activities. Our understanding of how, why, and to what extent transportation investments affect these physical dimensions of cities is rooted in traditional urban location theory (Alonso 1964; Muth 1969). This theory holds that people and institutions search out accessible locations so as to minimize transportation costs and maximize, in the case of households, housing and lifestyle preferences and, in the case of businesses and firms, profitability.

For the most part, theory is borne out by actual experience. Capital-intensive improvements like new rail systems and high-performance, grade-separated expressways exert the greatest land-use impacts because: they deliver the greatest incremental gains in regional accessibility; and as fixed, sunk investments, they are location-specific, providing clear, predictable signals to developers. Non-capital improvements—like operational changes to one-way streets and traffic-calming —exert fewer land-use impacts because their relatively marginal accessibility gains are never guaranteed (e.g., bus services can be cut back).

Rail Transit: Theory

Assume a new light-rail line is built along a fast-growing corridor, and the bold decision is made to provide only modest amounts of park-and-ride lots and to zone nearby land permissively to accommodate whatever the market will bear. Classical location theory holds that businesses and residents who might otherwise have gravitated toward a highway corridor might capitalize on the improvements in accessibility by locating near transit stops. Stations are the gateways between a neighborhood and the surrounding region. Because of their accessibility advantages, they function like magnets, producing clustered patterns of growth. Overall, real estate conditions around the station should be healthy—high rents, high space absorption, and low vacancy rates. Offices and shops will often command the choicest sites near stations, outbidding others. Ancillary, or business-serving, land uses will seek to be as near offices as possible, and a few blocks farther on might be apartments and duplexes; and, of course, where residents locate, so do convenience shops, grocery stores, movie theaters, and other "population-serving" activities that cater to them. In short, a light-rail investment should, in time, spawn clustered, mixed-use, higher rent land development within a half-kilometer or so radius of the station. The same activities that traditionally are scattered throughout the suburban landscape are instead huddled near rail transit's chief access points—stations. It is this very notion that rail stations are "under-exploited" assets that can function as nodes for targeting growth that has given rise to the "transit village" movement in states like California, New Jersey, and Oregon (Bernick and Cervero 1997).

Rail Transit: Experiences

For the most part, these expected outcomes of rail investments are borne out. Experiences in Toronto and the San Francisco Bay Area show that, under the right conditions, rail investments strengthen urban centers, promote subcentering, induce significant property-value increases within station catchment areas, and occasionally spawn reinvestment into once-declining urban districts (Huang 1996; Cervero 1998). As the marginal accessibility benefits of new rail tend to be greater in highly congested megacities in rapidly growing areas, so too do the land-use impacts. Land-constrained cities like Hong Kong and Singapore simply could not support their extremely high-rise development patterns—and what some argue are the resulting economic agglomeration benefits—were it not for underground rail systems and their surface feeder connections (Tong and Wong 1997; Prud'homme and Lee 1998). An important feature of these well-managed cities is close integration of rail transit and urbanization—

such as air-rights development above subway lines and vertical mixing of uses within buildings. Office rents for buildings served by Hong Kong's rail system have increased at double the rate of comparable office buildings in the central business district (Meakin 1990).

Highway and Freeway Improvements: Theory

What if a freeway, rather than a light rail line, were to be built along the same hypothetical corridor as outlined above? Impacts will likely be similar, but the physical form of land-use changes are apt to be much different. As with a transit stop, activities focus on the main access point, the freeway interchange. Higher-end commercial activities, like regional shopping malls and entertainment centers, often congregate up to two kilometers from the interchange, for several reasons: they can amass more land more cheaply; the same vehicle—the automobile—is used as both feeder and line-hauler to and from the freeway, relieving the need (unlike transit) to be right at the regional access point; and they are better buffered from the negative externalities of car and truck traffic. Thus, a notable difference between rail and highway improvements is that highest-end land uses typically cluster at the premium access point in the former case, but not in the latter.

Highway and Freeway Improvements: Experiences

Research suggests the land-value impacts of urban highways tend to be redistributive—prices increase in areas previously not very accessible, yet fall in areas historically well served by roads (Fujita 1989). Overall, the value-added per square meter from new roads is considerably less than from a rail system; however, because accessibility gains tend to be spread over a much larger geographic area, the aggregate benefits of road improvements tend to exceed those of rail projects—not surprising given that personal-vehicle travel normally comprises a much larger share of regional trip-making than does public transport, at least in the developed world where most research has been conducted.

While road improvements bring about more diffuse and segregated patterns of land development, it is not accurate to say that major roadways simply induce sprawl (thinly spread, skipped-over, scattershot development). On balance, major road projects bring about concentrated forms of decentralized growth, such as clusters of office parks and shopping malls. Today, there are generally fewer one-room school houses, "mom-and-pop" corner stores, and health clinics than a century ago. Many such activities have congregated in large-scale mega-complexes, well served by roadways and often enveloped by parking. However, land-use activities in many auto-oriented regional centers are not often well integrated.

Impacts on Regional Economic Productivity

Considerable controversy remains over the development impacts of road improvements in two areas: whether they induce real economic growth; and whether they function more as a "lead" or a "lag" factor with respect to growth.

Because transportation functions as an intermediate input into the production process, in theory roads that reduce travel times (e.g., for workers, raw materials, or product distribution) should lower output costs and increase economic productivity. Research suggests, however, that, at least in advanced economies, individual transportation projects fail to tip the scales in favor of generating new investments or attracting new businesses to a region. The net economic impacts of urban transportation infrastructure investments tend to be *redistributive* as opposed to *generative*. While impacts may amount to spatial shifts, this does not diminish the fact that highway improvements can give a region a competitive edge in economic development.

Studies of regional variations in economic performance suggest the effect of public transport investments are stronger in more rapidly growing regions than in those that are declining (Mera 1973; Eberts 1986; Kessides 1993). The same generally holds for road improvements. Shah (1990) examined the impacts of public capital, including transport and communications, on the productivity of 34 private-sector industries in Mexico from 1970 to 1983. He found that *ex post* rates of return to the industrial sector from public investments in infrastructure ranged from 5.5 to 7.3 percent, similar to rates of return from private capital. Studies of Seoul and Bogotá have shown that city centers with good infrastructure can serve as "incubators" for the growth of new industries, particularly small and medium-size firms that cannot afford the capital cost of providing their own infrastructure (Lee 1985; 1989). Productivity benefits also accrue from enlargement of the effective laborshed and "transactive space" of metropolitan areas, and lowering indirect costs, such as for product marketing (which in some emerging areas can be 25 to 60 percent of final prices) (Creightney 1993); and from the creation of positive spillovers to surrounding suburbs, exurbs, and rural hinterlands (e.g., improved access to institutional credit, technological diffusion, and reduced farm-to-market transactive costs). Evans (1990) argues that transport infrastructure is most effective where it can strengthen and spur exchanges among settlements, such as between rural areas and urban markets. Highways depend, as does transit, on other supportive factors, such as zoning, to help leverage their influence, quite often with impacts accruing over extended periods.

Non-Capital Improvements: Systems and Demand Management

Many supply-management programs, like synchronizing traffic signals, aim to expedite traffic flows. They enhance mobility, often at the expense of reducing site accessibility along corridors, producing redistributive land-use impacts. In the case of one-way streets, properties adjacent to fast-moving lanes often disbenefit, expressed in terms of lower property values. It is often activity centers connected by one-way couplets (that enjoy the greatest accessibility gains) that reap the greatest benefits, such as increased retail sales and higher rents. Similarly, traffic calming measures, such as speed bumps and curvilinear road alignments, exert largely redistributive impacts—residential neighborhoods experiencing less through-traffic gain (e.g., less noise, safer environments) and those receiving the diverted traffic tend to be worse off. However, traffic management schemes can be more than a zero-sum game if the deflected traffic goes to corridors where adjacent land uses benefit from its presence—namely, commercial districts. Indeed, much of the success with pedestrian zones and traffic calming in Europe lies in diverted traffic being channeled to commercial districts and inner-city beltloops (Hass-Klau 1993). Recent research suggests that withdrawing road capacity can cause as much as a 25 percent "evaporation" in motorized traffic, as former motorists switch to buses, trains, bicycles, walking, and tele-travel (Goodwin, Hass-Klau, and Cairns 1998).

If there is any central lesson to be learned from transportation investments, it is that land-use benefits are not automatic, even in the best of circumstances. Notably, there is a role for pro-activism within the public sector—to help "prime the development pump" by providing clear signals regarding long-term regional growth objectives, and rewarding good development through supportive infrastructure improvements, zoning, and risk-sharing.

The Institutional Context for Coordinating Transport and Urbanization

The need for pro-activism is underscored by the many inherent difficulties of coordinating transport and urban development. Regional land-use patterns—which set the stage for travel—are quite often the product of local, incremental decisions on where to locate a new shopping plaza, whether to rezone a particular land parcel, and so on. Rarely do these decisions shape into a coherent vision of the future. One of many institutional impediments to transportation-land use coordination is the mismatch between where decisions on land development are made—locally—and where the transportation impacts are felt—regionally. The effects of poor coordination get played out all too often as inefficiencies, negative spillovers, and fiscal disparities.

Ideally, jurisdiction over transport and land-use matters would match commutersheds—similar to the regional context in which water resources (watersheds) and air resources (airsheds) planning occurs. In practice, decision-making is fragmented across many jurisdictions and service providers. In Bangkok, for instance, over 30 government agencies are responsible for the city's transportation policy, management, and operations. Where private operators dominate the local transit scene, coordination is excruciatingly difficult. In Rio de Janeiro, over 60 private bus companies currently serve the city. Fragmentation not only produces inefficiencies and duplication, but also leads to uncoordinated services and, quite often, fare structures that penalize those who must transfer across transit systems. It also invites stagnation. Like Rio, São Paulo is stymied by institutional inertia. The city's last comprehensive plan was drawn up in 1968, calling for 100 kilometers of new metro rail lines and 135 kilometers of new freeways. Since the plan, not a single freeway, and only 43 kilometers of rail line, have been added. São Paulo's traffic engineers estimate that, on a typical day, traffic jams extend for 85 kilometers across the city; over an entire year this costs residents some US$10 billion in time delays.

There are other institutional impediments to effective coordination of transport and land use, such as differences in the pace of change. Local and subregional growth often occurs incrementally, in fits and starts. Land-use maps are continuously changing because of zoning amendments, variances, and new subdivisions. In contrast, decisions on regionally important transportation improvements often occur in two-to-three-year time increments, and are hard to reverse or change in response to unfolding land-use patterns. Thus, whereas land-use changes are fluid and on-going, large-scale transportation projects tend to be rigid, and occur over much longer time horizons.

Also hampering coordination is the reality that the benefits of careful transport-land use integration are often not evident for a decade or more. This is inherently at odds with political systems that demand short-term payments. Elected officials are much more likely to embrace a large-scale road project that immediately relieves congestion and generates lots of jobs, than transit villages, jobs-housing balance, New Urbanism, and other longer-term urban planning strategies.

The following case studies highlight institutional issues as well as important dimensions of transport and land-use co-development. The first, on Mexico City, examines the niche-market roles played between the public and private sectors, especially where little effort is made to manage growth regionally. The second, on Jakarta, reviews institutional challenges of recapturing land-value benefits of road improvements in the effort to rationalize road finance.

Integration of Transport and the Spread-Out Metropolis: Mexico City

As one of the world's largest metropolises, Mexico City poses unparalleled mobility challenges, with an official 1990 population of 15.1 million and an unofficial one of well over 20 million. About one-quarter of Mexico's population resides in greater Mexico City, which covers just 1 percent of the country's surface area.

Nearly 3 million private automobiles are registered in the metropolis, and vehicle ownership has risen at least twice as fast as the region's 2.5 percent annual population growth rate. During peak hours, traffic crawls at an average speed of 9 kilometers per hour. The crush of automobiles has produced some of the worst smog conditions anywhere, exacerbated by mountains that ring the valley and contain the pollutants. The Federal District has imposed a "Days off the Road" scheme that restricts vehicles from operating at least one day a week, according to the last digit of license plates. Studies suggest, however, this strategy has been counterproductive by spawning a market for cheap, second-hand vehicles (for use on banned days) that are the worst pollution offenders (Eskeland and Feyzioglu 1997; Wirth 1997).

Hierarchical Public Transport

Mexico City's congestion and pollution would be much worse without the dynamic and wide-ranging transportation system that has evolved in response to explosive growth. Notably, a hierarchy of transportation services—both public and private—has emerged, providing a rich mix of travel options in terms of geographic coverage, vehicle carrying capacities, and levels of integration. At the top of the hierarchy and forming the backbone of the network is the Metro, whose nine lines crisscross the District, totaling 158 kilometers of guideway and 135 stations. With average peak-hour headways of around a minute, and daily ridership nearing 5 million, Metro is one of the most extensive and highly patronized rail transit systems in the world (larger in size and claiming more riders than all others in Latin America combined).

Equally vital have been the network's capillaries—the extensive system of paratransit feeder services, known locally as *peseros* and *colectivos*—23-seat minibuses that burn unleaded fuel. Presently, there are about 100 paratransit routes in Mexico City, and each route averages around 15 deviations or branches. Paratransit has emerged as an indispensable feature of Mexico City's transportation landscape, in many ways the workhorse of public transport. *Colectivos*, *peseros*, and taxis today handle around 40 percent of motorized trips in the Federal District, and 37 percent of trips in the State of Mexico.

What has evolved is a hub-and-spoke transport network that closely mimics predominant travel patterns, and facilitates transfers. Institutionally, the arrangement has clear lines of responsibility—government is the provider of mainline services, and the private sector takes care of branch connections. However, supplementing the private paratransit sector, though more in the background, have been several publicly supported surface transportation modes—notably, the Ruta–100 bus network (recently returned to private concessionaires), 19 trolleybus lines, and the 30-kilometer Tren Ligero light rail system. Hierarchically, these public surface routes function more as distributors, filling in mainline service gaps of the Metro and serving more intermediate-distance trips.

While Mexico City's paratransit sector is nominally regulated, the sector is self-policed through route associations that secure authorizations for branch routes and organize the allocation of vehicles on these routes, assist owner-members in obtaining vehicle loans from banks and the government, settle accident claims, and represent members in dealings with government officials. These have become indispensable organizations for coordinating and rationalizing paratransit service delivery, while protecting and promoting the interests of their members.

Responding to, Rather than Shaping, Urban Form

As to land-use implications, Mexico City presents a context where the inter-workings of the marketplace have shaped urban form, and transport's role has been to respond to, and serve, the unfolding settlement patterns. Over the past several decades, the network of radial rail lines and branching paratransit feeder services has allowed a spread-out, polycentric metropolis to take shape, relieving pressure on, yet maintaining the pre-eminence of, the central core. While not an example of transport-shaped urbanization, nonetheless the region enjoys a gloved-hand fit between existing regional transport services and the regional settlement pattern.

To date, there has been little clustering of urban development around Metro stations. Except for a few downtown skyscrapers that pre-date the Metro project, Mexico City's urban density gradient does not noticeably rise near subway portals. Only a few outlying stations have spurred new office construction, a result of pro-active planning. Such leveraging of private development has been rare, however, because Mexico City has had neither the institutional capacity nor the luxury of doing advance master planning—urbanization has occurred so rapidly that government concentrates on immediate needs. Limited land-use controls have produced a hodge-podge of commercial activities around stations—small restaurants, repair shops, and street vendors—which, coupled with other perceived nuisances, like street peddlers and swarms of *colectivos*, have deterred middle-class housing construction.

Decentralization Trends

Metro's greatest impact on urban form has been to further spur decentralization. Rich and poor communities alike have taken form near and beyond Metro's terminal stations over the past several decades. In a largely unregulated regional land market, the combination of relatively cheap peripheral land, proximity to Metro's outer reaches, and less crowded conditions has led to mammoth new town developments on the fringes. To the south and west, new towns, like San Angel and Bosque, cater mostly to the region's burgeoning middle and upper-middle classes. To the east and west, often downwind from industrial belts, are large concentrations of unskilled laborers, poor households, and rural in-migrants. Some of the region's densest and poorest municipalities, like Netzahualcoyotl and Tlalnepantla, border the Federal District. Metro's busiest stations—Indios Verdes and Pantitlan, each handling 170,000 to 190,000 customers a day—mostly serve the factories and residents of these poor outlying areas. The high dependency of the peripheral poor on Metro services results in a predominantly captive ridership: over half of Metro's passengers earn below minimum wage, and only one in eight has access to an automobile (Benitez 1993).

Decentralization has resulted in exceedingly long average trip times—in 1994, 46 minutes for the region as a whole, and 53.5 minutes for those residing outside the Federal District. The Mexican government has announced plans to significantly extend Metro services: new extensions and lines will add 31 kilometers by the year 2003. And by 2020, if all goes according to plan, 27 Metro lines—a combination of subways and elevated commuter tracks—will weave an elaborate pattern across the metropolitan landscape, more than doubling Metro's current trackage. These announcements have brought on fears that Metro expansions will only fan the flames of galloping sprawl. A consequence of spread-out development has been high rates of intermodal transfer—35 percent of regional trips in 1994 involved a change from one mode to another (INEGI 1994). In the absence of a regional transportation authority, owing mainly to political squabbling, there has been very little coordination of intermodal services. One finds the greatest degree of service coordination in the private transport sector, mainly in the form of route associations. It has required the natural workings of the marketplace in a loosely regulated paratransit sector to close the coordination gap.

Capitalizing on Freeway Investments: Jakarta, Indonesia

Jakarta, Indonesia's capital city with a metropolitan population of 17 million, has embarked upon one of the most ambitious road-building programs anywhere. Much of the region's road development has been financed through BOT arrangements between the Indonesian government and foreign investors. While toll revenues are being used to pay off construction bonds, public-private co-sponsorship has also been motivated by the prospect of value capture.

Recent research that I conducted with a student (Cervero and Susantono 1999) suggests that road access substantially enhances the value of commercial property in Jakarta, with proximity to freeway interchanges being meaningfully capitalized into office rents. Capitalization effects provide opportunities for improving road finance. Returning portions of the capitalized value-added from road or transit improvements stands as an efficient and fair means of partly covering public expenditures for new capital facilities (Mohring 1961).

Betterment taxes have generated substantial amounts for local road development in Bogotá for several decades, but so far have met with resistance in other parts of the developing world (Bahl and Linn 1992). In fact, Jakarta has had a betterment tax, called *Pajak Khusus,* on the books since 1972; it allows city authorities to recover 60 percent of the estimated cost of new and improved infrastructure, but *Pajak Khusus* has not lived up to its expectations. Overall receipts dropped sharply from about US$500,000 in 1983 to under $20,000 a year during the mid-1990s. While tax objects (i.e., benefiting properties) could be easily identified, often tax subjects (i.e., legal landowners) could not. Even when landowners are identifiable, *Pajak Khusus* has suffered from lax administration, such as delays in sending out tax payment notices, and corrupt practices among poorly paid civil servants. Collecting money from low-income households has also been nearly impossible. While on paper landholders might be financially better off as a result of a road, unless they sell their land or engage in viable commercial ventures that benefit from improved accessibility, many have no liquid assets or cash.

For these reasons, the focus of betterment taxes in places like Jakarta should shift from residential neighborhoods to fast-growing commercial districts. Because offices are often the "highest and best" land uses, our research disclosed that they tend to reap the greatest dividends from accessibility improvements. From a practicable standpoint, therefore, it would be easier to implement a betterment tax program target at commercial-office uses, if for no other reason than the fact that compared to residences they are far fewer in number and are universally part of the official land registry. Moreover, recent transportation improvements in megacities often focus on rapidly growing commercial districts, making these areas more easily identifiable as the beneficiaries of new infrastructure. And, in terms of ability-to-pay equity criteria, betterment taxes targeted at high-end office land uses would rate highly. While they would raise the cost of offices doing businesses in Jakarta, the resulting accessibility gains (as suggested by significant capitalization) would more than offset these costs, making cities more competitive in the global marketplace.

Rationalizing road financing is especially important in countries like Indonesia, for past road finance policies have directly contributed to the nation's recent economic downturn. In 1994, Indonesia was spending over US$1 billion a year on road construction and oil, considerably more than it was receiving from road-user revenues and domestic oil sales. The difference was covered by government borrowing. Over the two decades prior to the present economic crisis, Indonesia borrowed more than US$6 billion in foreign exchange from multilateral and bilateral aid agencies just for road projects (Hook 1998). Also, private toll-road companies borrowed heavily from private banks. When Indonesia's rupiah collapsed in 1997, the cost of repaying this debt in foreign exchange skyrocketed, leaving the nation's road construction program in a dire financial condition. Value-based finance—derived from closely coordinating land and transport development—is especially needed in fast-growing megacities like Jakarta in order to place road finance on a more fiscally sound and equitable footing.

Paradigm Shift: Toward Accessibility Planning

The dominant urban planning model of modern, industrialized societies has been one of maximizing personal mobility. It is questionable whether this paradigm is sustainable. There needs to be a shift away from mobility-based planning toward a focus on accessibility. Replacing auto-mobility planning with accessibility planning means that social considerations take precedence over individualistic ones. It also recognizes what cities are about—first and foremost *people* and *places*, not *movement*. Efficient, well-managed cities minimize the need to travel, enabling residents to spend time more productively than fighting traffic. Accessible communities bring activities closer together by in-filling, inter-mixing land uses, and promoting tele-travel. Broadening our objectives to include accessibility inescapably leads to a wider array of approaches to physical planning, including better land-use management.

Table 9.2 contrasts different transport planning approaches when objectives are framed in terms of enhancing accessibility rather than auto-mobility. Planning for personal mobility works on the *supply side*, aiming to increase the speed and ease (and in so doing, the amount of energy consumption and emissions) of moving about the spread-out city. Accessibility planning, on the other hand, emphasizes *demand management*. It recognizes that new roads unleash new trips and thus provide only ephemeral congestion relief. Instead, it seeks to manage physical space and resources so as to avoid or minimize motorized travel and, where motorized trips are made, to reward travel by efficient and more environmentally sustainable modes. Auto-mobility planning focuses on the individual's movement, while accessibility planning focuses on the good of the community, making physical movement subservient to the city and the places within it.

Today, few, if any, metropolitan areas are carefully tracking trends in regional accessibility as part of their long-range comprehensive planning. This raises both efficiency and equity concerns. Without explicit attention to accessibility trends, it is unclear whether resource allocation decisions are cumulatively, over time, helping to promote broader environmental and societal goals, such as containing VKT per capita.

So far, the Netherlands has made the most headway in reforming regional transportation planning to give equal emphasis to accessibility and mobility. Dutch planners draw *mobility profiles* for new businesses, that define the amount and type of traffic likely to be generated. They also classify various locations within a city according to their *accessibility levels*. For

Table 9.2.   Transportation Mitigation Approaches Under Contrasting Planning Paradigms

Auto-mobility planning	*Accessiblity planning*
Road construction/expansion	*Land use management/initiatives*
Motorways/freeways	Compact development
Beltways	Mixed uses
Interchanges/rotaries	Pedestrian-oriented design
Hierarchical networks	Transit villages
Arterial expansion	Traditional neighborhoods/ new urbanism
Intelligent transportation systems/ smart highways/smart cars	*Telecommunication advances*
On-board navigational systems	Telecommuting/teleworking
Vehicle positioning systems	Telecommunities
Real-time informational systems	Teleshopping
Transportation system management (TSM)	*Transportation demand management (TDM)*
One-waying streets	Ridesharing
Rechannelizing intersections	Preferential parking for HOVs[a]
Removing curbside parking	Car parking management and pricing
Ramp metering	Guaranteed ride home programs
Large-scale public and private transport	*Community-scale public and non-motorized transport*
Heavy rail transit/commuter rail	Light rail transit/trams
Regional busways	Community-based paratransit/ jitneys
Private tollways	Bicycle and pedestrian paths

a. High-occupancy vehicles
Source: Author.

example, "A-locations" that are well served by public transport, that are connected to nearby neighborhoods by bicycle paths, and that feature mixes of retail shops, receive high accessibility marks. Such locations are targeted for land uses that generate steady streams of traffic, like college campuses, shopping plazas, and public offices. More remote areas that can be conveniently reached only by motorized transport tend to be assigned land uses that need not be easily accessible by the general public, like warehouses and factories. Thus, to make sure the right businesses get in the right location, Dutch planners see to it that the mobility profile of a new business matches the accessibility profile of a neighborhood.

Recently, the United Kingdom has also embraced the principle of accessibility. A study that contrasted the travel behavior of two fundamentally different new towns—the unabashedly auto-centric new town of Milton Keynes and the more walkable scale and bicycle-friendly Dutch new town of Almere—revealed that physical landscapes can exert a very strong impression on travel choices; whereas nearly half of all trips by Almere residents were by bicycling or walking, in Milton Keynes only one in five were non-motorized (Roberts and Wood 1992). In response, the British Ministries of Transport and Environment issued a joint guideline that requires localities to adopt policies that will promote re-urbanization, site major activity centers in urban cores, and promote alternative modes, including walking, bicycling, and public transport.

In an ideal world, of course, such centralized planning initiatives would be unnecessary, because land uses with the greatest accessibility needs would outbid all others for the most accessible sites, and many activities would co-locate to minimize travel. However, frictions to efficiently performing markets, like exclusionary zoning, neighborhood opposition to infill development, underpricing of automobile travel, and fiscalization of land uses, often require pro-active government responses. In many countries, pro-active land-use planning is needed as a "second-best" means of bringing about more efficient and sustainable patterns of urbanization in view of the inability to price resources (e.g., land, clean air, travel time) at their true social costs.

Whether the past 150 years of accommodating urban decentralization, and the enhanced mobility it requires, is sustainable for another 150 years is uncertain. Mobility planning needs to give way to accessibility planning as the dominant planning paradigm of the twenty-first century. Making this transition, however, will not be easy. In recent years, billions of dollars have been spent worldwide on making roadways and cars smarter, relying on the kind of technology and intelligence gathering once reserved for tactical warfare. New-age technologies could very well spell a future of even greater automobile reliance and an even more spread-out cityscape. Continuing advances in information technologies, telecommunications, and internet commerce are apt to decentralize growth further; this, according to most thoughtful observers, could very well end, on balance, by stimulating physical travel more than substituting for it (Castells 1997).

The difference between advancing these costly technologies as opposed to designing new kinds of sustainable communities is the difference between auto-mobility and accessibility. Auto-mobility is about physical movement. Accessibility, in contrast, is about creating places that reduce the need to travel and, in so doing, help to conserve resources, protect the environment, and promote social justice. As reported in their timely book, *Factor Four: Doubling Wealth—Halving Resource Use*, Ernst von Weizsäcker, Amory Lovins, and L. Hunter Lovins (1997) show that initiatives that enhance accessibility—from the creation of car-free communities to the integration of urbanization with busways—not only conserve resources but also increase economic productivity as well. When complemented by other resource-conserving policies, like the use of more water-conserving electrical appliances, and passive solar heating, efficiency-minded physical planning and conservation steps work together to promote social and economic, as well as environmental, sustainability.

References

Alonso, W. 1964. *Location and Land Use.* Cambridge, MA: Harvard University Press.

Bahl, R., and J. Linn. 1992. *Urban Public Finance in Developing Countries.* Oxford: Oxford University Press.

Benitez, B. 1993. *Ciudad de Mexico: El Metro y Sus Usuarios.* Mexico City: Universidad Autónoma Metropolitana.

Bernick, M., and R. Cervero. 1997. *Transit Villages in the 21st Century.* New York: McGraw-Hill.

Button, K. 1993. *Transport Economics.* Aldershot, UK: Elgar.

Castells, M. 1997. *The Information Age: Economy, Society and Culture.* Cambridge, MA: Blackwell.

Cervero, R. 1986. *Suburban Gridlock.* New Brunswick, NJ: Center for Urban Policy Research.

Cervero, R. 1998. *The Transit Metropolis.* Washington, DC: Island Press.

Cervero R., and S. Sesskin. 1995. *Transit and Urban Form.* Washington, DC: National Research Council, Transportation Research Board.

Cervero, R., and B. Susantono. 1999. "Rent Capitalization and Transportation Infrastructure Development in Jakarta." *Review of Urban and Regional Development Studies* 11(1): 11–23.

Creightney, C. 1993. *Transport and Economic Performance: A Survey of Developing Countries.* Washington, DC: World Bank.

Eberts, R. 1986. *Estimating the Contribution of Urban Public Infrastructure to Regional Growth*. Working Paper No. 8610. Cleveland, OH: Federal Reserve Bank.

Eskeland, G., and T. Feyzioglu. 1997. "Rationing Can Backfire: The 'Day without a Car' in Mexico City. *World Bank Economic Review* 11(3): 383–408.

Evans, H. 1990. *Rural-Urban Linkages and Structural Transformation*. Discussion Paper No. INU 71. Washington, DC: World Bank.

Fujita, M. 1989. *Urban Economic Theory: Land Use and City Size*. Cambridge, England: Cambridge University Press, 1989.

Goodwin, P., C. Hass-Klau, and S. Cairns. 1998. "Evidence on the Effects of Road Capacity Reduction on Traffic Levels." *Traffic Engineering Control* July: 348–54.

Hass-Klau, C. 1993. "Impact of Pedestrianization and Traffic Calming." *Transport Policy* 1(1): 21–31.

Hook, W. 1998. "Hurdles to Easing Congestion in Asia." *Habitat Debate* 4(2): 20–21.

Huang, H. 1996. "The Land-Use Impacts of Urban Rail Transit Systems." *Journal of Planning Literature* 11(1): 17–30.

INEGI (Instituto Nacional de Estadistica Geografia e Informatica). 1994. *Encuesta de Origen y Destino de los Viajes de los Residentes del Area Metropolitana de la Ciudad de México*. Mexico City: INEGI.

International Institute for Energy Conservation. 1996. *The World Bank and Transportation*. Washington, DC: International Institute for Energy Conservation.

Kelly, B. 1994. "The Transportation-Land Use Link." *Journal of Planning Literature* 9(2): 128–45.

Kessides, C. 1993. *The Contributions of Infrastructure to Economic Development*. Washington, DC: World Bank.

Knight, R., and L. Trygg. 1977. "Evidence of Land Use Impacts of Rapid Transit Systems." *Transportation* 6: 231–47.

Lee, K.S. 1985. *An Evaluation of Decentralized Policies in Light of Changing Location Patterns of Employment in the Seoul Region*. Urban Development Discussion Paper, UDD–60. Washington, DC: World Bank.

Lee, K.S. 1989. *The Location of Jobs in a Developing Metropolis: Patterns of Growth in Bogota and Cali, Colombia*. New York: Oxford University Press.

Leinbach, T. 1995. "Transport and Third World Development: Review, Issues, and Prescriptions." *Transportation Research A* 29(5): 337–44.

Meakin, R. 1990. "Hong Kong's Mass Transit Railway: Vital and Viable." *Rail Mass Transit for Developing Countries*. London: Thomas Telford.

Mera, K. 1973. "Regional Production Functions and Social Overhead capital." *Regional and Urban Economics* 3: 157–86.

Midgeley, P. 1994. *Urban Transport in Asia: An Operational Agenda for the 1990s*. Technical Paper No. 224. Washington, DC: World Bank.

Mohring, H. 1961. "Land Values and the Measurement of Highway Benefits." *Journal of Political Economy* 69: 236–49.

Muth, R. 1969. *Cities and Housing*. Chicago: University of Chicago Press.

Newman P., and J. Kenworthy. 1996. "The Land Use-Transportation Connection." *Land Use Policy* 13(1): 1–22.

Newman, P., J. Kenworthy, and F. Laube. 1997. "The Global City and Sustainability: Perspectives from Australian Cities and a Survey of 37 Global Cities." Paper presented at the Fifth International Workshop on Technological Change and Urban Form, sponsored by the Commonwealth Scientific Industrial Research Organization, Melbourne, Australia, held in Jakarta, Indonesia, 18–20 June.

Prud'homme, R., and G. Lee. 1998. "Size, Sprawl, Speed and the Efficiency of Cities." Paris: Observatoire de l'Economie et des Institutions Locales, Université de Paris XII; and *Urban Studies* 36(11): 1405–12.

Roberts, J., and C. Wood. 1992. "Land Use and Travel Demand." *Proceedings of Transport Research Council: Twentieth Summer Annual Meeting*. London: PTRC Education and Research Services.

Shah, A. 1990. *Public Infrastructure and Private Sector Profitability and Productivity: Microeconometric Foundations for Macroeconomic Policies in Mexico*. Washington, DC: World Bank.

Shen, Q. 1997. "Urban Transportation in Shanghai, China: Problems and Planning Implications." *International Journal of Urban and Regional Research* 21(4): 589–606.

Tong, C., and S. Wong. 1997. "The Advantages of a High Density, Mixed Land Use Linear Urban Development." *Transportation* 24: 295–307.

Varella, F. 1996. "Auto Dreams Collide with Reality." *World Press* 43(12): 6–7.

Weizsäcker, E., A. Lovins, and L. Lovins. 1997. *Factor Four: Doubling Wealth, Halving Resource Use.* London: Earthscan.

Wirth, C. 1997. "Transportation Policy in Mexico City: The Politics and Impacts of Privatization." *Urban Affairs Quarterly* 33(2): 155–81.

Zegras, C. 1998. "Clearing the Skies in Santiago." *Habitat Debate* 4(2): 23.

Index

(Page numbers in italics indicate material in tables, figures, or boxes.)

Printed in the United States
67410LVS00001B/61-96

9 780821 347386